FREE JAZZ / BLACK POWER

American Made Music Series
Advisory Board

David Evans, General Editor
Barry Jean Ancelet
Edward A. Berlin
Joyce J. Bolden
Rob Bowman
Susan C. Cook
Curtis Ellison
William Ferris
John Edward Hasse
Kip Lornell
Bill Malone
Eddie S. Meadows
Manuel H. Peña
Wayne D. Shirley
Robert Walser

FREE JAZZ/ BLACK POWER

By Philippe Carles and Jean-Louis Comolli

Translated by Grégory Pierrot

University Press of Mississippi   Jackson

www.upress.state.ms.us

The University Press of Mississippi is a member of the Association of American University Presses.

Cet ouvrage publié dans le cadre du programme d'aide à la publication bénéficie du soutien du Ministére des Affaires Etrangères et du Service Culurel de l'Ambassade de France représenté aux Etats-Unis. This work received support from the French Ministry of Foreign Affairs and the Cultural Services of the French Embassy in the United States through their publishing assistance program.

Free Jazz Black Power
By Philippe Carles and Jean-Louis Comolli
Originally published 1971 by Editions Champs Libre
Copyright © Editions Galilée 1979
English translation copyright © 2015 by University Press of Mississippi
All rights reserved
Manufactured in the United States of America

First English printing 2015
∞
Library of Congress Cataloging-in-Publication Data

Carles, Philippe.
 [Free jazz/black power. English]
 Free jazz/black power / by Philippe Carles and Jean-Louis Comolli ; translated by Grégory Pierrot.
   pages cm. — (American made music series)
 Includes bibliographical references and index.
   ISBN 978-1-62846-039-1 (cloth : alk. paper) — ISBN 978-1-62846-157-2 (ebook) 1. Jazz—History and criticism. 2. Free jazz—History and criticism. 3. African Americans—History—1964– 4. Jazz—Social aspects. I. Comolli, Jean-Louis. II. Pierrot, Grégory translator. III. Title.
ML3561.J3C3213 2015
781.65089'96073—dc23   2014017692

British Library Cataloging-in-Publication Data available

contents

Preface: . . . And in 2014   vii
   Philippe Carles and Jean-Louis Comolli
Free Jazz/Black Power: An Introduction   x
   Grégory Pierrot
Translator's Note   xix
Translator's Acknowledgments   xix

Introduction (1971)   3

Part I: Not a Black Problem, But a White Problem
   1. Jazz Today   11
   2. Economic Ownership of Jazz   25
   3. Cultural Colonization   31
   4. The Blind Task of Criticism   47

Part II: Notes on a Black History of Jazz
   Three Preliminary Remarks   51
   5. What the Blues Say   53
   6. Black Music before Jazz   77
   7. In the Margins of Jazz History   99

Part III: Contradictions of Jazz in a State of Freedom
   8. Free Fragments   151
   9. Music/Politics   168

Preface to the 1979 Edition   181
Preface to the 2000 Edition: Free Jazz, Off Program, Off Topic, Off Screen   183

Notes   195
Discography   227
Works Cited   242
Index   251

preface... and in 2014

Philippe Carles and Jean-Louis Comolli

Philippe Carles: It has been about forty-three years since *Free Jazz/Black Power* was first published, and as the English translation is in the works, we learn of the death of LeRoi Jones/Amiri Baraka. Had we not read the writings of this African American poet, musicologist and activist—among which the unavoidable *Blues People*—I wonder if our book would have been much less lively, or if it could have been at all.

Jean-Louis Comolli: Our work was profoundly inspired by LeRoi Jones's book. But we used it in a particular way: we set out to connect the history of jazz to that of the liberation and struggle of black people in the United States. We still believe that music, whatever genre it may be, refers more or less directly to the real lives of those who make and listen to it, and even more to the themes that animate its times. The conjunction of Black Power and free jazz is one of those encounters one might call *logical*, the same way Rimbaud spoke of "logical revolts."[1] Behind the four words that make up this title—*Free Jazz/Black Power*—are four histories that, back in the 1930s or 1950s, did not seem like they could converge or interact. As sometimes happens in the history of humanity, those elements then *crystallized*. By contrast, I would say that the current buffering of black demands, the destruction of all desire for revolution through violence and fear in the United States and elsewhere, make the English translation of this book absolutely necessary. It is undoubtedly a testimony of times past, but its aura and sound waves still manifest themselves in our present.

PC: Many of the ideas and/or theses that make up *Free Jazz/Black Power* have since its first publication been more or less absorbed (and often ill-digested, if not corrupted) to the point of being considered commonplaces bereft of all dilemmas and edges. Initial attacks and reactions from *moldy figs* and/or those who believe that "music is a beautiful mute"[2] have been replaced by finer, more learned, and at times intricately perverse critiques.

Thus questions and criticism have often focused on the fact that a discourse considered so "radical" and "provocative" in 1971 would be held by two Frenchmen born in Algeria in 1941. Early accusations and suspicions of crypto-Marxism—or even zhdanovism[3]—were in time followed by varied allegations of racism on our part. Beyond the simplistic criticism asking how and in whose name could these French-speaking whites dare analyze, gauge, and explore the history and present of an African American art, more punctilious readers believed they could find a form of "post-colonial" condescension and hierarchizing distinction when we depict connections, exchanges, and influences between creators from the jazz sphere and the works of composers of classic or contemporary European music.

If the notion of a jazz "oeuvre," no matter the style or the time, is in a variety of ways inseparable from that of the "given moment," so much could be said of our book. Like the words making up a slogan in a demonstration, the words in this book's title announce its context, its time, and its locations.

JLC: Some critiques (alas!) deserve no response. Let us simply underline the fact that most of the historians of any given culture or artistic movement belonged neither to that culture nor that movement. Physicists and philosophers have taught us that the *critical locus* builds itself as *foreign* to the critiqued thing. In order to explore an inside, one must not be caught in it, even though undoubtedly, "The observer is part of the observation," to paraphrase Einstein. So much is true, yet one takes part through difference and distinction. Any serious observation supposes proximity and distance, familiarity and foreignness, flattening and perspective.

French criticism did much to spread appreciation and understanding of jazz musicians and their oeuvre (as it also did for Hollywood cinema). I, like you, have been troubled by an accusation I did not expect: that of having "despised" so-called contemporary music. I believe the exact opposite is true. In our book, we perceived a deep relation between what was then at stake for "classical" musicians and "free" jazzmen. Like the two banks of the same musical river, both groups were immersed in the same questions about length, time, about involving the body and sound matter of instruments themselves. The questions that occur to creators and the answers they find follow similar preoccupations, determined here by what happens in the field of mass culture, there by the music industry, etc. In the end, I welcome the kind of critique that calls for debate.

PC: Over the past four decades the jazz sphere has expanded; music and its commercial and/or taxonomical labeling have never stopped diversifying, multiplying, as if after the explosions of free jazz, an infinity of aftereffects, corollary productions, and changes generated a kind of universal polyphony. It is as if the free jazz phenomenon had pollinated almost clandestinely and in all directions, including some that seemed impervious to its effects and echoes. Today, in a time when terms like "free jazz" or "black power" are likely to be seen as obsolete museum pieces, it is important to look for and analyze their avatars and offspring, whether they be natural, adulterine, or adopted.

JLC: Yes, of course. To borrow Bourdieu's terminology, there has never been such a thing as unity in artistic fields.[4] Power relations have always divided them, and in turn divided the divisions within them. One could call it vitality, of course, or a multiplication of commercial supply. Yet what is happening with the persistence of free jazz forms is of a different order. Free jazz picks up on all sorts of desires for liberation and improvisation, not only in jazz but also in a variety of cultures. It would be a mistake to assign a territory or a time period to free jazz. Here, there, everywhere, desire for freedom rises. The more formatted the forms (musical or not) become, the more artists refuse the mold and open up the field. Free jazz may well only have been *the continuation of jazz by means other* than those set by previous successive traditions. Jazz historians and aficionados alike have always asked: "What do we call jazz/what is this thing we call jazz?" The answer we give in this book is that all of jazz came from this deep need for *freedom*. What the African American people, the descendants of slaves have reminded us of—and continue to—through their music is this one word: *freedom*!

free jazz/black power: an introduction

Grégory Pierrot

Jazz is commonly regarded as having gone through several cycles. It rose from its roots in the blues to early development in the ragtime form, commercial explosion in the 1920s and settled into mainstream popular music prominence in the late 1920s, early 1930s swing era. Jazz experienced its first radical turn in the early 1940s with bebop, the genre brought about by the likes of John Birks "Dizzy" Gillespie and Charles "Bird" Parker. Formally turning away from the danceable, entertainment format of swing, bebop gave jazz at large an increased level of respectability, brought it a step closer to Western criteria for art. The innovations of bebop were soon swallowed by the mainstream, but the cooling of jazz brought its own reaction: in the early 1960s, a number of young jazz musicians began doing away with formal, melodic, and rhythmical limits, taking jazz far from the borders within which it had developed. This new music went unnamed for a while; some called it the "New Thing." In 1961, the late African American jazz critic, poet, and theorist LeRoi Jones declared about these musicians: "There is definitely an avant-garde in jazz today. A burgeoning group of young men who are beginning to utilize not only the most important ideas in 'formal' contemporary music, but more important, young musicians who have started to utilize the most important ideas contained in that startling music called bebop."[1] The iconic 1960 LP *Free Jazz: A Collective Improvisation*, by one of the new music's figureheads, multi-instrumentalist Ornette Coleman, eventually provided the new music with its most lasting, and arguably most descriptive label. The music was weird, grating, iconoclastic, and provoked reactions as extreme as its departure from jazz listeners' expectations. The free jazz wave from the United States took no time to reach foreign shores, and soon the new sound was grating the nerves and challenging the beliefs of people the world around. The book you are now holding is a testimony to the impact free jazz had on post-1968 French culture.

As its title makes fairly clear, *Free Jazz/Black Power* is a treatise on the confluence of avant-garde jazz and radical African American politics. Forty-some years after it was first published, it still stands as a testimony to the long ignored encounter of avant-garde African American music and politics with French left-wing theory and criticism. The authors Philippe Carles and Jean-Louis Comolli set out to undertake a novel task about a novel music: to show that the strong and mostly negative reactions to free jazz by classic jazz critics on both sides of the Atlantic could be better understood by analyzing the social, cultural, and political origins of jazz itself. In the authors' words, the book was meant "to study the ideological discourse of jazz criticism in its cultural, economic, and aesthetic implications and its consequences on the evolution and understanding of black music." In surprisingly self-aware fashion, Carles and Comolli analyzed the circumstances of the production of jazz criticism as discourse, producing a work of cultural studies in a time and place where such was virtually unknown.

The Authors

Philippe Carles has been a central figure of French jazz criticism since the mid-1960s. He was an editor and writer for *Jazz Magazine* for six years before becoming its editor in chief in 1971. He currently produces and hosts jazz programs on the French radio station France Musique. In these positions Carles has interviewed innumerable jazz artists, among them George Russell, Charles Mingus, Sun Ra, Sy Oliver, Jimmy Giuffre, Cecil Taylor, Anthony Braxton, Ornette Coleman, and Billy Strayhorn. He wrote texts for *The Eye of Jazz: The Photographs of Herman Leonard* (Viking Adult, 1990), for *Jazz Meetings* (Editions du Layeur, 2003), for Christian Rose's collection of photographs *Instants de jazz* (Filipacchi, 2006), and Giuseppe Pino's *Jazz My Love* (Vade Retro, 2003). He has co-edited *Le Dictionnaire du jazz*, and written liner notes for albums by Archie Shepp *(Yasmina, a Black Woman*, Get Back Italy, 1969), Anthony Braxton (*Saxophone Improvisations Series F*, Inner City, 1972), Sun Ra (*Cosmos*, 1976), Paul Bley (*Homage to Carla*, Owl Records, 2001; *Ramblin'*, Sunspots, 2002), and the Verve Records "Jazz 'round Midnight" series. In 1989, one of his dreams—the re-formation of the trio of Jimmy Giuffre, Paul Bley, and Steve Swallow—came true after he suggested it to Jean-Jacques Pussiau, owner of Owl Records, who was then searching for new projects.

Jean-Louis Comolli wrote for the prestigious French magazine *Les Cahiers du Cinéma* between 1966 and 1978. He was the magazine's chief editor between 1962 and 1971. He also wrote for *Jazz Magazine*, and with André Clergeat and Philippe Carles, he co-edited *Le Dictionnaire du jazz* (1988; Robert Laffont: Paris, 1994). He has acted in the films of his Nouvelle Vague fellows, such as Jean-Luc Godard (*Alphaville, The Riflemen*) and Eric Rohmer (*La Carrière de Suzanne*). He has directed some forty films, most of them documentaries, from his first *Les deux Marseillaises* in 1968 to his latest, *Le peintre, le poète et l'historien* in 2005. He currently teaches at the University of Paris VIII, La Fémis (French National School of Sound and Image Professions), and the University of Barcelona. He has written several books on film, including *Voir et pouvoir* (Verdier, 2004), for which he won the Film Critica Prize in 2005.

The Context

Free Jazz/Black Power has a solid, if ambivalent, reputation among jazz musicians and scholars in the United States. It has been mentioned or quoted in several classics of jazz and music studies (Ekkehard Jost's *Free Jazz* [Da Capo, 1994], Jacques Attali's *Noise: The Political Economy of Music* [University of Minnesota Press, 1985], among others), but has until now remained accessible only to readers of French. *Free Jazz/Black Power*, first published in 1971, is comparable in intent and in its theoretical foundation to Frank Kofsky's *Black Nationalism and the Revolution in Music* (1970), which may well explain its relative anonymity in the United States. Yet it is unique in its exhaustive scope and thorough research, and obviously in the fact that it was written by French authors.

Written a few years after French society and culture were shaken to the core by the student uprisings of 1968, *Free Jazz/Black Power* undeniably bears the marks of that tumultuous period. Carles and Comolli's writing clearly positions itself in a Marxist perspective; but it was and remains unique in French theory for what it owes to African American cultural and political thought. In the introduction, the authors recognize and celebrate the influence of LeRoi Jones/Amiri Baraka's seminal *Blues People*, but they also cite E. F. Frazier, W. E. B. Du Bois, and Sterling Brown, references all the more important given that, in the late 1960s, these authors were still ignored by many in their own country. Carles and Comolli's goal in writing was to defend free jazz, a musical label vilified by classic jazz critics on both sides of the Atlantic and even by some musicians.

Carles and Comolli cite African American authors in no small part as a political gesture. If one is to expose the ties that bind free jazz to African American culture, history, and the political struggle that was still raging in the early-1970s United States, one should show awareness of the African American archive. This gesture alone set them apart from the already storied tradition of French jazz criticism. Though the French had been among the first to take jazz seriously, their studies had early been tainted by profound racial and cultural prejudice, Eurocentrism, and condescension. Thus, if early twentieth-century century critic Hugues Panassié can be recognized as a pioneer of jazz criticism, notably for his archival work on the origins of jazz, this very endeavor was inseparable from a disturbing tendency toward racial essentialism on his part. That Panassié would eventually lead the charge against what he considered to be the abominable innovations of bebop is a testimony to the toxic outlook characteristic of early French jazz criticism. In a proto-ethnographic mode, French adepts purported to proclaim the Truth about music and people they barely knew, to offer taxonomies of forms, styles, and musicians whose opinion they rarely sought. Carles and Comolli reflect on the legacy of French jazz criticism in the light of African American texts and contexts. They propose that to fully understand free jazz and the reactions it provoked in the United States and abroad, one must be aware not just of African American history, but also of African American intellectual traditions.

Art or Propaganda?

With this book, Carles and Comolli choose sides in a longstanding debate tied to African American culture, one which in 1928 the critic Alain Locke described as "the one fundamental question for us today—Art or Propaganda?"[2] Locke's text was a response to W. E. B. Du Bois's famous phrase in "Criteria of Negro Art" (1926): "All art is propaganda and ever must be."[3] Writing at the height of the so-called New Negro Movement, or Harlem Renaissance, Du Bois was reacting against such artists as Countee Cullen, whose dedication to art for art's sake he considered anathema. In his rejoinder two years later, Locke vowed, "Our espousal of art thus becomes no mere idle acceptance of 'art for art's sake,' or cultivation of the last decadences of the over-civilized, but rather a deep realization of the fundamental purpose of art and of its function as a tap root of vigorous, flourishing living." Locke and Du Bois were concerned with African Americans' status as second-class citizens in the United States, and each thought in his own way that art should be a tool for racial uplift. Both agreed that it should represent the best African Americans could produce and demonstrate worth through excellence. At the same time, the young poet Langston Hughes proclaimed that African American music, as the most direct emanation of folk forms of expression, spoke from the very essence of the African American community. While Hughes' argument was in no small part class-based—and as such, a reply to the patrician disdain of Du Bois—it also smacked of racial essentialism, and in this regard did not necessarily challenge the romantic racism that often fueled white fascination with black music in the United States and Europe.

It bears noting that for the most part, Du Bois and Locke at best ignored jazz, when they did not voice outright distaste for it. They discussed high art, poetry, drama, classical music, and looked at the popular music that was taking the world by storm with a certain measure of disdain. This was not the position of other African American artists and critics, such as James Weldon Johnson—who had a career as a songwriter for Tin Pan Alley in the early 1900s—or Langston Hughes, whose poetry celebrated blues, jazz, and the black working class. Hughes and other younger artists saw in jazz the most authentic expression of African American culture. The patrician Du Bois found the music's lightness, its dedication to entertainment, and its licentiousness an embarrassment.

This question—"art or propaganda?"—drove critical outlooks on African American literature throughout the twentieth century, the pendulum swinging in cycles from one side to the other. When Carles and Comolli wrote their book, the notion that art should serve the African American people underlay the activities of the Black Arts Movement and its figurehead, Amiri Baraka. In his essay "The Myth of a Negro Literature," Baraka had made the provocative argument that while African American literature was characterized by utter mediocrity, "Only in music, and most conspicuously in blues, jazz, and spirituals—'Negro music'—has there been a significant contribution by Negroes."[4] His *Blues People* explored African American musical traditions in the light of social and political history. Baraka's groundbreaking text had its detractors, foremost among them the author and musician Ralph Ellison. In his review of *Blues People* for the *New York Review of Books*, Ellison explained his frustration with Baraka's sociological outlook:

> The blues are not primarily concerned with civil rights or obvious political protest; they are an art form and thus a transcendence of those conditions created within the Negro community by the denial of social justice. As such they are one of the techniques through which Negroes have survived and kept their courage during that long period when many whites assumed, as some still assume, they were afraid.[5]

Baraka and Ellison's disagreement echoed in many ways the earlier discussions between Du Bois and Locke; it also bore the marks of its time, the civil rights and Black Power era. Ellison's pointed criticism notwithstanding, Baraka's unabashed cultural nationalism was in no small part a strategic move meant to force white commentators to question their own social, economic, and political positioning.[6] This concern is crucial to Carles and Comolli's endeavor. Translated to a white, European critical milieu, it nevertheless retains some of the problematic aspects that Carles and Comolli criticized in their forebears.

The Reception

The publication of *Free Jazz/Black Power* was the culmination of an ongoing debate between old and new guard of French jazz criticism over the import of politics into the New Thing and its potential impact. In a 1966 radio debate with Jean-Louis Comolli, French jazz critic and composer André Hodeir expressed his fear that making free jazz political would prevent cultural exchange, and preclude its becoming "worldwide music."[7] In a rare contemporary review of the book in an American journal, Isabelle Leymarie, echoing Ellison's criticism of Baraka, states that "the main defect of this essay is its overemphasis of social and economic variables at the expense of musicological analysis."[8] More recently, other jazz scholars similarly criticized the French jazz criticism of the late 1960s for being too focused on social and political perspectives detrimental to the music itself. Stephen Lehman argues that free jazz musicians in France "met resistance when their music crossed tacit cultural boundaries."[9] He further argues that "in many ways, the French jazz press and its evolution over the course of the 1970s demonstrate a kind of cultural nationalism" that saw "certain cultural and musical domains, such as through-notated forms and intellectualism, as uniquely French or European."[10] Significantly, though he mentions Carles's articles, Lehman does not specifically discuss *Free Jazz/ Black Power*. Doing so would indeed require considering this outlook in the wider French political and cultural context, but also in light of its international relevance.

Indeed, Carles and Comolli's analysis, in making an effort to move away from race and focus instead on class, places itself against a tradition of French jazz criticism that essentializes race. For Jedediah Sklower, this partakes of a French tendency to idealize the free jazz musician as an "avatar of the 'proletarian/African American musician' essence created by the capitalist system" to the detriment of more aesthetic analyses of the music.[11] Yet, as Eric Drott notes, the authors "imagine the fusion of African Americans into a single political bloc in Marxian terms: it is not to be achieved through the collective recognition of 'blackness,' but through the collective recognition of exploitation—exploitation that had been enabled and perpetuated by the American racial hierarchy."[12] Drott makes the crucial argument that French jazz criticism must be read in the light of its socio-historical circumstances, in France and beyond. Carles and Comolli's book was not just a treatise on free jazz; it was also an intervention into wider French debates over worldwide proletarian revolution, post-colonialism, and racism. Drott argues that *Free Jazz/Black Power* can be seen as

> a sublimated reaction to France's colonial past. . . . In this context jazz became a surrogate by means of which the more immediate, local questions raised by decolonization and immigration could be negotiated. . . . According to this interpretation, knowledge of American race relations, made possible through critics' contact with jazz musicians, afforded French listeners a venue where they could confront certain social dynamics that were perhaps less pro-

nounced (but still present) in French society, dynamics that would come to the fore in the wake of decolonization.[13]

The French Left saw the African American struggle as one of many revolutionary movements throughout the world. Carles and Comolli strive to depart from the cultural nationalism of a Baraka by way of a Marxist analysis that presents the African American struggle as a single branch of the worldwide class struggle. Such reading is in fact fairly similar to the ways in which Black Power thinkers such as Stokely Carmichael/Kwame Ture and Huey Newton integrated the anti-colonial critique of Frantz Fanon into their revolutionary theory. Born in the French West Indian island of Martinique, Fanon joined the Algerian National Liberation Front in his fight against French colonial rule. His 1961 book *The Wretched of the Earth* became a fundamental reference for the Black Power movement, and echoes of its reflection resonate in Carles and Comolli's take on the correlation between cultural production and politics. Thus, Fanon writes:

> When the native hears a speech about Western culture he pulls out his knife—or at least he makes sure it is within reach. The violence with which the supremacy of white values is affirmed and the aggressiveness which has permeated the victory of these values over the ways of life and of thought of the native mean that, in revenge, the native laughs in mockery when Western values are mentioned in front of him. In the colonial context the settler only ends his work of breaking in the native when the latter admits loudly and intelligibly the supremacy of the white man's values. In the period of decolonization, the colonized masses mock at these very values, insult them, and vomit them up.[14]

Reading African American free jazz's innovations through an anticolonial lens makes it almost necessary to reject its similarities and connections to white European avant-garde efforts. For this musical revolution to be proletarian and black, it had to reject bourgeois influences—including European-style avant-garde—but also to eschew European influence by asserting its rootedness in African tradition. Such a position forced the music into a somewhat paradoxical position, in which it was expected to be both iconoclastic and traditional at the same time. Yet this paradox was an important topic of discussion at the time, one that *Free Jazz/Black Power* addresses without pretending to solve. This political vision of music can certainly be criticized, and the four decades that now separate us from the time when it was first put in print allow us to put it in historical perspective. Nevertheless, we cannot overlook the fact that it expresses an opinion for its time, a time when radical African American leaders were routinely targeted for execution by the American government through the FBI's Counter Intelligence Program, a time when black revolution seemed not only probable, but also necessary. In "Black Art," Amiri Baraka called for "poems that kill": that Carles and Comolli would think that free jazz should "vomit up" Western norms and values should not be so surprising.[15]

Free Jazz/Black Power was in 1971 and remains a militant book, with the flaws pertaining to such endeavors. Columbia professor and Association for the Advancement of Creative Musicians (AACM) member George E. Lewis's constant praise for the book also shows that *Free Jazz/Black Power* found even then many among free jazz musicians who agreed with its message. In a 2004 article, Lewis offers an explanation for the reservations of American critics in particular about Carles and Comolli's book: "In contrast to post-1990s American scholarship, French critiques of the 1970s positioned free jazz as a postmodernist, rather than a modernist phenomenon."[16] Carles and Comolli's book is an educational treatise about the origins and contexts of a movement relatively unknown and misunderstood in France. Critics' reservations confirm that *Free Jazz/Black Power* is a book with an agenda; as such it is indispensable as a reflection of both its time and the unsung cultural and political connections that then tied a certain America and a certain France and, to a great extent, still do.

Conclusion

The impact of this book on French readers in particular and European readers at large is not to be underestimated. While regretting the book's quasi-sociological angle, Ekkehard Jost nevertheless deemed Carles and Comolli's endeavor "imperative" and "productive" in the introduction to his seminal 1974 book *Free Jazz*. It is safe to say that Jost, like most European jazz aficionados, had read and learned from *Free Jazz/Black Power* before writing his own essay on the topic. As noted by George Lewis, after the book was released, "Commentators across Europe quickly signed on to Carles and Comolli's Jones-influenced assertion that the new black music was a direct expression of black power ideology."[17] As noted in Mike Heffley's *Northern Sun, Southern Moon: Europe's Reinvention of Jazz*, German free jazz luminaries Ulrich Gumpert and Guenter "Baby" Sommer credit this book with changing their view on their musical practice: "It made us mine the potential of jazz as a gesture of resistance. It forced us to politicize, rather than just musicalize, our lives more."[18] In his review of Heffley's book, Lewis declares that "*Free Jazz/Black Power* articulated a proto-postcolonial emphasis which stood in sharp contrast with nearly all

American accounts of the history of black music."[19] In this contrast, one can measure the distance between (African) American culture and its French interpretations, and catch a glimpse of the complex and rich world that develops in the interstices of cultural translation.

In the past ten years, scholars in the humanities have begun looking at cultural phenomena from resolutely transnational perspectives. Jazz is regularly featured in these studies as a major transnational cultural vehicle. Carles and Comolli's book is both a tool for research and an archival item. It occupies a central place in the complex network of cultural and political ties that bound artists, intellectuals, critics, political activists, and audiences together across the Atlantic in the period between the mid-1960s and early 1970s. *Free Jazz/Black Power*, for what it shows of the French cultural Left's attachment to American culture and liberation movements, is crucial to the mapping out of this period. It is indispensable in the attempt to form a complete view of the international nature and impact of free jazz. This book not only caught the spirit of its time; it also shaped it. Its translation into English is long overdue.

translator's note

Beyond the stylistic issues one expects in translating from French into English, the main problem I encountered in Carles and Comolli's text had to do with unrecoverable English-language sources. The authors cite many interviews with American musicians published in French jazz magazines that were originally conducted in English. I did not have access to the original recordings; neither did Philippe Carles, and I therefore had to retranslate them. All quotes from *Jazz Magazine*, *Jazz Hot*, and *Les Cahiers du Jazz* are therefore translated from the French in which they were published.

I worked from the 2000 Folio edition of the book published by Gallimard. In some cases, the sources indicated in the original text were either erroneous or absent. I corrected those errors where and when possible and indicated in footnotes when I could not locate the original text.

translator's acknowledgments

This translation was a long time coming. I thank the authors Philippe Carles and Jean-Louis Comolli for writing this book in the first place; for the intellectual stimulation it has provided from first reading to last; and for their patience and help throughout this long and arduous process. I also thank my colleagues Paul Youngquist at the University of Colorado, Jonathan Eburne, Aldon Nielsen, and Kevin Bell at the Pennsylvania State University for their help and support at different stages of this adventure. Tabitha McIntosh was tremendously helpful in the last stretch; so was Robert Jefferson Norrell, who kept my writing honest. I am eternally grateful to both.

Finally, I cannot express enough gratitude to Katharine Tune Pierrot, without whom nothing would ever get done; and to Chloë Pierrot, around whom little ever seems to get done, but who taught me that "Can You Get to That?" is a question that demands an answer.

FREE JAZZ / BLACK POWER

Pointless to seek any longer an explanation for coloured people suddenly breaking, with an incongruous extravagance, an absurd stutterer's silence: we are rotting away with neurasthenia under our roofs, a cemetery and common grave of so much pathetic rubbish; while the blacks who (in America and elsewhere) are civilised along with us and who, today, dance and cry out, are marshy emanations of the decomposition who are set aflame above this immense cemetery: so, in a vaguely lunar Negro night, we are witnessing an intoxicating dementia of dubious and charming will-o'-the-wisps, writhing and yelling like bursts of laughter. This definition will spare us any discussion.
    —Georges Bataille[1]

Introduction (1971)

The appearance and fast development in the USA of so-called "free jazz" and its difficult entry in France have provoked a veritable trauma in the small world of jazz criticism.

From the start, there was something *intolerable* about this music for many listeners, and even for music specialists. The music was shocking, to say the least: it hurt, quite literally. Ten years later, after Ornette Coleman, Cecil Taylor, Sun Ra, Albert Ayler, Archie Shepp, Don Cherry, Pharoah Sanders, the Chicago Art Ensemble, its shock power remains intact. Free jazz still triggers violent reactions, rejection, insults, and derision.

Some free jazz musicians show a deliberate partiality for sonic aggression; but this is not enough to explain the aggressiveness with which they were received. The new music broke away from well-supported, good old jazz traditions and the habits, certainties, and comfort that had come with them. It suddenly challenged a certain idea of the function and beauty of music, an idea of aesthetic pleasure and cultural consumption that was governed by the dominating ideology of capitalist societies and therefore marked with the seal of Western civilization.

The new music was not only produced and played according to aesthetic norms and cultural codes different from ours; it did not only transgress most of the rules then held to be specific to jazz—it also purported to testify to the oppression of black Americans, to express their revolt, and even to play a role in their revolutionary struggle. In short, it was mixing the unmixable: music and politics. This, indeed, was intolerable for jazz critics, they who had toiled to raise jazz to the level of art, but had done nothing to think about art in terms other than those used by bourgeois aesthetics and consumed by Western culture.

Criteria and definitions weathered by thirty years of jazz and criticism were suddenly useless. They should have been revised; but, instead, free jazz was received with jeers and whistles yet unable to cover up the *silence* of jazz critics. They seemed to have nothing left to say (beyond accusing the very few defenders of free jazz of wishing "the death of jazz").

The works of black critic (and poet and playwright) LeRoi Jones constituted the first global approach to the free jazz phenomenon. They study both free jazz's complex relations with jazz history and forms (which free jazz rejects, rewrites, and reactivates) and the way free jazz is determined by the black American socio-cultural field. In an era of Black Nationalism, LeRoi Jones focused on the study of Afro-American culture and arts, on propagating them among black masses, in the lumpenproletariat of the ghettoes (under pressure from intellectual and political militants, the long-ignored Black Studies entered black-university curricula—but for this very reason, they have been reserved to students and the future elite of the black bourgeoisie).

Black is beautiful: in order to fight against the integrationist policies that were discouraging them and perpetuating their exploitation, the black masses had to regain pride in their skin color and in their race. Referencing the values of African civilizations, educating on the feats of black history, systematically promoting proofs of the non-inferiority of African Americans (such as revolts, sports exploits, religious and political concepts, artistic creation, etc.) are the weapons of choice in this struggle waged on *ideological grounds*, in order to counterbalance the effects of the racist ideology of white American capitalism (according to which the black race is inferior and can only rise above by imitating whites).

Of all the forms of expression of black Americans, their music, jazz, is both the most prestigious and the most representative of African American culture. In his articles, and more specifically in his book *Blues People*,[1] LeRoi Jones has taken on the task of *giving back* to black people their own music, because though created and illustrated by blacks, jazz has long been offered to the musical influences, commercial interests, cultural pillaging, and aesthetic values of white America, and Western civilization at large. Some black musicians have denounced this situation of cultural and economic dependence. Most critics (being, to some extent and among other things, agents of this dependence), although informed on the subject, do not see the consequences of this twofold colonization on the very evolution of the musical forms of jazz. LeRoi Jones was the first to retrace the history of jazz and complete it with a history of the many pressures it has suffered. This has led him to present free jazz as an attempt at liberation from some of these pressures.

The *black point of view* on jazz therefore operates a reversal of orders and values that cannot be ignored. In connection with the works of LeRoi Jones, informed by them but also by this new phenomenon in the jazz world that is the politicization and radicalization of free jazz, a few French critics[2] have started reexamining the admitted "truths" of jazz. Free jazz is no longer defined as a musical aberration born of mysterious motivations; an effort is being made to understand the way it interacts, on the one hand, with anterior forms of jazz, and on the other with the sociopolitical context in which it is produced.

Our work is part of this necessarily collective enterprise.

Everything we owe to LeRoi Jones's theses leads us to depart from them on one important point. The facts and determinations he pointed out make possible a political reading of the evolution of jazz forms. Yet LeRoi Jones stops short of this particular reading. He notes the extent to which the songs and musical forms of the slaves are connected to economic and cultural conditions, to the racist oppression of slavery. He emphasizes the primordial role of the blues, a stalwart of permanence in the evolution of jazz. He denounces the cultural and economic exploitation of jazz by white America. He valorizes the African sources of black music, and presents free jazz as a rejection of Western influences and constraints and a recognition of African civilizations. But in the networks that constitute "black music in white America," he only sees multiple embodiments of a unique contradiction that opposes whites and blacks, Africanness (or Afro-Americanness) and Western identity. We think that the contradiction between white and black values—seen at work in the colonizations of jazz and in the resistance to these colonizations—is but one of the moments in the *main contradiction*: between colonizers and colonized, exploiters and exploited; between capitalism and its prey. Racist ideology, the devalorization of a race and a culture for the benefit of another, are but the effects, the products of capitalist expansionism, and they serve to legitimize it. Western civilization has only glorified itself as universal and superior so as to obfuscate and impose its economic imperialism. The cultural differences between African and Western civilizations were leveled, in the case of African Americans, by capitalist exploitation (in its primitive form, slavery, and in its modern forms) and its ideology. Rejecting this ideology to replace it by Afrocentrist mythology and culture is clearly not enough to suppress its conditions of existence, its base: capitalist exploitation itself. The history of African Americans is not solely made of cultural resistance and battles, but also of political struggle, which point to a revolution that is more than just cultural.

The *cultural nationalism* LeRoi Jones has adhered to (under the name of Imamu Amiri Baraka, he heads the *United Brothers* organization in Newark), and whose other leaders are Ron Karenga and Stokely Carmichael, is strongly opposed by the black revolutionary militants of the Black Panther Party, who see it as a demobilizing force, and ultimately as an accomplice of American capitalism and racism. To Stokely Carmichael's statement that "what counts in our struggle is culture," the Panthers ironically answer that "power flows from the sleeve of a dashiki."[3] The study of the contradictions and struggles between two cultures, among black Americans and in their artistic productions, implies taking into account the *ideological instance*, and therefore politics and the way politics is determined by class struggle.

We have tried to show some of the ways in which jazz and free jazz work jointly with black struggles, movements, and political programs, with the development of revolutionary consciousness among African Americans. This work posed a certain number of problems. On a cultural level, our being white Westerners threatened—precisely—to disqualify us in the appreciation of black political, cultural, and musical phenomena.

But, on the one hand, recent evolutions in music and in black political movements have gone *beyond* the mutual exclusion of the two races and cultures: black free jazz musicians play with white musicians when their collaboration challenges what jazz was and the Western values grafted onto it, when it is the common effort of those who, for racial and/or political reasons, refuse those values. Similarly, black revolutionary militants accept alliances with white revolutionary militants (while they reject the influence of the white liberals who long "guided" black movements), their common goal being the destruction of the capitalist system (in America and in the world).

On the other hand, jazz, an Afro-American music, not only has been commercially and culturally exploited by whites (capitalists, musicians, and politicians); its history, its aesthetics, its analysis have been exclusively undertaken by white critics, in the USA and in Europe. Our work follows the work of LeRoi Jones, which deconstructs the white history and aesthetics of black music. We are therefore engaging the dominant ideology of a society and the cultural system of a civilization *in which we are*.

Therefore, it is important to say precisely *what we aim at* when we fire at Western (American and European) jazz criticism as we often do in this book. Of course, certain jazz historians and critics in America and Europe have produced relevant knowledge about, and valuable assessments of, black music. But these critical and historical discourses are sometimes contradictory fragments emanating from a common ideological discourse that says what they do not say. We are not as interested (not always) in the precise ways in which jazz criticism can be applied as in the problems criticism exposes, more or less unknowingly, when it discusses jazz without questioning the very location, conditions, and contradictions of its own production as critical discourse. Western criticism is coterminous with cultural axes, values, aesthetic norms, and ideology that, even with the best of intentions, come to plague its object, jazz, and weigh *on and against* it. We have tried to study the cultural, economic, and aesthetic implications of the ideological discourse of jazz criticism, as well as its consequences on the evolution and understanding of black music.

It is remarkable that one of the main problems that black American political activists face nowadays is that of the influence of the dominant ideology on the black elite and part of the black masses. They have to fight against the feeling of resignation and the illusion of progress that American capitalist ideology feeds to the masses. It is no less remarkable that free jazz has appeared as a reaction against the co-optation of black music by this same ideology.

Part 1. Not a Black Problem, But a White Problem

1. Jazz Today

We see jazz as one of the most meaningful social, aesthetic contributions to America. It is that certain people accept it for what it is, that it is a meaningful, profound contribution to America—it is anti-war, it is opposed to the U.S. involvement in Vietnam, it is for Cuba; it is for the liberation of all people. That is the nature of jazz. That's not far-fetched. Why is that so? Because jazz is a music itself born out of oppression, born out of the enslavement of my people.
—Archie Shepp, "Point of Contact: Discussion," *Downbeat Music '66: The 11th Yearbook* (1966), 20.

a) The "Free" Movement

In 1960, saxophonist Ornette Coleman, considered by all critics and by the great majority of jazz aficionados as an "avant-garde" musician and composer of difficult, unpleasant, "hermetic" music, recorded with a *double* quartet—an exceptional formation—a 36' 23" piece entitled *Free Jazz*. This was collective improvisation music, deliberately played outside of the stylistic norms and structures of both "classic" jazz (1920–40) and what was then considered "modern" jazz (coming from bop, cool jazz, etc.). The piece was a scandal, at least musically speaking, and only in the very small world of jazz aficionados, musicians, and critics. Since Ornette Coleman was already known for scandal in this small world of jazz, this could have been just another one—if the radically novel character of his music had not immediately taken on meaning as a manifesto of sorts, and its title become a slogan, for those young black jazzmen outraged at the recent formal evolutions of their music. This "free jazz," being itself a reaction to the dominant tendency of jazz at that time, could only respond to the expectations, and focus the experimentations, of musicians who, in isolation and with difficulty, were attempting to resist the freezing of jazz, its gradual weakening into increasingly precious styles (the Modern Jazz Quartet, Third Stream, cool), its stereotypes. It responded to this opposition—but it also revealed and centered it (see III).

Dubbed "free jazz," "new music," "the new thing," or simply—in opposition to "jazz" as a music invented and played by blacks but culturally and economically colonized by whites—"black music," a movement sprang onto the jazz scene that was more than another style or school, and which would create a rift among musicians, listeners, and critics, triggering the most violent controversies jazz had known since the birth of bop (1940–1947, see I. 3.e).

Ornette Coleman himself gives an idea of what these seemingly exclusively musical controversies hide: "Well, for myself, I'm a Negro and a jazz man. . . . And as a Negro and a jazz man, I just feel miserable."[1] Much like bebop but even more clearly, free jazz not only challenges musically the forms and styles that precede it but acts beyond the strictly musical in the cultural and ideological fields. It quickly presented itself as an act of cultural resistance, the retaking—with the changes that necessitates—by black American musicians and listeners of a music that was originally theirs, that they had made in historical, social, and cultural conditions (deportation, slavery, poverty, and racism) *that were exclusively theirs*. Yet immediately, and for over half a century, under pressure from commercial, social, racial, cultural factors, this music was *leeched* and *exploited* precisely by that which had enslaved Africans, had given birth to racist ideology and used it against them, and which continues to exploit and oppress them today: white American capitalism, its ideology and value system. Not only did American society economically and culturally profit from jazz, but in exploiting it for profit, has incessantly controlled and influenced its stylistic development. It has imposed its aesthetic and commercial norms, forms, and a finality that were not only not those of the original black music, but, moreover could not, and *would not*, provide to black Americans what they were seeking in their music. Thus they aimed specifically at separating blacks from their music by performing cultural expropriation.

Free jazz resists this expropriation, rejects the musical and extra-musical values of dominant ideology—which in the United States is capitalist *and* white—and attempts to achieve cultural freedom, echoing the struggles of black Americans for their political and economic freedom. It endeavors to regain and *build* a specifically Afro-American culture. "Free" in free jazz does not simply indicate the rejection and/or sublimation of certain musical norms that once were jazz's; it also confronts a colonized music with a music and a culture involved in, and produced by, anti-imperialist and revolutionary culture. This situation, at the crossroads of the cultural and the political, is well explained by Archie Shepp: "New jazz is old jazz. Nothing really new here, except a message that could never be expressed until now. . . . For a long time a point of view that was not theirs was imposed on black Americans."[2] What purely musical innovations happen in free jazz are first and foremost effects and symptoms of a more general change in the relation of black Americans to their culture and in the role culture plays in their political struggles. Analyzing and assessing only the musical transformations performed by free jazz would amount to obfuscating what determined them at the political level, and thus ultimately obfuscating the political itself.

b) The Black Power Stage

The political history of black Americans is as rich and long as it is poorly known—and this is no accident: the ideological apparatuses of American society (school, the press, cultural networks, etc.) have systematically obfuscated and interfered with it. We study its different stages further in relation to the evolution of jazz (see II). Let us for now note that the birth of the "free jazz" slogan and the development of the free movement were contemporaneous with a clear radicalization of the political struggles of American Negroes (1960–1970). This radicalization operates on three levels.

1) Organizations
The famous boycott led by the blacks of Montgomery, Alabama, which forced the transportation company to desegregate its buses in 1956, marked the beginning of a new kind of protest movement: the civil rights movement. Its aim—the recognition of black Americans' constitutional rights—was similar to that of the traditional black organization, the National Association for the Advancement of Colored People (NAACP), founded by W. E. B. Du Bois, yet it privileged direct action at the local level (through demonstrations, sit-ins, boycotts, etc.) over judicial and administrative recourse such as lawsuits and petitions to centralized authorities. The NAACP and black church militants performed these local and completely nonviolent—if not excessively gentle—actions. But their increasing number and relative success in the racist South triggered on the part of the local white authorities and population an extremely violent repression that in turn contributed to toughening the movement. The necessity of coordinating these varied anti-segregationist demonstrations led to the birth of the Student Nonviolent Coordinating Committee (SNCC) in 1960, a group that would notably lead a significant battle to register blacks on electoral lists in the southern states. This extremely rough campaign had rather disappointing results. In 1963, SNCC refused to agree to an electoral compromise with the Democratic Party, the terms of which would necessarily have been unfavorable to blacks. White liberals and the traditional integrationist organizations they support disavowed SNCC, and finally the call for insubordination by black conscripts ordered to Vietnam (1966) forced SNCC to go beyond its initial "apolitical" stance. In 1966, SNCC's president Stokely Carmichael introduced the slogan *Black Power*. It drew a firestorm from whites—

liberals included—and led some to call racists the very victims of racism. It further widened the rift between SNCC and integrationists and black bourgeois elites.

2) Ideology

With his speeches and articles, Malcolm X played a considerable role in the political radicalization of blacks, first as a member of the mystical sect the *Black Muslims* (headed from 1932 by the "prophet" Elijah Muhammad, and influential in the black ghettoes of big cities), which preaches the rejection of all things white and the glorification of the Negro at all levels (religion, culture, history), and then, beginning in 1964, outside of the sect. Malcolm X's action was twofold: at the ideological level he strove to "decondition" black Americans, to make them critical and suspicious of *their own ideas* insofar as they were undergirded by the dominant ideology and manufactured by white society:

> You know why they always say Negroes are lazy? Because they want Negroes to be lazy. They always say Negroes can't unite, because they don't want Negroes to unite. And once they put this thing in the Negro's mind, they feel that he tries to fulfill their image. If they say you can't unite black people, and then you come to them to unite them, they won't unite, because it's been said that they're not supposed to unite. It's a psycho that they work, and it's the same way with these statistics.[3]

This leads him to underline black history and culture as signs of the worth of black Americans:

> One of the things that made the Black Muslim movement grow was its emphasis upon things African. This was the secret to the growth of the Black Muslim movement. African blood, African origin, African culture, African ties. And you'd be surprised, we discovered that deep within the subconscious of the Black man in this country, he's still more African than he is American. He thinks that he's more American than African, because the man[4] is jiving him, the man is brainwashing him every day.[5]

Overall, through him the black struggle took an important political step (joining W. E. B. Du Bois's Marxist conclusions) by subordinating the entirety of racial, legal, social, and cultural demands to a more directly political demand: the struggle against American capitalism, which became the main enemy.

3) Action

As if synchronized with the radicalization of militant organizations and the politicization of their agendas, in 1964 and 1965 bloody urban riots exploded in several black ghettoes (Harlem, Detroit, Watts, etc.), terrifying white America and accelerating the transformation of protest into a pre-revolutionary struggle characterized by illegal activity, armed resistance, and the formation of revolutionary movements such as the Black Panther Party. This demonstrated that a part of the black masses refused integration, no longer followed the old leaders, and was becoming aware of the fact that it had "nothing to lose."

At the same time, after the end of the war in Algeria decolonization accelerated in Africa, at the cost of violent struggles in which colonizers lost, on top of everything else, the heroic role that was theirs in colonial myths. Third world resistance to American imperialism in Cuba, Vietnam, and South America was of direct concern to black Americans; it put an end to their feeling of isolation, and by shattering America's trademark image as all-powerful and liberal, it lifted their spirits:

> In my estimation, [the United States] is one of the most vicious, racist social systems in the world—with the possible exception of Northern Rhodesia, South Africa and South Vietnam. I am, for the moment, a helpless witness to the bloody massacre of my people on streets that run from Hayneville through Harlem. . . . I ask only: don't you ever wonder just what my collective rage will—as it surely must—be like, when it is—as it inevitably will be—unleashed? Our vindication will be black as the color of suffering is black, as Fidel is black, as Ho Chi Minh is black.[6]

c) Black Beauty

Under the pressure of these converging forces, the political maturation of black militants and black masses was accompanied by important changes at the ideological level and in the cultural field: the ideological hierarchy was upended; the black man and Africa were valorized against the white man and the West, against the "Tom" who imitates them. The Black Muslims adopted Islam and renounced their "slave names," replacing them with an emblematic X. After Islam, African religions and civilizations were called upon; many musicians took on Arabic or African names. Black universities created Black Studies departments, and in the ghettoes militants such as LeRoi Jones taught black youths a different history, a different culture, and different myths from those presented as "universal" in white schools:

16   Not a Black Problem, But a White Problem

> History has been so "whitened" by the white man that even the black professors have known little more than the most ignorant black man about the talents and rich civilizations and cultures of the black man of milleniums ago. I have lectured in Negro colleges and some of these brainwashed black Ph.D.'s, with their suspenders dragging the ground with degrees, have run to the white man's newspapers calling me a "black fanatic." Why, a lot of them are fifty years behind the times. If I were president of one of these black colleges, I'd hock the campus if I had to, to send a bunch of black students off digging in Africa for more, more and more proof of the black race's historical greatness. The white man now is in Africa digging and searching. An African elephant can't stumble without falling on some white man with a shovel. Practically every week, we read about some great new find from Africa's lost civilizations, all that's new is white science's attitude. The ancient civilizations of the black man have been buried on the Black Continent all the time.[7]

It is interesting to note how Malcolm X does not mind couching the value of African civilizations in a reference to the kind of interest "white archaeologists" have in them. The struggle for black history and culture is waged at the ideological level, against the teachings and prejudices the white system inculcates in blacks. To manifest "black beauty" is not simply to value one's race and culture; it is also to forcibly extricate oneself from a mode of thinking and a scale of values that systematically devalue all that is black. It is to reject the dominant ideology in oneself, to renounce one's very self-image. Rap Brown also discusses this topic:

> Negroes have a hard time accepting anything Black unless it's been legitimized by white people. . . . If the white man was to package horseshit, put a name on it and advertise it on t.v., "Barbecued Horseshit," negroes would go buy it, because the white man said it was good. But that's the way it's going to be as long as white people have the power. Anything you don't control is a weapon against you. . . . The Black college student, if he is revolutionary, can help Black people to purge themselves of the misinformation that they've been fed all their lives. White nationalism has been instilled into us whether we know it or not. . . . America has negroes in the dilemma of thinking that everything Black is bad. Black cows don't give good milk; black hens don't lay eggs; black mail is bad; you wear black to funerals, white to weddings; angel food cake is white, devil's food cake is black. And all good guys wear white hats. And Black people fall for it. Everything Black is bad. That's white nationalism. And they tell you, you can't talk about Black nationalism.[8]

Black nationalism therefore appears as a *necessary stage* in the development of the black struggle in America, the moment of *battle on the ideological field*, against all the white myths that befuddle the consciousness of the black masses, from those directly linked to capitalism ("make a fortune," "work in order to be integrated") to those that indirectly support and justify it: "American democracy," "equality," "freedom," etc. Indeed, in order to survive or live better, a non-negligible portion of black Americans strive to adapt to the ideological conditions of white capitalism (and its black replicas). This fringe of the population slows down the politicization of the black masses by duplicating white ideology, and its class-race collaboration must therefore be denounced.

Yet the influence of dominant ideology is not confined to the black middle and upper- middle class. Through different ideological apparatuses (foremost among them school, the news, and advertising), this ideology controls the black masses' "way of seeing," which is torn in an insolvable conflict between the immediate and invariable reality of their skin color—of which they are constantly reminded by everything in American society—and the scorn and rejection one *must* feel about this color:

> Among the so-called Negroes in this country, as a rule the civil-rights groups, those who believe in civil rights, spend most of their time trying to prove they are Americans. . . . When they look upon themselves upon the American stage, the American stage is a white stage. So a black man standing on that stage in America is in the minority. He is the underdog, and in his struggle he always uses an approach that is a begging, hat-in-hand, compromising approach.[9]

This contradiction undoubtedly creates considerable inertia for American Negroes: political struggle against their living conditions should begin by questioning the way they are represented, including by their peers, on the "American stage." Politics is not *visible* without a critique of dominant ideology. Far from being—as some have argued—a "return to the past," to origins, or even "reverse racism," 1960s black nationalism acted in the history of the black struggle as an ideological counter-attack both anchored in and allowed by the level of development of this struggle. It was also a condition necessary for the next stage: with Malcolm X, H. Rap Brown, and the Black Panther Party overall, the transition from *Black Power* to *All Power to the People*, from black nationalism to proletarian internationalism.

d) Revolutionary Culture

Indeed, the same black political leaders who had campaigned for Black Power and Black Beauty, African civilizations and conspicuous signs of Africanness, sublimated this "culturalist" phase. This was no easy feat: many militants advocated cultural nationalism as an end in itself, shutting themselves into it. They suspected any revolutionary ideology that was not "purely African" of being a compromise with the white world, all social systems, including capitalism, appearing acceptable as long as they were black. Thus black revolutionaries denounced the demobilizing potential of taking satisfaction in such fantasies as learning to speak Swahili, dressing in African garb, etc., which were all substitutes for revolutionary action. At the same time, in order to break down the many social, cultural, and political barriers such as isolation in the ghettoes, the Africanist cultural circle, the black nation as racial minority, activists emphasized the fact that black Americans were victims *among other victims* of American capitalism: the people of the Third World, the colored *majority*. H. Rap Brown thus declares:

> Half of the Black "militants" ain't nothing but a bunch of potheads, bootleg preachers and coffeehouse intellectuals. They are caught up in that whole identity thing. They just discovered that they were Black, because they were working so hard all their lives to be white. They're further away from being revolutionaries than the poor people who are not militantly political. But the coffeehouse intellectual, the Black militant, thinks he's political because he reads Fanon. Books don't make revolutionaries. I contend that the Black people who burned down Watts and Detroit don't have to read. These cats have lived more than the intellectual has read. So they are political by having learned from their existence. Oppression made these cats political. The militants spend all their time trying to program white people into giving them some money. "The man" has created a new type of Tom. They are willing to be anything, as long as they can be Black first. Black capitalists, Black imperialists, Black oppressors—anything, so long as it's Black first.[10]

And further: "Because most of the laws in this country are built on attitudes, not justice, not equality, revolution is necessary. Racism, capitalism, colonialism and imperialism dominate the lives of people of color around the world—the people of Africa, Asia, Latin America, the colonized minorities who live inside the united states."[11] Malcolm X had already emphasized the deep connection between the liberation of American Negroes and that of the people exploited by American imperialism, in order to avoid putting Negroes alone on the "American stage."

The birth of the Black Panther Party in 1966 announced the elaboration of a coherent revolutionary political doctrine analyzing the situation of American Negroes in its interdependent relations with anti-imperialist struggles the world around. The BPP changed the political, ideological, and psychological characteristics of black struggles. It is organized like a revolutionary party rather than like traditional associations and civil rights groups; it teaches politics and weapons handling to adherents recruited among the lumpenproletariat of the ghetto. They do not hesitate to parade in arms and uniforms in front of the police, systematically defying the "pigs" (police, judges, civil servants, white politicians and their allies, etc.) with offensive words and acts, undertaking armed self-defense against increasingly frequent and deadly attacks by the government and its police force (twenty-eight party leaders have been killed; hundreds have been jailed, wounded, or lynched, either figuratively in court through special proceedings, or literally, by "friends of the police"). They lead mass demonstrations (the campaign to free Huey Newton, Eldridge Cleaver's presidential campaign, etc.) and organize for urban guerilla. Through daring acts of exorcism (publicly insulting the most powerful whites with ghetto slang, which proves to the black masses that whites can be frightened, pushed back, that they are not always the strongest), total commitment to the struggle (jail, death, or victory), the impact of its propaganda, but also through its Marxist-Leninist political analyses (blacks are first and foremost victims of capitalist exploitation, the struggle against the USA is international), the BPP has definitively moved black demands from the shifty terrain of asking America to respect its own legal and moral codes, to anti-capitalist revolution. The BPP sees black liberation as a consequence of the toppling of the American capitalist system in international anti-imperialist struggles. Rejecting all racism, whether black nationalism or "culturalism," the BPP accepts alliances with white clandestine revolutionary movements in the USA. It also replaces an exclusively Africanizing culture with the concept of revolutionary culture:

> Concerning our political educational work, in the black community we've opened what is called Liberation Schools for young black people and adults; for the young children we have classes in elementary school subjects, such as science and mathematics; then we have what is called black history and the teaching of African languages, but these teachings are not based upon a historical retreat into Africa. For instance, some people in the Congo speak Swahili but Swahili has not freed them. Africans in South-West Africa or in Mozambique wear African robes and have not lost their African cultural patterns but at the same time they're slaves to colonialism and neocolonialism, so that our teachings for both adults and young black people is the necessity to have a revolutionary culture. Our education and culture is the culture of the gun and the culture of resistance to racism and imperialism. The reason we say that the only culture worth keeping is the revolutionary culture of revolution-

ary agitation is that in revolution there is change—there is complete, radical, absolute and total change. That is, if we merely retreated back into our African past, we would not be engaging in complete change. For instance, the culture of the people may be defined as the total ways of the people. And therefore, in order for us to defeat racism, neocolonialism, and imperialism, our total ways must be revolutionary. . . . In other words, our dances, our songs, and the way we embrace one another must be geared towards resistance."[12]

e) The Place of Jazz

The relationship of black Americans to their music—blues, jazz, free jazz—is complex and often contradictory. For instance, the more or less westernized kind of jazz that is mass broadcast on the radio, TV, and in films never fails to satisfy a great number of blacks. Others prefer rougher genres played exclusively by blacks, such as rhythm and blues or soul music. Some of the bourgeois elite only have a taste for the most watered down jazz, closest to the white American variety. Others, the intellectuals, artists, activists, have no issue adopting free jazz.

Black musicians have played a central role in the history of jazz that has been recognized—and therefore preserved—by white elites: Louis Armstrong made the cover of *Life* magazine, Monk that of *Time* magazine, Ellington and Gillespie acted as world ambassadors of American prestige. In relation to this, and in spite of the many differences in taste, most black Americans recognize themselves in jazz, more than in fiction or poetry. This recognition is as ideological, if not more, as it is cultural, which is problematic. Outside of boxing, music is the career where blacks have met the least racial and social obstacles in the USA; needless to say, this is because American society finds commercial and ideological profit in it as well as entertainment. The image of the grinning Negro (Armstrong) is dear to the hearts of white Americans: it perpetuates the notion that black people are entertaining and futile children. Let blacks in turn choose this image as a model or a reference, and it becomes difficult not to see in this "choice" the effect of ideological pressure.

Yet this recognition is also undeniably cultural. The color line includes black musicians among black people: "Essentially there is no difference, as long as you're black, where you come from," notes Cecil Taylor. "The thing that unites us is the sameness in the oppression that we have undergone at the hand of the white man."[13] Even though the majority of blacks do not constantly listen to jazz and prefer its derivations (the white variety or black R&B), they are aware of its cultural significance as a black creation and "gift" to white America, as well as its fundamental proximity to their vital problems: the foundations for a wider adhesion to jazz by the black masses do exist. There are some politicians who have noticed as much, and refer to jazz both as a testament to black originality and as a vector of mobilization.

To the extent that political activists were invoking it, jazz could not remain outside of black movements and struggle. It became a field for ideological conflict between two conceptions of jazz (westernized and Africanized); two conceptions of music (entertaining or functional); a conflict between what pertains to commodity and art and what pretends to activism (see III).

However politically aware, however involved in activism, musicians are all directly implicated in the development of the black struggle. They all have to suffer the same oppression as the black masses: economic exploitation compounded by racism, which in its hatred levels all that are black: intellectuals, artists, but also workers, turned into sub-proletarians. Both economic exploitation and racism are factors of politicization: "Every Black person belongs to the Movement, whether he's been on a demonstration or not. The lives of Black people are political, because Black people carry on a constant war against 'the man.' So I was political, even before I knew the word."[14] Under the pressure of American living conditions and the weight of dominant ideology, the politicization of blacks becomes inescapable. For musicians, the very people whose aesthetic practice might appear to contradict political commitment, class consciousness builds parallel to, and through, race consciousness.

But it is especially in free jazz that jazzmen become more politicized, or at least more aware of politics. Their statements make this very clear:

Many among us want to kill, because we were treated like animals and fascistic methods were used against us. (Charles Mingus)[15]

Already it's not easy for whites to be artists in a white world.... In the United States, if you're black and a jazz musician, it's very hard not to go crazy. (Marion Brown)[16]

The kids are rebelling because they have learned that America has made the white, the black, the rich, the poor kid each an orphan unto himself, and this reason alone has created the most searching stage of youthful expression. (Ornette Coleman)[17]

I never really paid attention to politics. Religion is much more important to me. But in the United States, [the race question] is part of the problem. You can't forget you're black. You have to always be aware of it. As for me, I do my best to help my colored brothers. (Don Cherry)[18]

> To me, Jomo Kenyatta is still the one who leads from the darkness to the light. (Robin "Kenyatta").[19]

And declarations such as the following by Archie Shepp must be considered against the lasting silence of Western musicians:

> The black musician is a reflection of the black people, as a cultural and social phenomenon. His goal must be to free America of its inhumanity, on the aesthetic and social levels. The inhumanity of the white American towards the black American, or the inhumanity of the white American towards the white American, are not fundamental in America: they can be exorcised. I think that blacks, through the violence of their struggle, are America's only hope of salvation.[20]

Free jazz musicians are starting to think of their own aesthetic practices in terms of political commitment, thanks to the growth in political consciousness among the black masses and to struggles on the ground. The very dynamic of those struggles let them conceive of, and perform, their musical practices and productions as *part of social practices*, connected to liberation movements and revolutionary forces, rather than under the dominion of the classic bourgeois characteristics of art: separation, isolation, and ruin. The black musician produces among his people, for the people, and that makes up his music: "When you listen to Coltrane, he tells you about the life of black people from New Orleans origins to today." (Archie Shepp)[21]

On the other hand, black activists and political leaders are becoming increasingly aware of the importance of jazz as a black cultural manifestation, i.e. as a *propaganda* weapon, and they have begun using it as such. See Stokely Carmichael: "The music of Archie Shepp is the great black beauty of black power."[22] Or Malcolm X:

> And in that atmosphere, brothers and sisters, you'd be surprised what will come out of the bosom of this black man. I've seen it happen. I've seen black musicians when they'd be jamming at a jam session with white musicians—a whole lot of difference. The white musician can jam if he's got some sheet music in front of him. He can jam on something that he's heard jammed before. If he's heard it, then he can duplicate it or he can imitate it or he can read it. But that black musician, he picks up his horn and starts blowing some sounds that he never thought of before. He improvises, he creates, it comes from within. It's his soul, it's that soul music. It's the only area on the American scene where the black man has been free to create. And he has mastered it. He

has shown that he can come up with something that nobody ever thought of on his horn.

Well, likewise he can do the same thing if given intellectual independence. He can come up with a new philosophy. He can come up with a philosophy that nobody has heard of yet. He can invent a society, a social system, an economic system, a political system, that is different from anything that exists or has ever existed anywhere on this earth. He will improvise; he'll bring it from within himself. And this is what you and I want.

You and I want to create an organization that will give us so much power we can sit down and do as we please. Once we can sit down and think as we please, speak as we please, and do as we please, we will show people what pleases us. And what pleases us won't always please them. So you've got to get some power before you can be yourself. Do you understand that? You've got to get some power before you can be yourself. Once you get power and you be yourself, why, you're gone, you've got it and gone. You create a new society and make some heaven right here on this earth.[23]

Note the rhetorical form used in this passage, borrowing from black churches its flow, repetitions, call and response, punctuated with words of approval from the audience. Note also Malcolm X's constant effort to link cultural liberation and political liberation. The creative force of black Americans has so far only expressed itself to a limited degree, but it needs political strength to express itself further. Finally, his allusion to "heaven right here on this earth," like the form of this speech, aims at the religious reflexes of the black masses.

That politicians would in this way refer to black music as the vanguard of Afro-American culture—and therefore the proof of its existence and worth—and, more broadly, their focus on ideology meant to change the cultural moorings of the black masses, could only make musicians more conscious of the cultural role they could play at the juncture of political struggles. In free jazz, one can witness the *political positioning* of music, through activist preoccupations and their influence on aesthetic experimentation and the very conception of music.

Free jazz appeared at first to be a purely musical phenomenon, which is to say its determination by politics remained invisible. But under the pressure of political forces around and *within* it, free jazz was soon conceived by those who made it and those who listened to it as not only having a *social function*—which old jazz also had in its own way—but also a *political status and function* in the cultural realm. In eleven years (1960–1971) it has evolved to the beat of black political struggles. Thus its entry onto the American cultural stage was made possible by the advanced state of political struggles in the United States and around the world, and their theorization by black American activists. The reflection of these struggles on the ideological instance made it possible both for free jazz to develop and for its specific contribution to be formulated. The reach and stakes of free jazz's cultural role have widened, from the original reaction against the colonized forms of jazz and the search for references to African music, to a more global protest against the cultural values of Western civilization, the building of a specifically Afro-American music, and the practice of music as a revolutionary art in the service of revolution. In parallel, the political evolution of black struggles—and the qualitative leap tied to the Black Panther Party—transformed the question of black culture and black art. From the assertion of authentically black culture and art referring solely to extinct African civilizations, we moved to more internationalist art and culture, turning towards all cultures (African, Asian, Indian) suffering from Western imperialism. In this new stage, musical production opens up to a great variety of trends and influences outside of Africa, which Afro-American music, strong in its self-assertion, no longer fears to associate with.

2. Economic Ownership of Jazz

> It seems that production and publicity are so closely related that they turn into the same thing. What I mean is, in jazz the Negro is the product. The way they handle the publicity on me, about how far out I am and everything, it gets to be that I'm the product itself. So if it's me they're selling, if I'm the product, then the profits couldn't come back to me, you dig?
> —Ornette Coleman, quoted in A. B. Spellman, *Four Lives in the Bebop Business*, Pantheon Books: New York, 1966, 66.

In its first stages, jazz was only known and played in black neighborhoods, red light districts (New Orleans's Storyville) and black cabarets and dancehalls (in Chicago and New York). The rare ethnomusicologists interested in it then recognized it, at best, as a limited and *extra-artistic* folk music. At worst, they saw it as an evocation of primitive savagery, an exotic oddity. For the few whites who could hear it, jazz was a special kind of mood music, associated with sexual debauchery and race mixing. Associated early by its very name ("Jass" was slang for sex) to orgies both shameful and savage (African), jazz had virtually *no chance* to be broadcast widely in white Puritan and racist America, nor to reach commercial success. For jazz to be widely circulated and commercialized, *white musicians had to take it over*. They plagiarized it, *valorizing* it by "whitening" the genre, by exorcising its blackness and the related fantasies of repulsion among racist white populations, but also by *making a profit* from it, since in a capitalist system—and even more so in the US—profit is a guarantee of value. Capitalist logic demanded that Puritanism and racism defer to the priority of trade.

Introduced by *minstrels*[1] long before the historical birth of jazz, the commercial exploitation of black music could only be performed on a grand scale after the emergence of industrial capitalism. The invention and industrialization of sound-reproduction techniques (piano rolls, then records) mark jazz's transformation into an object of trade—and, *therefore*, into an object of art. Indeed, only piano rolls and records could ensure the conservation of music that was then unscored, and almost completely improvised (if often repeated).

But during the 1910s, the music industry, as would later be the case with radio, was in the hands of white capitalism alone. The jazz market was also first and foremost made up of a white audience, for its financial means and numbers. A small black middle class existed, but busy as it was mimicking white ideology, it rejected anything below itself as a reminder of its origins and condition. In general the black middle class despised jazz, accepting only its most westernized variations. The black audience for jazz only built slowly, hampered by the cost of record players and records, but also, as noted by LeRoi Jones, wary of what the radio and the industry offered up as "jazz"—Paul Whiteman et al.

This situation—white labels and a white audience—explains why, although many great black bands existed (King Oliver, Freddie Keppard, New Orleans marching bands, etc.), it was the Original Dixieland Jass Band, a white band, that had the honor of recording the first jazz record. Similarly, it was another white band, Paul Whiteman's—even further removed from authentic black music than the ODJB—that for a majority of Americans and later on for Europe represented jazz. Whiteman (who was dubbed the King of Jazz) inaugurated the long series of white musicians who owed their fame and wealth to the pillaging of black music: Benny Goodman (the so-called King of Swing), the Dorsey Brothers, Harry James, Artie Shaw, Glenn Miller, Charlie Barnet, Stan Kenton, Woody Herman, Gerry Mulligan, Dave Brubeck. . . . In 1956, Lucky Thompson explained how "colored musicians are fully aware that since the beginning of jazz, their music has been exploited in such a way that they only get minimal profit, even as people try to take away their privilege as creators of the music."[2]

Not just black musicians, but also black critics and writers denounce this cultural and economic spoliation: LeRoi Jones, of course ("Black Man, Black Man, The White Man Owns You"[3]), but also Harold Cruse, who wrote in 1963:

> In America the entire industry of popular music writing, publishing and selling was established by white appropriation of the whole body of Afro-American folk music—the only original music in America with a broad human appeal. This music has been cheapened, debased and commercialized for popular appeal. The American music industry has been exploiting, cheating, stealing from, browbeating, excluding, plagiarizing Negro singers, jazz musicians, composers, etc., for decades and getting away with it. The cultural exploitation established by white America in the early years of the twentieth century by the white appropriation of Afro-American folk-music was the first great manifestation of the racist development in the economics of American culture. This racist cultural doctrine, once established in music, spread through the entire field of cultural expression in America. It has had its poisonous effect on American theater, both musical and dramatic, and a distorting influence on American dance. Today it is still rampant in the jazz

fields. The racial attitudes behind American cultural developments were the basic problem of cultural competition between white and Negro. The whites very quickly realized that from the lowly Negro in America came the only rich vein of untapped and completely original material for song, dance, music and theater.... The economic benefits derived from the creative and artistic use of Negro cultural ingredients were reaped by the whites through the simple practice of cultural appropriation of aesthetic ideas not native to their own tradition. As a result there came into being a long line of white creative artists and performers who either enriched themselves or got their start by using Negro material—the Al Jolsons, the George Gershwins, the Amos 'n' Andys, Eugene O'Neill, Ridgely Torrence, Marc Connelly, and more, plus scores of plagiarizing white composers (including very big names). Booking agents and managers have for decades made millions by the shrewd exploitation and manipulation of Negro performers and creators over whom they held the life and death economic power to hire or fire.[4]

LeRoi Jones and Harold Cruse both emphasize that this parasitic relationship is cultural and economic, but they do not analyze the connections between the two fields of action. More precisely, they do not address how the economic imperatives of American capitalism may determine the forms of black music, nor how many elements of the music are filtered out because they do not conform to the established ideological frame. For the most part, these are the essential Afro-American elements. To steal their music away from blacks amounts to stealing blacks away from their music, to drive them away. Cecil Taylor says,

> I don't want my music to be called jazz, but I feel it is jazz. Jazz is what some exploit for profit, which would be fine if musicians benefitted from it. Jazz comes from the black community. It is the musical manifestation of a subculture and has nothing to do with the fancy places where you can listen to it. You can hear it on the radio, but not really on television—no doubt because some might find Negroes on the screen shocking.... No one wants to invest money in jazz, people would rather take money from jazz."[5]

Indeed, white commercial interests want to profit from their economic domination of jazz, but further still they aim to ensure that this profit remain steady, and to that effect they influence the very development of the music. New trends, styles, and musicians are regularly introduced, bolstered by advertising campaigns; the press and the radio inculcate taste for such and such music genre to the public. In the process, the musical forms and musicians that go against the grain are blocked; commercial interests control the schools, careers, and potential collaborations between musicians. The white public's tastes in jazz are not rooted in any of the founding histories or cultures of jazz, and for that reason they are extremely flexible. Ready for any conversion that will not challenge their norms, the record and radio industries manage to manufacture fame and trends (such as swing or cool jazz) while simultaneously impeding the work of forces of production they cannot immediately recuperate. Contrast Ornette Coleman's decade of misery and labor, or the difficulties faced by Sun Ra and Cecil Taylor, with Dave Brubeck and Cannonball Adderley's[6] quick fame. Think about the immense and sudden success of the musician presented in ads as the gravelly-voiced trumpeter born in New Orleans—no, not Louis Armstrong: Louis Prima.

The consequences of the constant—and in this place and time, inevitable—intrusion of commerce in the very evolution of jazz are ultimately serious. Some are easily noticed: one-hit wonders, commercial coups, etc. Others that participate in the repression and censorship of forms originating outside of the programs of the industry are more difficult to see. Let us simply mention what remains the rule for most musicians recording their first albums: they have to play with accompanying musicians they do not choose. About such intrusions, Ornette Coleman said: "I thought that as long as they were white, they all had the same thing in common, to control and rule you."[7]

Finally, among the schemes and censorship generated by commerce we also have the adulteration of the musical forms themselves (see further in Chapter 3.a). The emergence of free jazz has only emphasized the issue of (white) commercial domination over jazz. Everything about the New Thing clashed with the habits of jazz lovers; on the other hand, the black masses, those for whom the music was being played, either took time to discover and recognize it, or decided instead for the simpler violence of *soul music*. Despite early hopes, the big record labels showed little urgency in supporting free jazz: Sun Ra had already been among the first to create his own label, Saturn. ESP, a brand new label founded by a white jazz lover named Bernard Stollman, recorded Ayler, Pharoah Sanders, Byron Allen, the New York Art Quartet (with LeRoi Jones), but also Sun Ra, Marion Brown, Frank Wright, Sunny Murray, Milford Graves, etc. More importantly, free musicians formed several union-like associations: the Association for the Advancement of Creative Musicians (AACM),[8] the Jazz Composers Guild.[9] "I believe the Guild was Bill Dixon and Cecil Taylor's idea," says Archie Shepp. "They mostly wanted to fight against the dictatorship of club managers, record labels and critics. They knew our time would come sooner or later. Musicians who belonged were to only play in a club if the Guild accepted the conditions it offered. It was the same for recordings. This way musicians would no longer be exploited."[10] Crippled by infighting and racial conflict, the Guild disappeared and was replaced by the Jazz Composer's Orchestra Association, led by Mike Mantler and counting among its members Charlie Haden, Carla Bley, Andrew Cyrille, Ron Carter, etc.

Free jazz musicians are fully aware of their economic dependence on American capitalism (on record labels and radio stations, but also, on a smaller scale, on club owners, concert organizers, agents, etc.). They also know well that the nature and aim of their music means it will never be very "commercial," which leaves them relatively unarmed, much like all black musicians. They have to face the same capitalist exploitation as the rest of jazz, with the difference that their music is infinitely less likely to be co-opted by commerce and ideology, because of its focus on politics and cultural resistance. Free jazz is played amid the same economic contradictions as the rest of jazz. Yet it strives to cancel out the effects of such pressure at the aesthetic level by adopting a position critical of the ideology and culture dominant even within jazz, and by positioning itself in political struggles.

Thus the political commitment and activism of most free jazz musicians appears necessary to sublimate their own exploited position within the capitalist system of the music industry. Ornette Coleman declared in 1966:

> This is the worst kind of suffering. This psychological suffering of knowing that you're being exploited, whether it's whites doing it to whites or whites doing it to blacks or blacks doing it to blacks, it's still the same thing. But I'll tell you this, I'm thirty-five years old, and I don't believe I'll live to see the time when blacks will be exploiting whites.[11]

The economic colonization of jazz by American capitalism is but one aspect of the colonization and commercial exploitation of blacks by the same system; awareness of the intolerable character of this exploitation is what brings musicians and the masses alike to the necessity of revolution. It is therefore not by chance that all jazz critics (A. B. Spellman and LeRoi Jones excepted) in their histories and commentaries have modestly minimized—when they have not flatly ignored—the gravity of the capitalist exploitation of jazz in the name of aesthetic purism. To emphasize the exploitation would amount to exposing the wider capitalist exploitation of black people, of which jazz exploitation is but a detail. They obfuscate those economic contradictions specific to jazz (which, though denounced by musicians, have been ignored by critics) and the entire economic field in the process, thus forbidding the possibility of political analysis of the situation of black people in America.

We know the efforts made by capitalism, using its ideological apparatuses, to encourage the belief that its domination belongs to the natural order of things, and that economics is but one element of the issue, etc. In the case of America, because the "Negro question" is ultimately about the exploitation of part of the population by the class in power and its allies (racism, it deserves to be repeated, is a product of ideology), it is easy to understand how that class might benefit from hiding the economic reality of its domination behind a series of endless and insoluble debates on the race issue, the psychology of black people, their sociology, religion, morals, civil rights, and even aesthetics.

3. Cultural Colonization

I have certainly learned more in the black ghetto of Boston than in the conservatory.... Why do we have to spend so many years learning European musical traditions, when none of the teachers or musicians knows anything about Harlem or Afro-American traditions? The criteria they use are particular to their music, after all! But what is Louis Armstrong's idea of beauty? Who cares about that? And even if they cared, their opinion does not interest me, simply because they can't imagine that we would have our own criteria.
—Cecil Taylor, quoted by Daniel Berger in "Cecil Taylor à la trace," *Jazz Hot* (February 1967), 19.

a) White "Jazz"

The appearance and development of the free jazz movement led many musicians to refuse to call their music "jazz" (see Cecil Taylor above, and Charles Tyler: "I think jazz will free itself from being jazz, or at least from what the public thinks jazz is"[1]). This shows the distance gradually taken by jazz itself and jazz musicians from what has long passed—and still does pass—for "jazz" to the white public, American and European critics, historians, etc. "Jazz" in quotation marks refers to a long period in this music's history in which the commercial interests of white capitalism, their determination of musical forms, white ideological norms, and white musicians all prevailed. That period spans roughly the time between the commercialization of jazz (1920s) and the rise of bebop (1940–45).

The worldwide commercial success of jazz after 1930—along with the imperative condition and consequence of this success: the necessity of fitting the "tastes" of the white majority—make this a period of utter alienation for what remained of black music in "jazz." On the commercial and musical planes, this was a phase when the inventions of the preceding era, the formulas and recipes created during jazz's gestation period, were intensely exploited. Of course, *in the margins*, black musicians kept creating music that resisted the ossification of jazz; but the major trend during those twenty years was commercial, white, and mostly uninventive, a series of variations on the original forms, a work of infinite reiteration. "Jazz" acquired rules, aesthetic structures, and a definition recognized and perpetuated by those who made it, those who heard it, and those who exploited it. "Jazz" was either swing or big band; it was made for dance and entertainment; rhythmical fixity was emphasized, themes were valorized, and invariability in song structure (the length and placement of "improvisations," a mechanical adjustment of the ratio of each part to the other) was preferred. Jazz criticism was established during the same period in the US and Europe, took note of those dominant characteristics, and with beautiful recklessness promoted them as the transhistorical *values* of jazz. Blind to the historical, social, and ideological determination of these characteristics, critics offered them to musicians as references and models. Musical and aesthetic criteria whose origin, moment, and location of emission had not been questioned took hold of jazz, molded it, and fixated it in a series of *exact copies*, differentiated only by variations in details and accessories. What was made took on force of law, and since all that was made was what commerce and ideology demanded, the criteria of "good" and "true" jazz were white. Only black musicians became alarmed—the black masses either followed white fashion passively, or focused their interest on the primitive forms (blues) and on the few black musicians who, in spite of the multiple *adaptations* to which they had to submit themselves in order to survive, prolonged as well as they could the forces of black music. They did so in interpretation (Armstrong), reference (Ellington), and rhythm (Lunceford) rather than on a strictly regulated formal plane.

It is therefore not surprising that black musicians would have been the first to consider "jazz" a *long misadventure for black music*. Faced with the success of white jazz, the pillaging and dilution of their own music, black musicians felt constantly robbed. This theft added to a long list of despoliations in all domains, as this anonymous musician quoted by Eric Hobsbawm testifies to:

> You see, we need music. We've always needed a music—our own. We have nothing else. Our writers write like the whites, our painters paint like them. Only our musicians don't play like the whites. So we created a music for ourselves. When we had it—the old type of jazz—the whites came, and they liked it and imitated it. Pretty soon it was no longer our music....
>
> You see as soon as we have a music, the white man comes and imitates it. We've now had jazz for fifty years, and in all those fifty years there has been not a single white man, perhaps leaving aside Bix [Beiderbecke] who has had an idea. Only the colored men have ideas. But if you see who's got the famous names, they're all white.
>
> What can we do? We must go on inventing something new all the time. When we have it, the whites will take it from us, and we have to start all over again. It is as though we were being hunted.[2]

Yet, without minimizing the importance of the economic and musical pillaging of black music, the fact that only white musicians profited from the invention and production of new forms by blacks, that American variety and popular music owed everything to jazz (Bing Crosby, Sinatra, etc.), all these despoliations make but for one aspect of the parasitism of black music by white businessmen and musicians. The other aspect was their influence on the very evolution of jazz and on its aesthetics. In the imitation, the vulgarization, and the adaptation of black music by whites, the music was distorted and filtered: its most assimilable, constitutive elements (simple and regular rhythms, pretty melodies, for example) were valorized, while those less easy to incorporate (rhythmical and structural complexity, violent sounds, etc.) and altogether undesirable elements (the social function of black music, references to its racial and African origins) were censored.

We have seen how the cultural colonization of jazz by white aesthetic and commercial values started with the advent of the music under white control. Jazz owes it only to its white plagiarizers and vulgarizers for turning it into a business, and later into an art recognized and normalized by a section of the Western elite: whites had to start playing jazz for other whites to feel allowed to listen to it and to justify their interest by calling it art. In order to be accepted, what had initially been the music of black Americans *could no longer belong to them exclusively*.

In this first change of roles black music lost economically *and* culturally. Under the joint pressure of commercial interests and dominant ideology, what in jazz pertained to black struggle—which had produced jazz as its expression—was obfuscated in priority. Jazz was first "universally" defined as *entertainment music* (by opposition to "serious" classical music), because the label was popular and did not emphasize *color*. When discussing jazz as art finally became acceptable, it did not change a thing: color was not to be emphasized.

The strict regulation of jazz by commerce and capitalist ideology came with, and perpetuated itself through, aesthetic reshaping and cultural redefinition of jazz: to be accepted as art, jazz necessarily had to be seen as *compatible* with Western criteria of musical and artistic normativity. This meant that white translations of jazz had to be aesthetically and ideologically vetted and authenticated by jazz historians and critics. The crowning of jazz as art, considered everywhere a "progressive" victory over conservatism, actually perfected the colonization started by commerce.

b) White Criticism

There is between jazz and jazz criticism an obvious contradiction, which has only recently been discovered, in LeRoi Jones's first writings in the early 1960s. Whereas jazz is for the most part made by African Americans (it is a product of their history, of their social insertion and their cultural traditions), the criticism, theory, and history of this music have been since their first manifestations, and continue to be exclusively, the domain of white specialists, in the USA or in Europe. Jazz performance is the domain of black musicians; but when it comes to commenting on jazz, analyzing it, judging its aesthetic value, jazz becomes the private domain of white historians, critics, and musicologists.

The fact that apart from LeRoi Jones, his fellow poet A. B. Spellman has been the only black to play any role in jazz criticism can be explained first by the importance and longevity of the cultural obstacles set up by white society against African Americans. As far as access to education and the nature of education are concerned, everything (racism, overt and indirect segregation, poverty, the necessity of working young in order to survive, the cost of studies, the inadequacy of curricula, the rare and disappointing if not downright illusory nature of career opportunities) has worked towards barring blacks from going to school and conspired to turn them away from it. Only in 1960 did the scholarly results of blacks reach levels comparable, though inferior, to those of whites. In 1962, the average length of schooling for whites age 14 and older was 11.5 years, compared to 9 years for blacks; in 1961, 6.2 percent of 3,721,000 American high school students were black, while blacks made up 10.5 percent of the country's population and 12.1 percent of its student population.

Even more influential is the prejudice of the black middle class against everything that distinguishes it from the white bourgeois it tries to emulate, especially in rejecting all cultural connections with working class blacks, whom they despise as much as the whites despise them. E. Franklin Frazier, Malcolm X, and Rap Brown all have emphasized in their writings how this black bourgeoisie—from which are recruited the proponents of integrationism, nonviolence, and collaboration with white liberals and capitalism—has mitigated black social and political demands. In the words of Rap Brown:

> When a Black man looks at Black people with a Black mind and Black soul, it is immediately apparent that Black people possess certain unique characteristics which not only distinguish them from whites and negroes, but which have greatly contributed to the survival of Blacks. Whites recognize this and have always attempted to eradicate these characteristics or discredit them. In instances where they have succeeded, negroes have been created.... Negroes know that whites prefer institutionalized Blacks, i.e., Blacks who give their allegiance to white cultural, political, social and economic institutions.... Any action or behavior which is not endorsed by whites, negroes consider "acting a nigger." What was "acting a nigger" two years ago is now accepted as "soul."

Naturally, this was endorsed by whites before being accepted by negroes. . . . Negroes say: Nobody but niggers listen to the blues.[3]

Or Malcolm X:

> This modern, twentieth-century uncle Thomas now often wears a top hat. He's usually well-dressed and well-educated. He's often the personification of culture and refinement. The twentieth century uncle Thomas sometimes speaks with a Yale or Harvard accent. Sometimes he is known as Professor, Doctor, Judge, and Reverend, even Right Reverend Doctor. This twentieth century Uncle Thomas is a professional Negro. . . . By that I mean his profession is being a Negro for the white man.[4]

This attitude of submission to white ideologies explains how jazz can be scorned by its own people. LeRoi Jones writes:

> Until relatively recently, those Negroes who could become critics, who would largely have to come from the black middle class, have simply not been interested in the music. Or at least jazz, for the black middle class, has only comparatively recently lost some of its stigma (though by no means is it yet as popular among them as any vapid musical product that comes sanctioned by the taste of the white majority). Jazz was collected among the numerous skeletons the middle class black man kept locked in the closet of his psyche, along with watermelons and gin, and whose rattling caused him no end of misery and self-hatred. As one Howard University philosophy professor said to me when I was an undergraduate, "It's fantastic how much bad taste the blues contain!" But it is just this "bad taste" that this Uncle spoke of that has been the one factor that has kept the best of Negro music from slipping sterilely into the echo chambers of middle-brow American culture. And to a great extent such "bad taste" was kept extant in the music, blues or jazz because the Negroes who were responsible for the best of the music were always aware of their identities as black Americans and really did not, themselves, desire to become vague, featureless, Americans as is usually the case with the Negro middle class. . . . Any Negro who had some ambition towards literature, in the earlier part of this century, was likely to have developed so powerful an allegiance to the sacraments of middle-class American culture that he would be horrified by the very idea of writing about jazz.[5]

Most black intellectuals of middle-class extraction have inherited middle-class prejudice and have not yet shed it, and therefore jazz, this "savage music, nigger music," has suffered from discrimination on the part of the very people—i.e. black professors, black historians, black journalists—who would have been more apt than white critics to study it and reflect on its cultural status. They did not, which gives an idea of the power of dominant ideology over the dominated. ("Racism systematically verifies itself when the slave can only break free by imitating the master: by contradicting his own reality."[6]) To white prejudice—against blacks, against black musicians likened to clowns or pimps, and more generally against "artists" and their debauched lives—was added the *white bourgeois prejudice* of "integrated" blacks.

Black culture only gained value in the eyes of the black elites when black intellectuals eventually rejected and deconstructed dominant ideology, thanks to the political work of mostly autodidact militants (on the importance of this ideological struggle, see I. 1.b). Black culture, and, with it, jazz, could finally pretend to the status of object of study.

c) The First Jazz War

The misadventure of Western jazz criticism began shortly after the misadventure of black music also known as "jazz." It began when "jazz" was rejected by bourgeois intellectual elites in the US and in Europe.

Commerce was in the process of taking over black music and, in order to reach the white audience, broadcast pale reproductions of it as "jazz." Presented as and considered true jazz, these reproductions were scorned by bourgeois music lovers, and by those who were simply attached to traditional forms of Western classical music, even if they found them boring. "Jazz" — [Paul] Whiteman's jazz!—was condemned as "jungle music," "vulgar" music, non-music. The moral, religious, and cultural authorities in the US and Europe supported such judgments: "Governments should ban jazz like morphine and cocaine, as this music does nothing but degrade the taste and morale of the public."[7]

The first jazz critics were forged in this battle. From the start, their purpose was to defend a music they liked—and which had only remote connections to black music, a fact they were not aware of—in spite of their culture and musical habits, and to defend it against both the moral guardians of the Western bourgeoisie and the music lovers and musicians jealous of classical music traditions: a mixture of cultural and racist prejudice. In 1920, one could read the following in the French *Revue Musicale*:

> To speak cynically, jazz is an orchestra of brutes with non-opposable thumbs and prehensile feet, in the forest of Voodoo. It is all excess, and therefore it is

worse than monotone: the ape is left to himself, without morals, without discipline; fallen into the undergrowth of instinct, exposing his naked flesh with every bound, together with flesh even more obscene, his heart. These slaves must be subdued, or masters are no more. It is shameful that they reign. There is shame in ugliness and in its triumph.[8]

Ideological, cultural, and aesthetic implications are already inseparably mixed. These lines give an idea of the tone used by the opponents of jazz—especially when one takes into account that French colonialists thought themselves much more progressive than American slavery apologists.

Encouraged by the fact that a certain number of intellectuals and musicians, in reaction to the bourgeois tendencies of their society, had pronounced themselves in support of jazz, the first wave of jazz criticism worked at convincing skeptics that 1) jazz was indeed music; 2) jazz was not savage music, if only because it was influenced by Western music; 3) jazz was exotic, yet assimilable by Western aesthetic criteria; 4) jazz was not exclusively, nor mainly, black music: white jazzmen were more numerous; 5) in consequence, jazz was indeed an art, *which reiterated the ideological effects of all these arguments*.

The "defense" of jazz had no other weapon but a quest for compromise. It had to obfuscate all signs of jazz's alterity, soften them into exotic traces in order to produce a more acceptable *image* of jazz, *in spite* of its more or less concealed or concealable differences with Western musical norms. Jazz critics therefore reiterated the filtering and adaptation of jazz undertaken by commerce, *without even knowing it*. This retreating defense of "jazz"—which was *itself a retreat* from the original black music—*twice* erased the African American social and cultural traits of jazz, both from the musical foreground and the aesthetic foreground.

On one hand jazz was defended through dissimulation, by downplaying differences and reinterpreting and recuperating them culturally. On the other hand, the goal of this defense being the artistic consecration of jazz, the battle was waged on the field of aesthetics. This was choosing the enemy's field; indeed, jazz was being rejected on aesthetic grounds, a dignified façade to cover the ideological repulsion and moral interdictions that such rejection involved. Jazz *forms* were criticized, as if only forms counted, as if this critique came from a place where all forms were treated equally, and all arts and cultures were accepted according to principle and judged on a level plane.

Western bourgeois aesthetic criteria would therefore serve to "define"—elect, set aside—the specific characteristics of jazz. In order to both valorize and assimilate certain jazz forms, such as collective improvisation, the dialogue between instruments, or the importance of vocalization, critics automatically mentioned old forms of European music such as polyphonies, canons, etc., in reference. This concern for ennobling jazz by rubbing it against musical or extra-musical Western values[9] rested on the belief that a victory on the aesthetic front would make ideological hang-ups crumble. Recognized as a cultural object, jazz would no longer be despicable—which implied that its market would grow. But this did not so much destroy hang-ups as obscure *their cultural significance*, and their relation to *one* civilization, the Western civilization, which sees itself as superior to and exclusive of all others. Such a repression, in providing the means to "understand" jazz in its relative proximity, took away the means of thinking about jazz's differences and alterity.

To illustrate the castrating approach characteristic of most of Western criticism—and not only in its early writings—let us look at two excerpts from André Coeuroy's *Histoire générale du jazz*. His point of view is more than outrageous, but as such it shows the symptoms of the historical and cultural determination typical of the first wave of jazz criticism:

> Jazz therefore appears to be an instrumental *concerto*. It is a concerto in its abrupt irruptions of *tutti*, in its infinitely ornate phrases, and in the multiplicity of cadences thanks to which each soloist can display his virtuosity and his gift for improvisation or variation (when in modern symphony and concerto-symphony, space is *no longer*[10] given to these two qualities), in the new existence of a continuous metric and harmonic bass. . . . But it is a concerto permeated with vocal and polyphonic habits, one that evokes dance through its beats. It provides space for a kind of savagery that Western music, out of stylistic modesty, *had*[11] until now repressed. But this is a controlled release: that is the point. The *European* feel of the music is what keeps the Negro in check, what resolves seemingly inexplicable anomalies. One often marvels at the fact that Armstrong, who is so animalistic when he sings, becomes such a tasteful virtuoso when he plays the trumpet. In his good era [sic], never did he play adulterated tones nor muted notes, but always a pure and sober chant, even when it was poignant, and a style of improvisation that, though weak, was never anarchical. This is because Armstrong possesses a sure sense of harmony, and he applies at every instant the modal rules that dictate composition in European countries.[12]

All the elements are here: legitimacy provided by classical music, notions of "taste," "purity," "sobriety," the rejection of the "animalistic," the "adulterated," the "anarchical." Jazz forms are molded after, and shown as descending from, classical forms—as if the latter had anticipated the former in the concerto, the continuous bass *(continuo basso)*, modal rules, etc.

Coeuroy concludes the chapter entitled "Black and White" with these words:

> All the "musical material" at the origin of jazz (religious or social songs, ballads and dances, *spirituals* and blues) bears the mark of the tribute paid to Europe.... One can therefore conclude that jazz has found its *unity*[13] by mixing in the European mold of variation and concerto European harmonic technique (from Liszt to Ravel and Debussy), melody inherited from *protestant choral*, half-black and half-white rhythm patterns, and a specific use of instruments. Jazz is not a Negro art: it exists, in the words of Hoérée, in the margin of Negro art. Those who hate Negro art therefore do not have to hate jazz. It belongs to whites as well as blacks. If blacks first put it to good use, it is up to whites to get their own back. It has already started.[14]

While these comments do not represent the wide scope of Western criticism, they have the merit of illustrating how intertwined the aesthetic and ideological (commercial) planes have been, and how they have merged: aesthetically whitened, jazz becomes an art that can be appreciated by those who "do not like Negro art." Noting signs of Westernness and rejecting signs of Africanness go together and serve no other cause than that of "jazz," both actions being determined by the obsessive fear that jazz might escape criticism (and commerce). "It belongs to whites and to blacks" actually means that the less it belongs to blacks, the more it belongs to us.

From the start, Western jazz criticism has been concerned with the recognition of jazz as an art. This concern has dictated its goals ever since. For this reason, jazz criticism has remained blind to its own complicity with a dominant ideology that on the one hand focuses on aesthetic issues, and on the other is concerned with commercial and advertising issues. To make audiences accept jazz was to render jazz palatable.

The causes of this blindness were simple: leading its crusade for jazz in the name of noble principles (tolerance, open mindedness, modernity, progressivism, etc.) and against the backward-looking and ideologically hermetic aspects of the Western elite, jazz criticism could only fancy itself in the role of the *pioneer* (with a dash of the prophet). That is to say that critics had to position *themselves* ahead (and even, in their view, outside) of dominant ideology and Western cultural trends. This is why the opposition between supporters and detractors of jazz, because of its very visibility, long passed for the main contradiction. In fact, those who defended jazz were *on the same side* as those who attacked it, not only because they all were caught in the *same* historical and ideological determination, but also because the defenders of jazz let the dominant ideology—and the commercial pressure that demanded that they talk about art as soon as possible—force on them the Western bourgeois conception of art as a frame for this debate. A double trickery for criticism, and a double trickery for black music: the object (jazz) had already been sanitized by commerce, and jazz's defenders positioned it in the most neutralizing of frames, that of Western aesthetics.

Critics and historians old and new, from the USA and Europe, forced themselves to devote long demonstrations to proving that jazz was deserving of artistic dignity, without realizing that the music at stake in and under the word jazz had nothing to gain from this dignity, and much to lose: it risked perpetuating its commercial and cultural exploitation. Even when critics spared themselves a demonstration they felt had already been made, the same contradiction still weighed down on their discourse: while they believed the contradiction to be resolved, it was only repressed, and the fragility of this "resolution" suggested that the contradiction might very well return. The argument for and against jazz (jazz as art or not) that has long occupied criticism has also served to mask the main contradiction between, on the one hand, a music determined historically, socially, and culturally by both a non-Western civilization and the worst realities of the capitalist system and ideology (slavery and racism), and on the other hand, the bourgeois aesthetic criteria—inherently part of Western civilization—that pretends to judge it.

Jazz has nothing to do with the aesthetic idealists who rule music and art in capitalist societies; historically and culturally produced by other forces, other needs, other perspectives, it does not belong to the history of Western arts. As the capitalist bourgeoisie has come to think of its own arts as Art, the ultimate reference and model, the measure of all the others, to pull African American music into that Art's domain inevitably ignores what in that music is irreducible to Art, what has constituted it as a form of resistance against Westernness and the bourgeois representation of Art:

> Even though the white middle-brow critic[15] had known about Negro music for only about three decades, he was already trying to formalize and finally institutionalize it. It is a hideous idea. The music was already in danger of being forced into that junk pile of admirable objects and data the West knows as culture.[16]

d) White Jazzmen

White-black opposition in jazz is one of the false quarrels grafted onto the one we have just exposed. From the start, more or less talented white musicians imposed their names and music on "jazz," and often became famous sooner than black musicians, a phenomenon that became only more common with time. Soon, then, the question about the connection between a musician's worth and the color of his skin was raised. This debate returned regularly, filling thousands of pages in books, magazines, etc., as it obfuscated more serious questions about the economic exploitation of jazz or the political struggles of blacks in jazz. Interestingly, with the exception of Hugues Panassié (a case we will study a little further), all critics, emphasizing more or less the importance of black musicians—and more and more so as the political role of blacks increased—reached the conclusion that a certain musical equality existed between whites and blacks. This amounted to not taking into account social inequalities or differences in historical, economic, and cultural determination and their respective political spectrums, in the name of humanistic egalitarianism and for fear of being called a reverse racist.

The great majority of black musicians—until free jazz, when the elements of the matter changed, politically speaking—agree that white musicians have only had a secondary role in the development of the music; yet jazz critics, following the tendencies of the white public and the black bourgeoisie that emulates it, seem to have overestimated their import. That the white public would do so is easily conceivable, not only in the light of the advertising efforts of the record industry, but also because of ideological recognition: in the words of LeRoi Jones, "You cannot, for instance, blame any white man for liking Andre Previn more than Cecil Taylor; it is his life that is reflected by his choices (is, in fact those choices). Most white men in America are closer to Andre Previn than CT or Duke Ellington either, for that matter."[17] This "spontaneous" recognition is therefore exploited and repeated by ideological apparatuses: the press, advertising, cultural commerce. But it is remarkable that it would also be repeated by jazz critics who were better informed, more aware. If the point of view of specialists—concerned with impartiality and objectivity—in fact confirms and authorizes with its comments the tendency of the majority of consumers to prefer *their* music to that of *others*, even when the former is borrowed from the latter and often less interesting, then setting racism aside at the critical level and refusing to reflect on its action and its consequences participates in its subtle perpetuation at the ideological level.

In fact, it seems that jazz criticism still confuses the direct participation of white musicians in a black music—which is on the level of more or less decent imitation, borrowing, or influence of black on white—with the game of influences of white on black, the Western influences on jazz. The fact that jazz was musically born of the assimilation and reinterpretation of a great number of Western musical elements (marching bands, dances, church music, borrowings from classical and contemporary music) does not make it *ipso facto* assimilable by Western musicians. Deported into a foreign civilization, black Americans have found themselves forced to ingest and digest a considerable mass of exogenous elements, *not only in music*: in religion, social systems, language and writing, morals, culture, ideology, philosophy, etc. The very fact of being absolutely subjugated to these influences with no possible choice is *what is specific* to the historical, social, and cultural situation of black Americans: and that is what cannot be imitated.

The black's double extraction, African and American, determines all of his productions in many and complex ways; but this multi-determination is itself the privilege of African Americans. A black musician uses the multiple Western traces present in jazz to *work* on the specific and original character of this multiplicity, this diversity that constitutes jazz as music. For a white musician, the work is different: it is undertaken not on a duality or on a multiplicity of cultural codes imposed on him *en masse*, but on what *could* (or just as well could not) come as a supplement to his membership in Western culture alone. For the white musician, black inspiration is a supplement of soul (when it is not just a supplement of profit). "Western influences" are for blacks precisely what they have not chosen, desired, or appreciated; they're what they have been forced to live with, to struggle with daily. In jazz, these influences are elements of internal contradiction, permanent conflict, one of the poles incessantly challenged by this music's dialectic development. The most recent and most violent of these challenges came from free jazz, which targets *both* initial Western influences and ulterior influences grafted onto jazz along its history.

By mechanically opposing white with black jazzmen, only to resolve this opposition in terms of an equivalence of principle, Western criticism has prevented itself once more from thinking of differences as productive and specific to jazz. To define jazz as "syncretic music," as "a synthesis of Western and African influences," might seem to constitute a recognition of those differences. But, in fact, it shows how little they are known, in that they are summoned but once in mythical accounts of the birth of jazz, and understood as having since been resolved, or more precisely, synthesized. Every time criticism mentioned these differences and, content with a mere mention, neglected to study them within the social and historical frame of their work—that is, not as accessories in the music's christening, but as a series of brutalities and resistances (conflicts)—it denied their specific importance and the power of this contradiction. Jazz is no ecumenical music; it is a music of divisions, of unresolved tensions and open wounds.

e) "True" Jazz

In the concert of Western criticism and its different phases, European criticism has played a relatively more important role than American criticism, culturally if not commercially. LeRoi Jones notes without elaborating on it that "there were few 'jazz critics' in America at all until the '30s and then they were influenced to a large extent by what Richard Hadlock has called 'the carefully documented gee-whiz attitude' of the first serious European critics."[18] We think that this had to do with the gap between European jazz lovers and the object of their passion. Of course, they could only have an indirect knowledge of jazz (through records, the press, and then concerts), but this remoteness threatened to decenter their critical reflection and give it a peculiar perspective.

In spite of its colonies, Europe's relation to blacks was of course very different from America's: as trauma only went in one direction, censorship was milder and less necessary. When in the USA the fear of a bloody political uprising made impossible anything but derisory depictions of black life, European colonialism, as if it had a clean conscience, gave itself the luxury of discovering exoticism and the Africas (in missions, in the beginning of ethnology, the Negro art craze, etc.). The "black character" of black music therefore appeared more readily and more quickly to European critics than to their American counterparts.

As soon as groups and musicians other than the Original Dixieland Jass Band and Paul Whiteman's Orchestra became known in France (Armstrong, Bechet, Ellington, Fletcher Henderson, etc.), the term "jazz hot" appeared, in contrast to the policed music of white bands. Around Hugues Panassié, French jazz fans gathered in "hot clubs." Panassié's first writings (his book *Le Jazz Hot* was first published in 1934) had tremendous influence in Europe and in the USA: he discovered and valorized Chicago and New York jazz as authentic. This was a true revolution in the growing world of jazz criticism.

Let us immediately state what the consequences were: on the one hand, this put a rightful emphasis on the true creators of jazz, revealed them to the European public, and gave a boost to the commercialization of original productions rather than white copies. On the other hand, critics were unable to conceive of this as a specifically black contribution to jazz (owing to the weakness of theoretical, critical, and musicological tools at the hand of the author). Panassié only dropped names, titles, described styles in epithetic cascades, separated the "good" from the "bad," without explanation. His excessive recourse to a terminology of *excitation* (the music gets heated, it burns, it shakes, it swings, etc.) went hand-in-hand with his refusal of any critical approach, which he saw as desacralizing the cult object.

In fact, Panassié's extreme and feverish agitation chose black music because it found ecstasy in it, but also myths of primitivism, of strength and violence; in short, the entire mythic and psychoanalytical arsenal of the regression to the "values" and "truths" of the past. Curiously, it is because of his own staunch backwardness that Panassié defends black jazz as the permanence of primitiveness, a refusal of modern progressive commercial developments and decadence. Thus, what he praises in jazz is not very far from what other "enemies of progress" despise in it. Panassié's compulsive glorification of everything black evokes the practice of another prophet:[19] Elijah Muhammad. Both of them, in the same time period, defended black superiority in all domains.

There were two notable differences: first, Panassié is a Catholic and not a Muslim, and he is white, not black. One can then study what for Panassié could only be a fetishization of blacks directly connected to the place of the black man in white American fantasies (as a rapist of white women). The second difference is that Panassié only valorizes the few primitive forms of expression always directly related to the physical, i.e. dance and music, boxing and running, while he completely neglects political (revolts, speeches, pamphlets, associations, etc.) and intellectual (poetry, black literature, political theory) manifestations. The double obfuscation of the cultural and the political of course implies complete contempt for the black liberation struggle: the more primitive the black—that is, the less "contaminated by whites," the more uneducated, and the closer to slavery—the better. Panassié did not really see blacks any differently from colonizers; he just liked them, while colonizers did not.

This sacralization of primitivity manifests itself in two ways in Panassié's "critical" approach: through his turn toward origins and his fantasies of purity. The two mechanisms managed to coincide perfectly in the author's first major crisis: at the end of his first trip to the USA (which served as a regression of sorts, a journey to the roots), Panassié recanted his initial judgment and *transferred* the purity of jazz to its historical roots in New Orleans, to which he sacrificed his first loves, Chicago and New York. Note here the mechanistic character and the religious connotations of his reasoning: purity lies in the point of origin. We will see that, while New Orleans style is close to the origin, it is far from embodying the primitive purity claimed by the author.

Panassié experienced a second, much more serious crisis after the birth of bebop. Panassié had not seen it coming, had not discovered it himself (his former disciple André Hodeir would be its main proponent in France), and bop constituted a musical disavowal of his anti-evolutionist conception. After a long hesitation that threw the faithful into great and terrible anguish (not knowing whether or not to like the music, to buy it or not), Panassié violently denounced bop as heresy, in the name of "true jazz."

The importance of the phenomenon must be noted. Until then, in jazz criticism, definitions and aesthetic criteria had been used either to "explain" and justify jazz in its entirety, or, more rarely, to valorize this or that musician or style. But with bebop came something more than a new style: this was a historical moment in black music, which saw the collective work of its greatest musicians (Parker, Monk, Gillespie, Coltrane...) condemned *en masse* by a European critic for deviating from the official party line. There is something ludicrous about Panassié, who thought himself trusted with the truth on jazz, pronouncing anathema on the very people who create black music, *their own* music. Black critic A. B. Spellman put it this way: "What does anti-jazz mean and who are these ofays who've appointed themselves guardians of last year's blues?"[20]

More disturbing yet was to see springing out of nothing what was claimed to be a bona fide aesthetics of jazz, with norms, scales of value, exclusive systems, and even traditions, when nobody (and especially not Panassié) had bothered to enunciate its theory or test its concepts. These aesthetics could only function on dogmatic pronouncements and revelations. Swing—whose role and definition are more or less those of the Holy Spirit—was either present in music or not; some could see it, others could not; dance was decreed constitutive of "true" jazz, as faith was to the "true" Christian; since bop could not be danced to, it was therefore not jazz. New Orleans musical structures were sanctified and declared untouchable: by daring not to respect them and by reacting against certain jazz traditions, bop lost its status as jazz, and, more or less implicitly, bop musicians were presented as traitors to the "spirit of their race," etc.

Of course, since this aesthetic foundation was especially inconsistent, Panassié had to rigidify it to the extreme, surrounding his pseudo-critical interventions with a considerably vindictive and insulting machinery. He slandered musicians and critics outside the dogma, accusing them of selling themselves to the mysterious "progressive" interests of a mafia of sorts. What this obscure organization would gain by pushing jazz towards all that Panassié reproaches it for (elitism, intellectualism, abandoning dance, etc.) remained unclear.

This "Battle of the True Jazz" began raging in 1949 and for about a decade occupied center stage, involving most of the forces of jazz criticism in France and around the world. The result of this thousand-page conflict[21] was twofold: through terror tactics, an aesthetic system was imposed on jazz, and debates bogged down in discussions of authenticity and the norms and principles of jazz, all notions forced onto the music. On the other hand, the specific importance of the bop revolution remained completely unknown, obliterated by long speeches on "modernism" and "tradition" in art and music, "progressivism" as decadence, etc.

Bop started in the margins of mainstream jazz (at the end of the swing era, and during the New Orleans revival) where it was created as an experiment in new forms in reaction against mainstream trends. As the music of certain black musicians fed up with the jazz they were commercially forced to play, it marked the realization by these musicians of the alienation of their music, of its then complete subjugation to white commercial interests and cultural values. The bop reaction aimed precisely at re-authenticating black music, at bringing it closer to its people. That it was carried out by integrating varied elements, "modern" (European experimentation) and otherwise (African resurgence), was not a drastic change if one looks at the birth and development of jazz, a culturally composite and conflictual music. It was not because bebop was more "modern" than old jazz that it was the less jazz: what made it different from the jazz that preceded it (and what brought it closer both to blues and to "primitive" jazz, which Panassié could not see) was an attitude of resistance to, and cultural rejection of, a state of colonization of black music. It is symptomatic that Panassié, self-appointed defender of black authenticity, remained blind and deaf to the recovery by blacks of their own music: his passion for blacks did not go as far as recognizing their struggles, which he no doubt also judged to be too "progressive."

We have lingered on this case because it represents the incapacity of Western jazz criticism to grasp its object in all its specificity: like *free jazz*, bebop put at the forefront of black music its social and cultural implications, and thus offered critics an opportunity to reposition jazz in African American reality. This opportunity was lost and buried under an accumulation of contradictions that did not belong to jazz, but indeed *to jazz criticism*.

4. The Blind Task of Criticism

> But one of the most persistent traits of the Western white man has always been his fanatical and almost instinctive assumption that his systems and ideas about the world are the most desirable, and further, that people who do not aspire to them, or at least think them admirable, are savages or enemies.
> —LeRoi Jones, *Blues People*, 18.

Along with jazz, the contradictions inherent to jazz criticism have taken—and overwhelmed—center stage as "issues," "quarrels," and "theses." Toxic redherrings such as these have contributed to the misunderstanding of jazz as much as to the understanding of it. Through these devices, critics presented their stories as history, their fiction as truth, believing that they were writing about jazz when in reality they were inscribing jazz within criticism, outside itself. In spite of their opposition to one another, and the noise of their quarrels notwithstanding, the different schools of criticism remain accomplices in that they are all connected to, and regulated by, the majority point of view of Westernness. Dominant ideology reigns at the center of these "contradictions" and varieties. It *produces* such "contradictions" and "differences" as surface effects, masks, blinds meant to cover and isolate *the place from which it speaks*, and *what it speaks of by speaking of something else*.

Once more, the West put itself in a position to judge an artistic practice that did not belong to it. Indeed, jazz is determined in complex ways by non-Western cultural traditions (African, Muslim) and by conditions of production (slavery, exploitation, racism) willed— but *neither suffered nor experienced*—by Western capitalist bourgeoisie.

Jazz's alterity in relation to Western civilization is therefore double: on the one hand, it comes from an *elsewhere* the West has long loathed but considered to be its own rightful possession. The West censors jazz's alterity just as it attempts to turn it into a niche for its own markets and missions, an endless reserve to tap for wealth. The West ignores or fights all that is not a source of profit, whether it be financial, political, or even ideological: indeed, one of the *benefits* of colonization is that it valorizes the myth of white supremacy. On the other hand, jazz is born in *the doubling of this elsewhere*, the place where this form of colonization was perpetuated and reinforced: America, land of slaves. Double the colonization, double the censorship of interests specific to the colonized, if they are not those or do not serve those of the exploiters.

The second level of censorship both confirms and justifies the first: as blacks supposedly had no culture in Africa, they must have even less outside of Africa. Beyond economic exploitation and racist repression, slaves necessarily suffer from the "influence" of their masters: their religion, their ideology, their value systems, etc. Such *compulsory* influence has a twofold objective: to erase the traces of original influences, and to prove in the same movement their inconsistency, their lack of value. Though forced to imitate his master, the Negro is despised for it. It is a classic trait of colonialism to twice diminish its victims: because colonialism rejects their civilization and imposes its own, its victims are considered twice as "inferior." LeRoi Jones writes:

> What made the American most certain that he was "superior" to the African. . . was the foreignness of African culture. This came to be the African's chief liability in the New World: in the context of slavery, the most undesirable attitudes the foreign slave and his many generations of American-born offspring could possess. In fact, twentieth-century American society finds many of these same offspring denying any connection with this culture in what may seem to most Americans a perfectly natural attempt to dive headlong into and immerse themselves completely in the tepid safety of the mainstream of contemporary America.[1]

We have seen that, after initial reticence, the "mainstream of contemporary America" eventually came to recognize jazz as a product for entertainment and cultural consumption and to support and love it, pressed by radio stations, advertising, commerce, but also by the new international prestige "its" music brought to the USA. For this assimiliation to happen, jazz had to make cultural compromises, filter and reshape itself, so much so that what of jazz made it to the market had little left in common with black culture. Only those aspects deemed ideologically acceptable, as they were or after adjustments, made the grade; the rest—i.e. this music's original traits, its history, its social function—were lost on the way.

Moreover, the assimilation could only be performed with the help and advice of critics. Criticism played *its* role—mediation and transmission—in the relatively successful molding and remodeling of jazz by the cultural and commercial interests of the dominant ideology. Critics did not see that what they were doing in the interest of jazz, and for its cause, they were doing first and foremost for an ideology and a culture that could only see themselves as dominant, and could only admit black culture and music inasmuch as they were dominated.

In pontificating wisely on jazz for forty years, Western critics therefore judged, according to their own criteria, values, and cultural assumptions, a musical production irreducible to them, remaining blind the whole time to their ideological underpinnings. Critics rewrote the history and aesthetics of jazz according to this ideology, sorting out all that they could understand about jazz. They then offered certain elements as currency: musicians' names, styles, rules, legends, etc., which they circulated at the ideological level. Because their selection itself was ideologically programmed, these currencies were adopted and consumed. Critics and audiences eventually acquiesced and mutually confirmed each other's opinions *about* jazz: two complicit elements in the same system, obfuscating and influencing jazz.

The consequences of this forty-year critical occupation of jazz have been particularly grave for jazz history. Completely hiding social and racial determinants was impossible, so they were instead modestly posited, from a sociologist's point of view, as *a kind of backdrop that explained nothing because it explained too much*. We know how in the USA the rush to sociological explanations for the "Negro problem" considerably muddled and distanced the *actual* issues faced by black Americans. The frenzy with which American sociologists have accumulated piles of observations, fabricated and endlessly compared statistics into floating reference networks, can be explained as an effort to replace the search for causes with the endless analysis of clues and effects. All "explanations" are invoked—sociological, psychological, legal, religious, psychoanalytical—all except economics and politics. This partial accumulation can only lead—indeed, it is its ultimate goal—to forbidding one from reading in the "Negro problem" the white problem: capitalism.

Echoing the ideology of such hardly innocent sociological works, jazz historians have kept to summary descriptions of the condition of black Americans—virtually silencing, for example, the entirety of black political demonstrations (uprisings, riots, pamphlets, organizations) throughout history, which is no small feat. Considering slavery "abolished," they have avoided examining the equivocal aspects of abolition and its aftermath in segregation and the economic exploitation of blacks. In other words, jazz historians have delivered limited information about the condition of black Americans, making sure to present it as a *reminder* of sorts—as if this were well-known information—and as a *supplement* to jazz history per se. In this way they could avoid connecting this information to, and showing its relationship with, musical phenomena.

Western criticism built its history of jazz on the idealist model of Western art history: as an autonomous, simple series of facts and names, regulating itself apart from History, *safe* from it. To be sure, it experienced variations, stylistic evolutions, different schools, but only as if they had self-generated, independently from the pressures of society and History. Trends and fashions followed each other, very much alike, and one would study their minutest nuances, detailing each musician's style, the debts he owed others, all of this taking place in isolation, in the white margins of History. Everything a musician might owe to his personal experience of life, what in his music bristled with conflict, what made such and such movement emerge when it did, all of this was ignored, because it exceeded the purview of art and entered different categories: sociology, politics, history.

Not by chance is art given "a place apart" in dominant ideology. This ideology's function is to reinterpret social relations by obfuscating relations of economic dependence and production in order to calmly perpetuate capitalist exploitation. To that effect, ideology has traced a series of borders and walls between the sectors of the social field: it has separated art from politics, and politics from law and education. These hermetic compartments supposedly all have their proper history, separate from the rest. The multiplication of these segmentary histories and their contradictions effectively prevents the recognition of their common determination by class struggle.

Ideology's domination over the work of criticism, aesthetics, and art history is only effective as long as such work does not examine the areas and conditions of its own production, the place where it is made and the place it makes in the process. Black jazz criticism, emerging again after a long absence, was first to undertake the task of deconstructing the myths of Western criticism. Speaking from elsewhere, as it were, it was able to see and show where critics had been speaking from until then.

Part 2. Notes on a Black History of Jazz

Three Preliminary Remarks

a) In these "notes on a black history of jazz," we propose to point out a certain number of facts and historical data that are *usually* left out of jazz histories. In other words, we will simply note the musical facts featured and extensively commented upon in these histories, or rather we will attempt to put them in relation to all the things that determine them, directly or indirectly: historical, economical, social, and political axes. We hope to show that what has usually been considered mere backdrop to black music, what has usually been neglected and repressed, has often played a major role in the history of black music. In any case, after the works of LeRoi Jones and free jazz, it is no longer possible to analyze black music as an autonomous art, a purely aesthetic phenomenon. Music—the blues and jazz—is the privileged mode of expression of black Americans; it holds a position in their social field, it plays a role, secondary or preeminent, in their political struggles. We think that the relation between music, society, and politics revealed in free jazz's political commitment actually predates free jazz. It is indeed a constant, an original, a constitutive element of black music. To understand it, and understand the role and historical position of free jazz, we think it indispensable to show *where*, and *under* and *against what* this music was built, and to reposition black music in white America and in black struggles.

b) The commercial valorization of jazz—after the initial embarrassment—and its use as an element of prestige by white America have increased the rejection of other black American forms of expression. This is in part because music (even unadulterated) was, of course, considered less "dangerous" than black literature, poetry, and thought, but also because the trademark dancing Negro image matched the expectations of the average American better than that of the black intellectual. This is why we decided to reposition black music among the artistic and intellectual productions of black Americans.

c) This twofold contextualization of the black music that preceded and generated free jazz gives us the means to appreciate the specific contribution and dimensions of the free jazz movement. It is indeed impossible to reduce free jazz to a "new style" once it is connected to the contradictions and forces at work in the common history of black music and struggles in America. To the extent that free jazz—which appeared as increasing numbers of black Americans began studying their own history, their past, their culture, and have started using them politically—revisits and reinscribes in itself the history of these struggles and the developments of jazz, we found it necessary to follow the same detour.

5. What the Blues Say

In song and exhortation swelled one refrain—Liberty.
—W. E. B. Du Bois, *The Souls of Black Folk: Essays and Sketches* (Chicago: A. C. McClurg and Co., 1903), 6.

All the histories of jazz published to this day consider the blues, ballads, gospel songs, and work songs as so many testimonies of black life in the United States. Yet only Paul Oliver,[1] A. B. Spellman,[2] and LeRoi Jones[3] distill from these documents the fact that black revolt, begun almost four centuries ago with the first slaves, is the essential trait of the history of black Americans.

Though forgotten, denied, or reduced to mere "accidents," manifestations of black resistance were numerous long before the word "jazz" appeared. There was resistance on the first slave ships crossing the Atlantic, when shipments of "ebony" were unloaded on American shores, and throughout the centuries of organized slave trade and after emancipation; and later these manifestations of resistance formed a direct counterpoint to the evolution of Afro-American music. But these acts of resistance—so old, so diverse, so violent—how could they not have influenced, how could they not have *traumatized* the prehistory of jazz? According to some white musicologists, that same jazz might have been born magically with the sole aim of making recently emancipated slaves dance, and soon all of an America tired of polkas and other imported European dance steps. Not by chance are the oldest songs kept by oral tradition *work songs*. These melodically and rythmically simple (functional) songs are the direct product of a system of economical and social exploitation: slavery. In the study of any form of black expression, it is obviously impossible to neglect the still overwhelming weight of this astounding aggression carried on until fairly recently against millions of people. "Black rage" is not a mood swing, black struggles do not come from nowhere. The scars have not been "erased."

a) Slavery: The Birth of White America

Marxist economists and sociologists have shown that slavery was the result neither of the "inferiority" of blacks, nor of the "perversity" of whites: it was simply a very profitable affair for slave traders, sellers, and breeders, and unevenly profitable for American planters. Racist arguments were produced after the fact to justify the law of profit, and spread in order to perpetuate it.

Indeed, beginning in the sixteenth century, the colonization and exploitation of American land was carried out under the sign of slavery; yet *the first American slaves were not Africans.* European settlers first attempted to use indigenous populations. But Indians were relatively weak, few, spread out over a territory whose limits were mostly unknown to explorers, and soon replaced by white workers: debtors, convicts, and indentured servants who would serve a settler for the amount of years judged necessary to reimburse the cost of their transportation across the ocean. In spite of the efforts of English tribunals that multiplied common law convictions in order to provide American colonies with white cattle, this source of labor eventually dwindled. It became expensive to keep servants, who were disobedient and often fled the plantations to participate in the conquest of the West.

Producing tobacco, rice, indigo, sugar, and eventually cotton on increasingly vast lands demanded numerous and cheap labor: settlers found it in Africa. Thus at the origin of the intensive exploitation of black slaves lies the development of large plantations, better adapted to monoculture.

"Plantation slavery had in strictly business aspects at least as many drawbacks as it had attractions. But in the large it was less a business than a life; it made fewer fortunes than it made men."[4] The issue of increasing slaves' profitablity and, more importantly, the fear of slave uprisings generated a strengthening of surveillance and the creation of codes regulating slaves' activities: they were forbidden to bear arms, forced to learn English (to be able to obey the overseer's orders), drumming was banned (as drums could be used to transmit messages), etc.

Supported by the French and English governments, the slave trade became a boon for the companies and ship owners who participated in it. In the United States, if massive slave importation remained confined to the South, it was less for humanitarian reasons than because the expansion of slavery ran into insurmountable obstacles in the North: the climate was first and foremost especially hard on recently transplanted Africans, but it also forbade exotic monoculture. Blacks were only profitable in monoculture, where labor requires no professional qualification, and the very principle of slavery excluded wasting time on education: the system could only survive if it prevented the intellectual development of its victims (northern colonies nevertheless profited from the slave trade: Rhode Island, for example, became one of the most important slave markets and owed a great part of its wealth to this traffic).

From the sixteenth to the nineteenth century, some two hundred million Africans (this number varies between one hundred and three hundred million according to the scholar) were transported all over the American continent. While Western Africa was thus bled of its human potential, the trade benefitted the capitalist countries of Europe, and the New World flooded the

European market with the products of its plantations, eventually becoming wealthy enough to be able to separate from the metropolis and become the United States of America.

Around the mid-eighteenth century, overproduction of tobacco and the collapse of the market led to the development first of rice culture and later indigo and sugar cane. By the end of the century, the economic decline of plantations (except in South Carolina and Georgia) brought some economists to question the efficiency of the slave system. But a technical revolution gave new life to slavery: in 1794, Eli Whitney invented the cotton gin. Bolstered by the rise of the textile industry in England, cotton culture boomed and the South became its kingdom, provider of cotton for the entire world. Planters—there were less than 400,000 of them—became capitalists, exploiting immense territories and having the disposal of entire armies of slaves. The value of a "piece of India" (the ideal Negro, six feet tall, aged eighteen to thirty-five) went from selling for between $100 and $200 in 1800 up to $2,000 in 1860, a year when slaves numbered four million in the United States (they were two million in 1830, and 750,000 when the United States declared independence).[5]

When in 1776 southern planters and northern traders began to feel unfairly treated by the laws of the mother country—which controlled the triangular trade, making it very profitable for the metropolis, but also difficult for colonists to trade with countries other than England, which also imposed multiple taxes, etc.—a political break occurred and the War of Independence broke out. Thus were blacks—and more precisely the repartition of the profits drawn from their unconditional exploitation—one of the deep causes of the independence of the United States. But in this war between whites there was no place, no role for them to play. If they were sometimes used, they were merely an economical way to spare white lives in the strategic game. With some officers having remarked that Negroes had nothing to lose (or to win) in this war and worrying about letting them use weapons, George Washington (and Congress with him) forbade the enrollment of Negroes. He nevertheless had to recant because the English were promising freedom to any slaves who joined their side—this is how thousands of Negroes deserted plantations and, in one instance, a slave led his master (a Virginian planter turned colonel in the Continental Army) to British lines. The American Congress then decided to limit enrollment to free blacks. Yet, following the terrible defeat at Valley Forge, every able-bodied man, white or black, slave or free, was welcome in the American army. Over a hundred thousand blacks gained their freedom during this colonial war (some escaped to Canada, to Florida, or to Indian tribes, while others followed the "Redcoats" to the United Kingdom), but the mass of slaves kept increasing thanks to the intensification of the trade.

In order to fight against the burgeoning abolitionist propaganda,[6] planters sought justification in science and religion. Thomas Dew, a professor from Virginia, thus attempted to demonstrate that "the Negro possessed the form and strength of a man but had the intellect of a child and was therefore unfit for freedom."[7] Also in Virginia, Reverend George D. Armstrong published *The Christian Doctrine of Slavery* and *Slavery Ordained of God*. New laws reinforced slavery: in 1857, the Supreme Court issued the Dred Scott decision, which asserted that the black American "had no rights which the white man was bound respect."[8] The court specified that Negroes "were at that time considered as a subordinate and inferior class of beings who had been subjugated by the dominant race, and, whether emancipated or not, yet remained subject to their authority, and had no rights or privileges but such as those who held the power and the Government might choose to grant them."[9]

Let us also recall this declaration from a representative of the state of Virginia:

> We have as far as possible closed every avenue by which light might enter [the slaves'] minds; we have only to go one step farther,—to extinguish the capacity to see the light,—and our work will be completed; they would then be reduced to the level with the beasts of the field, and we should be safe; and I am not certain that we would not do it, if we could find out the necessary process, and that under the plea of necessity.[10]

Slave owners went as far as replying to abolitionists:

> Supposing that we were all convinced, and thought of slavery precisely as you do, at what era of moral suasion do you imagine you could prevail on us to give up a thousand millions of dollars in the value of our slaves, and a thousand millions of dollars more in the depreciation of our lands, in consequence of the want of laborers to cultivate them?[11]

Thus justified by law, religion, and profit, slavery reduced Negroes to the exchange value they represented for their owners. To increase their productivity and profitability, owners used every imaginable device: torture, flogging, persuasion, "brainwashing," and every imaginable physical and moral abuse. Yet masters still had to maintain their slaves so that the "human machines" could function without great difficulty. Herbert Aptheker writes:

> Slaves were instruments of production, were means by which men who owned land were able to produce tobacco and rice and sugar and cotton to be sold, on a world market, and to return them a profit. Their existence had no real

meaning other than this for their employers. Profit must be gotten from these workers whom the bosses owned no matter what suffering this entailed, and the more profit the better.[12]

The planters' "hardware" landed in the United States in numbers of about twenty thousand Africans a year at the beginning of the nineteenth century, and six thousand by 1850. As soon as the trade slowed down, breeding took over. Landowners in Virginia and in the Carolinas brought to the verge of bankruptcy by the depletion of their lands were saved from disaster by intensive breeding of the "black cattle" they still possessed. Thus did her reproductive capacities make the black female a new source of profit. Breeding followed more or less scientific, but quite rigorous selection methods that were for Negroes yet another obstacle to having a family. Some males were turned into studhorses, while many black women were "specialized," numerous progeny being sometimes the way to preferential treatment. While testimonies and evidence attest to this system of breeding,[13] it is more difficult to assert that slave owners impregnated their most beautiful slaves specifically in order to participate in the increase of their cattle and its "improvement" through the increase of mulatto children. Bastard mulatto children were generally used as servants, and blood relation got in the way of maximum profit during sales. In his *Autobiography*, Malcolm X confirms the privileged status of mulattoes (he himself was, like his mother, rather light-skinned): "I actually believe that as anti-white as my father was, he was subconsciously so afflicted with the white man's brainwashing of Negroes that he inclined to favor the light ones, and I was his lightest child. . . . It came directly from the slavery tradition that the 'mulatto,' because he was visibly nearer to white, was therefore 'better.'"[14] He adds, "Out in the world later on, in Boston, in New York, among the millions of Negroes who were insane enough to feel that it was some kind of status symbol to be light-complexioned—that one was actually fortunate to be born thus. But, still later, I learned to hate every drop of that white rapist's blood that is in me."[15]

There were about sixty-five thousand slaves in the southwestern states in 1820; forty years later, their number had increased tenfold. Similar increase could be witnessed across the country: there were less than ninety thousand slaves in 1790, 3.2 million in 1850, and 4 million in 1860. About a quarter of the slaves worked on plantations holding fewer than ten slaves; another quarter worked in bigger plantations of fifty slaves or more. The remaining half worked in plantations of between ten and fifty slaves. A mid-nineteenth century census showed that close to four hundred thousand slaves lived in cities, where they worked as servants, artisans, and manual laborers.

Opposite this "black cattle" were two and a half million free families living across the South, among whom were 384,000 slave owners concentrated between Georgia and Louisiana. While most slaves were field workers, many were rented out by their masters to individuals and companies such as textile factories, blacksmiths, tobacco factories, etc. In 1842 in Richmond, Virginia, the Tredegar iron works began using slaves in order to improve their profit margin. Following a strike by their white laborers, they fired all of them, thus gaining the capacity to compete against northern industry thanks to their low production costs. Factories throughout the southern states followed this example. Railway companies, mines, building companies, all resorted to slave labor. This unavoidably generated rivalry between black slave labor and the white proletariat. The status of specialized slaves was superior to that of white workers inasmuch as the latter did not benefit from the kind of protection demanded for the precious human material of the former by their owners.

This "renting out" system allowed a certain number of slaves—the most professionally qualified among them—to buy their freedom, thus forming the embryo of what would become the black petty bourgeoisie (truly a proletariat for which wage slavery replaced slave labor). Documents and testimonies about the daily life of slaves have accumulated in the past few years (autobiographies, interviews of former slaves, archival research into the records of the slave trade, the Black Codes, etc.[16]) as future black militants were growing in political awareness. Malcolm X devoted an important part of his activities to the study of the African American past:

> The field Negroes—those were the masses. . . . The Negro in the field caught hell. He ate leftovers. In the house they ate high up on the hog. The Negro in the field didn't get anything but what was left of the insides of the hog. They call it "chitt'lings" nowadays. In those days they called them what they were—guts. That's what you were—gut-eaters. And some of you are still gut-eaters.
> The field Negro was beaten from morning to night; he lived in a shack, in a hut; he wore old, castoff clothes. He hated his master. I say he hated his master. He was intelligent. That house Negro loved his master, but that field Negro—remember, they were in the majority, and they hated the master.[17]

b) Abolition, Secession, Reconstruction

Intense work, insufficient food and comfort, and inadequate or nonexistent medical care are so many elements that explain the short lifespan and high mortality rate among the servile population.[18]

Beyond the movements generated by the ambition of Northern capitalists for whom the abolition of slavery was just a means to ruin southern planters, other whites (the Quakers, most particularly) deplored the condition of slaves. Following the example of the Society for the Extinction of the Slave Trade created in 1823 in England,[19] the American abolitionist movement—whose followers belonged for the most part to the middle-class—attacked slavery from an idealistic and religious point of view. Considered fanatics, abolitionists were persecuted, sometimes even assassinated.[20] The actions of abolitionists, though isolated from the activity of other whites, would help northern capitalists find moral authority and justifications in their effort to thwart planters' expansion. Anti-slavery activism was also bolstered by the passing of the Fugitive Slave Act, which ordered the restitution of fugitive slaves to their masters. Abolitionism shifted from moral stands to action with the inception of the Underground Railroad, a clandestine network helping escaped slaves.[21] The progress of abolitionism in turn led to an increase of racism in the South.

Nevertheless, economic rather than ideological rivalry was at the origin of political opposition between the North and the South. As a cotton-exporting region and the customer of the industrial North, the South needed manufactured products and was a strong supporter of free trade, whereas the North, feeling insufficiently industrialized, felt a need for customs barriers. As retaliation against this protectionism, European countries such as England increased their tariffs and started looking for alternative sources of cotton. The price of cotton fiber dropped from fifteen cents a pound in 1824 to a little under ten cents in 1830, and planters suffered: the South was the victim of retaliation occasioned by northern attitudes.

This economic conflict was soon compounded by a political and electoral conflict. North and South fought for control over the federal government. In a compromise that had made the formation of the United States possible, the North had accepted that the representation of slave states in Congress be calculated on the basis of their white population, increased by three-fifths of the number of their slaves. Thus privileged, the South controlled all the important committees in the Senate.

North and South were also in disagreement not so much on the principle of slavery as on its expansion. As the country reached further west, a question was raised: would slaves or free men settle the new territories? For the slavery party, expansion was necessary inasmuch as the use of slave labor exhausted the land quickly; having impoverished lands in the East, planters and their armies of slaves were now moving west. Northern businessmen were also attracted by the West, which they were hoping to monopolize for their own profit. There had been country planning; there were now compromises. The opposition between the two American "empires" was reaching the point of no return. War was the predictable outcome of this conflict.

When eleven southern states organized themselves into a confederacy rather than obey the majority, they therefore did so less out of anti-abolitionist reaction than to avoid economic collapse. Southern planters and northern capitalists had common economic interests; owners in the North and the South tended to unite against the social forces (small farmers, workers, and slaves) that had started to threaten their privileges. The North often reluctantly played its role as "liberator." During the first year of the Civil War, for example, blacks were not allowed to bear arms. But as the North pushed further, thousands of slaves joined its troops. They were alternatively pushed away, treated as "spoils of war," or used as auxiliaries and irregulars; they posed an embarrassing problem for northern generals. Black soldiers under white command nevertheless reached two hundred thousand. Forty thousand died in battle. President Abraham Lincoln was among those northern men who doubted the military valor of Negroes. In an oft quoted 1862 letter to Horace Greeley, he explained that his "paramount object in this struggle [was] to save the Union, and [was] not either to save or to destroy slavery."[22] Although he had often condemned slavery in speeches, his reticence about the complete emancipation of slaves "was based on his conviction that Negroes and whites could not live together in the same community."[23]

In 1863, slaves were emancipated in the rebel states; two years later, the Thirteenth Amendment made slavery illegal in the United States;[24] Lincoln became the Great Emancipator and started the Reconstruction Era. While planters were deprived of their right to vote, and emancipated slaves gained voter status. Under the control of governmental troops and thanks to universal suffrage, Negroes and poor whites were able to install a democratic regime exalting economic and political equality for all in the South. For many white historians, these were the "terrible years,"[25] while black historian W. E. B. Du Bois speaks of "an upheaval of humanity like the Reformation and the French Revolution."[26] Dictatorship of the proletariat, blacks and poor whites participating in constituting assemblies, an increased number of *Union Leagues*, the creation of popular black militias, twenty-two black representatives in Congress—everything seemed to be in place for a more popular form of government: "The general government of the republic has, by proclaiming the emancipation of the slaves, commenced a great social revolution in the south, but has, as yet, not completed it."[27] Wendell Phillips, one of the leaders of the revolutionary branch of the abolitionist movement,[28] added: "That proclamation frees the slave and ignores the Negro."[29]

During Reconstruction, some seven hundred thousand Negroes were registered on voting lists. But several restrictive measures would come to hurt the amendments guaranteeing their right to vote: conditions of residency, voting taxes too costly for most Negroes, the *grandfather clause* (which forbade voting registration for anybody whose father or grandfather had not held the right to vote on January 1, 1867, a date when Negroes had not yet been granted voting rights), *white primaries* (closed meetings of the Democratic Party reserved for white members, during which candidates would be designated prior to elections), etc. To justify these attacks on democracy, a campaign began that meant to exacerbate the racial prejudice that had once kept anti-slavery activism in check. The Ku Klux Klan was the main instrument of this counter-revolution. Its main objectives were to reestablish planters' privileges and defend their possessions against Negroes, to put Negroes back into servitude, take away political rights from freed slaves, and, finally, to "maintain the purity of white blood."[30] With rifles, ropes, and fire, Negroes were gradually kept away from ballot boxes and all political or simply civic activities in which they naively thought they had gained a right to participate:

> We knowed freedom was on us, but we didn't know what was to come with it. We thought we was going to get rich like the white folks. We thought we was going to get richer than the white folks, 'cause we was stronger and knowed how to work, and the whites didn't, and they didn't have us to work for them any more. But it didn't turn out that way. We soon found out that freedom could make folks proud, but it didn't make 'em rich.[31]

In fact, on top of being swindled out of their voting rights, Negroes were also the principal victims of the change in ownership of the big plantations of the South. Some plantations were given back to their original owners; southern bourgeois or northern capitalists acquired some mortgaged plantations. Free but just as destitute as before, Negroes remained on the plantations as agricultural workers or *sharecroppers*. Yesterday's slaves became proletarians. Forced into debt alongside ruined small white owners, they found they had come out of slavery only to fall back into utter misery under the control of planters. This was the beginning of disenfranchisement.[32] Racial segregation soon added up to economic impasse and political exclusion.

The threat of a common front between Negroes and poor whites led planters and their supporters to dig an insurmountable gap between the two communities. In most of the former Confederate states, Jim Crow laws[33] were implemented that forbade interracial relationships and marriages, enforced racial separation in public transportation and all public spaces, including cemeteries, etc. Some poor whites justly analyzed this effort to separate the races: "You are kept apart that you may be separately fleeced of your earnings. You are made to hate each other because upon that hatred is rested the keystone of the arch of financial despotism which enslaves you both. You are deceived and blinded that you may not see how this race antagonism perpetuates a monetary system which beggars both."[34]

Segregationist maneuvers were reinforced by the conciliatory and conservative attitude of the rare black elected officials, who generally hailed from the free black class and/or former "favorite" slaves, and who mostly tried to satisfy everybody. One of them would declare to his white colleagues:

> I believe, my friends and fellow-citizens, we are not prepared for this suffrage. . . . We may not understand it at the start, but in time we shall learn to do our duty. . . . We recognize the Southern white man as the true friend of the black man. It is not our desire to be a discordant element in the community, or to unite the poor against the rich. The white man has the land, the black man has the labor, and labor is worth nothing without capital.[35]

Similarly, the rise of the black bourgeois elite only occurred under the control of white liberals; for example, varied philanthropic foundations financed by northern capitalists helped some Negroes get a college education: "Negro teachers who were beneficiaries of the [Peabody] Fund were expected to conform to the racial policy of this foundation. . . . This was especially true in the case of the beneficiaries of the Rosenwald Fund. . . . It was hostile to any Negro who showed independence in his thinking in regard to racial and economic problems."[36]

Booker T. Washington belongs to this first generation of black intellectuals. In 1876 he began asserting himself as the first black leader recognized by white figures of authority. His obstinate conservatism and his taste for compromise are exemplary of the "gradualist" reformism that W. E. B. Du Bois and all black radicals would come to oppose:

> Mr. Washington came, with a simple definite programme, at the psychological moment when the nation was a little ashamed of having bestowed so much sentiment on Negroes, and was concentrating its energies on Dollars. His programme of industrial education, conciliation of the South, and submission and silence as to civil and political rights, was not wholly original.[37]

Booker T. Washington preached nothing but resignation. Washington's message was to work hard, learn a trade, favor technical over higher education, earn money, own property, abstain from politics, and you will be accepted into American society.[38] Though such advice helped some Negroes achieve incontestable professional and intellectual improvement, it also encouraged blacks to renounce all African American tradition and culture on the one hand and all revolutionary activism on the other. It also gave free rein to the racism rising at the end of the nineteenth century. Booker T. Washington, then head of the Tuskegee Institute, would become the perfect instrument of cultural repression for his students: "Art and music, for people who live in rented houses and have no bank account, are not the most important subjects to which attention can be given. Such education creates want without a corresponding increase of ability to supply these increased wants."[39]

Having convinced part of the future black bourgeoisie, Washington was in great part responsible for the deculturation—regarding all *African* American traditions—that E. Franklin Frazier considered one of the characteristic traits of the black bourgeois,[40] and which translated into their contempt for black music (spirituals and later jazz).

In spite of the "collaborationist" attitude of this minority (once favorite slaves, now bourgeois), the radical demands of the black community would not lose intensity; the spirit of revolt had been for four hundred years part of the African American cultural heritage.

In direct action, protest, novels, poems, newspapers, religious ceremonies, work songs, and spectacles, manifestations of black consciousness always participated in a common (more or less conscious) will to transform the condition of the African American people—in spite of the diversity of these actions and the violence that often made them spill out of strictly cultural frames, and in spite of the contradictions inseparable from white, Christian, capitalist, colonialist oppression. Once freed from the insidious and spontaneous censorship of chroniclers, novelists, and filmmakers conditioned by the dominant white American ideology, the history of blacks struggling for their freedom shows us a "Negro" much different from the one here described by English historian Sir Harry Johnston:

> He is possessed of great physical strength, docility, cheerfulness of disposition, a short memory for sorrows and cruelties, and an easily aroused gratitude for kindness and just dealing.... And, provided he is well fed, he is easily made happy.... He has little or no race-fellowship—that is to say, he has no sympathy for other negroes; he recognizes and follows his master independent of any race affinities.[41]

c) Revolts

There were innumerable mutinies and collective suicides on board slave ships, and permanent passive resistance on plantations (through sabotage, systematic negligence, etc.[42]), and revolts broke out in American colonies as soon as slaves were settled, demonstrating that more or less organized struggle could precede artistic manifestations and political consciousness.

In 1526, twenty-four years after the Church had justified slavery (in the name of the Christian truths proclaimed to destitute Africans by the Spaniards), black slaves revolted in the colony established by Lucas Vasquez de Ayllon (now South Carolina). A century later, in Jamestown, Virginia, a black child born on American soil was baptized for the first time.[43] In the meantime, Massachusetts had become the first colony to recognize lifelong slavery.

As early as 1663, black slaves and white indentured servants organized a plot that was thwarted following its betrayal by a servant, who gained his freedom in exchange[44] (while, as of 1971, a coalition of white and black workers remains a political pipe dream in the United States). Half a century later, also in Virginia, a group of black rebels found allies in local Indians. In New York in 1712, six slaves committed suicide as twenty-one of their companions were executed following a major revolt. In South Carolina, rebel slaves were exiled, hanged, or burnt at the stake.

Successive failures and fierce reprisals necessarily led to escalation. Little by little, revolts became better organized, and slaves chose leaders. In the same movement, subversion and repression grew more efficient, which is to say bloodier. In 1739, thirty whites were killed during an action led by the slave Cato in South Carolina. Two years later, in New York, a new white and black plot emerged: a hundred and fifty slaves and their twenty-five white accomplices were hanged, burned alive, and exiled. Massacres followed in North Carolina, South Carolina, Virginia, and Louisiana.

After 1800 (the year when Nat Turner and John Brown were born), almost all revolts would be organized with quasi-military care. On August 30th that year, Gabriel, slave of Thomas Prosser, gathered an "army" of ten thousand slaves to take over Richmond, Virginia. Betrayed, he was captured and hanged on October 7th. In Norfolk, the black man Tom Copper was arrested along with a few hundred slaves and white accomplices. In 1811, Charles Deslandes was defeated by federal troops in New Orleans.

The end of the eighteenth century also saw the American Revolution and numerous discussions on the Rights of Man and the theories of John Locke and Thomas Jefferson. It is unlikely that these influenced the increase in slave revolts, but the revolts were all thought out, premeditated, and organized; they were no longer spontaneous reactions to particular acts of cruelty.

Aware of the fatal consequences that would follow if they were caught in an act of rebellion against their masters, many fugitive slaves would regroup and attack and pillage the most remote white colonies. Such outlaw communities would settle in mountains, forests, or swamps in the southern states. Several military expeditions were organized to destroy them. In Alabama, such a group was defeated as they were about to build their own fort.

Long before Archie Shepp declared, "Our vindication will be black. . . as Fidel is black, as Ho Chi Minh is black,"[45] black slaves knew how to find allies in other communities oppressed by American colonialism. Like the Cubans, like the Palestinians and the Vietnamese, American Indians were also "niggers." And Andrew Jackson's troops had to fight a real guerilla war in order to subdue the maroon communities settled in Seminole territory in 1818. Welcomed and supported by the South Carolina and Florida tribes, blacks and their Indian allies resisted governmental troops for two years, until the battle of Seewanee.

With Denmark Vesey, we see the beginnings of a true political consciousness. A slave, Vesey won the lottery and bought his freedom with the earnings, settling as an independent carpenter. Now a member of a privileged minority, the free blacks, he could have become uninterested in the condition of his former fellows, like many others (in 1830, 3,777 black families owned slaves!). But he kept in his mind tales of the French Revolution and dreamed of liberating his people, as Toussaint Louverture just had in the island of Saint-Domingue. Bolder and better informed than his companions, he attempted to convince blacks that they were equal to whites, but also that they possessed the *power* on which, some hundred and thirty years later, Malcolm X and Stokely Carmichael would base their propaganda. If whites were able to maintain blacks in slavery, it was only because they held the power. Blacks would only be free if they used their own power—which, for the time being, meant using physical strength:

> Even whilst walking through the streets in company with another, [Vesey] was not idle; for if his companion bowed to a white person, he would rebuke him, and observe that all men were born equal, and that he was surprised that any one would degrade himself by such conduct,—that he would never cringe to the whites, nor ought any one who had the feelings of a man. When answered, "We are slaves," he would sarcastically and indignantly reply, "You deserve to remain slaves."[46]

With the complicity of a few whites and thousands of blacks, he organized in 1822 one of the most important revolts in United States history, in Charleston, South Carolina. It was thwarted by a slave's betrayal: Vesey was hanged along with thirty-six of his companions.

Nat Turner's famous plot in Southampton County, Virginia, also deserves to be noted, inasmuch as it can be considered the indirect consequence of white Christian oppression. Turner interpreted the 1831 solar eclipse as a divine sign and, along with about sixty other slaves, prepared in accordance to accomplish the *terrible design*: the massacre of several families of planters. Contrary to the aforementioned revolts, Turner's was not very well organized. A devout Baptist, Turner spent most of his time praying for the triumph of his cause rather than organizing his followers. They were all caught soon after the alarm was sounded, and they were hanged. But the incident would traumatize blacks and whites alike in the South. It marked the mythology and history of slavery. Other revolts happening in the period suggested for a time the possibility of a vast plot. Turner's rebellion remains most famous for having occasioned a written confession.[47] For Malcolm X, Nat Turner, because "he wasn't going around preaching pie-in-the-sky and 'nonviolent' freedom for the black man," succeeded in "put[ting] the fear of God into the white slave master."[48] Soon after the black prophet Nat Turner's rebellion, whites passed laws forbidding blacks from preaching.

As we have seen, black rebels were not without allies: white indentured servants, Seminoles, etc. were at their side. Their most prestigious ally in the eyes of blacks themselves was without a doubt the abolitionist John Brown. In the words of Malcolm X, "He was a white man who went to war against white people to help free slaves. He wasn't nonviolent. . . . If we want white allies, we need the kind that John Brown was."[49]

With twenty-one men, including five blacks, John Brown, whose main objective was to organize secret camps for fugitive slaves, attacked in 1859 the armory at Harper's Ferry, Virginia. They were caught by the troops of Robert E. Lee, future general of the Confederate Army, and executed. Brown's sentence caught the world's attention, and famously brought Victor Hugo to write his open letter "To the United States of America" published in all the free newspapers of Europe: "Yes, let America know it, and ponder on it well—there is something more terrible than Cain slaying Abel: It is Washington slaying Spartacus!"[50]

Today still, John Brown is considered a hero by white liberals and black militants alike. In the years following his death, blues and ballads reminded blacks of his tragic action. He became an exemplary historical figure, alongside Nat Turner and Toussaint Louverture. This appears clearly in this text by Charlotte Forten, a black teacher who after emancipation taught in the Sea Islands off the coast of South Carolina:

> After the lessons, we used to talk freely to the children, often giving them slight sketches of some of the great and good men. Before teaching them the "John Brown" song, which they learned to sing with great spirit, Miss T. told them the story of the brave old man who had died for them. I told them about Toussaint, thinking it well they should know what one of their own color had done for his race.[51]

During the years of the slave trade, many slave revolts took the form of mutinies on slave ships. They were so common that "loss by mutiny" became a traditional column in ship owners' record books. The two most famous slave mutinies led to the hijacking of ships, long before Fidel Castro and Cuba. In 1839, under the leadership of Cinquez, son of a tribe chieftain from Sierra Leone, some fifty blacks recently acquired by the Spaniards killed the captain and took over the ship they were being transported on, the *Amistad*.[52] After disembarking the crew[53] they forced their former masters to sail towards Africa. But the navigator deceived them and sailed to Long Island. The ship was taken and the mutineers accused of murder. A trial opened in New Haven; the American Abolitionist Society organized the Amistad Defense Committee and, following an eight-hour plea, the abolitionist lawyer John Quincy Adams (then seventy-three years old) obtained the liberation of the mutineers and their return to Africa.

Two years after the *Amistad* trial, the unwilling passengers of the *Creole* repeated Cinquez's feat. After landing in Nassau, the mutineers were freed by British authorities in spite of pressure from the American Secretary of State, Daniel Webster.

Slave revolts were long minimized in the United States, and for the most part were studied and recorded only by radical historians. One among them, Herbert Aptheker, estimates that about two hundred and fifty conspiracies were organized by blacks in the United States.[54]

Beyond more or less organized collective violence, because of the constant surveillance by white masters, resistance often took the form of individual actions. Most of the crimes committed by blacks during the time of slavery were truly raw expressions of individual revolt. In Virginia, for example, of 346 sentences for murder, 194 victims were white: 56 slave owners, 7 overseers, 11 wives of slave owners, two sons of slave owners, and 111 other whites. Of the

60 unidentified victims, we can imagine that a majority were white. Of 111 sentences for attempted murder, there were only two cases where the victims were black.[55] Thus, we can agree with Michel Fabre:

> In the light of slavery considered as both a historical moment of the African American experience and a specific American institution, contemporary manifestations of black power and the resistance opposed to them by white society in the United States seem disconcerting and less characteristic of our time. For the students of slave revolts, the explosions of violence in the ghetto and the self-defense tactics of the Black Panthers are quite logically located within a secular tradition of protest.[56]

As abolitionist movements developed among white liberals (such as the Quakers) and "evolved" blacks, slave revolts changed. They either turned into violent and spontaneous urban uprisings anticipating the 1965 Watts riots, or into more politically structured, organized protest, like W. E. B. Du Bois's *Niagara Movement* and the action of twentieth-century black leaders. This transformation came with the influx to northern cities of the fugitive slaves and freemen who would constitute the core of the black intellectual elite, which would play an increasingly important role.

d) Organizations and Demands

The multiplicity and diversity of the movements edging for political leadership of the black masses in the twentieth century seem to have always been inscribed in African American forms of protest. Freed slave Paul Cuffee took thirty-eight freed slaves back to Africa in 1816, long before Marcus Garvey[57] and in much more practical fashion;[58] in 1822, the country of Liberia, created with the oversight of the American Colonization Society, gave freed slaves an opportunity to become colonizers. It remains the only example of a black nation realized by Americans.[59] But most blacks considered that the goal to reach was to live free in the United States.

In 1829 David Walker wrote *An Appeal to the Coloured Citizens of the World*, which incited slaves to fight their masters;[60] there was Sojourner Truth,[61] a former slave and the first female abolitionist lecturer; Harriet Tubman,[62] an escaped slave who traveled to the South nineteen times to help some three hundred slaves escape, among them her own parents (Southerners put a $40,000 bounty on her head); William Still;[63] David Ruggles; Prince Hall, one of the founders of the *Negro Masonic Order* in 1787;[64] Absalom Jones and Richard Allen, who in 1778 created the Free African Society;[65] Robert Purvis; Charles Remont; Theodore Wright; the slave Dred Scott, who in 1847 filed a suit for his freedom at the St. Louis Circuit Court;[66] pastors Samuel Ringgold Ward and Henry Highland Garnet, born in slavery, the former of whom became a man of letters and the latter a diplomat, dedicating their lives to the liberation of their former fellow slaves. "Brethren, arise, arise!" Garnet exclaimed during the 1843 National Negro Convention in Buffalo:[67]

> Strike for your lives and liberties. Now is the day and the hour. Let every slave throughout the land do this, and the days of slavery are numbered. You cannot be more oppressed than you have been—you cannot suffer greater cruelties than you have already. Rather die free men than live to be slaves. Remember that you are FOUR MILLIONS!... In the name of God, we ask, are you men? Where is the blood of your fathers? Has it all run out of your veins? Awake, awake; millions of voices are calling you! Your dead fathers speak to you from their graves. Heaven, as with a voice of thunder, calls on you to arise from the dust. Let your motto be resistance! resistance! RESISTANCE![68]

All these black men and women who, after living through slavery, opened the way of freedom to their people, show that the political and social consciousness of African Americans did not wait for the creation of the NAACP, SNCC, or the Black Panther Party to manifest itself with strength and perfect lucidity: "There shall be no peace to the wicked. . . . This guilty nation shall have no peace, and...we will do all we can to agitate!"[69] "If there is no struggle there is no progress. Those who profess to favor freedom and yet depreciate agitation, are men who want crops without plowing up the ground, they want rain without thunder and lightening. They want the ocean without the awful roar of its many waters":[70] these statements worthy of a Malcolm X or an Eldridge Cleaver, were delivered in the 1840s. Their author, Frederick Douglass, was born in 1817 of a black slave mother and a white man who did not recognize him. He grew up a slave. In 1838, he escaped Maryland and settled in Massachusetts. He had been lucky enough as a child to have a mistress who taught him how to read and write, and was able to write an autobiography[71] that would become a weapon for abolitionist propaganda. An anti-slavery militant and a brilliant orator, he collected by his lectures sufficient funds to help slaves escape. A journalist, he dedicated the first issue of his *North Star* "to the cause of our long oppressed and plundered fellow countrymen." A friend of the white abolitionist John Brown, Douglass organized regiments of black volunteers during the Civil War and was one of Lincoln's advisers. He hoped to accelerate the liberation process by putting blacks alongside Northern troops during the war. In fact—*and the theories of 1971 radical militants are no different*—he thought that blacks had to gain freedom on their own, without the help of white liberals. The case of Douglass is the perfect example of the importance of literacy in the evolution of African American protests and demands (young Douglass's master had predicted to his wife: "If you teach that nigger how to read... there will be no keeping him"[72]).

As early as 1773, literate slaves wrote a petition to Boston officials requesting not only their freedom, but their return to Africa:[73] this was the first manifesto written by black slaves.

e) Writings, Pamphlets, Newspapers and Poems

Long before the Civil War broke out, pamphlets, petitions, and other protest writings had been the only means for blacks to make public and explain their objections to the oppressive system. The themes treated of in these documents are all symptomatic of the social injustice inherent to slavery's reign: living conditions of slaves, request for compensation of slave labor and for the abolition of slavery, education for blacks, fair wages, electoral demands, etc. Thus from the eighteenth century was established an entire literature perfectly representative of the life and interests of the black community[74] and which—of course—was only revealed and studied recently.... The tone and terminology of these texts are often influenced by the style of early black preachers (many of whom were the authors of the pamphlets and petitions), which literate blacks emulated, hoping to reach an audience used to the language of sermons. This deliberate reference to a Christian/religious context also helped to allay the worries of whites, and sometimes even to draw their sympathy or support.

Black churches were the only available meeting places for slaves. There they were able to talk relatively freely about the oppressive social conditions under which they lived. Some of these sermons and manifestos were printed and distributed, which helped develop this "subversive" literature. In 1794, Richard Allen—a former slave and the founder, with Absalom Jones, of the first African Church in the United States—published a relatively moderate manifesto. His *Address to Those Who Keep Slaves and Approve the Practice* referred to the enslavement of the Hebrews in the Old Testament.[75] In Baltimore in 1810 there was published *A Dialogue between a Virginian and an African Minister*. The author was the Reverend Daniel Coker, "a descendant of Africa, Minister of the African Methodist Episcopal Church," and the text was "Humbly Dedicated to the People of Colour in the United States of America."[76] His commitment to the critique of slavery and—much like Allen—his role in the creation of an African church brought him to leave America with black emigrants to Liberia in 1820. He resumed preaching in Africa and founded a church in Sierra Leone. Preacher for the First African Baptist Church, Nathaniel Paul attempted to demonstrate that all would benefit from freeing the slaves in his 1827 *Address, Delivered on the Celebration of the Abolition of Slavery, in the State of New York*. Emphasizing the aberrations of a system still in use in the rest of the country, he anticipated the arguments of William Hamilton (*Address to the Fourth Annual Convention of the Free People of Color in the United States*, 1834), who saw "evil purposes" behind the actions of the Colonization Society and declared that reason would have no "full sway, until the community shall see that a wrong done to one is a wrong done to the whole."[77] A *Treatise On the Intellectual Character, and Civil and Political Condition of the Colored People of the United States* (1837) written by Reverend Hosea Easton, "A Colored Man," prefiguring the work of Malcolm X, compared the historical barbarity and warmongering of European nations to the artistic and pacific traditions of black peoples, thus countering the arguments of white supremacists....

If these texts often suffer from a pompous style of rhetoric influenced by the pedantic sophistications inseparable from the cultural and literary conditioning of the first literate African Americans, they nevertheless reveal a constant: the desire to obtain full political and civic freedom in all aspects of life.

Though Franklin Frazier considers the black press "the chief medium of communication which creates and perpetuates the world of make-believe for the black bourgeoisie" and asserts that "although [it] declares itself to be the spokesman for the Negro group as a whole, it represents essentially the interests and outlooks of the black bourgeoisie," he also recognizes that "the Negro press, like the press of other ethnic and racial minorities in American life, began as a medium for the expression of the opinions of the small intelligentsia among Negroes."[78] Developed along with elementary instruction, easier to circulate and read than books, the press played a crucial role in the awakening of black consciousness. It was born of the needs of abolitionist propaganda, before the Civil War. After the *Freedom's Journal*, created in 1827 by the two freed slaves Samuel Cornish and John Russwurm (the first black man to graduate form an American college), followed the *Weekly Advocate*, the *Colored American*, and the *Mirror of Liberty*. In 1847, Frederick Douglass announced the goals he had set for his *North Star* (later renamed *Frederick Douglass's Paper*) in his first editorial: "Giving no quarter to slavery at the South, it will hold no truce with oppressors at the North."[79] These first newspapers mostly covered the issue of slavery and protested racial discrimination, but their distribution was limited to free blacks in the North (the literate minority). After the Civil War more bourgeois, less radical publications replaced them. These were the days of Booker T. Washington's compromise. The rise of the black press corresponded to an increase in the migration of free Negroes to the cities. According to W. E. B. Du Bois, the black press in 1898 included three magazines, three dailies, eleven school newspapers, and one hundred and thirty-six weeklies, more than sixty of which were published by religious groups or more or less secret organizations. The three dailies were published in Norfolk, Virginia, Kansas City, and Washington, DC. At the beginning of the twentieth century, the two most important vehicles in the black press were the *Guardian*, published in Boston by black scholars struggling for equal rights, and the *New York Age*, which defended the sedative positions of Booker T. Washington.

The same way black newspapers were first simply "an organ for the Negro protest,"[80] the first books written by Negroes were testimonies, autobiographies telling about (and commentating on) the experience of slavery. Beyond the infamous *Confessions of Nat Turner*,[81] compiled in 1831 by his lawyer (and fictionalized in 1967 by white writer William Styron, whose adaptation/hijacking of this first autobiographical testimony on black revolt drew the ire of black intellectuals), let us mention *The Interesting Narrative of Olaudah Equiano*,[82] the first published account written by a former slave, books by Charles Ball,[83] Henry Bibb,[84] Henry "Box" Brown,[85] William Wells Brown,[86] Henry Bruce,[87] Frederick Douglass, *The Refugee, or Narratives of Fugitive Slaves in Canada*,[88] Moses Granby,[89] Josiah Henson (who served as a model for Harriet Beecher Stowe's Uncle Tom),[90] Lunsford Lane,[91] Jermain W. Loguen,[92] Sojourner Truth,[93] Henry Watson,[94] Samuel Ringgold Ward,[95] etc. Most of these books were published in the mid-nineteenth century, when the abolitionist movement solicited and supported propaganda through direct testimony.

However, black fiction authors manifested themselves only later. William Wells Brown published in London in 1853 what is considered the first black novel: *Clotel, or the President's Daughter*.[96] The novel is semi-autobiographical and doubles as a plea for the abolition of slavery.

Six years later appeared *Blake, or The Huts of America*,[97] of which only an incomplete version remains. In this novel, rather violent for its time, author Martin Delany distinguishes himself from traditional abolitionists by delivering a quasi-Marxist analysis of slavery, which he defines as first and foremost a system of labor exploitation. His protagonist attempts to organize a general slave uprising throughout the South. Addressing field workers rather than mulattoes and other "favorite" slaves, he appears like a proletarian leader *avant la lettre*.

In *The Garies and Their Friends*, published in 1857, Frank Webb is less interested in issues related to slavery (he hailed from the free black community of Philadelphia) than in civic and economic emancipation and discrimination at large (as it relates to marriage, etc.).[98] In chronological order, the Civil War,

Reconstruction, integrationist demands, the impossibility of interracial love, and late nineteenth-century white terror were the favorite themes of Frances E.W. Harper, Walter Stowers, William A. Anderson, J. McHenry Jones, and Charles Chesnutt.[99]

A special spot must be reserved for the pastor Sutton Griggs and the contradictory character of his works. Resigned and conciliatory to the point of servility in *Pointing the Way*,[100] he shows uncommon violence in *Imperium in Imperio*.[101] Presented as a "black patriot," his main protagonist leads a secret society of students whose goal is black revolution. They join a clandestine revolutionary government that intends to take over Texas and make it a black nation separate from the United States. The anti-white and anti-mulatto sentiment of the novel is reminiscent of early Malcolm X speeches.

The success met by Paul Laurence Dunbar was less surprising; his works are a testimony to the unsorted contradictions and psychic confusion once characteristic of parts of the black elite. Dunbar's father was a plasterer in a Kentucky plantation; despairing of ever being able to obtain freedom, he escaped to Canada through the Underground Railroad and came back wearing the uniform of the Union during the Civil War. He married a former slave who taught herself to read and write and managed to take night classes in spite of working as a washerwoman. Paul Laurence Dunbar was born in 1872, his only knowledge of slavery coming from the carefully edited stories told by his mother.[102] In his first novel, *The Uncalled*, he tells the story of a young white man forced into a career as a minister, and his rebellion against priesthood (Dunbar's mother wanted him to become a preacher). Dunbar became famous as poet, though. A great admirer of the classics and of the British and American Romantics, a friend of Frederick Douglass, a prodigal son (he started writing in elementary school, when he often found himself the only black person in class) who was unable to finish his schooling for financial reasons, writing at the time when Booker T. Washington was spreading his conciliatory message, he can now be considered the exemplary product (if not the victim) of the ideological confusion dominating his period. On the one hand, much like southern whites, and with similar nostalgia and retrospective optimism, he sings of "the good old time of the plantations" (which he himself only knew through his mother's tales): masters were good, slaves happy and faithful, and when they saw one another, they fell crying in each other's arms. . . .[103] And when he offers short glimpses of the atrocities of slavery, they are soon dispelled by renascent optimism: in the memories of his favorite characters, old slaves, the most painful images are repressed through a classic mnesic device. . . . In "When Dey 'listed Colored Soldiers," he expresses sympathy for the Southern grey as much as the Northern blue. In fact, he bears witness to the ideology of planters—which he seems to have more than tolerated—like no other black author had, in a rather equivocal manner, to use the least severe term used by critics—some white—to define his stance. His portrait of freed slaves is a true betrayal in that he takes no account of the effects of white ideological conditioning and presents an image of the Negro similar to that spread by white southerners:

> Willfully created and spread by the colonizer, this mythical and degrading portrait ends up by being accepted and lived with to a certain extent by the colonized. It thus acquires a certain amount of reality and contributes to the true portrait of the colonized. . . . It is common knowledge that the ideology of a governing class is adopted in large measure by the governed classes. . . . By agreeing to this ideology, the dominated classes practically confirm the role assigned to them.[104]

It bears noting that, under the influence of Booker T. Washington, compromise was the word of the day. However—and this reveals unavoidable contradictions—Dunbar was also the author of an "Ode to Ethiopia," wherein Ethiopia is presented as the glorious incarnation of the black race. In 1903, he paid homage to Frederick Douglass:

> Ah, Douglass, we have fall'n on evil days
> Such days as thou, not even thou didst know . . .[105]

In "Slow through the Dark," he loses some of his optimism and represents the improvement of the condition of the black race as a slow climb through the dark. In "The Haunted Oak," he describes and condemns a lynching and dares to present a judge, a doctor, and a pastor—three local Ku Klux Klan officials—as the authors of the crime:

> Oh, the judge, he wore a black mask,
> And the doctor one of white,
> And the minister, with his oldest son,
> Was curiously bedight.[106]

He shows racial solidarity in his vernacular poems, asserting himself—almost in spite of himself—as a Negro facing a white audience. This audience preferred his vernacular poems to those written in received English, which deeply humiliated Dunbar. A band accompanied Dunbar when he recited his poems in public, and, with gestures, added to his poems a rhythmic commentary closer to African American musical traditions than to Anglo-Saxon meter. . . . Music (what would soon become "jazz") was no stranger to Dunbar's inspiration. In their rhythmic structures and patterns of repetition, some of his poems show obvious relation to African American music and song. In "The Colored Band," Dunbar goes as far as comparing white and black musicians as he describes a black band marching down a city street, playing a ragtime version of a Sousa march.[107] A similar network of references is summoned in "When Malindy Sings" (a poem that Abbey Lincoln, the wife of jazz drummer Max Roach, would put in music half a century later[108]), where the poet remembers his mother singing spirituals. In his love poems, Dunbar even anticipates the proponents of the slogan *black is beautiful*: he praises the dark eyes, nappy hair, and ebony skin of a young woman, sings of the purity of blackness with a certain amount of scorn for mulattoes:

> Dely brown ez brown kin be
> An' huh hair is curly. . . .
> She ain't no mulatter;
> She pure cullud,—don't you see
> Dat's jes' whut's de mattah?
> Dat's de why I love huh so,
> D'ain't no mix about huh.[109]

Although clearly capable of overcoming the prejudice determined by a society in which he had no more chosen to live than his ancestors, Paul Laurence Dunbar was also torn by conjugal strife at the social and racial level. The son of a washerwoman, "black as sin," Dunbar married (against the wishes of his future parents-in-law) a New Orleans teacher who, like him, wrote verse, but came from a bourgeois family and whose skin was almost white. Throughout their life together she reproached him for associating his name with minstrel shows (he wrote lyrics for black musicals), and was infuriated when critics called him "the Prince of the Coon Song Writers."[110]

More for their contradictions and hesitations perhaps than for their literary qualities alone, Dunbar's writings (and his life) reflect and illustrate the conflicting impulses, diverging tendencies, and antagonistic cultural and social references that tore black consciousness in the troubled period that the end of the nineteenth century was in America. The issues of interracial love depicted by James Edwin Campbell,[111] the heavy comedy borrowed from minstrels by Daniel Webster Davis, and the dreams of magical whitening of J. Mord Allen were so many fragmentary visions of a universe that Dunbar himself had already entirely surveyed.

The only poems older than Dunbar's that have reached us are those of the slave Lucy Terry, published in the second half of the eighteenth century, which have "nothing specifically Negro about them;"[112] the spiritual sermons of Jupiter Hammon, whose main credit was to be the first black American to see his poetry in print; and of course the works of Phillis Wheatley, who did not let the very classical form she used prevent her from asserting an already marked racial consciousness:

> Some view our sable race with scornful eye—
> "Their color is a diabolic dye."
> Remember, Christians, Negroes black as Cain
> May be refined, and join th' angelic train.[113]

By comparison, in George Moses Horton's "The Slave," protest remains embryonic:

> Because the brood-sow's left side pigs were black,
> Whose sable tincture was by nature struck,
> Were you by justice bound to pull them back
> And leave the sandy-colored pigs to suck?[114]

Many other literate blacks attempted to parallel their abolitionist activism with their poetry. The results were overall as mediocre and boring as the works of some of their white counterparts, tied as they were to literary trends of a certain romantic tradition that mixed monotony and lament. After listing all African American poets, no matter the literary quality of their work, Jean Wagner writes:

> How much fresher, by comparison, how eternally youthful is the lyric poetry of nameless folk poets! How much more eloquently it pleads in its naive spontaneity for the cause of black humanity out of whose suffering it has arisen! Everything here has been truly lived; it is inborn and authentic. Song is an immediate upwelling; issuing directly from the heart, it blithely disregards all accepted metrical notions. However, years had to elapse before the incomparable beauty of folk poetry could be recognized. The prestige of the singer determines the prestige of the song: this often is the aesthetic criterion. It was not until these millions of slaves had been declared free men under the law that anyone deigned to listen, although over the centuries they had, by their singing, abundantly demonstrated their membership in the human race.[115]

6. Black Music before Jazz

> And finally, when a man looked up in some anonymous field and shouted, "Oh, Ahm tired a dis mess,/ Oh, yes, Ahm so tired a dis mess," you can be sure he was an American.
> —LeRoi Jones, *Blues People*, xii.

Before LeRoi Jones, Alain Locke,[1] a black scholar representing both the black bourgeoisie (its concern for respectability, its understanding of the differences between black and Western art as differences in degree, its intellectual inferiority complex) and a certain black intellectual elite (bent on valorizing black cultural contributions, cataloguing all black creators, alluding to the innumerable obstacles met by black artists in American society, etc.) had through his research underlined the importance of black music in the United States. But it is only with LeRoi Jones that the appearance and evolution of the African American musical phenomenon began to be studied in its relation to three essential elements: the persistance of Africanisms, the influence of an oppressive social context, and the continuous presence of protest in all vocal and instrumental black manifestations in America—this third element being inseparable from the second.

a) African Music in America

The music of the first generations of slaves (those born in Africa) could only be a *reconstitution* of African music. Prisoners in a foreign land whose language they could not yet speak, forced into a kind of labor and a pace they were not used to, they tried for a time—it seems—to adapt to the monotony of agricultural work in American colonies the songs and chants that traditionally accompanied both profane and sacred activities in Africa. The former Ibo slave who gained freedom in 1766, Olaudah Equiano (Gustavus Vassa), writes in his autobiography: "We are all of a nation of dancers, musicians, and poets. Thus every great event, such as a triumphant return from battle, or other cause of public rejoicing, is celebrated in public dances, which are accompanied with songs and music suited to the occasion."[2] Each musical style, each dance, represents some interesting scene of real life, such as a great achievement, domestic employment, a pathetic story or some rural sport; and as the subject is generally founded on some recent event, it is therefore ever new. This gives our dances a spirit and variety which I have scarcely seen elsewhere. We have many musical instruments, particularly drums of different kinds, a piece of music which resembles a guitar, and another much like a stickado. These last are chiefly used by betrothed virgins, who play on them on all grand festivals.[3]

At the beginning of the slave period, Africans tried to perpetuate their musical traditions. For a time colonizers did not think to oppose it—as long as it did not hamper productivity. But, little by little, obstacles were raised that made the preservation of African cultures impossible. This progressive "disafricanization" saw elements of the culture disappear, African elements banned or replaced by new (colonial or Western) elements.

Slaves first lost the instruments necessary to play their music (drums, balafons, etc.); therefore, as soon as they had the opportunity (or the authorization), they either made new ones from memory, or learned to use Western instruments when they could procure them. More decisive was the disappearance of the tribal context. Musical manifestations were almost always collective in Africa, but during slave sales Africans were not only separated from other tribe members, but also from family members—they were thus cut off from the people likely to stimulate and appreciate their musical production. African music was also almost always associated with—if not completely integrated into—the religious traditions of each tribe. In changing continents Africans lost their gods, partly because these gods corresponded to climatic and geographical elements of Africa that they did not find in America, but also because the white masters (especially Anglo-Saxon protestants) soon forbade "niggers" to perform their "orgies," "sabbaths," and other ritual devilries. Traces of these cults subsist in *voodoo* ceremonies—especially in the Caribbean, colonized by the Spaniards and the French—or in *Macumba* ceremonies in South America. One can imagine, along with LeRoi Jones, that "in the essentially Catholic New World cultures, the many saints were easily substituted for the many *loa* or deities in the various West African religions. But in Protestant America this was not possible."[4] One must add that Anglo-Saxon Puritans considered music and dance devilish manifestations, detrimental to work, seriousness, and morals. The fact that slaves used African music and songs as means of communication was another reasons for colonizers to be wary of them: "The slave-owners found to their cost that drums which beat for dances could also call to revolt, and thus it came about that in many parts of the New

World the African type of hollow-log drums were suppressed, being supplanted by other percussion devices less susceptible of carrying messages."[5]

In several southern states, laws were enacted that forbade slaves from drumming—the Black Codes of Georgia and Mississippi made it illegal to "beat drums or blow horns." Thus the percussion instruments traditionally used by the Ashanti, Yoruba, and many other Western African tribes as means of communication disappeared; transplanted along with their users in a foreign universe, this system became a secret code and therefore a potential means of major revolts. Soon after Nat Turner's rebellion in 1831, a series of laws made it illegal for blacks to learn to read or write, or to *play music*, as music might have reawakened violence among slaves or bolstered rebellion.[6]

As African musical elements were gradually eliminated, diluted, or simply ignored, the process of uprooting slaves also brought inevitable transfers and substitutions. We know that most African music and songs are functional, or at least circumstantial; they accompany, stimulate, or celebrate traditional activities, and beats and percussion are used in initiations. Deprived of their essential sources of inspiration (fishing, gathering, hunting, war, celebrations, religious ceremonies, etc.) and forced to dedicate all their energy to new and monotonous work (and the automatism dictated by monoculture), plantation slaves adapted their songs to the colonial system of reference that brutally replaced African systems.

Another decisive factor for the future of black music in America was the obligation to change linguistic systems. Slaves were unable to find other speakers of their native tongues (as a tribe's members were generally dispersed during sales), and if they did, the master or the overseer, always wary of potential revolt or escape, would use the whip to discourage conversation. This forced silence, along with the necessity of understanding the overseer's orders, made it necessary to learn the colonizers' language—Portuguese or Spanish in South America, Spanish, French, or English in the United States.

The gradual disappearance of ancestral cultures should have been followed by the acquisition of the masters' cultures. But this substitution, or rather its second step, acculturation, happened with singular slowness: all the restrictions on relations between blacks and whites imposed by the slave system slowed down the "civilizing process." The only teaching allowed was professional; educating slaves was contrary to custom and, sometimes, law. Thus, between the loss of a network of traditions thousands of years old and the impossibility of integrating completely or easily into a civilization of a new kind, blacks found themselves for a time in a *cultural void* of sorts. In order to gain control over such a disturbing situation, they had to *invent an original, inevitably heterogeneous system of references by using the remaining African ele-*

ments they still had access to, but also by practicing a kind of cultural poaching in their new surroundings.

The first consequence (or, at least, the most obvious to white observers): the appearance of hybrid languages (black French, black English) that preceded and anticipated the formation of African American dialects. Colonizers did not understand African dialects, and they understood no better the patois invented by their slaves; not only did African accentuation transform European (English, French, Spanish) words, but the very form of sentences seemed to indicate a complete incapacity to assimilate European syntax. Colonizers considered African American speech to be a linguistic jumble demonstrating blacks' intellectual inferiority. It was in fact the product of a collision between European vocabularies and African syntactic systems: slaves organized English words in the grammatical frameworks they possessed. Rather than "gobbledygook," this linguistic product was one of the last active manifestations of African culture, a new testimony of the cultural in-between where slaves were kept, proof of their resistance to abandoning African dialects, but also of the lack of instruction in European grammatical systems. In spite of the dilution and gradual disappearance of African linguistic elements, the black people of the United States would keep the particular accent that gives its "exotic" color to all their vocal manifestations and which white minstrels caricature, which poets (like Dunbar) use, and which would give birth to *jive* (the black slang present throughout white clarinetist Mezz Mezzrow's autobiography[7]) and be valorized by black jazzmen in the 1950s (see II. 2. g).

Linguistic phenomena are inseparable from the social and ideological context in which they appear and the vocal and musical manifestations of all human groups (song, influenced and conditioned by language, can also in turn have an influence on language); it is therefore possible to consider language, social, political, and economical conditions, and vocal and instrumental music as three perfectly parallel and connected axes in the evolution of the black American people. No wonder *soul music*, for example, was contemporaneous with nonviolent activism and the evangelical language of Martin Luther King Jr (see II. 3. g).

Thus, from the pure African dialects linked to a time of freedom and intact culture, blacks taken in the slave trade moved to a "double," African-English linguistic system, where their nostalgia for Africa and their resistance to enslavement (by the rejection or interdiction of the colonizer's syntactic system and by maintaining African words, songs, and beats) intersected with their desire (or need) to integrate the imposed dominant cultural system. These attitudes led to a *situation of conflict* repeated at all stages and in all domains of African American history (opposition between "favorite" slaves and rebel slaves, house servants and field workers, mulattoes and Negroes, voodoo and Christianity, "bourgeois" integrationists and radical proletarians, Booker T. Washington and W. E. B. Du Bois, vernacular poets and "integrated" poets, etc.). From this permanent duality—the double consciousness discussed by W. E. B. Du Bois—contradictions, imbalance, and hesitations would spring up that, added to the conditioning and trauma of colonization, slavery, discrimination, racism, and lost illusions, would get in the way of the political and ideological union of Negroes in America. This duality was of course fed by colonial and capitalist society in that it made enslavement easier (see 1. b, c, d): "The history of the American Negro is the history of this strife—this longing to attain self-conscious manhood, to merge his double self into a better and truer self."[8]

Because of the primordial importance of the word in African civilizations, this linguistic struggle would prove crucial. Its consequences were the evolution of music (song is speech, speech is rhythm) and the substitution of one religious system for another (the word creates through the Word of God: "God spoke and the breath of his word was creation"[9]).

Du Bois writes: "What are these songs, and what do they mean? I know little of music and can say nothing in technical phrase, but I know something of men.... They are the music of an unhappy people, of the children of disappointment; they tell of death and suffering and unvoiced longing toward a truer world, of misty wanderings and hidden ways."[10] He also states further:

> The human spirit in this new world has expressed itself in vigor and ingenuity rather than in beauty. And so by fateful chance the Negro folk-song—the rhythmic cry of the slave—stands to-day not simply as the sole American music, but as the most beautiful expression of human experience born this side the seas. It has been neglected, it has been, and is, half despised, and above all it has been persistently mistaken and misunderstood; but notwithstanding, it still remains as the singular spiritual heritage of the nation and the greatest gift of the Negro people.[11]

b) Work Songs

If the *work songs* of slaves[12] are "rhythmed chants," it is not only because of the importance of rhythm in African music: cutting sugar cane or picking cotton—much like pulling barges on the Volga—is less taxing when done to the rhythm of a song whose structure matches the succession of movements necessary to the task at hand. First, the functional value of work songs explains why colonizers did not forbid them. Secondly, these songs produce a kind of throbbing drive (tension and release) that can be compared to the rhythmic cadence of early blues, and which we also find in chain gang songs[13] by prisoners experiencing collective subjection in post-slavery times. Prison is much less exceptional for many black Americans than whites might think. The high percentage of blacks delinquents and convicts is in part due to the particular severity of judges—influenced like the rest of their compatriots by the dominant racist ideology—and to the phenomenon now considered classic by most sociologists whereby delinquency is bolstered by a socially oppressive and miserable environment. Thus many Negroes, even among the most famous, have recognized the crucial influence their prison stays had on their lives and ways of thinking. Malcolm X and Eldridge Cleaver started reacting *politically* to the condition of black Americans while they were serving terms in prison, the former for robbery and the latter for rape. The bluesman Leadbelly and the writer Chester Himes also spent long years behind bars.

Reading certain testimonies,[14] one might be struck by the often benign, resigned, if not happy and carefree character of work song lyrics. It seems that colonizers only tolerated these songs to the extent that they helped increase production (this attitude is comparable to that of certain "modern" cattle breeders who broadcast in their stables music scientifically chosen to improve milk production in their cows; analogous experiments have also been undertaken in our factories), and therefore were never melancholy or nostalgic. There could be no criticism of plantation life or, of course, any exhortation to revolt. The same concern for production explains how slave ship captains regularly forced slaves to dance on the deck: the "cattle" had to be in good shape for the sale. Thus, from the first contacts between Negroes and their exploiters, the content and meaning of black songs were systematically censored, *bent towards entertainment, a word that later became traditionally synonymous with "jazz" or "black music" for a majority of white Americans.*

c) African Memories

In spite (or because of?) these diverse repressions, interdictions, and constraints, references to, and more or less denatured memories of, Africa remained in the family traditions of many Negroes. Despite a series of laws meant to end the slave trade, it had not stopped at the beginning of the nineteenth century, and Africans were still being deported to ensure the reign of "King Cotton" in the South. Thus connections to the African continent were not severed, contrary to what one might think. Until 1859, slave ships regularly dropped off their human cargoes on American shores. This explains how even in the time of minstrel shows (the second half of the nineteenth century), some Africanisms in black American speech, songs, and music testified to a relatively recent past. In *The Souls of Black Folk* and *Dusk of Dawn*, W. E. B. Du Bois remembers his ancestors, and through them, a certain Africa:

> He [*Jacob Burghardt, Du Bois's great-grandfather*] married a wife named Violet who was apparently newly arrived from Africa and brought with her an African song which became traditional in the family.... With Africa I had only one direct cultural connection and that was the African melody which my great-grandmother Violet used to sing. Where she learned it, I do not know. ... But at any rate, as I wrote years ago in "Souls of Black Folk," "coming to the valleys of the Hudson and Housatonic, black, little, and lithe, she shivered and shrank in the harsh north winds, looked longingly at the hills, and often crooned a heathen melody to the child between her knees, thus:
>
> Do bana coba, gene me, gene me!
> Do bana coba, gene me, gene me!
> Ben d'nuli, nuli, nuli, nuli, ben d'le.
>
> The child sang it to his children and they to their children's children, and so two hundred years it has traveled down to us and we sing it to our children, knowing as little as our fathers what its words may mean, but knowing well the meaning of its music.[15]

African elements also persisted in instruments. Many testimonies discuss the "savage music" of early slaves, the best known being the account written by architect Benjamin Henry Latrobe on a trip to New Orleans and Congo Square, where slaves were allowed to gather at night:

> The music consisted of two drums and a stringed instrument. An old man sat astride of a cylindrical drum about a foot in diameter, and beat it with incredible quickness with the edge of his hand and fingers. The other drum was an open staved thing held between the knees and beaten in the same manner. ... The most curious instrument, however, was a stringed instrument which no doubt was imported from Africa. On the top of the finger board was the rude figure of a man in a sitting posture, and two pegs behind him to which the strings were fastened.... [Another instrument], which from the color of the wood seemed new, consisted of a block cut into something of the form of a cricket bat with a long & deep mortice down the center. This thing made a considerable noise, being beaten lustily on the side by a short stick. In the

same orchestra was. . . . also a calabash with a round hole in it, the hole studded with brass nails, which was beaten by a woman with two short sticks.[16]

Herbert Asbury notes that in 1817, Congo Square was

> designated by the mayor of New Orleans as the only area to which slaves might resort, and thereafter all such gatherings were held under police supervision. The dancing was stopped at sunset and the slaves sent home. Under these and other regulations the custom of permitting slave dancing in Congo Square continued for more than twenty years, when it was abolished, for which the city records do not make clear. It was resumed in 1845. . . . [and] reached the height of its popularity during the fifteen years which preceded the Civil War.[17]

Municipal authorities forbade gatherings on Congo Square during the troubled period that followed the city's occupation by Union troops. During the 1880s, George W. Cable witnessed similar musical and choreographic performances in a vacant lot on Dumaine Street. His extremely precise descriptions of the instruments and of the physical characteristics of dancers underline the still very African traits of the music and of the slaves themselves.[18]

d) Religious Songs

The "concerts" on Congo Square seem to have been an exception in the history of black music, which can be explained by the traditionally paternalistic attitude of the French and Spanish Catholic colonizers who constituted a majority of the white community in Louisiana. They were generally more tolerant towards slaves than the Protestant colonizers from England, Germany, etc., who dominated in the other North American colonies, where slaves could only go to the fields to work, to their quarters on the plantations to sleep (at the beginning of the nineteenth century, a law declared that any slave found further than eight miles from the house of his master would be considered a fugitive and therefore susceptible to the most severe corporal punishments[19]), or, possibly, to church.

From the beginning of the colonial period through the twentieth century, Christianity has played a permanent, decisive, and singularly ambiguous role in the history of Negroes in America. Detribalized, deprived of their ancestral gods, slaves were soon disposed to listen to pastors' sermons; by adopting the religion of their masters, they were likely hoping to understand the reasons for their enslavement, and also find in the new ritual manifestations offered to them an opportunity for respite, if not merely a distraction from the monotony of their work. (We know that to this day, in prisons, religious ceremonies attract a great number of prisoners whether or not they correspond to particular religious convictions). Among the causes for the Christianization of slaves, on top of the interdiction against practicing African cults, LeRoi Jones adds "a traditional respect for [the African's] conqueror's gods. Not that they are always worshiped, but they are at least recognized as powerful and placed in the hierarchy of the conquered tribe's gods."[20] Moreover, the adoption of Christianity—though one can suppose any other religion would have worked—permitted slaves to recover the kind of collective psychological current[21] so essential to tribal society. The need to imitate the behavior of whites is another determining factor that explains why the first converts were "favorite" slaves, the servants living closer to the masters. Through their diversity and contradictions, the causes for Christianization were also responsible for the twofold aspect of the Afro-American religious phenomenon. The church was both the main center of Negro social life and the most efficient tool of control at the hands of colonizers. While the majority of slaves turned to the Baptist and Methodist churches, which Negroes had discovered during the Great Awakening at the beginning of the eighteenth century (missionaries of the time organized mass, open-air camp meetings that were accessible to Negroes, where the faithful would sing religious hymns together), house slaves, servants, "favorites," mulattoes, and free men generally belonged to the Episcopal, Congregationalist, Presbyterian, and sometimes even Catholic denominations, those that, they thought, got them closer to their white models, and put them at a distance from other Negroes.

Initially watched and controlled by whites, black churches would nevertheless generate more than purely ministerial vocations; they saw the rise of the first black nationalist leaders, as well as the first supporters of a kind of gradualist and integrationist collaboration. Headed by black preachers, these churches would constitute the "Invisible Institution,"[22] as the ensemble of the non-institutionalized congregations reserved to Negroes was designated in the United States. There the first quasi-political meetings took place; there scriptures were *interpreted* in different ways in order to either justify slavery as a "divine curse," or instead to reveal to Negroes the injustice and hypocrisy to which they were subjected in the name of the principles of love and justice. There the first "subversive" manifestoes were also broadcast "live."[23] There, finally, were created the first black religious songs: spirituals, gospel songs, groans, moans, etc.

To the extent that church was the *only place* where Negroes could express *together* their repressed feelings, spirituals cannot be considered merely religious songs: they also have to be heard as testimonies of the violence prominent in the slave's life (like African chants told the history of the tribe as transmitted through oral tradition). The first preachers were often the most educated slaves. As true race leaders, they took care of their constituents' spiritual lives as well as their secular problems. Thus did the black church begin to play a social and political role. Following slave revolts in the nineteenth century, services where only Negroes gathered were forbidden. "The Invisible Institution" became a true secret society, and the spiritual a code of sorts through which Negroes could communicate unbeknownst to their masters. Spirituals became code between fugitive slaves and "conductors" of the Underground Railroad. This way of using hymns, unexpected by white preachers, was evoked by Frederick Douglass[24] and Martin Luther King Jr.:[25] Canaan was Canada, Pharaoh stood for white masters, the Hebrews were the Negroes, etc. Discussing the spiritual "We'll Soon Be Free," a black soldier explained to T. W. Higginson that all the people who sang the verse *"De Lord will call us home"* thought, *"de Lord mean for say de Yankees."*[26] If most spirituals, much like Christianity at large, promised paradise to those who had known hell on earth, it remains that the frequent use of the words *free* and *freedom* must have had a completely different meaning for slaves, in spite of the explanations of some southerners:

> The haunting melody of these "spirituals," their notes of sorrow, aspiration and jubilance, have given rise to a common belief, demonstrably false, that in these songs we have the negro's expression of suffering under slavery and of his joy at liberation. Without pausing to expose this fallacy in detail, one needs only to call attention to the fact that a strain of supposed melancholy is a common property of folk-songs everywhere and does not always reflect a really melancholy mood.[27]

Following Jean Wagner,[28] one can simply oppose to such an argument the unambiguous lyrics of some of these songs:

> No more auction block for me
> No more, no more,
> No more auction block for me
> Many thousand gone[29]

Or:
> White man use whip
> White man use trigger,
> But the Bible and Jesus

Made a slave of the nigger.[30]

The recurrent references to Old Testament passages recounting the enslavement of the Hebrews in Egypt even suggest hopes of vengeance:

Oh Mary, don't you weep, don't you moan,
Pharaoh's army got drowned.[31]

Thus, we find that resignation and carefree happiness were not the essential characteristics of slaves' vocal manifestations, which, as a collective phenomenon, testify to an ever-present protest tendency in black consciousness, even in areas where one might think it had been put to sleep by promises and good words.

Paradoxically, this aspect of the spiritual is not what has caught the attention of most specialists (musicologists, sociologists, ethnologists, etc.). Black and white intellectuals seem to have preferred to study a different—and much less urgent, of course—issue: that of the origin of the spirituals. Were they African? Anglo-Saxon? Both? Call and response, hand clapping, collective improvisation and trance, all constants of the spiritual, can also be found in songs of Western Africa; but many spirituals are undoubtedly inspired by Methodist hymns. African and European elements meet in variable proportions in spirituals as in any other form of African American music, a *mixed music* whose history is overall the history of mixing and of the many different outcomes and *conflicts* it occasions. Everything about this music—whether it be religious or secular—seems to suggest that it obstinately refuses to conform, thus preserving its original productive contradictions.

e) The Blues

The origin, gestation, and evolution of the blues are no less complex than the spirituals', but they are more obscure in that the location of their birth is not confined to the temple or the church, and in that this birth was not determined by religious sentiment or religious occasion. LeRoi Jones was right to note—against those historians that make the blues into a second nature for Negroes—that Africans did not sing the blues as they walked out of slave ships.

Through their content and their social inscription, the blues already constitute the Negro's *response* to his situation as a slave, the Negro's *personalized reaction* to white America. And this reaction is thought out and sung in *English*.

The first differential trait of the blues is that it is sung in the singular, by an individual who is the subject of the song. Spirituals are collective and generally speak in the plural. In the blues, the black subject is in the forefront; it is a monologue of subjectivity. This calls for two remarks. First, that the formal structure of the blues can be an adaptation of the necessarily collective call-and-response principle of African origin to individual performance, notably through the repetition of the first verse. This adaptation/preservation of the form reintroduces Africa in an English-language song with American themes and collectivity (thought of as the listener or the interlocutor to the singer) in individual expression. Second, that one of the blues' original elements is most likely the *field hollers*—those shouts and calls that helped the slave communicate with his fellows around the plantations—which reinforces the occult, driving role of the collective in the blues.

Another important element in the central role played by the blues in African American music is the fact that it was initially repressed: since masters forbade melancholy and protest songs, the blues was forced underground throughout slavery. It was sung at night in cabins, in solitude, but it did not constitute a *spectacle*, which settled its character as an interior monologue.

Finally, the importance of speech in African civilizations is here multiplied by the fact that the Negro rarely possessed musical instruments, that he had lost his own, that he obviously was not allowed to quit his job in order to start *playing* music, and finally that the instruments he could use were without exception European instruments. The blues, sung alone, often without other accompaniment than the noises the singer could make, was the response to instrumental deprivation, to the emphasis on spoken language, and to the need for discretion and secrecy.

All these factors, confirmed by the themes and content of the blues (commentary on the life of Negroes, their problems, etc.), lead us to hold the blues as the major formation of African American music, with jazz only an adaptation of it, an instrumental translation, a musical compromise struck with the different orders imposed by white America: an instrumental and entertaining music designed for spectacle.

What returns in the blues is what white America repressed first in the slave, then in the poor black: his subjectivity, either completely denied or ridiculed by the masters ("Negroes have no soul"), his need to locate himself at the center of his own mode of expression, to be the subject of his own story. Another symptom of this return of the repressed in the blues resides in the "dirtiness," the "obscenity" not only in its vocabulary (the blues transgresses dominant moral and social codes with its language: sex, money, and filth are the leitmotivs of the blues) but also in its tone (bawdy or bemoaning), both assaulting the codes of social "distinction" and the "measure" of white music and society.

The blues grunts, cries, moans, slurs: the "bad nigger" sings it and the blues talks about him, this "bad nigger" who is the dark and dangerous other side of the "stage nigger," the *minstrel*, the whitened Negro.

Finally, one must note that the blues, the confessions and complaints of the black Subject, was throughout the history of jazz both the form of black music that whites were the most resistant to and the music the black masses most easily identified with. It indeed puts in place a process of identification between the singer and his listeners: the issues and tribulations of *this* Negro are in fact the issues and tribulations of *all* Negroes: the Subject here is but the spokesperson of black ideology (see III. 1).

The first famous blues—which were chronicles in song—date back to the Civil War; they multiplied around the time of emancipation. The bluesman was often a kind of vagabond, an emancipated or freed slave migrating from the southern farmland to the industrial cities of the North. According to Frederic Ramsey, what we call the blues today were once also called *reels* and *cornfield songs*.[32]

For *white listeners*, one of the most surprising characteristics of the blues is the appearance of *blue notes*, these modulations already present in *field hollers* and in the calls of southern street vendors.[33] Although *blue notes* are not part of the (temperate) Western scale, any European instrument can reproduce them. They were therefore interpreted by the majority of Western musicologists as the result of a difficulty, if not an inability on the part of Negroes who had been taught European hymns by missionaries, to produce the third and seventh degrees of the Western scale, those degrees being absent in the primitive, five-tone scale.[34] Sidney Finkelstein replies,

> These deviations from the pitch familiar to concert music are not, of course, the result of an inability to sing or play in tune. They mean that the blues are a non-diatonic music.... Many books on jazz ... generally describe the blues as a sequence of chords, such as the tonic, the subdominant and dominant seventh. Such a definition, however, is like putting the cart before the horse. There are definite patterns of chords which have been evolved to support the blues, but these do not define the blues, and the blues can exist as melody perfectly recognizable as the blues without them. Neither are the blues simply a use of the major scale with the "third" and "seventh" slightly blued or flattened. The fact is that both this explanation, and the chord explanation, are attempts to explain one musical system in terms of another; to describe a non-diatonic music in diatonic terms.[35]

Similarly, to generally accepted definitions of "classic" blues as black American folklore, fixed-form poems comprising several stanzas of three verses each, twelve bar themes, etc., one can reply with this statement by Archie Shepp: "Certainly Blind Lemon Jefferson and Huddie Leadbetter must have played 13, 17, 25 bar blues."[36] The blues should therefore be defined through its meanings rather than its musical "anomalies"; "The blues," says singer Chester Burnett (known as Howlin' Wolf), "mean trouble. When a man has no money, no job and has to take care of his family, when nothing goes right for him . . . that's what I call the blues, when nothing goes right."[37] "No white man ever had the blues," adds Huddie Leadbetter, or Leadbelly.[38] In *White Man, Listen!*, Richard Wright gives several examples of another aspect of the blues: its expression of a revolt already obvious in "religious" songs ("If I had-a my way/ I'd tear the building down/ Great God, then, if I had-a my way/If I had-a my way, little children/If I had-a my way/I'd tear this building down"), which from recalling the harm suffered, often turns to telling the story of criminal acts against masters or death wishes against whites:

> We raise the wheat
> They give us the corn;
> We bake the bread
> They give us the crust;
> We sift the meal,
> They give us the husk;
> We peel the meat,
> They give us the skin;
> And that's the way
> We skin the pot,
> They give us the liquor,
> And they say that's good enough for nigger.

Or:

> Yes my old master promise me;
> But his papers didn't leave me free.
> A dose of poison helped him along.
> May the Devil preach his funeral song.

Or again:

> I wish to God that east-bound train would wreck
> I wish to God that east-bound train would wreck
> Kill the engineer, break the fireman's neck.[39]

Sometimes the singer also talks of the duality in which Negroes are condemned to live:

> Me and my captain don't agree
> But he don't know, 'cause he don't ask me
> He don't know, he don't know my mind
> When he sees me laughing
> Laughing to keep from crying
> Got one mind for white folks to see
> Another for what I know is me.

Despite black churches and spirituals, these songs sometimes allude to the injustice of masters who pretend to be Christians:

> Our Father, who art in heaven
> White man owe me 'leven, and pay me seven,
> Thy kingdom come, thy will be done
> And ef I hadn't tuck that, I wouldn't got none.[40]

This prayer-poem by W. E. B. Du Bois strikes a similar tone:

> Doth not this justice of hell stink in Thy nostrils, O God? How long shall the mounting flood of innocent blood roar in Thine ears and pound on our hearts for vengeance? Pile the pale frenzy of blood-crazed brutes, who do such deeds, high on Thine Altar, Jehovah Jireh, and burn it in hell forever and forever! *Forgive us, good Lord; we know not what we say!*[41]

Though Christianized, black slaves were equated with animals, "soulless creatures." Slavery, institutionalized and justified by some members of the clergy, was a permanent denial of the teachings of Christ. The religious definition of marriage was ceaselessly betrayed by the sale and dispersal of families, while black women were at the mercy of the sexual appetites of their masters. . . . Christian principles were challenged every time they were confronted with the reality of slavery, which explains why the religious fervor of Negroes was not as widespread as some historians have claimed. The blues acts contrary to the spirituals, and often refutes them.

The blues appeared and was practiced by the people long before jazz, but jazz did not replace it: it is jazz's source, and remains its secret force, its subterranean undercurrent.[42] We will therefore have to speak again of the relations of coexistence and sometimes conflict with jazz, and even free jazz (see II. 3 and II. 1).

f) The Ballads

The ballad is another black vocal form, just as *mixed* as the spiritual. Transmitted through oral tradition, it consists of as many African elements (improvisation, more or less mythical tales told by the tribe elders) as European references (traditional English ballads imported by immigrants), and tells the tales of black heroes (such as John Henry, who died of exhaustion digging a railroad tunnel in a race against a steam-powered hammer), the tribulations of a *bad man* such as Stackolee, or dramatic tales of love like "Frankie and Johnnie." Often considered by whites "more entertaining" than the blues in spite of their relatively "subversive" allusions (a critique of the man-crushing machine, references to more or less heroic outlaws, etc. . . .), these songs started the exceptionally meaningful phenomenon of the minstrel shows (see further, i).

g) The Dirty Dozens

The inferiority of blacks, the passivity of slaves, the religious fervor of Negroes: so many myths easily debunked through the merest examination of facts, myths which were nevertheless carefully perpetuated by white chroniclers.

The musical productions of Negroes were expunged and censored as soon as they began to be published. Some, whose character was judged "subversive" or "immoral"—protest songs deemed too violent, obscene or profane lyrics, etc.—were not published at all. Only black militants such as Richard Wright, LeRoi Jones, or Rap Brown lifted the hypocritical reservations of white historians and insisted on the importance of *obscenity* as displayed in the singing and rhyming duels known as the *dirty dozens*. Insults, obscenities, and slander—much like in the vocabulary of the Black Panthers[43]—were means of protesting the cruelty and hypocrisy of the pseudo-Christian white world.

The dozens are somewhat comparable to the songs of recrimination and palavers of Africa and the *hain-tenys* of Madagascar.[44] You need two people to play the dozens, a game that remains very popular in Harlem.[45] One of the players throws increasingly barbed, insulting remarks at his adversary until he leaves or, to the contrary, responds with even more barbed insults, or blows. For Rap Brown, playing the dozens is basic schooling for kids in the ghetto:

> The street is where young bloods get their education. . . . Hell, we exercised our minds by playing the Dozens.
>
> I fucked your mama

Till she went blind.
Her breath smells bad,
But she sure can grind.

I fucked your mama
For a solid hour.
Baby came out
Screaming, Black Power.

Elephant and the Baboon
Learning to screw.
Baby came out looking
Like Spiro Agnew.

And the teacher expected me to sit up in class and study poetry after I could run down shit like that. If anybody needed to study poetry, she needed to study mine. . . . The real aim of the Dozens was to get a dude so mad that he'd cry or get mad enough to fight.[46]

For Richard Wright, the deliberately dirty aspect of the dozens was first a reflection of the pessimism of Negroes: "These Negroes seem to have said to themselves: 'Well, if what is happening to me is right, then, dammit, anything is right.' The *Dirty Dozens* extol incest, celebrate homosexuality, even God's ability to create a rational world is naively but scornfully doubted. . . . This is not atheism; this is beyond atheism; these people do not walk and talk with God; they walk and talk about Him."[47]

The *dozens* are also improvised duels between soloists, the prefiguration and verbal equivalent of saxophonists' chases and trumpet players' battles.[48] The provocation, the insistence of the dozens will make them—along with bottles and bolts—the weapons of choice for black activists facing the *pigs* and the National Guard.

h) Attempts at "Serious Music"

Whether religiously inspired or profane, collective or individual, fictional and fantastic or realistic and activist, these diverse forms of vocal expression illustrate the state of mind of Negroes confronted with the oppressive white system, with infinitely more nuance and truth than the writings of contemporary black intellectuals (poets, novelists, etc.). Here again we see at work the duality inseparable from the process of socio-cultural stratification imposed by colonialism and capitalism. The spontaneous expression of the black masses stands opposite an already gentrified, self-censoring literature that seeks to translate concerns that might be palatable for whites. Only in the twentieth century would the members of the Negro Renaissance try to join poetry and popular lyricism,[49] or, with free jazz, musical innovation and activist music.

The musical field would not escape such whitening/gentrification, however. Alain Locke cites a few black, creole, and white musicians who in the nineteenth century voluntarily strayed from popular vocal and musical tendencies to compose or interpret works likely to satisfy European aesthetic norms: the violinist Edmund Dédé, born in New Orleans in 1829, was sent to the Conservatoire in Paris and composed an overture, *Le Palmier*. Joseph Write, a black man from Cuba, presented his violin compositions to music lovers in Boston and New York. The New Orleanian Louis Moreau Gottschalk authored a "Cubana" that would a century later inspire a very popular rumba, "The Peanut Vendor," and several pieces in which he attempted to associate a romantic style with Louisiana references ("Bamboula," "Negro Dance," "Le Bananier," "The Banjo," "La Savane," etc.). Elizabeth Taylor Greenfield, nicknamed "the Black Swan," was compared to the greatest sopranos of her time; Anna and Emma Louise Hyers became famous for their interpretations of great lyrical duets. Thomas "Blind Tom" Green Bethune was a blind virtuoso pianist whose success is very reminiscent of the advertising campaigns organized around other blind black geniuses (such as pianists Art Tatum or Ray Charles). As Phillis Wheatley in the eighteenth century (a slave born in Senegal, she had learned Latin and written her first poem by the time she was seventeen; admired as a curiosity by the Boston elite, she was sent to England where she became "a sensation" in literary salons[50]), most of these black artists were presented to white elites as circus freaks. They were simply imitating the white musicians of the time, and in this way they reassured whites and comforted them in their social and racial prejudice. The attitude of whites toward specifically black aesthetic manifestations appears to have been scornful and ignorant: inferior to whites, Negroes could only be admirable or exceptional when they did their best to resemble whites. Black folklore, in turn, only became "interesting" or "entertaining" through minstrel shows in which white actors caricatured black singers, dancers and musicians, parodying black speech, *dressing up* like Negroes. *Black imitators of whites* or *white imitators of blacks* both bolstered the obfuscation of purely black forms of expression and perpetuated the only image of the Negro wished for and supported by whites: resigned, if not self-content, happy, carefree, and naive, *capable of progress* only when he deigns to forget his natural laziness and tries to imitate his masters.

i) Minstrels

This "ideal" portrait of the American Negro—already sketched out by some favorite slaves summoned by their masters to entertain their guests—was spread out and commercialized from the end of the eighteenth century by European immigrants who, unlike American planters, had seen in black folklore an inextinguishable source of inspiration and profit. On December 30, 1799, at the Federal Street Theatre in Boston, an all-white audience gave a triumphant welcome to Johan Christian Gottlieb Graupner, a German musician and remarkable interpreter of Haydn and Mozart. His face blackened with burnt cork, he sang "The Gay Negro Boy" [sic], accompanying himself on the banjo. He admitted himself that the tune was only an adaptation of a melody he had heard in the South, a paradoxical homage to the music of Negroes who were forbidden from the stage.[51] Singing and dancing *Negro boys*, Negro dances, *blackface entertainers*, *blackface singers*, *Zip Coon*,[52] and of course Jim Crow would provide circuses, music halls, and theatres across the United States with entertainment throughout the nineteenth century. Success with white audiences was guaranteed since, as Constance Rourke noted, "To be black is to be funny."[53]

Irish-born Thomas Dartmouth "Daddy" Rice asserted himself in 1830 as the "father of minstrels" and became the inventor of "Jim Crow." A music-hall artist, he was seduced during a tour in the South by the grotesque and melancholy character of a tune sung by a black stableman:

> First on de heel tap, den on de toe,
> Turnabout and wheel about an' do just so
> An' every time I wheel about, I jump Jim Crow![54]

When he introduced this new dance and its accompanying song to the audience of the Pittsburgh municipal theatre, it was a triumph. There were eighteen encores! To achieve a more "realistic" effect, Rice had borrowed a black porter's tattered clothes, wore a nappy wig under a straw hat, and the song he had heard in Kentucky had become:

> O, Jim Crow's come to town, as you all must know,
> An' he wheel about, he turn about, he do jis so,
> An' every time he wheel about he jump Jim Crow.[55]

His dance and outfit provoked hilarity that was only topped by the surprising appearance on stage of the clothes' rightful owner, who had begun to worry backstage.[56]

"Jim Crow" immediately joined the long list of nicknames and racial slurs used throughout the history of black presence in the United States to designate black people—such as burnt wood, piece of India, darky, burnt cork, yaller, coffee, brown, coon, crow, etc. There were "Jim Crow laws"; cars reserved for black people on American trains were called "Jim Crow cars," "Jim Crow churches," etc. "Jim Crow" became more than merely a synonym for Negro: it came to embody anti-black racism, to the point that C. Vann Woodward entitled his book on the history of racial segregation *The Strange Career of Jim Crow*.[57]

Like their white imitators, freed blacks began organizing minstrel shows as soon as 1821: *The African Company*, William Henry "Juba" Lane ("this extraordinary youth who, we doubt not, before many weeks have elapsed, will have the honor of displaying his dancing attainments in Buckingham Palace," wrote an anonymous English journalist in 1848[58]), *The Ethiopian Minstrels*, banjo-player Horace Weston and the *Georgia Colored Minstrels*, etc.

The composer and lyricist Stephen Collins Foster, for his part, was inspired by the work songs of the coal-trimmers and stevedores of Pittsburgh and Cincinatti, the religious hymns he heard in the black church where his parents' mulatto servant would sometimes take him, and, as he himself admitted, by all the black melodies he discovered in his travels. Among *white* musicologists and historians he acquired a reputation as "folk-song genius of America,"[59] and was among the main forces behind the spread and authentication of a mythical portrait of the Negro likely to satisfy all the demands of "well-bred" Americans. James Weldon Johnson would write, "It was from the minstrel show that millions of white Americans got their conception of Negro character.... To the minstrel stage can be traced the difficulty which white America finds in taking the Negro seriously.[60]"

If the minstrel phenomenon is a perfect example of the cultural and economic recuperation and colonization of black music, dances, and songs (numerous white composers and interpreters became the first variety "stars" of America thanks to minstrel shows), if it anticipated the triumph of white jazzmen/imitators of the twentieth century and the extraordinary success of pop music "idols" (who, from Elvis Presley to the Rolling Stones, do not hide their multiple borrowings from black American instrumental and vocal forms), then it was also a place of crystallization—the true melting pot, white and for whites, of jazz experiences—which would prepare the rise of jazz and of all American popular music. Minstrel-show programs featured more or less caricatural spoken and sung sketches of Negroes (defining the "professional

Negro," or "Negro for whites" evoked by Malcolm X that we also find in American cinema—from the "black" judges of D. W. Griffith's *Birth of a Nation* and the roles that have become Sidney Poitier's specialty, to the carefree and naive character of Zeke in King Vidor's *Hallelujah*), songs in black dialect-mixing borrowings from all vocal form of black folklore (spirituals, blues, work songs, ballads), dances (tap dance, clog dance that anticipated the success of... Gene Kelly and Fred Astaire), some of which—such as the Jim Crow dance, which already contained the future steps of the *Black Bottom*—would become the fashionable dances of the twentieth century, and exhibitions of instrumental virtuosity (tambourine, banjo, or piano solos). In this frame certain characteristic traits of future jazz were beginning to appear. *Jazz* is a product of minstrel shows that attempts to save and recover, rather than deny and lose, the *blues*: it is the result of a conflict between two polar opposites, white and black, between which jazz oscillates under the pressure of history.

j) Marching Bands

To the extent that a military career is a "serious" thing, before emancipation few Negroes were allowed to join marching bands and learn how to use those instruments that would play an essential role in jazz: horns. Although there were then no regular black regiments, Alain Locke indicates that a few black marching bands became famous in the nineteenth century. The most famous appears to have started in Philadelphia in 1839. Conductor, composer, arranger, and trumpet player Frank Johnson led it until his death in 1846. He was so successful that he toured Great Britain and received a silver trumpet in praise of his virtuosity from the hands of Queen Victoria herself. Joe Anderson led the band until 1874, when it split into two bands: the *Excelsior Band* and *Frank Jones' Orchestra*. According to reports of the time, these orchestras were constituted of accomplished musicians and included string sections in order to play works by "classical" composers on top of their repertoires of marches and hymns.

To be accepted and listened to by white audiences, these pre-jazz orchestras had to integrate into their music elements of "respectability," such as virtuosity (as defined by Western academic criteria of technique), the presence of "noble" instruments (violins), and absolute rigor in execution. Similarly, the *Fisk Jubilee Singers* choir gained fame in the United States and throughout the world thanks to the (very "classical") beauty of its sopranos, bassos, and contraltos, the "dignified" look of its members (wearing dark, sober suits), and their cultural references (the eighteen members of the choir were students at Fisk University, one of the foremost black universities in the United States).

Convinced that they were carrying to the white world their people's "message" (they sang in 1874 in several European countries, and toured Australia, South Africa, and New Zealand in 1877), they also strove to eliminate all "savagery" liable to shock Western ears from the spirituals in their repertoire. Once more, repression and self-censorship forced Negroes to act a part, to become "professional Negroes," i.e. ideologically white Negroes—Negroes who knew their place.

7. In the Margins of Jazz History

I think that music, being an expression of the human heart, or of the human being itself, does express just *what is happening*. I feel it expresses the whole thing—the whole of human experience at the time that it is being expressed.
—John Coltrane, interviewed by Frank Kofsky, *Jazz and Pop* (September 1967), 26.

I think black people in America have a superior sense when it comes to expressing their own convictions through music. Most whites tend to think that it's below their dignity to just show suffering and just show any other meaning that has to do with feeling and not with technique or analysis or whatever you call it. And this to me is why the black man has developed in the field of music that the white man calls jazz. And basically I think that word, the sense of that word, is used to describe music that the white man feels is really inferior.
—Ornette Coleman, in A. B. Spellman's *Four Lives in the Bebop Business*, 142–43.

This, then, will not be about telling, repeating what is called "the history of jazz," cataloguing once again the musicians, orchestras, records, or styles that constitute it. We will instead attempt to recover, to bind anew the ties that always existed—though often went unnoticed—between the American social field, the ideology that dominates it (and what other ideologies are dominated within it), and the diverse musical (and non-musical) manifestations of black Americans. Except by LeRoi Jones and, to a lesser extent, the German Joachim Ernst Berendt, the history of jazz has not been studied for what it is: a network of complex relations, a location where artistic practices are articulated with non-artistic fields such as society and politics—the product of a series of conflicts between these antagonistic determining factors. These absences, then, the blank margins of the already written "history of jazz," are the spaces in which we inscribe our notes.

In some sense there is no such thing as a "history of jazz," because there is no jazz outside of history, and what is true for all art is even truer for this art: its "history" is that of the forces that make jazz as much as that of the forms that jazz makes. Mapping out the work of these forces is never easy, nor will it ever be finished, inasmuch as the ideological fascinations with the "splendid isolation of art" anchored in our cultural traditions are obstacles to the process. When the dominant ideology advocates the separation of art and politics, it *intervenes* in the aesthetic field to condemn all ideological intervention in the aesthetic field!

This is why obstinately bringing an artistic practice back to its context, the non-artistic fields it is entwined in always seems "reductive" and "sacrilegious." Such a process reduces the "artistic blur" so common in reflections on art; yet it is true that mechanical determinations and systematic indetermination also play a part. What all these approaches mean to elude is the complex and precise network of overdeterminations between all levels.

a) Blacks and Blues Turn Proletarian

From work songs to pop music and free jazz in the 1960s, singing as an individual form of expression—thanks to its diversity and plasticity—has ensured the continuity of black music, in its meaning, role, and testimony as regards social context. The resistance and permanence of the blues form, or even simply of the blues spirit (in free jazz, for example), has helped black music to develop, constantly change face, and lend itself to all imaginable experiments while resisting its economic and cultural colonization under the name of jazz. When, at the end of the nineteenth century, thousands of Negroes abandoned southern plantations for the industrial cities of the North, they often only took with them in traditions and family "memories" the lyrics of country blues in which their exodus was already inscribed.

If the blues has survived in such remarkable fashion, it is because whites always found it a difficult material to exploit and imitate culturally (only with the first white rockers did borrowings in the form of homage replace attempts at parodic imitation) and economically (Bessie Smith excepted, there were very few blues "stars" until the appearance of pop music). Testifying more or less directly to a specifically black experience, the blues addressed a faithful audience—black proletarians and lumpenproletarians—much more restricted than that of big orchestras, for example, and as such could only generate indifference in white businessmen and wary scorn among the first black "bourgeois." In their desire for advancement and social whitening, they only wanted to forget these "slave songs." This repression, as noted by James Baldwin, was never as perfect as they would have liked:

> It was Bessie Smith, through her tone and cadence, who helped me to dig back to the way I myself must have spoken when I was a pickaninny, and to remember the things I had heard and seen and felt. I had buried them very deep. I

had never listened to Bessie Smith in America (in the same way that, for years, I would not touch watermelon), but in Europe she helped to reconcile me to being a "nigger."[1]

Born in the South,[2] where slavery marked it and where oppression and repression were always worst, the blues testifies, takes note, describes, or at the very least suggests, but it rarely protests or calls for revolt. It says what Negroes see and live, and says it to an audience of Negroes who, unlike a white audience, ignore nothing of the living conditions inseparable from the blues, an audience born in the *World of the Blues*.[3] Neither adviser nor agitator, the bluesman simply testifies, files reports on his own experiences, thus letting his black listeners find out that their misery is not exceptional, that they are not the only victims of fate, i.e. of oppressive social structures, in America. Contrary to pastors who preach resignation and promise heaven to those who go through hell on Earth, the bluesman does not try to "sugarcoat the pill":

> You know, I'm going to put this a little blunt. I don't know if I should say it or not, because it might hurt the religious type of people, but when I sing the blues I sing the truth. The religious type of people may not believe that it's good, because they think the blues is not the truth; but the blues, from a point of explaining yourself as facts, is the truth, and I don't feel that the truth should be condemned.[4]

Though they do not explicitly encourage Negroes to revolt, the blues describe a revolting situation in its most minute details. Transplanted to northern industrial cities, former slaves and their children would substitute for the African nostalgia of the first generations of slaves the memories of a more recent past in the South, the countryside, life on the shores of the Mississippi. These were the first reactions of Negroes to a new oppressive frame: turned city-dwellers, though living most often on the outskirts of industrial cities such as Detroit or Chicago, they discovered another form of serfdom: wage labor, capitalist bosses, assembly line work, high rent, overcrowded slums. Even their sentimental and sexual relationships changed. Freed from slavery which—against the principles of Christianity—had developed without taking into account notions of family marriage, or love, they discovered the promiscuity that led to adultery, debt, and prostitution. Unemployment, an unexpected aspect of "free" work, replaced compulsory work:

> I would stay up North, but nothing here that I can do.
> Just stand around the corner and sing my lonesome blues.[5]

When he finds a job, the Negro, who now uses the referential system of whites, realizes that he is often badly paid:

> The white man he rides in a great big car,
> The brownskin man does the same,
> The black man he rides around in a T-model Ford,
> But he gets there just the same.[6]

Such comparisons only further the state of mind of blacks from the South, where the following stanza long served as a proverb:

> The nigger and the white man
> Playing seven up,
> The nigger win the pot,
> But he's afraid to pick it up.[7]

Money becomes a determining element in relations between man and woman:

> When I had my money it was hello sugar pie.
> Now I done got broke so it's so long country guy.[8]

In order to make this money, there remains hope of finding work in a big factory:

> Say, I'm goin' to get me a job now, workin' in Mr Ford's place,
> Say, that woman tol' me last night: say you cannot even stand Mr Ford's ways.[9]

After emancipation, Negroes looking for work began traveling around the United States. Yesterday's slaves traveled by train, sometimes even by car. They soon distinguished "friendly" and "unfriendly" highways within the United States road network. Route 49 from Biloxi to Jackson, Mississippi, Route 51 from New Orleans to Memphis, Route 61 through cotton country and, later, Route 66 that would direct the exodus of ruined black farm workers and poor whites towards California.[10]

Even black convicts would see their lives and deaths transformed by the industrial development of America:

> They're gonna send me to the old electric chair
> Wonder why they electrocute a man at the one o' clock hour at night?

> Wonder why they electrocute a man, baby, Lord, at the one o' clock hour at night?
> The current much stronger, people turn out all the light[11]

As laborers in the great auto factories of Chicago and Detroit, Negroes integrated the car, the symbol of social advancement in capitalist surroundings, into the thematic foundation of the blues:

> Well, the T-model Ford I say is the poor man's friend.[12]

To the point that a man's aging could be measured by . . . the bluebook:

> I had a man for fifteen years, give him his room and board.
> Once he was like a Cadillac, now he's like an old worn-out Ford.[13]

The car can of course become an erotic symbol:

> Come on and be my chauffeur.
> I want you to drive me,
> downtown.[14]

Or:

> Ain't nothing, mama, don't get scared at all.
> It's a long distance well, and it's running all its oil.[15]

If before emancipation whites were wary of Negroes becoming soldiers, the First World War would change everything, to the point that Negroes would almost pine for the forced neutrality of slaves in white conflicts:

> I'm going to Newport News, baby, take a battleship across the sea . . .[16]

Thus the reconversion period lived by the American Negro starting at the end of the Civil War much resembled the uprooting experienced by the first slaves: yesterday, they went from freedom (Africa), to an unknown and oppressive world (America); today, from the chains of slavery (slave quarters, the plantation), to the invisible but just as traumatizing chains of ghetto life and factory work. There is some "solace," however: rid of religious surveillance and of the Puritan morals of pastors, the Negro could fornicate, drink, gamble, and take drugs as he pleased. And the white man wouldn't stop him, either.

This kind of censorship lifted, sexual themes and allusions became an important source of inspiration:

Um-um, black snake crawling in my room.
Yes, some pretty mama better get this black snake soon.[17]

The titles of some blues were by now very explicit: "She Moves It Just Right," "I'm Wild About That Thing," "Warm It Up to Me," "Do It a Long Time," "It Hurts So Good," "My Banana in Your Fruit Basket," "My Pin in Your Cushion," "I Want Some of Your Pie," "Hard Pushing Papa," "You've Had Too Much," "My Pencil Won't Write No More," "Tight Like This" (recorded by Louis Armstrong in 1928), "Black Snake Moan," etc. Freed from the puritanical morals of white America, the bluesman tells without shame of his sexual, sometimes homosexual, adventures and fantasies:

Two times three is six,
Three times three is nine,
You give me some of yours,
And I'll give you some of mine.[18]

While in northern cities the Negro attempted to adapt to this newfound "freedom" and to his new slavery, in the South, Jim Crow laws, the Ku Klux Klan, and new modes of exploitation continued to crush the black sharecroppers and field workers who remained. For them, debt (loans on coming harvests, mortgages, etc.) and legal disenfranchisement were added to the fear of being suspected of random crimes (stealing, rape, relations with a white woman, etc.), or of being condemned merely for being accused by a white man or woman, or worse, of being lynched. In the February 1920 issue of his newspaper the *Crisis*, W. E. B. Du Bois listed black victims of Lynch law between 1885 and 1919. From 78 in the year 1885 and 71 in 1886, the yearly number of lynchings evolved as follows: 80, 95, 95, 90, 121, 155 (this record number in the year 1892), 154, 134, 112, 80, 122, 102, 84, 107, 107 (for 1990 and 1901), 86, 86, 83, 61, 64, 60, 93, 73, 65, 63, 63, 79, 69, 80, 55, 44, 64, 77, for a total of 3,052 in thirty-five years![19]

Not only did lynchings not decrease, but thanks to the conciliatory attitude of Booker T. Washington, the South had simply deprived the "emancipated" Negro of his right to vote, turned his status as a second-class citizen into law, and gradually reduced financial aid to the secondary education institutions reserved for him. In order to fight this new form of slavery, Du Bois summoned a group of black leaders to Niagara Falls in 1905 and organized a movement dedicated to the defense of Negro rights. The first convention of the *Niagara Movement* took place in 1906 at Harper's Ferry, where John Brown had been captured half a century earlier. The convention wrote a list of demands for the Afro-American community: the same civil and social rights as any American citizen, the end of racial discrimination, the right to have relationships with any consenting person, the enforcement of the law with respect to all without distinction of wealth or race, and the right to an education for all children. From this initiative would arise, in 1909, the National Association for the Advancement of Colored People, and one year later, the monthly the *Crisis* with Du Bois as editor in chief. By 1912, the circulation of this publication was already reaching sixteen thousand.[20] The NAACP asserted itself as a powerful instrument in the struggle for full-fledged citizenship, but the radical character of its demands would be gradually blunted by Du Bois' *Talented Tenth* program. According to Du Bois, the black masses needed leaders, and therefore an intellectual elite capable of playing those roles. The NAACP was soon run by black bourgeois and white liberals, and lost all popular representativeness. It remained the black organization most widely established throughout the country, though only from a quantitative standpoint. For the black masses, the NAACP became a sort of go-between, an advocate in dealings with white power. Other attempts were made in northern cites, New York especially, to facilitate the assimilation of thousands of black workers coming from the South. The Urban League was created in 1911 to fight against discrimination in employment. Subsidized by northern capitalists (Ford, Rockefeller, etc.) who encouraged the influx of labor for their factories, this welcoming agency—it acts as a professional placement and orientation body—still functions thanks to the fees paid by employers. Thus does it constitute another instrument of control of black proletarians by white capitalism.

While black bourgeois, the accomplices and dupes of more or less liberal whites, took over these protest movements one after the other with the naive hope of using them as springboards for their own integration, the majority of white and black workers found themselves further and further removed from these dealings. But as racial prejudice was carefully kept alive and well by the climate of violence that still reigned over the South, and through the *competition* that (underpaid) black labor represented for white labor (Irish, Polish, etc.), the American proletariat, incapable of uniting as a class, devoted the forces it could have used to oppose socially and economically oppressive structures to race riots (New York 1863; Memphis 1866; Atlanta 1906; Springfield 1908[21]).

The Negro would take stock of the system and its consequences in the blues, thus gathering a mass of evidence comparable to the *cahiers de doléances* [notebooks of complaints] of the French Estates General in 1789.²² Replacing "complaints" by "blues" in the following quotation is sufficient to imagine it was written by Paul Oliver, Samuel Charters, or any other specialist of Negro American songs rather than a French historian: "These assemblies formulated complaints that were very reasonable sometimes, sometimes very artless, some of them a little grotesque, but oftenest of all tragic."²³

b) White Wars and Black Struggles

The entrance of the United States into the First World War in 1917 would lead to decisive changes in the life and music of Negroes.

References to New Orleans in the first black orchestral manifestations that were presented white audiences—the New Orleans style—long led to the belief that New Orleans was *the* city where jazz had been invented. William Christopher Handy, the composer of "Saint Louis Blues," relates that in Memphis, Tennessee, in 1905, you could hear music very similar to that of New Orleans: "But we didn't discover until 1917 that New Orleans had such music too. Any and every circus band played this way."²⁴ To the extent that work songs, spirituals, and pre-jazz blues had all appeared in the southern states (see II. 2), it seems that the birthplace of jazz, the location where these diverse black vocal forms converged and crystallized, was, simply, the southern half of the United States.

Nevertheless, as Hugues Panassié often asserted, it remains that the music of New Orleans Negroes was, more than any other, representative of a certain jazz "purity." But if one admits that New Orleans style is exemplary of a privileged purity and authenticity of jazz, a quick survey of early twentieth century New Orleans society and music forces us to define this "pure" music as one essentially based on mixings and cultural contradictions. Jazz was the genre most marked by diverse white Western influences, while the blues, the principal yet underground current of black music, did not feel them as much, and therefore did not have to evolve much. New Orleans style therefore appears necessarily as the *first stage* of the westernization of black music that would peak in the *swing era*. It is only in this way that we can understand free jazzman Milton Graves's remark: "Because of slavery *and the New Orleans episode* (our emphasis), people have lost their identity, what drummers play has nothing to do with African music. That's the problem of all musicians in America: they have a Western conception of their music."²⁵

At the turn of the century, New Orleans was the most extraordinary mix of races, social classes (if not castes), and cultures one can imagine, the prefiguration of big northern cities after 1918. Descendants of French, Spanish,

British settlers; Italian, German, Slavic immigrants; aristocrats, poor whites, former slaves, artisans, dockers and black shop-owners; Afro-French, Afro-British or Afro-Spanish creoles[26] all lived in the city. . . . Musical trends and traditions were just as diverse, numerous, and contradictory: from the dance music (square dancing) and "classical" music (the importance of the opera, the preeminence of virtuoso pianists and violinists[27]) of the traditionally French aristocracy and (white and mulatto) bourgeoisie, to the neighborhood bands sporting the lyre pins of Napoleonic marching bands, and the religious hymns and profane songs of former slaves of Anglo-Saxon planters whose development we observed throughout the South.

More than any others, the *creoles*—sitting at the crossroads between white French culture and black African American culture—illustrate the duality and conflict depicted by Du Bois, and anticipated (as Jelly Roll Morton's autobiography shows well[28]) the contradictory attitude of the black bourgeoisie throughout United States history, hesitating between repressing its Negro "past" and asserting its originality.

It is also in the New Orleans region that the social differentiation of places *reserved* for black music appeared most clearly, prefiguring the Negro cultural ghetto. This musical segregation had an essentially moral and Christian character: black music was played on plantations (work), in brothels (sin), and in church (redemption). Slaves had disappeared from Congo Square (see II. 2. c), and free Negroes were allowed on certain occasions to play in the streets (parades, Mardi Gras, burials, etc.). Jazz would long be inseparable from "bad places," from notions of pleasure and sin, from the debauchery of the rabble. Brothels seemed to have been the only place where racial and social barriers were transgressed. To this, one must add the disappointment felt by even the wealthiest *creoles*, whom Jim Crow laws pushed away from whites, to whom they thought themselves equal. No longer allowed to patronize public venues now reserved for whites (theatres, operas, concert halls), they had to play their music—though it was much more "refined" than the music of bluesmen or black marching bands—in the brothels and dives of the red light district.[29]

In 1917, the United States entered the First World War to defend, *in Europe*, the economic and democratic values threatened by German imperialism. New Orleans became a war harbor. Thousands of recruits were garrisoned there. The military high command decided that Storyville,[30] the red light district, represented a threat to morale and should be closed down. Prostitutes and professional musicians found themselves out of work. A great number of them emigrated, joining black workers who managed to find jobs in the factories of Chicago.

This massive influx of Negroes opened infinite ways to make profit, economically and culturally, to musicians and businessmen. White workers, for their part, only saw the threat of competition for employment. Riots multiplied. On July 2, 1917, in East St. Louis, Illinois, Negroes were massacred in their neighborhood by a mob of poor whites who set houses on fire after blocking the doors and windows. Six thousand Negroes lost their houses, many died (several hundred according to some, forty-eight according to others[31]), half a millions dollars in material damages. In Houston (1917), Washington, DC, Chicago (1919), Tulsa, Oklahoma (1921), other bloody battles pitted the two communities against each other. Negroes at first only defended themselves, but newly discharged black soldiers back from Europe had learned a few things from their stint in the army.[32] Negroes, from then on, would respond to violence with violence: "Under similar circumstances, we would fight again. But by the God of Heaven, we are cowards and jackasses if now that war is over, we do not marshal every ounce of our brain and brawn to fight a sterner, longer, more unbending battle against the forces of hell in our own land."[33]

W. E. B. Du Bois was not alone in making such statements. All were judged "seditious" by white American authorities. Reactionary forces soon organized, as they had after emancipation and as they would after World War II in the form of witch hunts and McCarthyism. In 1919, the Senate published the results of a long investigation in a report entitled *Radicalism and Sedition among the Negroes as Reflected in Their Publications*:

> At this time there can no longer be any question of a well-concerted movement among a certain class of Negro leaders of thought and action to constitute themselves a determined and persistent source of a radical opposition to the Government, and to the established rule of law and order.[34]

There followed a list of the foremost seditious attitudes of black leaders:

> Ill-governed reaction towards race rioting; . . . the threat of retaliatory measures in connection with lynching; . . . the more openly expressed demand for social equality, in which demand the sex problem is not infrequently included; . . . the identification of the Negro with such radical organizations as the I.W.W. and an outspoken advocacy of the Bolsheviki or Soviet doctrines; the political stand assumed toward the present Federal Administration, the South in general, and incidentally, toward the Peace Treaty and the League of Nations. Underlying these more salient viewpoints is the increasingly emphasized feeling of a race consciousness, in many of these publications always antagonistic to the white race, and openly, defiantly assertive of its own equality and even superiority. . . . The boast is not to be dismissed lightly

as the ignorant vaporing of untrained minds. . . . The sense of oppression finds increasingly bitter expression. . . . Defiance and insolently race-centered condemnation of the white race is to be met with in every issue of the more radical publications. . . . The Negro is *seeing red*.³⁵

Thus is defined, fixated in history, "The dangerous spirit of defiance and vengeance at work among the Negro leaders."³⁶

Following the triumph of minstrels, show business began to organize as a true industry, the musician and the singer joining the mass of victims of capitalism. Soon the industry focused on a more insidious challenge thrown at the cultural values of white America by Negroes: their music, which they meant both to exploit and defuse. 1917, as American troops officially entered the war, white musicians recorded the first record in the history of "jazz" (the Original Dixieland Jass Band, see 2. c).³⁷ Hailing from New Orleans, the musicians of this all-white band had followed the Great Migration of Negroes northward. Their music, imitating that of "King" Oliver—whom they sincerely admired—was the first "jazz" that white northerners had the opportunity to hear, and even this "noisy and brassy" adaptation of Negro music by white "hicks"³⁸ shocked them and disturbed their cultural habits. Much the opposite of minstrels, the members of the ODJB were not trying to mock their models: they were presenting a *faithful* imitation, and spiteful caricature was not their goal.

At the same time, the black bands representing "New Orleans style" in Chicago (King Oliver, Freddie Keppard, Baby and Johnny Dodds, Jelly Roll Morton, etc.) were only known and appreciated by a local, mostly black audience, and a few white aficionados and musicians enthused by the "exotic" character of this music. As for blues singers, they were only popular in the black Chicago areas of the South Side and the West Side and their ways changed relatively little. In their economic marginality and ideological alterity, their chronicles of the black soul remain formally indifferent to the pressures of commerce, fashion, and taste (until their commercial recuperation in pop music, that is, and we will see the consequences of this late appropriation further on). Because of their formal solidity of sorts—whose principles were only reinforced by the variety of styles of bluesmen—the blues managed to remain one of the pillars of jazz, a reference against which jazz never ceased to define and redefine itself, in opposition to the commercial and Western temptations it faced throughout its evolution. The profound resistance of the blues translates into a certain structural invariability, and thus inscribes the history of Negroes—the diversity of their problems and of their reactions to white America—in reference to a *constant of protest*. Thus the blues is more likely than the composite jazz of New Orleans to be considered a guarantee of the authenticity of black music. The blues *reacts* against Western influences, turns them into contradictions: New Orleans-style jazz integrates these influences, assimilates them, neutralizes *them* and *itself*. Thus, every time a style or a fashion begins to fade, jazzmen will turn to the blues, not so much to find inspiration as to reconnect with the ideology of the black masses and to counterbalance westernizations that threaten to resolve African American cultural conflicts to the profit only of the elements of white origin.

The blues, whose obscenity is as sexual as it is social, will constitute for a very small part of the white public a means of cultural slumming. Bessie Smith did not become a true star in 1923 by the power of her voice alone. While, beginning in 1919, America was forced to follow the dry regimen of prohibition, in listening to and watching this southern black woman, whites found the sensual pleasure of diving into a socially forbidden universe of filth, sex, poverty, alcohol. . . . The exhibitionism of the singer (and of the blues in general) disgusted the white majority and black elite. But the whites it did arouse, and the Negroes to whom Bessie Smith addressed these portrayals of a life they knew well, made it possible to establish one of the first sales records in the recording industry: her recording of "Down Hearted Blues" sold two millions copies, but it was most particularly her "Empty Bed Blues"—banned for obscenity in Boston—that made her a success with white listeners. During the few years that her fame lasted, New York snobs and liberal intellectuals fought for her presence at their parties.

As white America opened up to jazz (to better strap it to its economic structures), post-war Europe opened wide to the great victors of the war: the Americans, their economy, and their strange music. Renouncing the isolationist politics that had almost prevented its entry in the war (despite the fact that the war, through the armament industry, was the indispensable engine of capitalism, as the Second World War, the Cold War, the Korean War, and the Vietnam War would later prove), the United States discovered that this Negro music they had until then rather despised, could become an extra instrument of seduction in the service of American imperialism. The military band of the Negro Jim Europe, the ODJB, and Sidney Bechet enthused European audiences, prefiguring Dizzie Gillespie's triumphal European tours sponsored by the State Department, and the non-negligible propaganda role played by radio station *Voice of America*'s jazz shows that were broadcast towards countries of the Eastern Bloc. It nevertheless took a few years before more specifically black jazz pieces—blues singers' works among them—spread around Europe. Yet, in the mind of a general audience not keen on finding out the agenda that posters and programs did not reveal (ODJB, George Gershwin's "Rhapsody in

Blue" by Paul Whiteman's great orchestra, the Southern Syncopated Orchestra—twenty-five backup singers and thirty-five musicians, including Sidney Bechet—led by Will Marion Cook, or the *Revue Nègre* presented at the Théâtre des Champs Élysées in 1925, with Josephine Baker), "Negro" beats and "symphonic" jazz asserted themselves as the most obvious signs of a sort of miracle "made in the USA."

They had no idea what the bluesmen were saying or singing at the time; instead, they were discovering the smile, the joy, the faces and puffed out cheeks of sympathetic Negroes who played a kind of music different from all they had been used to. They were also discovering "extraordinary voices," or "well played, well interpreted jazz, that would have deserved to be presented in a classical music concert hall." The entire world thought they were discovering "true" jazz and Negroes: in 1920, Blaise Cendrars published *Negro Anthology*; the following year, West Indian writer René Maran won the Goncourt book prize with *Batouala: A True Negro Novel*, which all black American intellectuals would read once it was translated into English. Many white American novelists used the Negro, this spontaneous, naïve, and marvelously primitive character, to condemn Puritan conformism and the ills of industrial mechanization.[39]

This is the time when Louis Armstrong broke away from "King" Oliver and immediately asserted himself as the perfect example of the "ideal" Negro dreamed of by white America. Whether blowing into his trumpet or singing, it is first and foremost as an *instrumentist*, a phenomenon/freak rather than a virtuoso, that Armstrong enthuses the crowds. He personifies the joy of living. . . in America, a country exceptional for its wealth and liberty. Audiences, critics, and record salesmen together made him one of the century's biggest stars. He was jazz, and jazz was America. Worried about pleasing the greatest number of people[40] and keeping his star status as long as possible, he strove to illustrate in songs such as "La Vie en Rose," "Tea for Two," "Hello Dolly," etc., the statement of the Creole Jelly Roll Morton (who always resented being associated with the Negroes of New Orleans and boasted of his French origins): "Any kind of music may be played in jazz, if one has the knowledge."[41] And Armstrong played just about *anything* throughout his career: through the "infinite grace" of jazz and his own genius, the most stultifying songs were supposed to turn into "the purest jazz," through some kind of magical process. . . . This theory was long the principal dogma in the "temples of the one true jazz." It conferred to jazz a veritable power of *sublimation* and led to the valorization of the worst fluff, industrially produced by manufacturers who specialized in ditties. Because jazz had been defined once and for all as the result of crossing influences, some *believed*—or wanted to believe, since all of the interest in jazz shown by show business rested on these virtues—in its infinite capacities for synthesis. The lure was nevertheless obvious: if Armstrong, like most other jazzmen, was able to make a "flattered" rendition of the most insipid melody, it is obvious that he could have played a more complete creative role by working on acceptable material, if not by practicing total improvisation. The conflict inherent to jazz was, once again, resolved in and for the benefit of, white music. Only a few remarkable traits of the famous black/jazz purity remained, drowned in the inherent poverty of the theme and the confusion of the arrangements. While there never was a true synthesis of the contradictory elements that constitute jazz, it nevertheless happened that one or the other element of this struggle of influences gained the upper hand, *an advantage always determined by the economic and political context of the time.*

By the 1920s, jazz was definitely launched as a product for mass consumption—with all the ambivalence this implied. It was dominated on the one hand by Louis Armstrong and his rising popularity, and on the other by the phenomenon of dance bands (black and white) that would regulate jazz production for the next fifteen years. The contradictions that would slow down or restart the evolution of jazz were put in place at that time: white musicians were more successful than blacks; black musicians were forced to conform to the demands of commerce and ideology; jazz's entertainment value was emphasized; the blues existed more or less underground; jazz was conceived of as a recipe for artistic and commercial success; the notion of interpretation (any possible theme, down to the worst standards[42]) replaced the notion of improvisation (the musician commenting on and directly intervening in his own music), and the notion of spectacle (big band, dance) replaced that which, behind the stage, continued to feed the blues: the notion of testimony. Together, these dominant characteristics of jazz were therefore directly determined by commercial interests and the white ideology: they defined jazz as a music that Negroes liked, listened to, danced to, and in which they *somewhat* recognized themselves (depending on how imbued in ideology they were), but which had little to do with black music and culture (the blues, improvisation, historicity, social condition) when it did not contradict the political and ideological struggles of the moment. These characteristics were the basis on which most Western critics built criteria of authenticity and normativity for jazz as a black music. The history of jazz is first and foremost the history of this taxonomic reversal.

c) American Dreams

From the beginning in around 1925, the works of Armstrong and Ellington (the two most prestigious and famous black musicians) could be pitted against each other, in that they each answered to one great ideological current of the black movement, *integrationism* for one and *separatism* for the other.

Very soon, due to its success, Armstrong's career appeared to illustrate black integrationism and the precepts of Booker T. Washington: Armstrong strove on the one hand to please the white public by producing a doubly reassuring image of the black musician, a marvelous combination of the contradictory traits of, on the one hand, the virtuoso instrumentist (his increasingly spectacular sonic feats had something of the athletic about them, and that athleticism gradually came to take over his music) and on the other the jolly entertainer, the funny "good Negro" (his voice, his way of singing come to be appreciated for being slightly caricatural elements of vocal blues such as *scat*,[43] for example, which reverses the classical vocalization of blues instruments by instrumentalizing the voice). On the other hand, Armstrong pleased the black public by showing in striking fashion how a Negro could assert himself in white society and even become wealthy, under the condition that he consent to make the necessary efforts.

Ellington's music seems to connect to a different trend: *Garveyism*. At the end of the 1910s, Marcus Garvey[44] started his nationalist/separatist movement. Garvey advocated racial pride, the union and organization of Negroes, and resistance to white oppression, and he soon conceived the notion that only the founding of an independent black state outside of white America could solve the problems of millions of Negroes who were traumatized by white society—and who, following World War I, wanted to fight for their own cause. He launched the *Negro World,* a newspaper that advocated a planned return to Africa supported by a strong economic base. He coined the slogan "Africa for Africans at home and abroad." Touching a chord among the black masses from the South now struggling in the industrial ghettoes of the North, this movement, which reestablished black pride and stood against dictatorship and oppression, gathered five million members. They were organized in military fashion (among Garvey's organizations were the paramilitary Universal African Legion, but also the Universal Black Cross, the Universal African Motor Corps, etc.). At the movement's first convention in 1920, Garvey denounced the colonization of Africa, and presented his movement as the army that would help Africans free themselves from white domination. Colonial powers reacted strongly: Garvey's newspaper was banned in several African colonies, and the American government was pressured to find ways to stop Garvey's endeavors. Yet the funds he raised were enough to let him charter a veritable transport fleet; he negotiated with Liberia the acquisition of a territory to which he sent crews of technicians and workers to start building a city. But soon, the schemes of colonial powers led to Garvey being accused of a plot to overthrow the Liberian government, and of fraud in the United States. All of the movement's possessions (the most considerable ever gathered by a black organization) were seized, sold, destroyed, and Garvey himself was jailed. The dream of a return to Africa collapsed as it was gaining in strength and reality.

The disappointment was huge, and the countershock paralyzed Negroes for a long time. But Garvey had succeeded in making Negroes realize their potential strength, by valorizing the black race and black cultures in the eyes of masses until then conditioned by the ideology claiming Negro inferiority in all domains. The movement was indeed first and foremost one of proletarian and sub-proletarian masses (like Garvey himself): bourgeois intellectuals and integrated elites condemned him and fought him forcefully. For the first time in a mass movement of this size, Garvey had had the political clear-sightedness to link the liberation struggles of American Negroes to those of colonized people around the world. He sent money and letters of support to leaders of people of color in Africa, Asia, and Latin America, and the walls of Harlem soon displayed slogans such as "Africa must be free," and "the Negro fought in Europe, he can fight in Africa!" The movement had the strongest impact in Harlem, where it generated and destroyed the most hopes. Harlem became the heart of black resistance: in 1925, Alain Locke devoted a special issue of *Survey Graphic* magazine to "Harlem, Mecca of the New Negro."[45] This area of Manhattan had not only become the biggest black city in the world, but overall the place where Negroes could become aware of their unity, of the communality of their problems and interests: southern, northern, West Indian and African Negroes found each other and organized economically and culturally in the ghetto.

Meanwhile, as black bands such as Fletcher Henderson's valorized the ideological themes and musical ditties of white subculture through painstaking work (arrangements, rhythm, rigorous performance, the elaboration of a music adapted for dance, etc.) to meet the "standards" of the time, Duke Ellington, for his part, undertook to make "American Negro music." A composer, he centered most of his themes around black life and history, and generally around Harlem, where he long lived: "A Night in Harlem," "Black and Tan Fantasy," "Harlem River Quiver," "Harlem Twist," "Black Beauty," "Hottentot," "Louisiana," "Harlem Flat Blues," "Mississippi Moan," "Jungle Nights in Harlem," "Drop Me Off at Harlem," "Harlem Speaks," "Chicago," "Ebony," "Puerto Rico Chaos," and "Cotton."[46] The orchestral style devised by Ellington reproduces in music the staging of the Negro and his setting: what the *jungle* style treats musically as an African jungle—resorting to all sorts of imitative sound effects such as animal shouts, strange noises, etc.—is the "jungle" of Harlem. Strictly through signs of savagery, primitivity, and chaos, Africa intrudes upon the ghetto, which from the moralistic and controlling point of view of whites indeed is a "jungle."[47] This can only play as a fantasy of exoticism both for Negroes, who in the jungle see mythical Africa, the primeval forest, the clichés of lost tradition, and *for whites*, who experience musical and sensual defamiliarization, transgression of all orders, a violation of the civilized.

Hence, even in its Afro-American references, Ellington's music is ambivalent. It bears the marks of the permanent conflict of jazz: it must speak about Negroes and please whites. On the one hand, Ellington installs the Negro in his music—and not merely in titles—and borrows and refers to the spirit and scenery of country and urban blues. On the other hand, he offers his white audience exotic thrills and troubling sensations vouchsafed by the safest cultural references: the appearance of classicism, rigor in writing and performance, propriety, the valorization of form, etc. This double and contradictory impulse therefore brings him to satisfy some white musicologists despairing over the "poverty of form" in jazz, and at the same time to question the economic norms of his time; his "Reminiscing in Tempo" suite[48] renewed the formal equipment of jazz, and, by widely exceeding the length imposed on jazz and popular songs by 78 rpm records, became a problem for phonograph companies in the same stroke.

On top of economic (attracting urban black audiences) and political determination (the rise of Garveyism, Africa on the agenda), another important cultural phenomenon came to bear on Ellington's project of "American Negro music": what has been called the "Black Renaissance." Influenced by the writings of W. E. B. Du Bois, who asserted in 1926 that "all art is propaganda and ever must be,"[49] black poets and writers (of popular extraction, some being self-taught, and almost all members of left or far left political organizations and unions) undertook to reevaluate the cultural past of black people and rehabilitate it in the eyes of the black elite, and to spread this knowledge among the masses; in short, to rid it of the mask and censorship imposed on it by slavery and racist ideology. In 1925, Alain Locke published a collective manifesto of young black poets, *The New Negro*,[50] in which Arthur A. Schomburg wrote:

> The American Negro must rebuild his past in order to make his future. Though it is orthodox to think of America as the one country where it is unnecessary to have a past, what is a luxury for the nation as a whole becomes a prime social necessity for the Negro. For him, a group tradition must supply compensation for persecution, and pride of race the antidote for prejudice. History must restore what slavery took away, for it is the social damage of slavery that the present generation must repair and offset.[51]

Claude McKay, Countee Cullen, James Weldon Johnson, Jean Toomer, and especially Langston Hughes have in common the influence of Marcus Garvey, Du Bois, C. G. Woodson,[52] political commitment (McKay and Hughes were members of the American Communist Party), Harlem (where they lived and which they used as one of their main themes), and their love of jazz. Langston Hughes wrote numerous blues and poems on jazz, and even borrowed the structure of these poems from the rhythmic patterns of jazz: "Jazz to me is one of the inherent expressions of Negro life in America: the eternal tom-tom beating in the Negro soul—the tom-tom of revolt against weariness in a white world, a world of subway trains, and work, work, work; the tom-tom of joy and laughter, and pain swallowed in a smile."[53]

"Jukeboxes blared Erskine Hawkins, Duke Ellington, Cootie Williams, dozens of others. . . . The biggest bands, like these, played at the Roseland State Ballroom, on Boston's Massachusetts Avenue—one night for Negroes, the next night for whites."[54]

"I didn't particularly care, because I was already speechless thinking about being somewhere close to the greatest bands in the world."[55]

"Every Benny Goodman record I'd ever heard in my life, it seemed, was filtering faintly into where we were [the men's room]. During another customer lull, Freddie let me slip back outside again to listen. Peggy Lee was at the mike singing. Beautiful! . . . She was a big hit."[56]

Arriving in Roxbury, the black neighborhood of Boston, and then in Harlem, Malcolm Little (who had not yet renounced his slave name), the future Malcolm X, did not resist the latest attractions of the *swing craze*.[57] Like millions of Negroes seduced and frightened by the ghetto jungle, seeking to forget the South as much as the hardness of the city, he discovered the magical solutions now open to Negroes: dance, alcohol, drugs, theft, and gambling to escape factory work or the misery of unemployment, and the illusion of being *almost* white thanks to chemical hair straightening (a process that made millionaires out of some black store owners).

Swing had begun to reign over America when Hitler took over Germany. The United States and Western Europe, from then on intimately linked, were coming out of the most terrible economic recession they had ever known. Poorly organized (A. Philip Randolph's projects of workers' unions were less popular than Garvey's African dreams), the victims of discrimination and of the hostility of white employers, black wage workers were the least prepared for the 1929 crisis. Thus they suffered from unemployment much more than white workers. In rural areas, Negroes were working for meager wages. In spite of the Urban League's efforts, 65 percent of able-bodied Negroes survived only thanks to public assistance in 1935. And even there racial discrimination was strong, especially in the South, where some "charitable" organizations, religious and secular, excluded Negroes from their soup kitchens. Rural flight toward northern cities increased.

The music industry and musicians were also touched by the Depression. But they also found a new economic impetus, a new raison d'être, and a new social function by turning en masse to dance and entertainment music: to dispel gloom, for whites and for blacks. It became the industry that we know today. To forget, people did not simply drink; they also danced. Black musicians, who like everybody else needed to work, supplied the demand. Many young Negroes who had gone to college to become doctors, lawyers, and architects, understanding that these jobs *were not for them*, turned to the only domain where they seemed to have a chance to prevail: jazz. Whereas New Orleans musicians had often been illiterate, this new generation of jazzmen knew how to read, both books and music. Dancers needed good bands, "swing machines" that would make them dance to popular songs. Bandleaders therefore needed qualified machinists. In the 1930s, black bands multiplied (Jimmie Lunceford, Bennie Moten, Cab Calloway, the *Blue Rhythm Band*, Lucky Millinder, Claude Hopkins, Earl Hines, Benny Carter, Teddy Hill, Andy Kirk), each more dedicated than the last to the efficient production of swing. With the exception of a few soloists, most musicians felt as if they were working on an assembly line like factory workers. Jazz became mechanical and used a magical lubricant: swing.

The Depression was for blues singers the occasion of a certain qualitative renewal: new themes[58] (although the great majority of the blues remained focused on sexual and sentimental issues), but overall the tone, once generally lachrymose, toughened up and became frankly aggressive, no doubt in reaction to the "freedom of misery" offered by the ghettoes. Jazz, in contrast, became watered down, formally and economically the music of *exhausted formulas*.

A music of *immediate consumption* born of the public's needs was instantly turned into law by businessmen and critics, swing jazz—musically and through its social position—constituted the faithful ideological product of this time of feverish expansion, a headlong rush, a massive repression of the horrors brushed against during the Depression. Through a kind of mimicry (characteristic of the art forms regulated by dominant ideology), swing jazz reproduced the dynamic image new American capitalism gave of itself. "Swing," this mysterious notion that Western critics presented as the privileged trait and necessary condition of jazz without quite being able to explain what it was (or maybe because of that), swing, through its finely honed, mechanical regularity, its *reassuring*, ever-repeated alternation between moments of tension and moments of release, with its *movement for the sake of movement*, is itself the emblem, the product, the brand name of the cult which capitalist ideology vows to comfort—rhythm, agitation, movement, everything that could exorcise the ghost of the recession in all things, if only nominally. The number of white jazzmen and businessmen that dominated the swing era suffices to show that swing was the music of easiness, artistically and commercially. Around Benny Goodman, the "King of Swing," successor to Paul "King of Jazz" Whiteman, white imitators and adaptors multiplied: the Dorsey brothers Jimmy and Tommy, Glen Gray and his Casa Loma Orchestra, Ray Noble, Bob Crosby, Charlie Barnet, Red Norvo, Artie Shaw, and later Glenn Miller, Bunny Berigan, Jack Teagarden, Woody Herman, Gene Krupa, etc. They played mostly for whites, and therefore became equally popular among the black bourgeois. But of all the white representatives of swing, Goodman was undoubtedly the king, and not only musically speaking. The economic crisis having turned the focus of black protest to economic matters, a new slogan was launched in the ghettoes: "Don't buy where you don't work." Benny Goodman immediately showed keen cleverness: he asked Fletcher Henderson to write arrangements for his big band. He was also the first white jazzman to "dare" to hire black musicians (Lionel Hampton, Teddy Wilson, Cootie Williams, Charlie Christian), which could only satisfy both whites and blacks.

Free jazz saxophonist Marion Brown defined the reign of swing in these terms: "The time when jazz conformed to Western ideas of metric division the most. With harmonics on the piano, regular rhythm, it was jazz close to white America."[59]

Through its mechanical music, rhythmic uniformity, and massive use of spectacular elements (such as *riffs*: the repetition of brief melodic sequences as rhythmic refrains), swing was not only a fixated form of jazz, presenting but a few Negro elements as surface effects, but unlike the blues, it was perfectly clean. Its violence and sonic excesses are perfectly controlled; the rare improvised choruses were bridled within a few measures; all parts of the band and all sonic elements are articulated, perfectly combined, well-oiled. We are far from the breaks, discordances and hoarseness of the blues. In fact, swing traded the socio-cultural functionality of Afro-American music for another function of escape and entertainment that answers an ideological need. This need to escape from daily trauma is not only common to whites and blacks, it also ultimately serves the interests of capitalist exploitation by demobilizing the malcontents. In valorizing certain external signs of black music (dance rhythm, blues *form*, soundscapes as "exotic" references), swing, in an example of perfect cultural parasitism, makes them serve an ideology completely opposite to what is at stake in black music: remembrance and confrontation, rather than escape and oblivion.

Let us clarify what use swing jazz makes of the blues: by citing or mechanically reproducing its formal structures, swing demonstrates *a contrario* that the blues—unlike Western aesthetic principles that place the differentiation between modes of expression in their formal differences—exists outside of its structural core, outside of its forms. Bluesmen constantly tinker with the simple, summary, base structure of the blues, incessantly working it over with their voices, their diction, their flow, through a set of parameters linked to the bluesman's personality (his voice, his life, his age, his technique, or lack thereof, in relation to Western norms of virtuosity, and generally what in his singing or playing is implicated in his life). When one goes from this intimate plane to the well-regulated scenarios of orchestras, it is obvious that only a few formal, unimportant characteristics of the blues remain: twelve bars, a certain sound coloring.

But the blues sung—and improvised—about personal adventures and feelings were only of interest to Negroes. The blues of the Depression Era, which testified to the misery of Negroes in the crisis of white capitalism (in spite of the New Deal and its policy of economic interventionism, discrimination remained the rule in some offices and administrations; federal urbanism increased the problems faced by inhabitants of the ghetto; agricultural subventions were beneficial for white landowners, while the decrease in harvests drove black agricultural workers out of the countryside) presented little commercial interest compared to the swing craze: white and black bourgeois that still had the means to buy records or to patronize dance clubs had of course no desire to hear about the tribulations of proletarians.

d) Middle Jazz, Music for the Middle Class

Though the New Deal nevertheless did help by offering work and cheap housing to some Negroes, the sympathy of Democrat politicians was overall directed towards black leaders. For the first time since the Taft administration, black leaders were named to political positions, which could only remove them from the black masses. Faced with the rise of the bourgeoisie, some unionists attempted to unite black and white workers, an effort that had until then been considered a perfect utopia. Black workers organized boycotts of white stores that did not hire Negroes and sought, if not a merger, at least equality between workers' organizations. Increasingly the representative of black bourgeois, the NAACP lost its popular audience. Du Bois resigned from the *Crisis* in 1934: the

NAACP was protesting voting and school discrimination (the bourgeois were dreaming of becoming full-fledged citizens) at the very moment when the black masses were expecting economic solutions! A. Philip Randolph, black unionist, supporter of mass action, and founder in 1925 of the Brotherhood of Sleeping Car Porters,[60] tried in 1936 to bring together unions, religious groups, and black brotherhoods into a united front (the National Negro Congress), only to face the reticence of ministers and black bourgeois.

Thus the traditional white-black opposition is complicated by another conflict, class struggle, which was always covered up by racial prejudice. Its true nature began to appear, and what had until then been considered the principal phenomenon, racism, was now seen by the most politicized leaders as a simple epiphenomenon, a mask (convenient enough for those living off of it) that needed to be torn off. Triggered by the achievements of the New Deal, the development of the middle class among whites and blacks (and it is certainly not by chance that some jazzologists called *middle jazz* the kind of music that satisfied the needs of this *middle class*) showed finally that racism is first and foremost a socio-economic phenomenon.

Negroes were always proportionally more exploited; therefore exploited whites had been able to dream that they were not part of the same class. The appearance of a few black capitalists, more than a sign of advancement among the black masses, only confirmed the reality of social classes. To answer the nostalgic needs of workers in the ghettoes, black store owners turned into businessmen and started chain stores, restaurants, and factories devoted to "southern specialties"; black phonographic companies recorded country bluesmen, etc. All these black businesses were of course helped or bankrolled, if not operated, by white capitalists, on the one hand because capitalists no matter the color of their skin are necessarily accomplices against the classes they exploit, and on the other hand because black bourgeois and capitalists, though they would staunchly deny it, do not yet have the disposal of the economic means that would let them definitively separate from the exploited mass from which they originally arose. "They had helped to create the myth of the vast purchasing power of Negroes which had become the justification for large corporations to employ Negro salesmen so as to exploit the Negro market."[61]

Following the great fear of 1929, all of America felt a frenzied need for reassurance and entertainment. For that reason, the apparent uniformization of musical tastes could give the appearance that the internal conflict of jazz had been resolved synthetically and that *middle jazz* constituted a perfect balance of white and black elements, that this was the "classical" period of jazz. If uniformity and monotony were obvious in the most commercialized sector of jazz (it is indeed impossible, if you're not a "specialist" or a musician, to tell swing era big bands apart), the quasi-clandestine permanence of the blues let some black singers and musicians react against them. Their commercial situation was relatively marginal, as they were of interest only to the black public, musicians, a few white intellectuals and snobs (particularly students, who became more and more numerous following the war), and "country" Negroes. Like Bessie Smith, Billie Holiday sang of sex, sadness, alcohol, and misery, in counterpoint to mechanical singers who concentrated their efforts on virtuosity and vocal performance.

If her songs do not all display the form and structures white jazzologists would like to box the blues into, Billie Holiday, as much as any black musician, always lived and sang within the universe of the blues. She would even go further than bluesmen in that, in her autobiography *Lady Sings the Blues*, she discussed her own confidence-testimonial songs. The most famous, "Strange Fruit," deals with lynching. Though she was friends with many whites, she asserted that for all whites, you were "still a nigger,"[62] thus echoing Big Bill Broonzy's blues "When Will I Get to be Called a Man." Lester Young, who would often be associated with her for the recordings in which he accompanied her but also in the very *spirit* of his music, also actualized the blues, revalued the melancholy sound climates banned from most "swing" works (as they had been by the first planters). Young made it possible for all that had been repressed in the flashy kind of jazz fashionable in his time to resurface in black music: "ugly" sonorities, indifference to the mechanical play and agitation of other musicians, solitary rhythmic endeavor were all practiced by Young, as if the saxophonist told and improvised a kind of dream, a meditation. Therefore critics often compared Lester Young's music to Billie Holiday's singing (whose voice was also judged "ugly" by Western standards), unaware that this was a sign of the continuity of the blues and blues singing, which underlies the entire history of jazz.

A special place must be made for pianist and singer Fats Waller. Both an example of this continuity of vocal blues (in the anecdotes, personal stories, sexual allusions, and dedication to obscenity) and of the function of the black musician-entertainer—in the image of the Negro as defined by minstrel shows and Louis Armstrong—he gained great success, a result of white and black ideological demands. He was the complete jazzman, dabbling in everything: a virtuoso, he willingly interpreted classical works (such as Dvorak's *Humoresque* and the waltz from *Faust*), which did not fail to seduce or amuse white audiences, whom he amused further by his half-minstrel, half-bluesman singing. This did not stop him from ridiculing and mocking some aspects of American society ("Loungin' at the Waldorf," in which he mocks the jet set, "The Joint is Jumpin'," a very realistic reconstruction of a noisy black party eventually broken up by the police). The case of Fats Waller is therefore also typical of the divisions and conflicts in which black musicians could not avoid getting caught, standing as they were on the fringes of American society and forced to satisfy disparate tastes, traditions, and discourses.

Equally marginal, the musical phenomenon that developed in Kansas City in the 1930s was the first collective effort at a renewal and a revalorization of black elements. This movement managed to emerge without suffering from white economic and cultural pressure, because Kansas City had been since the end of the nineteenth century the destination for an important migration movement of black peasants from the Mississippi shores. They had answered the call of Benjamin Singleton, the Moses of the "Great Exodus," who had invited them to migrate to this new promised land: Kansas. Some forty thousand Negroes followed suit. Such a concentration would help black music develop in a state of semi-freedom, in the cultural and social surroundings of country blues, and for an essentially black audience. There, big bands were more deeply marked by the blues than the bands in New York; in many different ways, musicians strived to give the blues an important role. It was there that Lester Young began defining his style by playing with Count Basie's orchestra before it gained a national reputation; there that boogie woogie, one of the piano forms of the blues, became one of *the determinant elements of the new orchestral language*; there that the *shout* asserted itself for singers such as Jimmy Rushing as the only way vocal expression could avoid getting drowned in the orchestral mass. Whereas, in the most representative orchestras of white swing, lyrics had no importance, the texts sung by *blues shouters* were audible, giving back to Negro speech the communicative function it had in the blues. It was also in Kansas City—in the orchestra of pianist Jay McShann, one of the main representatives of the blues revival—that Charlie Parker was able to work on a renewal of form anticipating the rise of *bop*.

Thus, almost unbeknownst to whites, Negroes were preparing the musical styles that would answer the colonization and exploitation jazz had fallen victim to, illustrating in an unexpected domain Malcolm X's assertion: "I would hate to be general of an army as badly informed as the American white man has been about the Negro in this country. This is the situation which permitted Negro combustion to slowly build up to the revolution-point without the white man realizing it."[63]

e) The First Black Revolution

Ten years after the first great capitalist crisis, new alarming symptoms appeared in the United States. Despite the New Deal and its interventionist policies (public works, the increased role of the federal administration in the country's life, social legislation), recession seemed to be gaining: economic activity was down 39 percent from its 1929 level; there were more than ten million unemployed in 1938, nine million in 1939. Capitalism proved incapable of developing harmoniously without further harming the proletariat. Only rearmament (starting in 1937) helped diminish unemployment by giving work to weapons factories. Only the USA's entry into the war momentarily resolved the contradictions that were leading to a new crisis: this time again, capitalism was saved by war, as it would be in the 1950s by the Korean war, and after that by the politico-military lobby behind the Vietnam war.

The 1940s were therefore marked by unemployment, war, the "national union" policy for victory, and the relative improvement of economic conditions thanks to the development of war industries.

On the union front, the working masses organized more during the New Deal: the AFL counted seven, totaling five hundred thousand members, and there were many massive strikes (1933, 1935, 1937), in spite of the brutality of private police companies, anti-union committees, and strikebreakers. In Chicago in 1937, the National Guard maimed and killed close to a hundred workers during a meeting.[64] The founding of the Committee for Industrial Organization in 1937 by AFL dissidents somewhat shook the union movement and led to more struggle, the CIO being more open and democratic than the AFL. The CIO was the first union to admit Negroes and, in some of its branches, to advocate wage equality between whites and blacks. This contributed to the politicization of black proletarians—to a small extent: few of them were specialized, and therefore unionizable, workers.

After long refusing to let Negroes join voluntarily, the American army eventually began to recruit them following a kind of *numerus clausus* (allowing in the armed forces the same percentage of Negroes present in the civilian population), and sending them into separate, for the most part non-combatant, units. Thus did the United States undertake to fight Nazi racism with an army organized according to racist principles: there were no supplies for black units, and segregation also applied to . . . blood in the Red Cross's pharmacies, although the creation of blood banks was for the most part the idea of black doctor Charles Drew. Black jazzmen, many of whom would end up wearing the uniform, were to fight in a war that did not concern them, and experience the military version of segregation and racism for the sake of "defending the homeland."

The Negroes who remained in the United States and sought work in the war industry had to deal with the ill will of employers. A West Coast factory advertised: "The Negro will be considered only as janitors and in other similar capacities. . . . Regardless of their training as aircraft workers, we will not employ them."⁶⁵ Convinced that "mass demonstrations against Jim Crow are worth a million editorials and orations," A. Philip Randolph warned the federal government in 1941 that if President Roosevelt did not demand the hiring of Negroes in war factories, "On to Washington, ten thousand black Americans! . . . If Negroes fail this chance for work, for freedom and training, it may never come again."⁶⁶ Immediately disavowed by the leaders of the NAACP and the Urban League, Randolph canceled the march after Roosevelt signed Executive Order 8802 (25 June 1941): "There shall be no discrimination in the employment of workers in defense industries and in Government, because of race, creed, color, or national origin." In spite of the creation of the Fair Employment Practices Commission, the order was barely enforced.

A hundred thousand Negroes ready to follow Randolph had to repress their protest momentum. Randolph's aborted action nevertheless remains a striking example of the political evolution of black leaders. Randolph's analysis of the situation and his idea of mass movement demonstrate his increasing politicization:

> As to the compositions of our movement. Our policy is that it be all-Negro, and pro-Negro but not anti-white, or anti-Semitic or anti-labor or anti-Catholic. The reason for this policy is that all oppressed people must assume the responsibility and take the initiative to free themselves. Jews must wage their battle to abolish anti-Semitism. Catholics must wage their battle to abolish anti-Catholicism. The workers must wage their battle to advance and protect their interests and rights.
>
> The essential value of an all-Negro movement such as the March on Washington is that it helps to create faith by Negroes in Negroes. It develops a sense of self-reliance with Negroes depending on Negroes in vital matters. It helps to break down the slave psychology and inferiority complex in Negroes which comes and is nourished with Negroes relying on white people for direction and support. This inevitably happens in mixed organizations that are supposed to be in the Negro.⁶⁷

Furthering the message of this speech, Randolph would later assert the absolute equivalence between American racism and European colonialism. Randolph's pristine analysis notwithstanding, there is no way to assert that the march would have avoided the 1943 riots in Detroit (a center for heavy industry) and Harlem (the "model" ghetto).

For Walter White, NAACP secretary, the Detroit riots were the consequence of southern white and black migration to the North, and of the obvious hostility that white workers bore blacks in the war industry:

> According to the War Manpower Commission, approximately 500,000 immigrants moved to Detroit between June, 1940, and June, 1943. . . . For years preceding this riot, there had been mob attacks . . . upon the homes of Negroes. In some instances there had been police connivance in these attacks. In practically no cases had there been arrests of whites who had stoned and bombed the homes of Negroes. During July, 1941, there had been an epidemic of riots allegedly by Polish youths which had terrorized colored residents in Detroit, Hamtrack, and other sections in and about Detroit. Homes of Negroes . . . close to but outside of the so-called Negro areas were attacked by mobs with no police interference.
>
> Early in June, 1943, 25,000 employees of the Packard Plant, which was making Rolls-Royce engines for American bombers and marine engines for the famous PT boats, ceased work in protest against the upgrading of three Negroes. Subsequent investigation indicated that only a relatively small percentage of the Packard workers actually wanted to go on strike. The UAW-CIO bitterly fought the strike. But a handful of agitators charged by R.J. Thomas, president of UAW-CIO, with being members of the Ku Klux Klan, had whipped up sentiment, particularly among the Southern whites employed by Packard, against the promotion of Negro workers. During the short-lived strike, a thick Southern voice outside the plant harangued a crowd shouting, "I'd rather see Hitler and Hirohito win than work beside a nigger on the assembly line."[68]

The racial hatred created, released and crystallized by the Packard strike played a considerable role in the race riot which was soon to follow. It was also the culmination of a long and bitter fight to prevent the employment of Negroes in wartime industry. But these riots, did they not in fact have even deeper causes, of interest not only to America? The editor of the *Michigan Chronicle* (among the most popular Negro newspapers in the Detroit ghetto) writes:

> We all know that for hundreds of years before Hitler anti-negro sentiment has been woven into the social fabric of American life. We know that one of the worst manifestations of that anti-Negro sentiment is the unwritten jim crow law which serves to oppress Negroes and to place a wrought iron ceiling over Negro development and progress. While most of the repressive measures against us were created in the Southland, the North has rapidly adopted these measures in order to solve the problems created by the influx of colored fami-

lies from Dixie. Another important aspect of this picture is the phenomenal rise of the Negro people themselves. Actually we have made progress faster than the dominant group has been prepared to expect. The comforting illusion of many whites that Negroes were really inferior has been knocked into a cocked hat and they see today that if the Negro is really given opportunities he will take adequate and sometimes extraordinary advantage of them. The truth is breaking in upon the mind of white America that the colored Americans are proving the democratic axiom that all men are created equal. Many whites hate to be robbed of their cherished illusions. . . .

The very character of this war—a war for freedom, for democracy, for liberation—has of necessity produced profound changes in our own thinking and has accelerated the hopes of all of us for a new America and even a new world. Two apparently irresistible forces are meeting in our society and the democratic forces are challenging the forces of reaction. This is what is meant when we refer to the World War as a world revolution. The increased tension between Negroes and some elements in the white population which results in rioting is a manifestation of the deep conflict between democracy and fascism.[69]

The summer of 1943 riots burst in several sections of the city: first between bathers at segregated black and white beaches, and the next day in Belle Isle, an amusement park near the city. As fights between blacks and whites increased at Belle Isle, in another neighborhood of the city seven hundred Negroes were waiting for the band to start the dance. Suddenly, a dancehall employee announced on the microphone: "This is Sergeant Fuller (a black cop). There's a riot at Belle Isle. The whites have taken a colored lady and a baby. Thrown them over the bridge. Everybody get their hat and coat and come on. There is free transportation outside."[70] Through doors and windows, the dancers hurried outside. A beat cop patrolling outside the dancehall attempted to stop them, to no avail. As there were not enough cars, vehicles driven by whites stopped at the red light in the intersection were requisitioned. At half past midnight, the police received a first call: the riot had spread beyond Belle Isle.

At the same time, in another neighborhood: "Several Negroes were beaten. . . . The rumor spread among the white people that a Negro had raped a white woman on Belle Island and that the Negroes were rioting."[71] Meanwhile, black rioters began attacking the whites they encountered in Hastings Street. The police intervened with batons and guns. Negroes responded by throwing stones, breaking the windows of white-owned businesses. No looting was reported until seven in the morning. The next day (June 21), police cars patrolled Hastings Street. Their modus operandi was to stop suddenly in front of a store and pick up all Negroes in the surrounding area, including people on their way to work: "To the Detroit police, all Negroes on Hastings Street were 'looters.'"[72] Things kept getting worse:

> Four white youths, all but one teen-aged, were held today in the race riot murder of Moses Kiska, 58 year-old Negro shot down the evening of June 21 as he waited for a street car.... Prosecutor Dowling said he had confessions from three of the quartet. They shot Kiska, he stated, for no other reason than that they had a rifle and wanted to "have some fun shooting niggers." Homicide squad detectives said the youths showed no more compunction about shooting Kiska than "normal men would show at going out to shoot clay pigeons."[73]

The mob of white rioters was not entirely made of hoodlums. A taxi driver confessed to one of his customers: "I was in that mob last night, and I killed one of those niggers myself! I've got the iron bar right with me, too. A lot of good American citizens were in there fighting." After blaming "recent mayors of Detroit for 'catering' to Negro voters and for permitting them to 'over-run' Belle Isle," the cab driver added, "This thing will never be solved until all the niggers have been put under.... I'm going to try and get a gun, and the first nigger that comes toward my cab is going to get it, full-blast."[74] According to the *Crisis*, policemen were hardly more kind: "Policemen would then tell the Negro bystanders to 'run and not look back.' On several occasions persons running were shot in the back."[75] While one journalist wrote, "We must keep in mind the kind of people we have to deal with in this connection. They are half-baked, half-educated people—white and colored alike,"[76] some thought that a conspiracy of German agents and Ku Klux Klan members might be at the origin of the trouble. After each riot, the choice of scapegoats by the American public obviously depended on the political context; after the 1866 Memphis riot, the Freedman's Bureau was accused; in East Saint Louis in 1917, union leaders were said to have incite violence; all the 1919 riots were blamed on the Bolsheviks; two years later, W. E. B. Du Bois and the chief editor of the black newspaper the *Tulsa Star* were blamed for the Tulsa riot. Others—the only ones with black militants and intellectuals not to seek culprits abroad or among foreign residents of the United States—blamed the First Lady for being too liberal:

> It is blood on your hands, Mrs. Eleanor Roosevelt. More than any other person, you are morally responsible for those race riots in Detroit where two dozen were killed and fully 500 injured in nearly a solid day of street fighting. You have been personally proclaiming and practicing social equality at the

White House and wherever you go, Mrs. Roosevelt. In Detroit, a city noted for the growing impudence and insolence of its Negro population an attempt was made to put your preachments into practice, Mrs. Roosevelt. Blood on your hand, Mrs. Roosevelt. And the damned spot won't wash out, either.[77]

One would be remiss to forget white, capitalist, and Christian America's traditional enemies:

> When those communistic Jews—of whom the decent Jews are ashamed—go around here and hug and kiss these Negroes, dance with them, intermarry with them, and try to force their way into white restaurants, white hotels and white picture shows, they are not deceiving any red-blooded American, and, above all, they are not deceiving the men in our armed forces—as to who is at the bottom of all this race trouble. The better element of the Jews, and especially the old line American Jews throughout the South and West, are not only ashamed of, but they are alarmed at, the activities of these communistic Jews who are stirring this trouble up. They have caused the deaths of many good Negroes who never would have got into trouble if they had been left alone, as well as the deaths of many good white people, including many innocent, unprotected white girls, who have been raped and murdered by vicious Negroes, who have been encouraged by these alien-minded Communists to commit such crimes. They are spreading their poisonous doctrine of hate among the Negoes and thereby making it impossible for them to live in peace with the white people around them. Communism is dying in Russia, or rather it is being run out of Russia by the Russian themselves, but it is still active in this country, as the records of these race riots show.[78]

Thus many Americans were already eager to follow Joseph McCarthy in his witch-hunt or take part in the struggle the John Birch Society would lead a decade later.[79]

Harlem, two months later: a black soldier on leave is shot down by a white policeman. Riot. Five dead. Responding to an article that saw in southern ideology the essential cause of this crime (at that time, black soldiers were often humiliated and brutalized by white policemen in southern states), the *Crisis* responds:

> Harlem's riot was not exclusively and solely the fault of Dixie. It was New York City's riot and New York City must bear its share of blame. All the old problems are there; and New York is a part of America, in many ways very like Dixie. But the stimulant in this particular instance did come from below the

Mason and Dixon line; every Negro feels that in his bones, and white men, in Richmond as in New York, should understand it. In the minds of Harlemites that Sunday night the gun in the hands of a good New York policeman doing his duty was the gun in the hands of Dixie cops shooting down men in the uniform, if you please, of the Army of Democracy. That's the fact, much too big and much too bitter to be laughed away.[80]

In Harlem still, during the war and during the riots, another *revolt* was hatching, being prepared in semi-clandestine meetings after hours of increasingly boring and mechanized work in big bands, between two rehearsals, backstage in theatres, cabarets, and dancehalls when the crowds of dancers did not force jazzmen to serve their function as machinists. On top of the racial discrimination and economic barriers all American Negroes have to deal with, jazzmen had to suffer the rhythmic constraints of dance music. The music they played, the arrangements they were given reduced improvisations to a few solos whose very length was predetermined by the melodic line of the main theme, the tempo chosen by the band leader, and the returns to the ensemble programmed by the arranger. They had to submit to these elements not only when they reproduced a score, but also in the moments when they were supposed to *create*. Simple executors, civil servants of jazz, they had to show diabolical technical ability if they wanted to express themselves in spite of the accretion of constraints, barriers, and other sign-posting methods. Forced to accept the imposed musical and economic order, they could only contest it at the risk of losing their material security and being kicked out of the band. Some would nevertheless attempt to go smoothly "from swing to bop"[81] by getting hired by "liberal" black band leaders open to "avant-garde ideas," such as pianist Earl Hines—a former collaborator of Armstrong's—in 1942, or in 1944, singer/trumpet player Billy Eckstine. Working in these bands, they could test ideas until then only formulated in small committees.

Minton's Playhouse, the club opened in Harlem by former saxophonist Henry Minton, was one of the venues in which the meetings of these musical plotters would take place.[82] There they played, improvised, experimented for an audience made up for the most part of black musicians, the only judges whose authority they recognized. Indeed, their attitude was characterized by complete indifference, if not disdain, for audience reaction. This was an aesthetic choice as much as it was a mood swing triggered by fatigue, routine, annoyance, but this is how bebop appeared at its birth: as the irrepressible need for black jazzmen to find themselves in their music, to purge their art of conventions imposed by business and by the aesthetic criteria of white, bourgeois squares. Thus their first experiments were sacrilegious to capitalist ideology:

they questioned the notion of music as commodity, as consumer product. Aware of the acommercialism of their music, they bolstered their protest of the economic system by "destroying" the raw material on which jazzmen had been working for over a decade: hit songs, refrains, and ditties were tortured, deconstructed, and rewritten, methodically and relentlessly.

Fashionable songs were deprived of what made them popular and made unrecognizable: their original titles, having lost all justification, were generally replaced, often with a certain dose of irony. "Whispering" became "Groovin' High," "Honeysuckle Rose" turned into "Scrapple from the Apple," "What Is This Thing Called Love" transformed into "Hot House," "How High the Moon" to "Ornithology," "Indiana" to "Donna Lee," "Cherokee" to "Warmin' Up a Riff," or "Koko."[83] Because of the words they chose, the way they dissected the harmonic structures of themes, their attitude towards the audience and bourgeois society (a mix of provocation and scorn, a refusal of jazz as spectacle), and even because of their religious choices (many boppers strayed from white America's Judeo-Christian traditions by becoming Muslims and adopting Arabic names), the inventors of bop were the first deliberately scandalous black musicians. Moreover, in the words of Count Basie, "It used to be that fifteen out of twenty couldn't understand their music and didn't like it."[84] Such almost unanimous incomprehension in fact indicated that they had reached one of their objectives: to force the white world to either love or hate black music, but no longer see it as a means of entertainment. Their revolutionary jazz evoked the same enthusiasm, the same hostility as any avant-garde experiment, and forced a change in methods of commercial exploitation. Yet their efforts were not supported by any rigorous awareness of political and economic phenomena, and rather participated in a kind of aesthetic activism. As a result, they were unable to resolve the problem of jazz's colonization by dominant economics and ideology. As inevitable and necessary as bebop was in the war and post-war contexts, as a revolution fomented by anti-bourgeois intellectuals and artists, bebop could only be appropriated by the very system it was attempting to destroy. Better yet, it eventually completely integrated it: "Now if people don't hear it," said Count Basie, "they wonder what's wrong."[85]

With Charlie Parker, the image of the dignified, even tragic black musician imposed itself for the first time: the misunderstood artist replaced the entertainer.[86] But if all did not understand Parker's music, it was *received*, felt and finally accepted, because above all it plays with emotion and tragedy. In many ways, Parker and his accomplices themselves were appropriated through romantic interpretations of their oeuvre and lives. Anecdote trumped analysis, and discussions focused rather on Charlie "Bird" Parker's tragic fate, or the mystery surrounding Thelonious "Sphere" Monk, his eccentricity of dress, his silence, or Bud Powell's self-destructive folly.

But it was also said that what they played was *no longer truly jazz*, that they were betraying or rejecting the blues and the traditions of their music and race. . . . Although jazz had appeared in the Western world over three decades prior, bebop's detractors used the same arguments and criteria as the enemies of "negro dances" at the beginning of the century: the sounds of Parker were judged "ugly," Monk did not know how to play the piano, etc. In sum: jungle music had become asylum music (and critics of this madness, which they turned into the new definition of black music, had of course no idea of the reality it covered up: that of the psychological alienation of Negroes in white society[87]).

What were the symptoms of this "madness"? Rhythmically, it manifested itself through explosions and diversifications that returned to percussion the *representative* function it had lost when the slaves were torn from Africa. Allowed more autonomy than in swing bands, drummers could improvise more and punctuate at will, opening the novel possibility of *creating* rhythmic figures, *phrases*, melodic lines by exploiting their drums' many timbres. Bopper slang itself was a phonic rendering of certain drumming patterns, references we can find in some titles ("Oop Bop Sh'Bam," "Obla Dee," "Budeedah," "Salt Peanuts"), some musicians' nicknames (Kenny 'Klook' Clarke, one of the drummers most responsible for this rhythmic renewal), and the very name of the genre (bebop or rebop). Bop singers developed the instrumentalization of voice as introduced by Armstrong into a pretext for vocal performance and instrumental imitation. The rediscovery of rhythmic and percussive freedom showed on the part of boppers a dedication to dewesternizing jazz by emphasizing certain traits characteristic of African and Indian cultures, where percussive sounds are signs as well as signposts.

The madness of bop was also in the use of themes no longer recognizable by anybody. The rhythmic complexity of the new music had already alienated a source of profit until then inseparable from jazz: dancers. Bebop, with its refusal of melodic banality and corniness, became incongruous and suspicious in the usual broadcasting and commercial circuits (radio stations, juke boxes, etc.)

Finally, it was their way of improvising on a theme by playing "whatever" instead of playing what might have echoed the initial method. . . . Saxophonist Coleman Hawkins demonstrated very clearly in 1939 the limits of methods consisting of valorizing and embellishing whatever thematic material was in use. Yet the transformation of the modes of improvisation participated in a rational evolution, rendered necessary as musicians reached the end of the inventory of the swing heritage, the result of diverse experiments and analyses on the harmonic structures of the traditional repertoire rather than a true revolution. Instead of breaking from the principle of the theme as starting point, boppers simply focused their effort beyond appearances (the melody) and deconstructed the structural core of themes (harmony). By improvising on the basic chords of a piece, they transformed it in depth. Moreover, a theme could provide several derived themes through harmonic reconstructions and combinations. This kind of work brought about a revaluation of improvisation's power to surprise.

The same taste for contrast effects was at play in the collaboration between two leaders of bop: to Parker's continuous drama, trumpet player Dizzy Gillespie opposed a mix of acrobatic virtuosity and a true gift for clowning. Where Armstrong entertained his audiences by exaggerating tics, faces, and other personal traits, Gillespie deliberately mocked all and everything, accumulating gags and winks, political references, puns. . . . Armstrong amused by acting his character of the jovial Negro, but Dizzy bolstered the sacrilegious activity of bop by protesting aspects of the established order through humor. He also attained artist status: Parker was stunning and worrisome; Gillespie stunned too, worried at times, but by substituting for Parker's tragic dimension the playfulness of his virtuosity as a musician, singer, and entertainer. Thus boppers, rather than effecting an actual, ideological, and economic revolution, managed to replace one racist scheme with another; the image of the Negro as stupid, naïve, involuntarily funny, "inferior," was replaced by that of the anti-conformist, mysterious, mad, drug addicted artist. Where appropriation by the dominant ideology remains a possibility, eccentricity becomes a trap: artists and intellectuals, because they are exploited and/or disturbing, are also the "niggers" of capitalist society. The economic and cultural exploitation of bop was about to begin.

Bebop big bands, foreign tours, clothing fashions, the appearance of bop singers, intellectualist bias (and the related bop snobbishness), publicity centered on quarrels between critics (ancients and moderns, *moldy figs* and *sour grapes*, jazz or non-jazz, progressives and purists, André Hodeir vs. Hugues Panassié, white music and Negro music), the appearance of the first white boppers: bebop was gradually accepted, commercialized, integrated. Even Dizzy Gillespie's Africanist/Negroist efforts through Afro-Cuban music and beats were eventually reduced to another sales pitch.

Bop allowed big bands to replace the processes and formulas of an agonizing swing with a system of writing and improvisation that was unheard of:

enriching and broadening the fields of harmony and rhythm made it possible for the soloist to emancipate himself. It also renewed connections with the blues, the hidden energy source of Negro American music that boppers had never rejected.

According to the writings of Langston Hughes, a black poet and jazz aficionado who long lived in Harlem, the relation of bop to the blues should only surprise those white musicologists obsessed by art for art's sake. Hughes created a hero (or close to it) in the image of the black readers of the *New York Post*, Jesse B. Simple, in fact a caricature of a Harlemite who says out loud what few black Americans dare even think. Simple is interested in jazz. Better yet, he analyzes it in ways that owe nothing to the study of harmony or counterpoint: "A dark man shall see dark days. Bop comes out of them dark days. That's why real Bop is mad, wild, frantic, crazy—and not to be dug unless you've seen dark days, too. Folks who ain't suffered much cannot play Bop, neither appreciate it."[88] In fact, Langston Hughes has the spirit of the blues speak through Simple's mouth. Negroes for whom the blues is something altogether different from the three-four bar structure associated with two altered tones from the European scale have lived enough of the blues to find it beyond the harmonic refinements of bop. Charlie Parker makes a constant in his oeuvre of this particular sound color/climate, this phrasing constantly rebooted in the blues. With him, the spirit of the blues invaded music, ignoring the labels/borders embodied by theme titles ("Cool Blues," "Blow Top," or "Hot Blues," "Blue Bird," "K.C. Blues," "Blue n' Boogie," "Blues for Alice"[89]) and trespassing into seemingly colorless pieces. Whites long believed that the blues was synonymous with slow, dragging, simple beats. Accompanied by Max Roach, Roy Haynes, Art Blakey, or Kenny Clarke, all responsible for the evolution of drumming (polyrhythmic play, irregular emphases, breaks, and other provocations meant to stimulate soloists, dialogues with other musicians during improvisations), Parker completed his demonstration: the blues could exist in the most diverse rhythmic contexts.

It appears that for Simple (and Langston Hughes), bop beats mean more than a desire to renew rhythmic formulas after the quasi-metronomic rigor of swing dance machines. According to him, the first bop recordings in the early 1940s could very well be musical reports—in the vein of blues narratives—of the 1943 Harlem riots:

> [Bop comes] from the police beating Negroes' heads.... Every time a cop hits a Negro with his billy club, that old club says, "BOP! BOP!... BE-BOP!... MOP!... BOP!" That Negro hollers, "Ool-ya-koo!Ou-o-o!" Old cop just keeps

on, "MOP! MOP! BE-BOP! . . . MOP!" That's where Be-Bop came from, beaten right out of some Negro's head into them horns and saxophones and piano keys that play it.[90]

It remains that bop's most significant victory regarding Negro-American music was to have *revitalized the blues*, through harmonic modernization, and especially with the return to the music's socio-cultural roots on the part of the musician as opposed to the mere interpreter, who remains foreign to everything he plays.

During World War II racial discrimination was the dominant factor for internal conflicts in the USA. Black musicians were nevertheless associated with the entire country's efforts to boost troop morale. Their most notable participation was the recording of *V-Discs*[91] exclusively for the armed forces, though boppers played a very limited role in it.

Lionel Hampton perpetuated the "good Negro" image best represented by Louis Armstrong and played "Flying Home" to celebrate aviation and the Air Force; Duke Ellington created his "Black, Brown and Beige" suite, which presents the evolution of the American Negro as a progressive integration into white American society. With this optimistic piece, seemingly confident in the government's intentions and the good will of the white community, he announced the Negro's accession to first class citizenship.

More aware and more politicized,[92] the writer Richard Wright testified in *Native Son* to the difficulties that a black nationalist would encounter even with members of the Communist Party of the United States (CPUS), inasmuch as most of them were—also—white. At least the practice of Marxist analysis helped Wright better understand the history of Negroes in the United States. In *Twelve Million Black Voices*, published a year after *Native Son*, in 1941, Wright defines the ghetto experience, its endemic criminality and confusion, as the logical consequence of slavery and the unpreparedness of Negroes for modern society. Like many black intellectuals rising after the Great Depression, Wright considered the racial struggle as a stage in class struggle. When boppers were trying to prove that black music was a serious matter, Wright's first books—*Native Son* and *Uncle Tom's Children*—showed that black literature could only be politically committed. Social critique would become a constant in Negro American fiction. Among the symptomatic themes often treated in black literature is the *nonexistence* of the Negro in American society, as in Wright's "The Man Who Lived Underground," "The Man Who Killed a Shadow"; Ralph Ellison's *Invisible Man*; and James Baldwin's *Nobody Knows My Name*. The Black Muslims' notion of replacing their family names (in fact, the names of their ancestors' masters) with an X or a Muslim name expresses this feeling of nonexistence. Many were the jazzmen who, after the advent of bop, showed absolute disdain for their American names and changed them to suit their fancy (Yusef Lateef, Sahib Shihab, Ibrahim Ibn Ismail, Sun Ra, Absholm Ben Shlomo, Abdullah Ibn Buhaina, Abdul Hamid, Liaquat Ali Salaam, Kenyatta, Rashied and Muhammad Ali, Kiane Zwadi, etc.[93]). This separatist attitude followed early-1920s Garveyism. During the war, the Black Muslims refused to join the army, and their leader, Robert Poole, known as Elijah Muhammad, spent three years in jail. After his liberation he would become a new hero for the black masses, and see converts and temples multiply. The war also saw the birth of the Congress of Racial Equality (CORE), a nonviolent protest movement inspired by Gandhi and led by James Farmer.[94] Farmer renounced a career as a minister in 1943, noting, "I did not see how I could *honestly preach* the *gospel* of Christ in a *church* that practiced *discrimination*." He was first helped by students and organized the first sit-ins in southern cities. He then transformed CORE, following Malcolm X's influence, into a more popular movement.

f) Chain Reactions

Change, upheaval, renewal: after the war, a craze for novelty took hold. There were nuclear bombings, the American victory foreshadowing the country's coming military-industrial omnipotence, but also a redistribution of political roles around the globe and the assertion of a victorious and strong socialist country in counterpoint to the USA. The titles of recorded jazz pieces of the time testify to this atmosphere: "Now's the Time" (Parker); "Things to Come" (Gillespie); "New World A-Comin'" (Ellington); "Things Ain't What They Used to Be" (Ellington), anticipating Ornette Coleman's "Something Else," "Change of Century," and "Tomorrow Is the Question." Forces of resistance soon opposed this theme of change in all areas of life. Soon the Cold War appeared, and the consequent freeze of socio-political situations in the USA. On returning to America, discharged black GIs discovered that their participation in the war against dictatorships and racism had not changed much in their relations with white Americans; it had not turned them as *beige* as Duke Ellington had hoped in 1943. It was in fact quite the opposite: the fear of Negroes paralleled the fear of Asians, of the Japanese first and soon the Chinese. White America admitted to being racist at home, but also across a world it already considered its property: Harlemites asked, "Why did they not drop their atomic bomb on Germany? Odd, isn't it?" Anticommunism, vigorously spread by all ideological apparatuses, developed in the middle class a systematic hostility to everything that in one way or another appeared to challenge the established order, democracy, America, the President of the United States, the moral and religious opinions of the (Protestant) majority, the very "tastes" of this majority, etc. ... Protesters, dissenters, parasites, and other troublemakers were of course Communists,[95] and generally speaking all leftists, Jews, liberal Christians (specifically Catholics), Negroes (those, in any case, who wanted to go "too fast" and refused to stay in their place: intellectuals, political militants, union leaders, avant-garde artists, boppers of course among them), criminals (and we know the proportion of delinquents in the black American community to be "traditionally" higher than in other social groups). America offered these firebrands a choice between economic misery or accepting the status quo. By the end of the 1960s, responding to radical militants' phrase *AmeriKKKa*, was an ultimatum in the form of a merciless bumper sticker slogan: *America, love it or leave it.*

After the Cold War and rearmament in Europe in 1950 came the war in Korea, in which President Truman involved the United States. On the eve of a new capitalist crisis (with industrial development slowing down, an increase in unemployment, an excess in food products, increasing income inequality, and restriction of the right to strike), a bit of war was welcome. For shaken capitalism, stuck in internal contradictions, war was once more the miracle cure, the perfect stimulus. Like Roosevelt, Truman had attempted to reduce unemployment (which went from 1,070,000 in 1945 to 3,395,000 in 1949 and 4,500,000 in 1950) with an authoritarian policy of full employment and public work projects, but this symptomatic treatment had proven insufficient. Americans, whose fear in the face of the "Communist threat" was carefully cultivated, had to believe that the source of evil was *elsewhere*: if there was something rotten, it could not be in the kingdom of freedom and capitalism. Invoking the solidarity of the "free world," the United States therefore launched their first official crusade against Communism: the Korean war would jump start their industry, support development in all areas (strategy, armament, chemistry, etc.), and keep some of the unemployed busy. From 1950 to 1953, all threat of economic crisis appeared to have been eradicated. But in order to preserve the optimism of the American dream, thousands of Americans would have had to experience the nightmare of a war whose necessity did not appear so obvious. Between the difficult weather conditions, the limits within which the war had to be conducted in order not to degenerate into a world conflict, the incessant cycle of advances and retreats—facing a guerilla war in an unknown country, against an invisible enemy, artillery barrages on ill-defined targets in trench battles mostly involving foot soldiers lying in wait—all these factors of confusion, doubt, and psychological tension added up in the minds of soldiers to the strange feeling that this might not be such a "good" war for America after all.[96]

The situation in the United States was no more reassuring. In order to prevent another rise in unemployment and preserve the supremacy and purity of the WASP dominant class, the government once more reduced southern European immigration with quotas. In 1952, the McCarthy era reached its pinnacle: thousands of artists, writers, film directors, unionists, journalists became suspects, were harrassed for un-American activities, interrogated by the agents of the many inquisitorial committees of Senator McCarthy. . . . Among the victims of this witch-hunt one can find intellectuals, of course—Langston Hughes, for example—and black militants suspected of leftist sympathies. 1952 was also the year when Robert Henry Welch, a former candy maker born in a North Carolina cotton plantation in 1899, began studying the communist threat and the life of John Birch, the first victim of the Reds in the Third World War.[97] From its inception, the John Birch Society found in the Ku Klux Klan a natural ally. They have the same goal: to protect America from blacks and Reds associated in a vast plot that threatened to upend American society and compromise the privileges of "real" Americans.

Doubly suspect as black artists in the eyes of a white America literally mad with fear, bop musicians were not spared the secondary manifestations of Americanist hysteria. At the end of the 1940s, high unemployment rates among the black population had already deprived them of significant swaths of their public. At the beginning of the 1950s, they were ostensibly excluded from the music business. White businessmen owned all that lived off of music in the United States—show promoters, venue owners, recording companies, specialized publications. No matter their position on the racism and anticommunism spreading around them, their professional policy was determined by those two aspects of dominant ideology—whether because they actually believed in a Negro-Communist coalition, or more simply because they would rather not displease part of their white clientele.

Even the most dated forms and styles of jazz did not disappear with the advent of bop. In his *Histoire du jazz moderne*, which begins with bop and ends in 1960, Lucien Malson emphasizes the fact that bop, even when it reigned supreme, was not all of jazz: on its periphery other styles and other musicians still existed, as jazz does not develop through succession and substitution of one movement for another, but rather by accumulating fashions, with the oldest remaining contemporaneous with the most recent, developing in parallel without influencing each other.

Boppers had only superficially shocked or amused the bourgeois (boppers' favorite outfit: the beret, thick rimmed glasses and goatee—so many signs of "intellectualism"). Even so, the fact that they reflected on their art meant that they refused to play a game whose rules were established by white critics. Disappointed by the behavior of these intellectualized, "whitened" Negroes—an attitude one can relate to the burgeoning hostility against students who used their knowledge to question capitalist values—Hugues Panassié and his disciples in Europe and America were forced to *invent* another, "purer" jazz, better fitted to their criteria of authenticity, since "bop was not jazz." Aware that they were pressed for time, they organized a kind of hunt for old musicians across the landscape, frantically recording all survivors of the New Orleans era, the last holders of the truth and purity of jazz. Besides the physical decrepitude of most of the musicians they dragged into studios, one must note that these veterans were often unknown (or "unsung'") because, in spite of the references and CVs compiled by their discoverers, at the beginning of the century they had only been obscure epigones. Sidney Bechet and Jelly Roll Morton were exceptions in the *New Orleans Revival*. The stories about the one and undiminished virtuosity of the other gave some the impression that they could go back in time and restart the history of jazz at its point of origin. Better yet: they could manufacture it, direct it at will, control it so as to protect it against heresy: finally, they could *own* it. According to Berendt:

> Soon the revival led to a simplified and cliché-ridden "traditional" jazz from which black musicians turned away. (With the exception of the surviving New Orleans jazz musicians, for whom traditional jazz was the logical form of expression, no important black musicians participated in the Dixieland revival—strange as this may sound to some.) Amateurs often worked against the commercialization of Dixieland, but they regularly fell victim to it themselves as they attained professional status.[98]

Berendt, who rightly notes how important white elements were to the revival, was nevertheless surprised by them, and seemed to see in them the effects of a "strange" paradox. White musicians on the one hand, commercial appropriation on the other: there indeed lay the twofold phenomenon we have called *cultural* and *economic colonization*.

Sidney Bechet came to show the French public and young musicians how, through a kind of legerdemain ("jazz magic"), one could turn the most stultifying tune into "real jazz." At every level, Bechet truly continued in Armstrong's footsteps: settled in Paris, he was responsible for perpetuating the cliché of the "ever resourceful, brave Negro," much like French colonial troops who give the image wished for and asserted by the metropolis. Simultaneously, another reaction to bop manifested itself: *cool jazz*, whose rise paralleled that of a new trend in American literature, the *Beat Generation*. Jack Kerouac, among the better known Beat writers, recognized this connection by referring to cool jazz in most of his novels.[99]

Birth of the Cool: under this title and after the fact were gathered a series of recordings made between 1949 and 1950 under the direction of one of Charlie Parker's former bandmates, trumpeter Miles Davis. To the nervosity, the exasperation of bop, he opposed muted, veiled sounds, simple beats, as well as the premeditated refinements of European polyphonies. This was *reasonable* music, in which composition and arrangement regained essential roles. A black music deliberately westernized—a kind of chamber bop devoid of all panic and sense of urgency: on generally slow beats, all musicians adopt a meditative, dreamy stance, and renounce the prolixity of bop improvisation. The music emphasizes softness, refuses the feverish rhythms of bop; it displays narcissism or introversion, revaluates writing, sometimes yielding to sophisticated sounds and sound combinations (showing the influence of European music: fugue, counterpoint, and dodecaphony). A group of young saxophonists playing in white clarinetist Woody Herman's band attempted in 1948 to integrate these moderating elements inherited from essentially white aesthetic traditions into Parker's jazz. But rather than a synthesis or a balance, the music they produced was a kind of delicate chimera, whose power of seduction was owing to its obvious fragility, its indifference to surrounding reality, its floating stance, its commitment to non-commitment (a harbinger of hippie disengagement). In the face of music and the world, they appeared to want to emulate Lester Young's attitude and extend it into hypertrophy, if not downright caricature. That some of these cool musicians resorted to narcotics reveals a desire for escape and retreat. Contrasting with the black rage of bop, cool music was symptomatic of the anxiety of America at large, especially among the generation most concerned by the Korean War. Most cool musicians migrated to California, partly for cultural reasons (Henry Miller was in Big Sur; beatniks and other dropouts went there looking for sun and to forget New York's hyper-Americanism), but mostly for economical reasons. Hollywood was gradually falling for cool, a subtle form of jazz capable of complementing image without disturbing it, like Monk's or Gillespie's music might. Moreover, in order to play the drivel of mainstream film music, big symphonic jazz bands were necessary. Jazzmen capable of reading music were more numerous among whites than among blacks. Finally, job discrimination there also played a part. Thus black boppers stuck to the few jazz clubs still open in New York.

This was the time when Charlie Parker recorded "La Cucaracha" and other fashionable songs—whose melodic banality he stayed true to for the first time—often backed by lachrymose violins or vocals. Many black jazzmen were forced to abandon music: trombonist J. J. Johnson, for example, went to work for the postal service, as pianist Cecil Taylor later would. White musician Chet Baker was elected "best trumpet player of the year" (beating Miles Davis, Dizzy Gillespie, and even the harmless Louis Armstrong). Dave Brubeck, Gerry Mulligan, Lee Konitz, and Stan Getz became stars; among whites, the most popular black band was the Modern Jazz Quartet, led by the very westernized and refined John Lewis, who apparently dreamed of becoming a black American Couperin or Rameau: he imposed on the blues the rules of the fugue and counterpoint, the toccata, the trite rondo. His many attempts at synthesis anticipate the Third Stream,[100] among whose main defenders he would soon figure. Charlie Parker died in 1955.

Miles Davis was therefore the only black musician to play a significant role in the cool episode (which he rejected years later), when other boppers were kept away from a movement that betrayed their essential contribution. Also excluded from cool, young black musicians would take advantage of this underground phase in order to prepare the new music. They would soon react against the cool reaction with an energy found for the most part by contact with the blues.

Still mostly ignored by the white public, the blues had nevertheless evolved out of economic and social pressure in the margins where it was kept. To respond to demand from the black working class, recording companies specialized early in production for black audiences—what critics and disc jockeys called *race records*. After the rise of Bessie Smith, the first blues singer whose commercial success spread beyond the ghetto, white and black blues fans and businessmen explored the black sections of industrials cities, the cabarets where factory and steel mill workers met, southeastern cities, etc., to find new singers. Blues artists were vagrants, unemployed people, itinerant field hands, sometimes delinquents,[101] but also local celebrities, who sometimes agreed to record two sides of a 78 RPM, take their money, and vanish, often without giving their real name. Records might become popular among the black public and the singer be impossible to locate. Known or unknown, these singers had an audience, and soon the bigger record companies included in their catalogues a selection for Negroes: the *race series*. Only a few ethnomusicologists and amateur sociologists were fascinated by these blues which, according to most whites, "all sounded the same." The smaller black-owned labels, black headhunters and artistic directors, became scouts in the black world for the big white labels that did not want to deprive themselves of an extra source of revenue, however minimal.[102]

This economic appropriation would soon be followed by pressure from the dominant ideology and the market, the effects of which were observable on the lyrics of blues, as well as its forms and composition. To the extent that the blues is first and foremost the American Negro's *reaction* to his surroundings, living conditions, social and individual connections, its critical character seems unalienable. The blues gives an account of black American collective and subjective issues, and this account from the black point of view necessarily testifies about white America, bears traces of revolt. More so than jazz, the blues appears apt to resist threats of commercial and ideological appropriation. Little appreciated by whites and despised by the black bourgeoisie, the blues is marked by both race and class in ways that throw it back towards the black working class, where it was born and where its audience is. But it would misunderstand the dominance of dominant ideology to think that it does not affect the exploited classes. The blues constitutes a veritable ideological vector as the discourse of an individual who puts his problems in common, who has common problems.

The black masses are also constantly affected by the ideology of American capitalism and Christianity, and to that extent, something of the dominant ideology necessarily passes into the blues, at the most explicit level of its lyrics. Therefore there are two types of blues: the first is a kind of primitive protest song, testimony, and critique, which we have exemplified earlier. Historically, this kind of blues was on the wane, and one had to wait for the politicization of black masses following the radicalization of political movements to find it again (see James Brown's "I'm Black and I'm Proud"[103]). The second kind, which quickly became the main kind, deals with intimacy: sexual and sentimental issues, daily life, etc. Of course, lived experience bears the deep marks of American Negroes' social, economic, and historical station. This kind of blues remains a reaction—at the individual level—to the different kinds of oppressions blacks have to face. But it is also the place where dominant ideas invest themselves, where ideology comes into play. The Negro's ideological and musical context, from radio stations, television, film, newspapers, and novels to white love songs, informs him about the kind of problems bourgeois society fetishizes. This imprint also bears on the blues. Through it the salient points of the dominant ideology reinscribe themselves on black popular ideology. Reinscription is always problematic: the honest, direct character of blues complaints and the graphic character of the lyrics (banned from the sentimental press and mainstream love songs) still act as defenses. Yet the blues cannot but speak of the very life of those who make and listen to it. Black existence in white America is marked by the hold of dominant ideology and white values on the black masses. The blues therefore testifies to the alienation of American Negroes even in the way dominant ideological themes shape them.

Yet thanks to the means specific to the blues—its music, its words, its tone—these themes are in a way stripped and revealed for what they are. Love songs describe feelings in order to distract from the tough realities of life, but here those feelings are reality; where love songs display an ideological valorization of jealousy, love, etc., the blues shows the work of suffering, the difficulty of controlling one's own fate. Like the Negro, like jazz, the blues is made of the never-ending conflict between what is imposed and what is refused, between the many socio-historical overdeterminations of American Negroes. The divided and conflicting nature of the blues is the basis to which black music, constantly under the threat of commercial and ideological destruction, must regularly go back to reconstitute itself. When white determinations reign for too long, antagonistic determinations, resistance, and contradictions are reactivated. This movement back and forth makes up the history of jazz, just as it makes up the history of the ideological struggle of Negroes.

During the *swing craze* another factor had revealed itself, inseparable from the fashion and trends (i.e. the ideology) of the time: the need to dance. In rent parties[104] the blues, now played on the piano, had already adopted the fast tempo and thumping drive of boogie.[105] In Kansas City, as soon as 1940 and in all places where the blues encountered black dance big bands, the blues and dance were combined to form a new mix: *rhythm and blues*, whose popularity never ceased to increase. It integrated Western elements, using new instruments *in a blues context*: blaring saxophones in a soloist role once left to *blues shouters*, organs, drums.

Since bop and especially with cool jazz, "progressive jazz" had seen its audience diminish; it became a music for initiates and snobs, a cultural commodity. Its commercial potential weakened also because its rhythm and its musical structures make dance almost entirely impossible. The great success of rhythm and blues in the early 1950s must be seen as a violent reaction by musicians and the black masses against the delicate, polished, and aestheticizing daydreams of cool jazz. What made this success especially unique was that rhythm and blues reached an important section of the white audience without renouncing any of the traits of authentic blues.

9) Soul Music and Soul Brothers

Reactionary forces, once triumphant with Senator Joseph McCarthy—finally disavowed by the Senate in 1954—seemed temporarily on the wane; with the onset of "peaceful coexistence," anti-Communist, anti-Negro, and anti-protest psychosis appeared to weaken. For a time, American capitalism showed its liberal side. Traditional black organizations began—timidly at first—to take action against segregation in the South. They received some support from the federal administration, reaping benefits and prestige from it abroad. The South, whose laws contradicted the country's constitution and supreme court decisions, remained Jim Crow's realm. Anti-segregation activism remained very cautious, supported as it was by white liberals and churches.[106] The struggle for integration deemed itself nonviolent, and appealed to humanitarianism, nobility, democracy, etc. Focusing its efforts on specific and exemplary cases of segregation, the movement garnered a few successes, by which it gained massive support among American Negroes and hatred among southern whites.

The civil rights movement, begun in 1962 by all black organizations (the NAACP, the Urban League, SNCC, CORE, SCLC), a few AFL-CIO[107] unionists, and liberals from the Southern Regional Council, developed after the relative success of sit-ins and a variety of integrationist actions performed locally: Freedom Rides, walk-ins, as well as a campaign supported financially by the Kennedy administration to register southern blacks to vote in areas where they had long been disenfranchised. These nonviolent actions were met with brutal police repression (over 3,600 arrests in one year as well as a number of deaths) and violent counter-protests by white southerners; racist attacks increased, the Ku Klux Klan resurged, and the White Citizens' Council formed, which would go as far as banning the broadcast of blues and other black music.[108]

The federal government took note of the violence but did not prevent it. When Kennedy appointed three notorious racists federal judges in the South, it destroyed the legalist illusions of the movement.[109] It then launched the famous March on Washington, immediately denounced by Malcolm X as one of the greatest swindles perpetrated against Negroes in any time. The failure of the electoral coalition with the Democratic Party marked the end of integrationist endeavors that had attracted a majority of the black middle class, but had left behind the masses in the North. King's influence remained important, though jeopardized by the Black Muslims and their theoretician Malcolm X (see 1. c).

Nonviolent ideology had no trouble rallying a majority of white students, who would play an increasingly important role in American political life. Anti-segregationist and legal campaigns in the South contributed in the training of black and white activists who would become politicized. The entrance of the post-war generation on the political scene was partly responsibility for the quasi-unanimous acceptance of rhythm and blues—and its immediate white derivation, rock and roll—by the white public. Cool music no longer held attention; Fats Domino, Little Richard, Chuck Berry, and Elvis Presley became "mixed" stars.

The appearance and success of white rock and roll were comparable to the ways in which swing had prevailed some twenty years earlier: following a grave political crisis, at a time when the effects of a strong demographic push were making themselves felt and racial strife was (apparently) less lively; as a response to the collective desire of Americans to forget the recent past with the help of music easy to listen and dance to. Music that posed no problem; music that whites and blacks could play, its white version being of course only the imitation and adaptation of its black counterpart. During the swing era, the repertoire of white big bands was made up of fashionable love songs; white rock integrated hillbilly music, cowboy ballads, and other elements from white American folk music. Their common foundation: the blues. Thus the recording studios of the "purest" form of rock and roll are located to this day in the Southeast (Nashville, Memphis, etc.). Though the majority of rock and roll stars were white, "purists" began to appear (blues aficionados who wanted to follow this new commercial offshoot of the black tradition, or proponents of a movement back to the roots). In this way black rhythm and blues singers and musicians in turn became popular among black and white audiences. The way rock replaced swing in dancehalls can also be explained by the fact that it was easier, financially speaking, to support a small group of musicians (guitar, bass, drums) than a big band (fifteen to twenty musicians). Overcome by the rock invasion, most big bands dedicated to dance music were disbanded. Their musicians went to find jobs in the recording studios where ephemeral big bands were sometimes put together for rock recordings. Others participated in the nascent soul-jazz movement; others yet would find employment in an orchestra backing a star such as pianist-singer-saxophone player Ray Charles. Black, blind, addicted to drugs, Ray Charles played for the white public the same role Bessie Smith or Billie Holiday had played in their day. His shouts, smirks, stutters, and jerks added to a strange, broken, and throaty voice made for a "true Negro" voice.

Jazz split at this time: black musicians reacted brutally to the advent of cool jazz, a genre far from their concerns and from which they were mostly excluded. Black music revisited its origins, leaving the white musicians of the previous season—as well as their audience and the commerce built upon them—speechless. Contrasting with the produced, perfect, clean feel of cool and of the Modern Jazz Quartet, black primitivity came back, inscribing itself in simple, raw, nagging beats, often in three-four time, waltzes of sorts. Sounds got dirty, funky, and improvisations took on the repetitive forms of the trances of black churches. The music reactivated elements of the blues (such as a kind of "ugliness" in the sound, a kind of musical "poverty") as well as effects borrowed from spirituals (repetition, unnerving rhythm and flow, violent expressivity). Facing this crude, reactive, rough, and heavy music, the latest in white fashion was the so-called bossa nova, a painstaking movement exploiting Brazilian rhythms. This may be why, in spite of the quick (and ephemeral) success of bossa nova, funk, or soul-style jazz, was extensively exploited commercially (after Horace Silver, the Adderley brothers were launched with much publicity by panicked labels, and pianist Les McCann knew worldwide success with no follow-up). Quickly appropriated in spite of—or rather, because of—its elements of black assertion, soul music also testified to the necessity for black musicians to tap into a cultural commons to reinvigorate their music.

The promotion of what cool jazz had repressed in black music is typical of the more or less efficient resistance black music puts up against anything that draws it away from itself. In soul music, the power of resistance was expressed not so much in the blues and spiritual effects—whose benefit can only be temporary in that they embody a regression through reaction—but in the *ideological valorization of these effects*. *Soul* became a password in the black community. It is a quality whites can neither have nor imitate; blacks are *soul brothers*,[110] and they identify easily and immediately with *soul music*. At stake here is a process of celebration, a communion similar to that expressed in "black is beautiful": it promotes self-recognition, self-definition sheltered from white values, and the tightening of racial connections to prepare for a common struggle. Yet soul music was quickly commercialized, became fashionable, and obtained the support of the white public—even when the music told whites that it excluded them, that it was not for them. . . . This paradox must be questioned: is emphasizing the most external, apparent, noticeable signs of black character enough to make this character unalienable? In soul, the white public found exactly what it expected from black music: rhythmic simplicity and violence, a picturesque and outrageous mask. Soul ceased to hold any meaning for those Negroes who projected themselves into it as soon as it reawakened and reinforced white notions of black music as savage and simplistic, with its simplifying effects, its black apparatus. Nothing about the "dirtiness" of funk could have unsettled certain themes of white ideology.

Parallel to the rise of soul music, black churches went through a political rebirth. On the one hand, Martin Luther King Jr and the SCLC pushed traditionally resigned churches into an active protest role. On the other hand, King's nonviolent ideology found a response and a contradiction in the brutal effects of soul music, in its image as a religious music tougher than the sermons of the time. Could this compensation be the way by which the violence banned from political life by the dominant ideological form—religiosity—reinvested that form itself?

Similarly, as a contradictory echo to nonviolent protests in the South, that is, in echo to the violent repression of these protests, came the music of Charles Mingus: "Fables of Faubus," the infamous governor of Arkansas, the man of Little Rock, an exemplary episode in the black struggle.[111] Black music itself offered a rejoinder to the integration and patience preached by King, the notion that whites would gradually gain awareness of the harm they had caused. The derision and hatred of old forgotten blues made their comeback in the music, the sounds and the forms. The shouts (instrumental and vocal), obsessive reiterations of rhythmic and melodic lines, the oppressive climate Mingus's musicians create all anticipated free jazz. Audiences began to realize that, in its very forms, this black music was made of rage and imprecations, the blows and insults received throughout history and given back in music in a kind of exorcism. With Mingus and his partner Eric Dolphy, violence took front row; it structured and played the music, thus preparing certain forms of free jazz musically and ideologically, and anticipating Archie Shepp's quip, "We are not angry men. We are enraged."[112]

Mingus's music was not alone in translating developing black political and ideological struggles. Following the entertainment phases in jazz history, before the political-commitment phase of free jazz, black music began eschewing the obfuscation of its socio-political determinations. The politicization of music originated in the very politicization of black movements, rendered inescapable by the transition from formal protest to direct action and open conflict with reactionary forces. Thus in 1962 (the year of sit-ins, and of the founding of the *Council of Federal Organizations*), bop drummer Max Roach recorded with his wife Abbey Lincoln *We Insist, Freedom Now Suite*.[113] That piece, 36' 03" long, in many regards has a place in the free movement—though neither Hawkins nor Roach play "free"—for its (exceptional) length; its political commitment (it pays homage to black students and Africa); Abbey Lincoln's vocal experimentations anticipating Patty Waters and Jeanne Lee's free singing (shouts, wails, brutal contrasts between soft phases and pitches that organize singing along a kind of orgasmic structure, erotic emphases inherited from the blues, which had disappeared in "modern" jazz singing and whose principles free jazz singers would systematically borrow). The rhythmic experiments of Roach and the African percussionist Olatunji lead to great rhythmic plasticity: the beat transitions from simple patterns, referring directly to African percussions, to complex moments where several rhythmic structures overlap. Finally, it references Africa: rhythmically, then, but also in the vocals, in the melodic tone, in the very lyrics that enumerate African tribes. It bears noting that *We Insist* was produced by a small label, Candid, run by journalist Nat Hentoff.[114]

The surge of Africa on the jazz scene dates back to the first recordings of Horace Silver and Art Blakey ("Safari," "Message from Kenya," in 1952) and to the latter's trip to Nigeria, where he studied African percussion, which would become an important element of his style and music. The Jazz Messengers would spread around the world an Afro-American music in which Africa began to play a politically and musically structuring role, rather than the nostalgic and exotic part it had played in Ellington's music, for example.

It must be noted that black music went "back to Africa" before the cultural Black Nationalist movement. One might see there the trace influences of Garveyism and the more direct influence of the Black Muslims. The music opposed the counter-myths of Africanness to the Judeo-Christian values and myths of the dominant ideology. A more easily attainable cultural return to Africa replaced Garvey's physical return.

Africanness, violence, negritude, black beauty (*Back to black, black is beautiful*), Black Nationalism: in the 1950s all of these elements could be found in the music (and more strikingly in titles that explicitly assert the new black consciousness) that perpetuated the "Negroizing" action of *hard bop*, a style performed by young black musicians eager to react against the mellow whitening of cool jazz. Clifford Brown recorded a "Hymn to the Orient," "Blue and Brown," the Africanizing "Daahoud' and "Delilah," and "Caravan." From 1958 onward, hard bop turned churchy, funky, soulful, in so many symbolic assertions of its black ownership, and references to Africa and American Africanism increased: "Garvey's Ghost," "Bronze Dance," "Black Diamond," "Airegin," "Ritual," "Dakar," "Tanganyka Strut," "Africa," "African Lady," "Message from Kenya," "African Waltz," "Dahomey Dance," "African Violets," "Bantu," "Katanga," "Man from South Africa," "Uhuru" (but also, around the same time, John Coltrane's "Alabama"), "Afro-American Sketches," etc. So do references to the black church: "The Sermon," "The Preacher," "Sister Salvation," "Wednesday Night Prayer Meeting," "Sister Sadie," "The Prophet" (a homage to Black Muslims), "Like Church," "Ecclusiastics" (mixing ecclesiastics and exclusion), as well as references to slavery ("Work Song"), black vernacular ("Dat Dere Dis Hyeah"), protest ("Justice," "Freedom" by Charles Mingus, "Emancipation Blues"), voodoo cult ("Devil Woman") and of course to black soul.[115]

This non-exhaustive list shows that a new ideological fabric had been woven among American Negroes. In its politicization, violence, and black culture, free jazz was already inscribed in the movements that preceded it and which it radicalizes and/or critiques.

Musically, culturally, and ideologically, free jazz is not born out of nowhere; it prolongs, takes over, and reworks old forces of black America. If free jazz decisively changes black music, the very possibility of such a change is determined historically, culturally, and ideologically. Its meaning and scope are connected to black history. The last manifestations of black music before free jazz reveal an intolerable situation, a confused reaction to white cultural domination, a point of no return that makes the leap of free jazz absolutely necessary.

Part 3. Contradictions of Jazz in a State of Freedom

8. Free Fragments

> Although modern science and technology are the same whether in New York, Paris, London, Accra, Cairo, Berlin, Moscow, Tokyo, Peking, or Sao Paulo, jazz is the only true international medium of communication current in the world today, capable of speaking creatively, with equal intensity and relevance, to the people in all those places.
> —Eldridge Cleaver, *Soul on Ice*, (New York: Delta, 1968), 203.

What is most striking in listening to free jazz compositions is their polymorphism, the multiplication/collision/juxtaposition at all levels and in all senses of material, codes, sources, worlds, and modes used, or referred to, by musicians. Everything happens with these jazzmen as if they had decided not to abstain from anything they could desire or need, at any stage in the creation process.

Compared with "jazz," a great mass of exogenous elements float on the surface of this music; it emphasizes the impression of a mix, underlines in fact the contradiction that preceding genres and forms of jazz tried to mask as "synthesis," unable as they were to control these elements. On top of this, the elements that white jazz critics had believed to be specifically attached to all jazz are now systematically unhinged. This is not to say that in this music attachments to tradition are always, globally, and finally destroyed; rather, they are stretched, drawn out, until they are barely perceptible, hardly identifiable, and open to the most complex detours. This makes for an exceptional, and previously unheard of, freedom of movement.

Looking for such extremely minute links is all the more difficult because they are almost always hidden by, or associated with, other connections made more recently: a sound coloration more or less referentially "exotic" or "nostalgic" (some pasts being as foreign to African Americans of the 1960s as Asia and even Africa can be), the apparent influence of immediate peripheral genres (popular and contemporary music) and the commitment to making music say something, on top of what it already says without meaning to. Any survey of these "characteristic" traits can only be provisional; whether new or resulting from a contestation/actualization of traditional elements, they correspond to so many particular cases, and are only exemplary of the musician or group (band, association) that elected to use them, often only for one given piece. However, they are all signs and manifestations of the double process of critique and affirmation that underlies the free jazz approach.

In order to tread into such uncharted territory, we have no other possibility but to take note of the most obvious characteristics of the music, being well aware that they can only be indicative of tendencies and moments in free jazz. Moreover, these "constants" can only be inventoried in relation to music already heard, i.e. the most recent forms of African American music.

In fact, what appears first and foremost is free jazz's departure from most of the traits of common jazz: the structure of compositions, the function and relation of instruments, the rhythmical conception, the relation of the musician to the audience, to other musicians, etc. are so many principles and habits that free jazz musicians seem to break away from. This decisive series of breaks, unheard of in the history of African American music, challenges more than a musical order; it challenges a cultural order. In a double movement (both centripetal and centrifugal), free jazz endeavors to reappropriate the Negro elements of African American music. In the same movement, it opens itself completely to all possibilities of musical and extra-musical enrichment offered by musical codes beneath or beyond the alleged field of action of jazz.

a) Theme

During the bebop era, some music lovers and critics complained about not being able to identify the melodic and harmonic springboards for improvisation that themes are. One of the main complaints against free jazz had to do with the absence of, the avoidance of, or the scorn for, theme in the new music. Some free jazzmen indeed seem to favor absolute spontaneity and athematism, while others, more numerous, try to invert and otherwise disturb the hierarchy according to which theme is a leading element of jazz because improvisation is necessarily predetermined by, and inscribed in, the theme structure. Displaced, reduced to its simplest expression, or on the contrary blown up, reiterated to the point of becoming punctuation in the beat, recited without modification, theme is no longer the decisive element of a free jazz piece. It can occupy a central position in the development of a piece—see Sun Ra, Alexander Von Schlippenbach—i.e., constitute a plateau, a pause, without necessarily being connected to the improvisation preceding and following it by anything more than contiguity. Theme is no longer necessarily what announces and concludes improvisation. No longer is it the support, the primary material, the melodic and/or harmonic guarantee. Therefore, the notion that theme and improvisation form an inseparable couple disappears. There is improvisation, and there is also, on the side, theme (sometimes even themes), but the former no longer depends on the latter. As a melodic segment, theme only intervenes as a citation, an element among others, a perfectly isolable and isolated fragment. By reexamining the function and place of theme as a melodic organism to which improvisation remains structurally foreign, musicians such as Albert Ayler can use theme as a mere sound object.

Through this effect of detachment, theme is now denied all commercial value. So engrained in our aesthetic habits is the need for melodic comfort and safety that until the appearance of free jazz, a misunderstanding, tacitly maintained for reasons of commercial and cultural colonization, had often measured jazz only by the "beauty" or charming power of its themes. Listeners had grown to listen to improvised segments only absent-mindedly, considering them more or less successful "recreations." The overestimation of the thematic element is obviously inseparable from the musical criteria of Western countries, where musicians—no matter the musical genre—were until very recently only expected to execute. The notion of the theme as commodity, object of enjoyment and aesthetic consumption, is resolutely rejected by the most radical free jazz musicians.

One of the first jazzmen to have called theme into question in this manner is the saxophone player Eric Dolphy. His *Music Matador* is a perfect example of the revalorization of improvisation (that only builds on the side of, or far away from, the theme) and the absolute limitation of the powers of the theme. Louis Armstrong and pre-bop musicians improvised on the most uninteresting themes in attempts to demonstrate the sublimating virtues of jazz. Contrary to them, free jazz musicians do not let preexisting melodic elements, however poor in melody or harmony, restrain their improvisations. Rather than be in the service of the theme, they use it for their own purpose.

But the most remarkable and decisive example of the evolution of the theme-to-improvisation and theme-to-musician ratio is incontestably the work of saxophone player Albert Ayler: the *isolation* of traditionally inseparable elements one from the other is one of its essential characteristics. By emphasizing, systematizing, and enlarging the dual nature (theme/improvisation, white/black, etc.) of his music, he transforms what was the simple contrapuntal relation of two elements into a kind of permanent conflict, a structurally insoluble contradiction.

Ayler's approach opposes, for example, that of John Coltrane in the early 1960s. Coltrane then seemed to be expecting from the most obstinate reiteration of a thematic segment a quasi-miraculous resolution/revelation for what, to him, was less a contradiction between theme and improvisation than a need to reach a musical beyond, bereft of all conflict. Coltrane, trained as he was during the bop era (bop improvisation was no longer the beautification of a melody, but rather the exploitation of its harmonic canvas), had to free himself from the harmonic ties judged liberating in the '40s and '50s. Although he had a determining influence on all the musicians (free or not) of his time, he could only realize this emancipation by studying at the school of the young pioneers of free. He submitted his music to the ordeal of collective improvisation (*Ascension*), placing himself in the necessarily equivocal situation of being both master and student (much like old Coleman Hawkins had in his time, by participating in the first bop recording sessions or, later, by playing with Thelonious Monk or John Coltrane himself).

Pharoah Sanders, one of the "official" disciples of John Coltrane, strives to conciliate stark oppositions of theme and improvisation such as practiced by Ayler with incantatory progression. He uses themes as means of tension and ascension, leading inexorably to explosive improvisations. Although he gestures towards a synthesis of these two approaches, he is also less radical than the more avant-garde free jazz musicians in that, to him, the repetition of a given melodic segment presupposes a revalorization of the notion of theme. In all of his pieces, the presence of a theme chosen for its charming powers, for its brilliance, occasions the inevitable resurgence of commercial implications (Pharoah Sanders has thus become one of the rare free jazzmen whose themes have become a non-negligible factor in commercial success).

Closer to Ayler's example, the Art Ensemble of Chicago (and more generally the AACM), who indeed appear as the true heirs of Ayler's spirit, only use theme as one of innumerable elements of the décor they create with each piece. Not only is theme neither enriched nor sublimated by improvisation, but it also seems to be chosen or built only in order to provide the musicians/torturers with prey. The theme, in fact, is reduced to the level of other musical and infra-musical elements, and participates, in this function, in the playful enterprise of the Ensemble.

So free jazzmen do not eliminate theme from their music; but, put simply, it is no longer privileged in relation to other elements. Desacralized, it is used, *played* (with). It can even be hummed; but it no longer exerts supremacy over the rest of the piece. Albert Ayler put it this way:

> I'd like to play something—like the beginning of *Ghosts*—that people can hum. I want to play the *songs* I used to sing when I was a child. Folk melodies everybody could understand. I'd use these melodies as a starting point, and several simple melodies would move inside the same piece. I'd like to go from a simple melody to complex textures, then back to simplicity, and from there go to the most complex, dense sounds.[1]

In fact, there is no longer a need for the themes used in free jazz to be complex or refined, i.e. replete with pretext for improvisation, because they are no longer the essence, the substrate of a piece. We no longer have *the* theme; now, we *also* have themes.

b) Instruments

When Sonny Sharrock declares, "I think the greatest artists are those who have no technique,"[2] or when Ornette Coleman replies to his detractors, "Some musicians say, if what I'm doing is right, they should never have gone to school. I say, there is no single right way to play jazz,"[3] they both point to a new axis in the transformation of black music, one centered on the role of instruments and their use.

The first jazz musicians—who often were self-taught—were already radically straying from Western academic norms in their technique: it was influenced by the intonation and other characteristics specific to Negro voices and songs; they used growling effects[4] and fiddled with sound matter in a variety of ways (for example, using multiple mutes on trumpets and trombones), they put an excessive emphasis on vibrato, etc. Jazzmen, in fact, have invented or reinvented most of their instruments: banjo, drums,[5] string bass,[6] saxophones,[7] etc. The adaptation of instruments to the contingencies of black music—the only possible response to the disappearance of African instruments—is radicalized by free jazz. Notions such as "virtuosity" and "instrumentalism" disappear. Like Thelonious Monk before them, free jazzmen are accused of having no "technique," of not knowing how to use their instruments.

In fact, many free jazzmen assert that it is not necessary to go through Western academic teaching in order to play African American music: their goal is not to play the works of classical European composers, but rather to play/create their own music; hence their often unorthodox way of using instruments, their need to go beyond the instrumental limits imposed by Western norms. What used to be exceptions, accidents, become new sound possibilities: reed whistles (once erased from Charlie Parker's recordings as defects or errors) are accepted, valorized as integral parts of the discourse; breath effects and other noises until then considered parasitical to the purity of sound are now used and perfected. These sounds constantly solicit an elsewhere, a place outside their usual field of action (high pitch register, incongruous noises, key sounds on the saxophone, etc.); musicians bypass the keyboard to directly strike piano strings, and use their bows to *hit* bass strings. . . . Sounds, asserts Ayler, are more important than notes, and the musician now seems to care little whether those sounds are (judged) "good" or "bad." Shouts, noises, shocks, growls, creaks: all infra-musical effects are now part of the improviser's discourse.

Free jazz uses instruments borrowed from faraway folklores (shehnai and bagpipe with Ayler, Pakistani oboe for Giuseppi Logan, Indian flute and gamelan with Don Cherry, balafon with Sunny Murray, etc.) and European classical music (oboe, bassoon with Joseph Jarman, fife and piccolo with Pharoah Sanders, tympani drums with Sun Ra's percussionists), from either the modern or the most "primitive" music (the rhomb of African children) or from unexplored domains of European instrument-making (sousaphones, bass and contrabass clarinets, and other "monstrosities," revalorized by the musicians of the Art Ensemble of Chicago and Anthony Braxton; Dewey Redman and the musette; Don Cherry and the pocket trumpet).

Boppers anticipated the widening of the instrumental field (the saxophonist Yusef Lateef, for example, integrated all the instruments of Arab music into his own); but for free jazzmen this systematic approach is less a "touristic" curiosity than a need to play with the entire scope and complexity of sound possibilities. To instrumental sounds are added those produced solely by the human body: mouth noises (Art Ensemble of Chicago, Don Cherry), finger snapping, etc.

Obstinately refusing all instrumental limitation is inseparable from contesting the notion of the "specialist" (from the point of view of technique); such stances led to the appearance of many "multi-instrumentalists." If saxophone players always had the possibility of diversifying their music by using all reed instruments (Eric Dolphy thus played alto sax, flute, and bass clarinette; John Coltrane played tenor sax, soprano sax, and the flute), it was rare to see musicians go from one family of instruments to another. First known as an alto saxophonist, Ornette Coleman, after a few months of solitary work, started playing the trumpet and the violin; Albert Ayler, not long before he died, played the bagpipe; pianist Alice Coltrane (John Coltrane's wife) plays the harp; AACM musicians integrate into their concerts/happenings all the instruments they have had the opportunity to discover (in any concert or recording session, each musician has some twenty instruments at his disposal); the trumpet/cornet player Don Cherry uses equally diverse kinds of flutes, the piano, and percussion instruments.

More clearly and systematically than traditional jazzmen, the free jazzman tries as much as possible to vocalize the sonority of his instrument, no matter what it is: the instrument is but a extension of voice and body. Like bluesmen who work their guitar style in reference and echo to their singing inflections, the free jazzman makes his instrument an appendage, an interchangeable and provisional substitute for his body; all physical impulses, including the most brutal, are transmitted through the instrument to the music, in which this *corporeality* is inscribed.

The need for complete, immediate, and faithful expression, which leads the free jazzman to shake off the rules and criteria of white academicism and all "professional qualification/specialization," is at the start of an absolute revolution in the band: the abolition of the distinction between solo and accompanying instruments. All musicians, no matter their instrument, can now improvise through a kind of democratization of relations within the band. Piano, bass, and drums no longer are there *to serve* trumpets and saxophones. Since improvisations on "theme harmonies" are no longer in fashion, the piano is no longer an instrument for harmonic sign posting. Drums and bass are no longer limited to formulating an explicit tempo and beat. They are, as much as other instruments, *sources of sound*.

c) Improvisation

In free jazz ensembles, no matter the size, a new principle replaces "the traditional conception of the big band where, while his band mates stay nicely seated in their chairs, the soloist comes to the front of the stage and delivers his solo in front of the microphone."[8] But it sometimes happens that "we turn back to collective improvisation, and the soloist—to maintain this terminology—becomes only an improvisation leader whose sound emerges barely above that of his partners."[9] Free jazz musicians are all soloists. This term—borrowed by jazz critics from Western musical literature and the *concertante*[10]—thus loses its significance, in that free jazz brutally breaks away from the hierarchical classification of musicians the term implies.

The function of "improvisations," their place and their status, no longer have much relation to age-old traditions: now, all musicians in an ensemble will often improvise together and each for himself. The restoration of the principles of collective improvisation reinscribes what some have called "New Orleans polyphony" into African American music. "We are trying to renew the old *New Orleans* idea that music can be played collectively and in a free form," says Ayler.[11] Moreover, even when they follow each other in time, free jazz improvisations supplement each other, contradict each other, build networks, strata: a multilayered assembly of sound lines, rather than a single line prolonged by musicians in relay. Thus the entire piece becomes an improvisation, in that its structure and its global form are born of the more or less expected crossing of individual lines. Polycentric, free jazz improvisation is in fact much more than the mere reactivation of the polyphonic system of New Orleans jazz (where the trumpet gave a general direction, supported by the clarinet's counterpoint or the bass punctuation of the trombone). Rather than mere improvisation—i.e. an immediate and unpremeditated composition, with the notion of performance and technical mastery implied by such a definition—free jazz improvisation is essentially random, provocative, risky, and playful.

The main risk it has to face is the probability of repetition. Since the harmonic points of reference and the melodic guarantees granted by thematic improvisation have disappeared from free jazz, the musician no longer has any means of control over the development of his discourse: the melodic line and the harmonic frame were also mnemonic elements. In a fixed chord progression, improvisation could not go several times through the same chord without the musician being aware of it. The free jazzman is no longer protected from his own melodic obsessions, personal clichés, idea or sound associations, and other automatisms. This explains the appearance of a kind of "free" academism, in the form of an absolute refusal of premeditation or repetition.

In order to keep collective improvisation both *free* and *structural* to the particular piece in which it inscribes itself, musicians have become more diversified in their approaches. Through the emphasis they put on preparation and on the writing/organization and rehearsal of their works, Bill Dixon, Sun Ra, Alan Silva, Cecil Taylor, Mike Mantler, Charlie Haden, Carla Bley, Sonny Sharrock, and Dave Burrell introduce a second moment for free music. A necessarily new system appeared as collective improvisation developed in the first orchestral manifestations of free jazz, and these musicians substituted for absolute spontaneity an always contradictory and unbalanced mix of points of references and indetermination: a network of the unpredictable, going from expected crossroads to blurred zones. This is not so much musical composition as the establishment of formal structures and points of sound condensation.

d) Rhythm

In 1967, Marion Brown said, "It is wrong to say that free jazz does not swing. It swings to a high number of beats. It is polyrhythmic. But it is hard for people listening to it to realize that. . . . Free jazz is closer to African beats than bop or swing were; African rhythm is very complex."[12] Drummer Milford Graves added,

> until now the drummer's job was to keep the beat. He did nothing else, even if sometimes he took off in a solo. Now, he has to create sounds according to what he plays and his means of expression. You can use any part of your drums, in any way, at any time. Now drums have become an instrument; you have to use it to make music, not to connect other instruments together. The drummer used to be clockwork, not an artist.[13]

Pianist Cecil Taylor asserts that to the extent that "rhythm becomes melodic and melodic instruments turn rhythmic... there has been a switch in traditional functions," and that "there are differences in intensity and speed in our music."[14] These declarations indicate that:
—free jazz musicians are heretics to the rhythmic orthodoxy of jazz as it has been defined by Western musicologists (who decreed that tempo must not vary in proportions perceptible by the ear);
—rhythm is no longer only the affair of "specialists" ("rhythmicians"); like improvisation, it is a collective phenomenon, which also means that:
—sounds, melodies, and rhythms cannot be considered divisions of music, independent one from the other; instead, they conjugate in an indivisible whole, in permanent conflict;
—the rhythmic complexity of jazz, which has not stopped growing since the rise of bop, corresponds less to a process of progressive sophistication than to a musical deconditioning and a work on African subtleties: the universe of rhythm(s) is the richest aspect of African musical culture;
—because it refers to African polyrhythms, swing cannot be limited by notions such as regularity, uniformity, unity; it is never synonymous with monotony or reducible to a kind of metronomic beat, and it participates in collective play, in challenging the comfort of the return to the familiar.

If, at the beginning, the "guardians of the one and unalterable true swing" often judged free jazz harshly (and often accused it of being completely arhythmic!), it is because in free jazz rhythm is located at all levels of sound production and in all sections of the band. Rhythms are born from timbre and register contrasts, from alternation between plainsong unison and scatterings of sound, from brutal or gradual variations in volume, from the opposition of the most simple melodic sequences to zigzagging and often contradictory rushes of collective improvisation, from the intervention of noises, shocks, breaths, and other traces of instrumental work, from variations of intensity in the overall play. These add up, superpose and cross, oppose each other, contradict each other, burst into secondary beats. As a result, we get the impression of a *complex resulting rhythm*, specific to each piece and each collective improvisation. Nevertheless, the possibility of traditional drumming and regular tempo is not denied, but like theme it has become just one of the many possibilities of space-time organization. Considered before free jazz to be in charge of the rhythmic pace, the drummer can now use rolls and accentuations as he pleases, without seeking to serve, push, or direct his band mates. He can accelerate or slow down so that, at his level *also*, a kind of rhythmic halo can be created that will be interfered with, crossed with digressions, parentheses, and contradictions, throughout the process of *sound* production. The drummer no longer produces a beat, but rather a *complete music* (listen to Milford Graves in "Nothing" or Andrew Cyrille in "What About?").

Where in traditional jazz the tempo and nature of swing was defined in the first bars of a piece, the rhythmic destiny of free jazz pieces remains obstinately and perfectly unpredictable: "Music has to be conducted in the moment. Life is in the instant, always new and fresh: it has to be the same with music."[15]

e) Africa

Duke Ellington, Marcus Garvey, Dizzy Gillespie, W. E. B. Du Bois, Art Blakey, John Coltrane, Malcolm X, Stokely Carmichael, Archie Shepp, Robin Kenyatta . . . Until a relatively recent date, rare were the leaders of black political movements and bands in the USA who had not referred to Africa at least once in their writings. As Eldridge Cleaver put it, "All blacks have known a phase of cultural nationalism, more or less starting in 1956, when Ghana became an independent country, when the bus boycott started in Montgomery, Alabama, and when the Black Muslims were beginning to be known."[16] In the same period, jazz went through a phase of intensive Africanization, at least in its explicit thematic references. With free jazz, the relation to Africa becomes less obvious, but also more subtle. This relation also loses its fashionable character: musicians participated in the revalorization of the African legacy; Afrocentrism and cultural nationalism added to a mass of experiences, memories, and references that make up the psycho-mythological cultural heritage of the African American community. More or less anecdotally, Africa is evoked/invoked by Sun Ra ("Ethiopia," "Ancient Aethiopia"), Charles Tyler ("Strange Uhuru"), Frank Wright ("Uhuru Na Umoja"), Don Cherry (through melodic references, use of African instruments—balafon, etc.), Sunny Murray ("Homage to Africa"), Clifford Thornton ("Ketchaoua"), the trombonist Grachan Moncur ("New Africa"), and, generally, by all the musicians who participated in the Panafrican Festival of Algiers in 1969. It was for most of them the first opportunity to see and hear Africa. This was not, however, the Africa that Marcus Garvey, Malcolm X, and all the "Black Moses" prophets of a return to a lost paradise had told them about. The Africa of jazzmen remains located in oneiric and mythical regions. Before he died, Malcolm X himself had started to gradually translate his "Back to Africa" program to a less utopian plane: he would only cite Africa as a potential collective reference. Originally, Africanity had been a way to assert and strengthen the solidarity of black Americans. But on the musical plane, Africanness was encouraged and valorized by the promoters of cultural nationalism, foremost among them LeRoi Jones.

In fact, if Africa still manifests itself in and through free jazz, it is less in the accumulation of more or less artificial references (titles, "exotic" citations and "African ambiance," or even stage dress, dashikis, etc.) than in the revalorization and actualization of specifically African musical traits: the prominence of rhythm, the new melodic functions of percussion, the use of instruments of Western cultural tradition in novel and "Africanizing' ways (Cecil Taylor plays "percussion" piano, using the keyboard with a velocity, rhythmical figures and melodic lines reminiscent of balafon players; Ornette Coleman and Alan Silva reduced the melodic possibilities of the violin in order to explore what Western musicians had until then neglected: its rhythmic power, much in the way of the old African one-string vielle).

This is especially clear in the reintroduction of vocality in the instrumental discourse, *an essentially black notion* that white elements at play in jazz had regularly attempted to minimize or obfuscate (as with the vibrato-less style of cool jazz, the sound "purity" of white saxophonists such as Paul Desmond, the mechanization of traditional jazz rhythms, etc.). Flow, (mis)treatments of sound matter, accent and even mispronunciations, expressivity and emotional nuances of speech (shouts, moans, harangues, rage, insults, etc.): all the qualities of human voice, the *phonè*, and through it the body, all *come back* in the music of Archie Shepp, Albert Ayler, Roswell Rudd, Don Cherry, Ornette Coleman. The constant connection of African music to speech, to the Word, to language, also finds itself in the music:

> Western distinctions between instrumental and vocal music are evidently unthinkable ... where the human voice and musical instruments "speak" the same language, express the same feelings, and unanimously recreate the universe each time that thought is transformed into sound. Consequently, the words with which they acclaim life are articulated in an equally careful manner.[17]

f) Exoticism

So as not to forbid themselves any possible source of formal renewal, so as to widen as much as possible their field of action, universalize their music and find correspondences beyond the ghetto in which cultural nationalists have tended to trap music, free jazzmen have not limited their references to African cultures and music. Probably to avoid falling into the trap of another westernization of their music, and under the more or less conscious influence of the Black Muslims, they have generally turned to the East. John Coltrane first pointed the way with pieces marked by the haunting and methodical sound explorations of sitar players ("India").

Sun Ra, as early as 1958, also recorded a piece called "India"; he went on to record pieces that referenced Ethiopia, Nubia, Africa, China ("Overtones of China"), and Egypt. Yet these multiple musical explorations generated Sun Ra's least complex pieces, limited as they were by the composer's choice to introduce exotic "effects" (soon replaced by the solar system and cosmic spaces). In fact, the referential trips undertaken by a few free jazzmen barely enriched or transformed African American music, in that they were typical of a curiosity common to most musicians (no matter their race, nationality, or culture) and only occasioned a very superficial approach to the cultural codes evoked in passing. Rather, they brought instrumental borrowings to jazz, previously unheard timbres, but also and especially another challenge to the status of instruments in black music. Once and for all, the instrument was brought down to a more humble dimension: *all* sound producing tools could be put in the service of jazz and widen its scope.

Nevertheless, these attempts at strengthening the non-white and non-Western elements of jazz are perfectly in line within the escapist themes of the dominant ideology in America. Fascination with the mythical East plays on blacks much in the same way it does on whites: in both cases, it works in agreement with the dominant ideology. The semi-failure of these "escape" attempts would demonstrate how ingrained contradictions between black and white culture are, if openings to non-Western worlds were not so overdetermined by the internationalist evolution of black revolutionary ideology.

g) Westernism

There is nothing surprising, of course, about free jazz borrowing, citing, referencing, and alluding to Western cultural elements. From its birth, the music of black Americans was marked by this embarrassing *presence*, and its entire evolution was a series of conflicts and imbalances between moments of white cultural predominance and moments where a more or less decisive revival of Negro elements occurred. But the appearance of free jazz corresponds to the first global attempt by black musicians to use a great number of white aesthetic products and cultural signs—while more or less systematically challenging and deconstructing them.

"Everything I've lived, I am," says Cecil Taylor. "I am not afraid of European influences. The point is to use them—as Ellington did—as part of my life as an American Negro."[18] An admirer of Bartok and Stravinski, he added:

> [John Cage] doesn't have the right to make any comment about jazz, nor would Stravinski have any right to make evaluations about jazz, because they

don't know the tradition jazz came out of. I've spent years in school learning about European music and its traditions, but these cats don't know a thing about Harlem except that it's there.[19]

Cecil Taylor's case exemplifies the conflict of two cultures in black musicians. He is without a doubt the free jazzman that has most often been accused of letting himself be influenced by modern European composers. In fact, like many middle class black people, Taylor received the kind of education where only Western cultural norms were considered worthwhile. He only discovered black musical traditions through the randomness of family tastes, encounters, and personal experience. He came to jazz as if by reaction to, or revolt against, a culture that had been imposed on him. At all levels, though, he was a musician by Western training. If this cultural baggage did not turn out to be an obstacle, it might have been because Taylor only kept of Western music what in it was already internal contestation: Bartok, who revalorized folkloric themes by imposing a resolutely modern approach upon them; Stravinski, whose mix of rigor and violence, reinforced by barbarian rhythms, announced Taylor's own ambiguities (Western/African); and, of course, composers of serial music who, long before him, had conceived of the piano as a percussion instrument. Taylor's music is the privileged location for a novel conflict between two modernities: that of the West, in more or less open revolt against its own traditions, and another one at play in polyrhythmic improvisations, attempting to reach the surface of black American man's music from an African depth.

With Albert Ayler, everything happens more brutally, schematically, but also in more exhaustive fashion, to the extent that the saxophonist tackles a great variety of Western musical genres: the subculture of marching bands, ditties, and other "minor forms" that bourgeois culture reserves for the working classes; the two dialectically opposed terms of his music (white references, black revolts) which he forces to contradict each other (by alternating them in his pieces). To these, he adds an intermediary element: strings and refined musical combinations treated in the European manner, which, far from solving the primary contradictions, complicates them. Then he uses all the elements of Western origin he can lay his hands on in succession in his works: Indian chants in "Love Cry" (an homage to the first colonized and despoiled people of the New Continent), the incongruously syrupy harpsichord of "Love Flower" and "Angels," up to the "'yeah, yeah yeah,' which the Beatles high-jacked from Ray Charles"[20] and the "less sophisticated (but no less Body-based) popular music of urban Negroes—which was known as Rhythm and Blues before the whites appropriated and distilled it into a product they called Rock and Roll."[21]

Ambiguous in Taylor's music, where two homologous and yet contradictory cultural strands interact, hypertrophied in Ayler's, where immiscible musical genres are deliberately and roughly opposed, this traditional antagonism is in both cases the object of an excess unprecedented in the history of black American music. Don Cherry's experimentations with white musician Jon Appleton (playing the cornet, the flute and varied other instruments, Cherry is confronted with a succession of electronic sounds programmed by Appleton) and the free jazz treatment applied by Dave Burrell to such great pieces as Puccini's "La Vie de Bohème"[22] are interesting as curiosities or sound happenings. Nevertheless, neither stages the white/black cultural conflict so powerfully as Cecil Taylor's and Albert Ayler's music.

The enormous enterprise undertaken by Archie Shepp is reminiscent of Taylor's and Ayler's approaches. Shepp restores to black music everything that could have marked it; he confronts it with people, events, and other musical genres that, one way or another, have played in jazz or on its peripheries. Commenting on his "On This Night (If that Great Day Would Come),"[23] a piece dedicated to W. E. B. Du Bois, he mentioned wanting to realize "a synthesis of my vision of contemporary America as a man of color.... In all these elements—and that is the essence of 'On This Night'—there is the presence of a people struggling for its emancipation. 'That Great Day' is the day of liberation." The sound climate of this resolutely black combat piece is undoubtedly rather surprising: it features a singer (a soprano of perfectly "classical" training, probably more used to singing Gustav Mahler's "Kindertoten Lieder" or Brahms melodies than the compositions of a free jazz saxophonist), who in fact echoes a characteristic of Ellington's music:[24] the taste for "beautiful" (according to Western norms) voices and dramatizations worthy of the masterpieces of European lyric art; a somber bass accompaniment played with a bow by Henry Grimes; and more strikingly, a pianist—Archie Shepp himself—more influenced by the Webernian instrumentists of Pierre Boulez's "Domaine Musical" than by the masters of boogie or the disciples of Bud Powell. Thus does Shepp, much in the way of Taylor and Ellington, accept in quasi-provocative fashion the most westernized aspect of his music (which others strive to reduce). Over time, from one piece to the other, he played with this contradiction (a bluesy theme following a militant *lied*), and also by associating/opposing a text of aggressive and demanding content to a completely discrepant vocal and instrumental sound context: soft, corny, inscribed in the European romantic tradition. This discrepancy, this opposition of the message and the music, in truth an insidious way to emphasize drama, can also be found in "Malcolm, Semper Malcolm" and "Le Matin des Noirs." On the contrary, when Shepp takes over such a futile thematic element as "The Girl of Ipanema," he strives to negrify/

dramatize it in order to, here again, isolate contact and rupture points between the culture of the colonized and the dominant cultural codes and ideology.

h) Jazz/Blues

What Archie Shepp's music takes charge of, more than anything, is the history of jazz. In almost all his pieces, there is first an obvious homage to Duke Ellington who—like Charles Mingus—he considers to have prefigured all the yet underexploited possibilities of black music. Faithful to Ellington's melodic lines and ambiances, Shepp also details them, emphasizes them; he accentuates their sentimental aspects, conducts a true rereading of them. Similarly, he plays and analyzes traditional blues, rhythm and blues, his predecessors' style (Coleman Hawkins, Ben Webster, Rollins, Coltrane), Monk's oeuvre ("Crepuscule with Nellie"), the life of bluesman Sonny Boy Williamson, rock (with Chico Hamilton: "The Dealer"), and marching bands. Concerned about authenticity, Shepp summons to sessions, *where the entire history of black music is rewritten and actualized*, the very people who participated in it: boppers Philly Joe Jones, Walter Bishop Jr, Roy Haynes, middle jazzman Don Byas, blues harmonicists Julio Finn and Chicago Beau. . . . The very makers of past forms of jazz now work at reconstructing it, play their own role as reference, self-citation, and reinscription.

Marion Brown also rewrites the history of jazz, but through that of his instrument, the alto saxophone—from Benny Carter and the Ellingtonian Johnny Hodges to Ornette Coleman.

For the musicians of the Art Ensemble of Chicago, jazz's past, New Orleans style, religious hymns, etc. are very clearly *targets*. Like Shepp, they reread and rewrite the history of Afro-American music, but their work on yesterday's jazz is more often ironic: they contest, contradict, and mock, like musical clowns of sorts. This enterprise of derision in some ways expands upon Ayler's own work. The difference is that Ayler sincerely and naively saw himself as the depository of the "joyous" forces of New Orleans jazz:

> The power of Bechet's timbre, for example, the power of his vibrato, that was fascinating. For me he represented the true spirit, the full power of life, which many old musicians had and musicians no longer have now. I hope I can replace this spirit in the music we play. We try to do now what musicians like Armstrong used to do: their music was joy. Beauty appeared in it. It was this way in the beginning, this way it shall be in the end. One day everything will be as it should be.[25]

The need for jubilation, the nostalgia for the "good old times" of New Orleans: Ayler looks for them in the marching bands and brass bands that walk down Canal Street on holidays and in the basic beats of rhythm and blues and rock and roll, or in the black churches and in sermon-like refrains.

i) Voices/Texts

Shepp's or LeRoi Jones's poems ("Black Dada Nihilismus," "Black Art") backed by brass, strings, and skins, caressed or brutalized; quasi-orgasmic alternations of howls and moans from the inheritors of Abbey Lincoln (Patty Waters: "Black is the Color of My True Love's Hair"; Linda Sharrock's "Black Woman"); the instrumentalization of the voice expands the range of virtuosity of bop singers, with Jeanne Lee (who was also influenced by the European techniques of *sprechgesang*, which she negrifies with blues intonations and rhythmical effects borrowed from *soul music*). Poems again, recited (like Mingus, like Coltrane in "Love Supreme") by the AACM musicians, chants and preachings from Albert Ayler (who introduces himself to his audience in the fashion of bluesmen), but also mouth noises (Anthony Braxton, the Art Ensemble of Chicago), laments of Native American origin (Maurice McIntyre, Ayler again), choirs added to Sun Ra's different Arkestras to comment on and announce the stages of his "trips into infinite space" ("Next stop Mars," "We travel the spaceways," etc.), the trills and vocalizations of Leon Thomas, who by Pharoah Sanders's side transforms scat's onomatopoeias into a kind of Negro yodel, the satirical sketches and happenings of the Art Ensemble of Chicago ("Old Time Religion"), Alan Shorter and Archie Shepp's aggressive yells at the Festival of Antibes (July 1970), Sunny Murray's poems. . . . From all directions, at all levels of free jazz, chants, discourses, poems, or voice-derived noises burst and respond to each other. Inheritance and actualization of the blues, confessions, critique, prayers, simple sound effects, all these vocal manifestations, through their extraordinary diversity, actualize the power of the word and the shout that is always at play in black history. But contrary to preceding eras of jazz, the discourses of free jazz, no matter their form (articulated or not, made of words or of the accumulation of quasi-visceral sounds), place themselves outside of the formal frames of the blues and traditional "songs" of jazz. They target the essence of the blues: their discourse and functionality. In freeing themselves completely from the structures imposed by singing, they evoke the work songs and dirty dozens, but also pamphlets, petitions, manifestos, slave complaints: "If my music doesn't suffice, I will write you a poem, a play. I will say to you in every instance: Strike the ghetto. Let my people go!"[26] The sound evolutions of free jazz have paved the way for, and made possible, this vocal explosion; the exasperation of timbres, the frantic vocalization of instruments, the appearance of extraneous noises, first tolerated and then encouraged, indicated the imminence of free jazz's shouts.

9. Music/Politics

> You can't blow up three children and a church without it somehow reflecting itself in some aspect of our cultural experience. That's what the avant-garde is about, I think.
> —Archie Shepp, "Blindfold Test," *Down Beat* 33 (1966).

In Chapters 5 and 6, we isolated certain points where Afro-American music interacts with the economic and social structures of white capitalist America and therefore with the political history of black Americans, which is itself produced by these structures as their repression and/or remnants. We have attempted to show how some jazz "styles," musical forms, and aesthetic choices have been linked to specific moments in extra-musical fields (economic conditions and their translation in ideological terms into political consciousness and cultural trends). From the beginning, black musical productions have *played* into the themes and ideological modes of white bourgeois American society, whether by achieving them, echoing them, explaining them, or instead by attempting to separate from them, defend and react against them. This music takes place in the contradictions of this society, not only because it bears the traces of its influence, but also because it is one of the forces struggling against it.

Black Americans relate in a variety of ways to the system that exploits them economically, socially, and culturally: resignation, acceptance, redeeming participation, resistance, nationalist or revolutionary struggle. Each option is echoed in the evolution of jazz, which appears as one of the privileged tools of black ideology and one of the central stakes of its struggle against dominant white ideology. Jazz is torn between these forces that simultaneously make it, structure it—and attempt, by excluding their counterpart, to use it for their sole profit. The economic, social, and racial contradictions at the origin of jazz have not disappeared. They have not been flattened by the development of jazz, by what we have long believed to be its infinite ability to "synthesize," because these contradictions have not been erased or sublimated in the wider social field. The vision of the origin and evolution of jazz as a crossroads of original influences gradually blended into each other, boiled down to a specific unit, is an ecumenical myth. There was no crossing or mix but a struggle between dominant and oppressed influences, the latter resisting only through increasingly marked emphasis on its *differences*. Free jazz takes up and radicalizes all these differences. Far from rejecting jazz history, it inscribes itself in it as both a break from the commercial and ideological domination of American bourgeois values, and as the inheritor of the many attempts at resistance against these values. That it continues this tradition determines the success of the break: the music of Ayler and Shepp bases its rejection of the colonized forms of jazz on, and reinforces it through, rewriting these forms, through quoting and recontextualizing styles, themes, and figures belonging to the "past" of jazz.

The term free jazz, as we have just seen, covers profoundly diverse musical styles. Ten years of development necessarily produced varied concepts and forms, among different musicians but also in the evolution of specific musicians. One must note that such evolution was rare in jazz before the advent of the free phenomenon: each musician, once he had found his "style," was thereafter defined by it. One could perfect it but would not challenge it. It took free jazz to upend the musical conceptions of musicians stemming from bop (Coltrane, Rollins), cool (Konitz), and even Dixieland (Lacy). Such diversity and contradictions make it impossible to reduce the free phenomenon to a "style" or a "school": as with bop, nothing unifies free jazz musically. Much to the contrary, its *specific*, principal characteristic is the *diversity* of musical material and forms. Yet these contradictions *within* compositions themselves do not float randomly: they are produced and regulated by this music's historical inscription. What defines the free phenomenon as an ensemble—what articulates and structures the multiplicity of its musical manifestations is their common overdetermination by history, by social relations, political and ideological struggles, and cultural attitudes towards previous jazz.

To the extent that free jazz was historically produced as the reaction(s) of certain black musicians against the dominant forms of jazz, free music defines itself first as a break/rejection, or a transformation/rewriting of these forms. Free jazz's formal experiments continue in musical form a critical reading of the history of jazz, its cultural and economic alienation. From the get-go, there is in free jazz's work on musical material a cultural, ideological, and political point of view connected to and inscribed in the wider cultural, ideological, and political struggles of black Americans. If, as we have attempted to demonstrate, the history of jazz is indeed the history of a struggle between black and white conceptions, between Afro-American and colonialist cultures, then free jazz intervenes in this history and the struggles that produced it as a *reflection*. This is why, whether they be explicitly politicized or not, free jazz musicians produce work that is inevitably politically inscribed, not only because these musicians live at the heart of the same economic and racial contradictions as the black masses (see 1. e), but also because their musical work targets the musical effects of these contradictions on jazz.

Free jazz mixes and works a multiplicity of cultural codes into itself; a true dialectics of opposites is at work in this music, which targets, quotes, and reinscribes different alienated forms of jazz, transgresses or rejects cultural taboos and aesthetic norms. Economic and political determinants long contained in a musical elsewhere return violently to music in free jazz. This complex combination of factors soon became an issue in the approaches to the movement of those (mostly white, as we have seen) jazz critics who only had at their disposal definitions of jazz they had themselves designed, references and links only to their own Western culture, wherein the notion of art holds a central and forbidding position.

Literally disoriented by the new music, jazz critics—as if they felt personally targeted for building up jazz as an art and aesthetically normalizing its forms—reacted with symptomatic rage. "Progressive" critics—those who had defended bop against the "true jazz" faithful, those who had coined the "modern jazz" label, who had encouraged the influence of contemporary Western music on jazz (Gunther Schuller's experimentations and Third Stream jazz)—did not hesitate, in order to mark the break, to pick up Panassié's old anathema: "This is not jazz." Indeed, this was not *the* "jazz" which white America and critics had systematically valorized and authenticated as "black American music;" this was not "white jazz," but this had more in common with black Americans than what passed for jazz had had in the previous thirty years.

Until recently, most jazz magazines, when they bothered to mention the likes of Ornette Coleman, Albert Ayler, Sun Ra, Archie Shepp, Don Cherry, Sunny Murray, Milford Graves, and even already famous musicians like Eric Dolphy, John Coltrane, or Sonny Rollins, accused them of not knowing how to play, of playing nonsense, of playing tricks on audiences. Critics also presented them as clowns or provocateurs, impostors or aesthetes lost in abstruse experiments and severed from the "popular roots of jazz." The first accusations simply denote the incapacity to musically and culturally appreciate music that upends certain deep-rooted habits and codes believed to be universal and eternal. The second—and very common—kind of accusations was a belated reactivation of Panassié's anti-intellectualism. First, one posits that since jazz is (or used to be) entertainment music, simple—and therefore somewhat primitive—dance music, it fit the masses, according to the ideology that the masses like the easiest—that is, the lowest—things. From there, one deduces that since free jazz is "incomprehensible music," it has nothing left to do with the masses, which will "understand it even less." This is truly about confusing the cultural demands of the masses and the cultural, *but also* political and economic demands of the dominant ideology. The question of what the cultural needs of black Americans could be is here masked by what dominant ideology attributes to them, inculcates in them, and formulates in their stead as *demand*. Because free jazz endeavors to challenge what *dominates* popular "tastes," what conditions the mass's demand, it strives not to cut away from the masses themselves, but from the ideology that runs through them, blinds them, speaks in their name so as to perpetuate their exploitation. In its critique of ideology, free jazz connects with the political demands and needs of the black masses. Free jazz is closer to the masses, and better addresses their interests by attacking the very idea that they have of *their own* music, the jazz that we have seen so often used to serve their enemies. Speaking suddenly in the name of the "popular nature" of jazz, critics not only misunderstand the role and the very notion of dominant ideology; they actually reinforce its domination. That some critics reject and hate free jazz shows that it constitutes, within the relative importance of aesthetics and culture, a danger for dominant ideology *and what it has produced as a function of music* (entertainment, escape, fantasy fulfillment) and art.

What is at stake in these reactions—which often only express themselves through insult—is not simply a quarrel between styles or generations. Nor does it merely amount to shaking up musical forms and formulas, or even the periodic readjustments of criteria of "beauty" and "ugliness" (Ornette Coleman tells the tale: "Once I played for ten minutes for a conference of the American Architects' Association—it was for a discussion entitled 'Beauty and Ugliness.' . . . They told me that I represented ugliness'"[1]). It is not only music and aesthetics that are at stake here.

Yet, we will note two things.

First, critics of free jazz—when they attempt to build an argument[2]—take pains to position themselves on a *strictly musical* plane, notably banishing from their discourse considerations of musicians' race in the name of antiracism, which here serves to cover up antihistoricity. They dismiss politics in musicians' statements or even such explicit signs of political commitment as appear in the titles or references of certain compositions. They do this in the name of the principle of *separation* between the personal comments of artists and the texts in their oeuvre, the latter alone being worthy of analysis. In bourgeois ideology the author is held—explicitly or implicitly—more or less irresponsible. Only the music, then, can be discussed, not the musicians' ideas, since music itself "expresses nothing." It is therefore only in the field of musicology, and in the name of jazz's musical values and truths alone, that these critiques intervene.

Second, free jazz indeed sets itself apart from previous jazz *musically* on a number of points we discussed in III: rhythm, theme, improvisation, structure, role of instruments. . . .

On the matter of *musical differences* between free jazz and jazz, critics are somewhat relevant: indeed, they reject free jazz precisely because of its musical differences, which they deem disastrous. These differences exist, and critics certainly have a right not to like them, and to choose certain forms and styles of jazz over others. We will go further yet: critiques about the musical traits of free jazz are *inevitably* and *automatically* relevant since they are based on, and programmed by, a conception of jazz that already pertains to a certain kind of jazz. Free jazz rejects both the conception and the music. This contradiction is precisely that to which critics remain blind. The *sum* of the differences between jazz and free jazz may be made of musical facts, yet it does not concern only musical facts; through them, it also influences a conception of music, that is to say something at the junction of the musical (aesthetic) field and the cultural field in their common relation to ideology.

What critics do not question (or see) is *why these striking aspects of jazz, rather than others*, are the ones from which free jazz musicians want to break away. These traits, and no other, because to free jazz musicians they are *the most heavily laden with non-musical* (cultural, ideological, commercial) *investments*. Critics do not see this because they have contributed to position, invest, and co-opt those characteristics of jazz contested by free jazz musicians. They have helped manufacture and valorize them so as to serve their own ideological and commercial interests, following their own cultural demand. When critics swear they are only speaking of musical facts, they are lying to themselves and misunderstanding all that is determined by the dominant ideology of a capitalist society and Western culture in their own aesthetic criteria and conception of art, in what they consider musical or not, etc. Consequently, by locating the debate only at the level of "musical differences" between jazz and free jazz, critics forbid themselves from even questioning the *raison d'être* of these musical differences. The evolution of free jazz is therefore magically put down to the growth of a malignant disease of jazz: "decadence." It becomes a kind of self-justification for critics, who "were right to love" such and such form of jazz.

A critical attitude is labeled "musical" that aims 1) to judge free jazz by the criteria of jazz; 2) to condemn free jazz as degenerate or inauthentic because of its distance from these criteria (which it rejects, but this is never mentioned); 3) to preserve jazz from any possible "contamination" by, or self-assessment through, free jazz: the counterfeit form cannot contest the authentic form; 4) for the public and for musicians (encouraged to keep playing music that is easily accepted) try to perpetuate under the name of jazz a neutral, harmless kind of music presented as location for and proof of cultural and racial integration; 5) to systematically devaluate the avant-garde work performed by free jazz because it is part of a wider political project on ideology; 6) finally, to confirm the—necessarily "beneficial"—influence of Western music and aesthetics on jazz; in other words, to justify the economic and ideological exploitation of the music of black Americans, and dispossess them of their music more or less completely.

Critics mobilize against free jazz because it no longer plays jazz's game—a game where until then capitalism and its ideology always won.

Ideology, commerce and Western criticism invested increasingly more into the forms of jazz, leading to a conception of jazz given as eternal and universal. Free jazz means to break with this "civilized" view of jazz regulated—more or less explicitly—by a very *Western* concern for clarity, balance, and elegance. It applies even to dashes of sonic violence, which like spices foster an excitement that does not compromise its satisfaction, its return to normal. Jazz owed its "universality" and commercial success to its value as distraction; in free jazz distraction collapses, perhaps to the benefit of its utter contrary, playfulness, which because it demands involvement and work on the part of the audience, annihilates distraction. It was asked that jazz be played without taking risks; that it provide joy, based both on a system reassuring for the regularity of smooth, automatic resolutions for rhythmic tension, and on the intensive use of a sound whose restricted register allowed only for those sounds immediately agreeable to the ear. Resolving rhythmic tension easily and satisfying norms of audibility are the two axes along which develop all the criteria and definitions used to conceptualize jazz. In its least co-opted manifestations,[3] free jazz cares little about these two laws. This showed in many reviews about the unbearable aggressiveness of free jazz, its "inaudibility," its upsetting character *at the sensory level*, which all point to the musical refusal of the notion that free jazz is determined by resistance that expresses bourgeois ideology and culture in a "conception of jazz." Not only do those reviews evoke the comfort of habits,[4] but they also testify to a value system: that of Judeo-Christian civilization, which conceives itself as the center of all civilizations, a unique and universal reference, where Art has a central and superior position. Art as an equivalent and substitute for God (terms such as "oeuvre," "creation," "genius," "inspiration" and their inflation in criticism, aesthetics, or even bourgeois conversation indicate the sacralization of artistic work) embodies in the Western system the "purity of Idea," conceived as transhistorical, bereft of contingences, contradictions, work, a place for boundless pleasure (the fantasy of capitalism), the place of the demiurgic/magical domination of the world. Yet everything in free jazz is done to upset this "purity," to counter its qualities: the multiplicity of cultural codes at play in free jazz alone opposes a polycentrism to Western ethnocentrism. Further yet, free jazz bears traces of toil (improvisation does not give music as *result* but as *production*), effort, traces of the physical, the corporeal: voices, gestures, the very sounds of instruments (whose material, touch, resistance are neither erased nor sublimated but indeed incessantly inscribed in the musical outcome; they mark it), phonics (shouts, grunts, onomatopeia, etc.), "infra-musical" noises (hits, percussions), and finally, inseparable from corporeality, a certain *dirtiness* (in non-academic playing techniques, non-harmonious sounds, amusical, raw, unformed vocals, violence and obscenity in singing and speaking). Note also the complexity and variability of formal structures, which cannot be reduced to a *unit* (of composition, tone, register, genre, etc.—the fantasy of unity in Art does not recognize how it is determined by the dominant ideology—it negates class struggle—or by theology). Note finally excesses that go beyond the *measure* that supposedly proves *mastery* in art (along the same ideological and theological determinations as unity).

Everything that the Western idea of Art censors in the arts lives in free jazz—which should suffice to show that it does not pertain to this civilization or culture, but to their refuse: another civilization and culture—and everything it strove to censor in jazz—returns in free jazz. Everything, including especially *political determination, banned from bourgeois art as "impure."*

But we have seen (Chapter 7) that all forms of black music have been more or less linked in their appearance and development to the political history of black Americans, to their social, economic, and racial situation (not to go as far back as the functionality of African music). For black musicians living and producing in a political situation, and working on an aesthetic practice built in reaction to social and political history (Shepp said in 1965 "we are convinced that the forms of jazz must be developed to coincide with a brand new artistic, social, cultural, and economic context. Some will find it strange that the word jazz would figure by realities as cold and tough as society or the economy; yet we cannot deny that the music's origins and its ulterior developments take root in social structures"[5]), the political place of their music *goes without saying*, though it never fails to clash with bourgeois conceptions of art as marginal, separated from politics, protected from social practice by society. Black Americans see their culture, their art, and their music as produced by, and lived as, moments in the social whole about which they testify, which they help reveal, among whose forces they number. For the dominant ideology in the West, culture, art, and especially music are *a supplement of pleasure.*

Musicians' statements testify to the force of this black conception of music:

If you don't live it, it won't come out of your horn. (Charlie Parker[6])

My music is alive and it's about the living and the dead, about good and evil. It's angry, yet it's real. (Charles Mingus[7])

I think that music is an instrument. It can create the initial thought patterns that can change the thinking of people. (John Coltrane[8])

It's always been a tradition to express their points of view and human, social and political demands in their music and poetry for Afro-American artists such as Huddie Ledbetter, Bessie Smith and Duke Ellington, to cite but a few. Everything from spirituals to Afro-American popular music reflects this without a doubt. That is why our will to use artistic effort as a basis to express human, social and political demands is very natural. (Max Roach[9])

Some of us are more bitter about the way things are going. We are only an extension of that entire civil rights—Black Muslims—black nationalist movement that is taking place in America. That is fundamental to our music. (Archie Shepp[10])

You have to connect people to the realities of life, and this apparently happens through jazz these days. Whether or not they feel aversion to what they hear, it is essential that they have a reaction. (Walt Dickerson[11])

Is music black? I don't believe you can say that it's black, white, green or colorless. What's obvious when I'm playing (if I'm sincere) is that, since I'm black, I play from the so-called black experience. (Bill Dixon[12])

The variety of (more or less radical) political options one can read in these statements reinforces their common concern with associating music to black issues and struggles. Such an attitude can only upset the Western conception of music as necessarily apolitical: histories of European music condescendingly allow a little room for so-called "politically committed" music, a "musical genre" among others, but the "poorest." First, bourgeois critics and aestheticians deem it impossible that music could be produced in circumstances that would not involve "inspiration," "grace," "the mystery of creation," ordinary, daily, collective circumstances ruled by the "sordid" class and race struggles, rather than the "sublime" conflicts of Matter and Spirit, of Form and Freedom.

Yet overall, according to (idealist) bourgeois aesthetics, music and the other arts are "autonomous," as if they were made outside of, and above, social relations, beyond economic, historical and social determinations. Art is the domain of transcendence, a protected zone reserved for the elites, the place where society sublimates itself, far and safe from its realities. Art thus serves in bourgeois societies to both localize and exploit fantasies of purity and perfection (actualizing the transcendental/divine Idea) but also to censor all that idealism condemns in the name of the same notions of purity and perfection: matter, disorder, social contradictions. We find again a string of oppositions; high/low, spirit/matter, art/politics, unity/contradictions, order/chaos, etc.: the bourgeois sanctification of Art is not innocent. In this aesthetic system, music is considered the epitome of art, on top of the hierarchy precisely because it *signifies nothing* (that is to say, it only signifies the absolute of creation, God). Contrary to artistic practices using language (poetry, literature, drama, cinema) and/or figuration (drama, cinema, painting), music exists away from messages, representation, and signification. Its material holds it out of the reach of the sensory issues with which other artistic practices have to engage—which is why they are less "pure"—and thus allegedly out of the historical and the social.

Stravinsky, who remarkably defined music from the most idealistic point of view ("In the pure state, music is free speculation"), deserves to be cited on the relation between music and politics:

> Modern man is progressively losing his understanding of values and his sense of proportions. This failure to understand essential realities is extremely serious. It leads us infallibly to the violation of the fundamental laws of human equilibrium. In the domain of music there is a tendency to . . . degrade music to servile employment and to vulgarize it by adapting it to the requirements of an elementary utilitarianism. . . . Art is not and cannot be "a superstructure based on conditions of production" in accordance with the wishes of the Marxists. Art is an ontological reality.[13]

Here a register and vocabulary symptomatic of idealist aesthetics join together with a denial of history, utter scorn for politics, and antimaterialism. The idea of music as what gives form to "the contrary of chaos," "order as rule and law against disorder,"[14] as the place for the highest spirituality and achievement of the notion of art in bourgeois societies, continues to dominate most musical conceptions and practices. Bourgeois ideology doubles up on the sublime exigencies of aesthetics in imposing on music the most noble task of being "pure entertainment."

It is remarkable that alone among the arts music generates such massive, almost delirious, idealist investment. Other signifying practices have striven—at least in their avant-gardes—to break away from the idealist conceptions that long ruled them, and build materialist theories. Resistance is stronger in music—undoubtedly because it has been laden with more "spirituality" than the other arts, and that it long was a "model" for them. It is also because materialist reflection is behind on the topic of music. Zhdanov's interventions on the subject did nothing to help: his dogmatism, mechanism, the brutal flattening of artistic practice under the political all denote on his part a complete inability to theorize the musical.[15] We do not pretend to intervene theoretically on the question of a materialist approach to musical practice (though urgent, such an intervention is premature precisely because Marxist theory is so behind on the topic). Yet we believe that the study of the free jazz phenomenon in its dual relation to previous forms of jazz and to the historical and social forces that determine it should at least lead to asking questions from a different angle. It should help question if not the way musical material interacts with the socio-historical, at least how it is inserted and factors into the socio-historical, and the fact that it pretends to an activist role beyond that of "pure entertainment."

In order to put in perspective the Western point of view on music, let us quote Cameroonian musicologist Francis Bebey:

> In the West music is considered as a pure art form. . . . Westerners are frequently at a loss to understand the music of black Africa: the concepts of Africans are so totally different. Africans do not seek to combine sounds in a manner pleasing to the ear. Their aim is simply to express life in all of its aspects through the medium of sound. But, whereas Western music is rather an inadequate form of expression, the same can by no means be said of African music. The African musician does not merely attempt to imitate nature by means of musical instruments; he reverses the procedure by taking natural sounds and incorporating them in his music. . . . Thus, music is clearly an integral part of the life of every African individual from the moment of his birth. The musical games played by children are never gratuitous; they are a form of musical training which prepares them to participate in all areas of adult activity—fishing, hunting, farming, grinding maize, attending weddings, funerals, dances, and by necessity, even fleeing rom wild animals. This explains why every conceivable sound has its place in traditional African music, whether in its natural form as it is produced by the object or animal in question, or reproduced by an instrument that imitates them as faithfully as possible.[16]

Free jazz more or less returns to the imitative nature of African music and its evocation of material and bodily sounds, which are considered scandalous in Western conceptions.

But this is not its most scandalous aspect: indeed, jazz's borrowings from exotic cultures are close to being accepted as folk elements. What is not so easily accepted is the social displacement of music, its restitution to functionality, its inscription in the relations of production. This, in our mind, is the point where the free jazz phenomenon is crucial: it puts up front its role in the political struggles of the avant-garde, and offers a practice of activist art where art no longer serves the dominant class. Bourgeois culture, idealist aesthetics, and the dominant ideology have long attempted to repress such a practice of art—and succeeded.

Needless to say, it is not our goal to renew Zhdanov's flattening of art in asserting that since black struggles are now revolutionary struggles, their music is, *ipso facto*, revolutionary too (and here we disagree with Stokely Carmichael: "Revolutionaries? Shit man, the only revolutionaries I've ever seen I met in a jazz cellar"[17]). Neither will the compilation of free jazz's "revolutionary" titles be enough; numerous as they are, there are such things as fashions and markets for revolution. It seems to us that it is the *overall strength* of free jazz's traits that justifies its qualification as militant. Free jazz is characterized by an emphasis on political signalization (in the musicians' statements, the titles of their compositions . . .), but its militant status is especially clear in that the contradictions between varied cultural codes, musical material, and multiple historical traces at work in this music (see Chapter 8) are productive contradictions to the extent that they are truly problematic. They are not simply cosmetic, as is the case, for example, in the many borrowings on which pop music thrives. These contradictions connect to and participate in the contradictions of the cultural, historical, and social in black America.

Free jazz's militancy is also clear on the ideological plane (see Chapter 1): black revolutionary forces work essentially against American capitalism's dominant ideology. Black Americans are a racial minority in white America: they represent 12 percent of the population (roughly twenty-three million people). This minority is divided—it does not constitute a class—though the great majority are either proletarians or unemployed. Yet, though small in number, the black bourgeoisie and petty bourgeoisie carry great influence because they are imbued with dominant ideology and convey it unto the masses. Yet this ideology carries its own contradiction: because of slavery, of segregation ("separate but equal," which in a capitalist system means all are equal in exploitation), social injustice, school and employment inequality, the black masses are more or less clearly convinced of their fatal "inferiority," a feeling reinforced by Christian ideology and the constant effects of racism. Yet constantly faced with harsh economic exploitation, endlessly made aware of their rejection by white society, the black masses live in a state of political struggle and have reached a point where they could massively fall to the side of revolution. Only the dominant ideology prevents them from doing so: we have seen how, in practice, this ideology is so often contradicted that it cannot operate durably. Political activists work on this breaking point. The goal is to make black masses aware of the nature of the painful exploitation they suffer daily. The cultural weapon is one of the means of achieving awareness: to spread black culture, to valorize black compositions, is to shake the foundations of white cultural domination, which is also economic domination. Speaking of knowledge and circulation of the culture of colonized countries, Michel Leiris declared:

> Such studies, showing that those cultures, reputed to be less advanced or cruder than ours, are worthy to be taken seriously and are often, indeed, marked by true greatness, can in fact only help those who are their more or less direct representatives to get rid of the inferiority complex that has been fostered among many by the colonial regime, a complex that induces too many of them to regard as the only "culture" deserving of the name that which they have learned from the Europeans, who constitute a privileged caste in their country.[18]

In a colonial situation, culture is directly determined by politics: culture either belongs to the colonized or to the colonizers. That is to say, if it is not revolutionary, culture is automatically at the service of dominant ideology and capitalism. There is no middle term; an Africanist culturalism that does not reject capitalism helps perpetuate it, and thus feeds the dominant ideology. There is no room for "autonomy" in the cultural sphere, nor for floating artistic practices: if art is not committed to serve the black masses, it serves the exploiters. The very harshness of social relations and the brutality of class struggle doubled by racism both contribute to radicalize the fields they determine, and forbid transitions. Black culture can only be either revolutionary or an accomplice: it is either rooted in the history of black Americans which the great majority of black artistic production takes into account,[19] or it diminishes the importance of black history, *excludes* itself from it, integrates into the master's history, by conforming to the system of repression and defense of American society. There is no third way, no point of synthesis between these two cultures, these two histories, because they are in a state of violent, antagonistic contradiction: every event in the dominant history produces an event in the other history, a kind of negative or refuse.

Black studies,[20] but also the work of political activists (from Garveyites and Black Muslims to black nationalists and Black Panthers in black universities and in the ghettoes) perform the huge task of exhuming black history and building a culture whose specificity is twofold: it has long been restrained, negated, hijacked, and masked; it has nevertheless begun to resist these assaults. The dominant ideology did not swallow or assimilate the dominated culture. The process of synthetic resolution of differences has stopped, and syncretism has proved a failure, for a variety of reasons. White society profoundly rejected blacks—it also attracted them, pushed them to servile imitation, enacting a double exclusion. Simultaneously, white society took what it wanted in black forms of expression, especially in music,[21] culturally pillaged them and profited from them in the same way it profited from the economic exploitation of the black masses: a double spoliation, rejection through scorn. Afro-American culture built along such rejections: it is the product of resistance to a system of interconnected, endlessly repeating aggressions; it is what *remains* of it, what remains to be taken and/or destroyed.

Free jazz has chosen its side: culturally, it testifies to black situation and struggles, and reacts against the hijacking of black music by white interests.

The effort of most historians and critics in keeping discussions on jazz and free jazz on the aesthetic plane is not innocent. Building Afro-American music as a sequence autonomous from the social whole, not taking into account its connection to other fields, valorizing it as "art," amounts to censoring its production process, its historical, social, and economic determinations, its conditions of production and existence, its economic dependence. Debates on style and form have modestly covered the economic and the political, *where the struggles of black Americans and the very possibility of their music are decided.* And such was indeed their function: by emphasizing aesthetics, by pointing exclusively at the stylistic, "purely musical" aspects of Afro-American music in order to valorize or devalorize them, those debates promote ideological interferences meant to deny the music its revolutionary character—not at the formal level, where all "revolutions" are accepted, if not required, but in social practice, and in relation to the place of the "artist" and of his productions in society. It is by changing the *very conditions* of artistic production that forms will be most radically changed. No doubt some would like to keep this hidden as long as possible.

Preface to the 1979 Edition

To the Soledad and Attica brothers
To Jonathan and George Jackson

Free jazz today is more marginalized than it has been in the past fifteen years;[1] clearly, it is still disturbing. The living and necessary force with which it breaks away from the commercial and cultural banalization of music is now more dominant than ever.

Free jazz, inasmuch as it had ever sneaked into the media, the big record company catalogues and institutional concerts, has now been thrown out of them. It is now barely tolerated on cultural radio stations; it has many times been declared dead and buried by so many docile critics eager to please. It has found refuge or been quarantined in peripheral festivals, clubs, and concerts; but *free jazz* resists.

Because under this name, or others, or under no name whatsoever, free jazz is the music that from their places of exile, of wandering and poverty, many young musicians get together to play, produce, and broadcast, whether they be black, white, American, or, increasingly, European, in spite of everything. It plays with and within contemporary musical creations related to the Western cultural network and therefore far from jazz traditions.[2] Yet the crucial aspect of the resistance embodied by free jazz lies in that today it is still played *in its full meaning*: as a music that refuses, that disobeys, that divides; a music that fights.

This sense remains in spite of the ideological variations and political avatars in the recent history of black struggles in the United States:[3] we emphasized that free jazz never could be reduced to a simple *musical representation* of these struggles, although it is intimately linked to them as a historically determined moment in Afro-American music. It was an effect of the struggles rather than a reflection; better yet, it was what was manifested of them and through them in the symbolic field. Free jazz was saying, and still is saying, that music is the stake of struggles and that there is no such thing as innocent aesthetics. Now that the Black Power of the 1960s is but the ghost of a reality, an exhibit in the political slogans museum, free jazz such as it is played is to be valued even more than before as the demand, the assertion, the radicalization of an ideological involvement in *music*.

No music is socially inactive, ideologically meaningless, or without effect on the cultural formatting of behaviors. Suffice it to observe the mass scale on which, above fashion and fads, dominant types of music nowadays tend to be unified by the media into a new musical order (from taxi-specific music on French radio stations to the neutrality of disco). Observe how, once it is advertised, normalized, automatized (who plays for whom? Who sings, who performs?) this mono-music trains bodies to listen indifferently, locks them into programs of more and more uniform rhythms and dances.

It is this social dream of regulation through music—among other things—that free jazz—among other turbulences—comes to disturb, if only in that it accomplishes, amplifies, and sometimes exacerbates the other image of the body—unchained, unpredictable, and rebellious—that jazz has always implied and put forward.

Media appropriation and management of music in our societies lead to the selection of dominant musical forms designed not to contradict each other, and tending—because this is how the media works—to a form of hegemony that should not only be thought of in quantitative terms, but also in qualitative terms: indeed, it monopolizes musical space, but it also levels differences through a syncretism of musical *brands*, censors the differentiated histories of musics and of their symbolic incidences.

In a world where the dogma of quietness and the love of security are being inculcated everywhere, the superb obstinacy of today's musicians in refusing to box their music in the frames of this disciplinary commercial order, in positing musical intertextuality in terms of contradictions and breaks rather than mixes and overlaps, in not wanting sound or social hygiene—each would be enough to render all free musics somewhat *unbearable*. As for us, we see urgency and necessity in these musics. And if to that which aspires to an eternal balance of tensions, anything that moves, be it beauty, is always violence? Too bad.

Preface to the 2000 Edition

Free Jazz, Off Program, Off Topic, Off Screen

What is in the love for jazz?
Beauty, emotion, nostalgia, excitement, youth, revolt; all of that, without a doubt.
But first, a taste for new paths.
A vivid desire for the unheard-of.
Not necessarily for new music, or new musical forms,
But for music constantly renewed.
Music that, even after you listen to it for the thousandth time, can still convince you that it's coming for the first time.
And that it could still be completely different.
And that if it isn't different, if it is
as it should be and how it will always be,
it owes it to the nameless beauties of chance.

If something's at stake in the life of jazz these days, this is it.
What does it mean to produce something new in music?
Something new in the world?
New forms, new beauties, new emotions. Always, already, already, the world has always already been used, will always have been used. And always it gives itself to us as a renewal. Improvisation is a form of faith. Faith in the first time; faith that there will always be a first time; faith that the first time can never be the last time. So much for the Gospels. All words have always-already tried to possess the world, and the world, from crisis to epiphany, dispossesses words of their power to imprison it, and in the process gives words back to poetry, this other power that charms and enchants, this power that awakes words ands gives us the dizzying feeling that those words had not quite appeared to us, had not quite been uttered. The same power of beginnings is at work in the improvisation that takes hold of the poet's and the comedian's words, in the dancer's and the musician's bodies. And musical forms get old, faster yet than words. Music is the abyss of fascination for the same, the drunkenness of the ever same note, of the minute change, the infinite repetition, the cycle, the rumination. Great is the undulatory temptation of music. To enter the circle of vibrations, to adjust to it. Return, repetition, variation: is there in all musical

constructions just an always-there that has to be rearranged in novel ways, or, quite the opposite, circulated (almost) identically until ecstasy, until ecstatic saturation? Repetition is a prayer, and music always threatens to topple to the side of religion. A world lulled by litanies is not a world of rupture; new beginnings there seem identical to each other, generations there only reproduce; history is lacking. Improvisation musics, while they have not renounced repetitive voluptuousness, have not limited themselves to it; they have vowed to accomplish in their own way the haunting fate that might be that of all music, by breaking the circle, rupturing the cycle: such music rejuvenates the world to all of our senses—not only to our ears.

It posits the world as change, change as history, the music of change as a music inscribed in human reality. Improvised musics rejuvenate themselves by surprising us, in appearing as one of the possible worlds in the making. They make the bet that it is not all over, that the game is not up; they make a bet on a bet.

One possible figure for the canvas slowly being woven: a tear in the fabric.

Musics today are spread and multiply more than ever. Automatized, they invade space and time. They act as the devoted auxiliaries of strip malls, fairs, commercial districts. Telephonic automatization is performed through bribes of music. Repetition.

Radio jingles accompany the inaudible noise of bombs in the night.

Automated music invades all.

Music that once may have been written by a desire called X or Y, Mozart or Beethoven, is nowadays desired by none of those who hear it on the phone, on the street, in bars, in the toilets of fancy hotels, anywhere at any time. Could this be about killing music with something else we still call music?

The jazz of eternal urgency is that which is invented day by day, not the kind played in loops in automatic music dispensers. Not all music, not all jazz can thus be formatted into loops. Some musics are too fragile, and threaten to break. Some are too strong, and threaten to break.

This jazz,
close to breaking,
implies that at some point in the work of music the musician and the listener gain the acute awareness that all of this could end abruptly,
from one moment to the next,
that the void,
the silence,
death are all a breath or a note away.
It could end.

That threat.
Which is no longer a game, but the end of play.
(unlike muzak, which only ends when the stores close.)

That it can end means that it's fragile,
that it only holds by a thread
between music and us,
a thread pulled so taut it could break.
We call this improvisation.
Because only in that case is it possible that the thread really break.
The threat is not formal, it is real. The game could end or change all of a sudden.
This break is all the more possible that it is not programmed.
Breath can be held, the note could be the last, or not.
It could end and it could start over, who knows. It is a matter of circumstances.
When circumstances are right, and especially when they conspire to scramble human messages, that moment can be called, possibly, the irruption of the real.

So-called free jazz is about experiencing the fragility of musical forms.
Births and deaths, jumps and falls, apparitions/disappearances, evanescences, uncaught.
We can never feel ourselves listening more than with these forms, themselves in danger, destabilized, disturbed, poked through, fragile, feeble,
And beautiful in their very weakness.
The essential fragility of musical form is present in jazz more than anywhere else.
Jazz as a music struggling with and against the wind in the fields and the noise of cities,
against machines and with them,
with and against inner silences,
bodily silences,
gut fear,
lust for life . . .
For us, this essential fragility is tied to improvised forms.
In musical improvisation such as jazz and free jazz have accomplished in this century, one encounters the strength of abandon.
Let's speak of free jazz.
The word that comes is abandon.
One could say, to give oneself to abandon.

Abandon
what submits us
to programs
Through which social domination is exercised...

Abandon programs
that think for us...
Abandon programmed
Languages...

Abandoning the score is not
renouncing to write but instead giving oneself
to a form of writing tied to chance.
The chance of real journeys.

To abandon is to put in abeyance the possibility to name and formulate. In other words,
to enter an abeyance of articulated language, an abeyance of reasoning, of causal chains, an abeyance not so much of the production of meaning but rather of the semantic mechanisms of meaning production, a momentary liberation from the law of language to which we, musicians or listeners, and even deaf and mute, all answer. In raising the curtain of words improvisation becomes a gesture, an act not yet said, a form not yet named, normed, honored. To abandon oneself to improvisation
first in order to free oneself from the musical narratives of the world which, however beautiful they might be, are already there, already beautiful, already world. To undo, O Penelope, the musical bandages that form the cocoon of sound around us that is not the world, but the ritualistic custom of a customary world.

Abandoned, improvisation gives itself to what floats around meaning,
around words,
around codifications,
it gives itself to intensity, to restraint, to momentum, to energy,
to the hardly nameable, in short
through which musical production
ties itself at every moment to the path of desire
simply because it is threatened with desire.
The desire that finds it could doom it.

Preface to the 2000 Edition

This question of improvisation . . .
This improvised jazz . . .
This free jazz . . .
Open to chance, to accident, to the unexpected, to encounters, to shock, to fear, to crisis.
Especially today, this is the place from which
music that escapes the program can still be produced.

In a world of finely honed scenarios, minutely calculated programs, spotless scores, well-placed options and actions, what blocks, what lingers, what stumbles and limps?
Limping indicates bodies,
body.
Limping points to a man with a fragile heel.
A god was holding him there. He was God by his heel. Gods limp when they are not hunchbacks.
Deregulation is of the body. What limps, what hurts, what doesn't hold straight, shortness of breath and the miracle of balance. Neither man nor music ever stand up straight. Bodies are not yet well regulated by the law of commodities.
It does not work. It suffers. It wears out. It makes mistakes. It escapes.
Too hot, too cold, too close, too far, too fast, too slow.
And in spite of it all it wants to hold on, it tries again, a little more, just a little more.
Here's what makes improvisation play.
The path in abeyance, distance in abeyance, excess itself in abeyance.
The place of the listener in improvised music is that of a body echoing the body played and at play in this music.
The play of the body in improvised music,
is precisely to play with
and against what the body permits and forbids,
but especially with
what it times with the beat of its own breathing.
Breathing,
what is awakened and falls asleep inside of us.
The acute sensation and the vague sensation, passing from one mental speed to another, from one mental duration to another.
Music plays with all this, and this also is the body.
Synthetic music does not breathe like the non-synthetic body. We live in an age of synthetic music and synthetic images. No synthetic bodies just yet. But

already ideas, feelings, but already voices and gestures, organs, flows are often fabricated synthetically, and it does not surprise us. Little by little, piece by piece, the perfectly designed body replaces the body with weight and the frightening flesh. Plastic is lighter, cleaner. Prostheses are optimistic. And the work of musicians, in jazz and outside of jazz, boils down to giving flesh to the tailor-made, precision-made instrument, to weigh it with a body, with shit, with sweat, all of which had not been factored in by the provider.

The music instrument is the opposite of the prosthesis. It is there for things to get worse. There is no purity without misery. The sound of the world is like the battle of the body in the world against the world without body.

Jazz is what still escapes,

What struggles against the synthetic, i.e. the calculating and programming thought, against the reduction of the world to a collection of calculated scenarios.

Unframed music. Music that spills out of the frame. There are all sorts of frames: capital, the market, the public, labels, contracts, agents, reviews, dictionaries, words, rules, scripts, plans, studies, no shortage of them. What is lacking is what does not bend. It is out of the frame because it will not fit.

Indiscipline of the body, indiscipline at the horizon of the greatest musical discipline.

The indisciplined body is within history because it bears history's marks,

visible and invisible,

inside and outside,

bodily and mental marks,

wear is historical, fatigue, excess are historical.

The perpetual improvisation of the body in its clumsy errand is historical.

In improvisation, the erratic body encounters musical discipline pushed to the limit, pushed out of its frame, off screen, given back to the encounter, given back to errand. Two limps meet.

Funny scene.

Free jazz is funny.

To spread noise,

to shake off,

to shake off the weight of jazz for it is not accumulated music but history, to shake history, the history of jazz, the history of the *Blues people*, the history of America struggling against itself, the weight of the ghosts of yesteryear, the weight of ghosts of slaves coming back at night to dance in our heads, the weight of bodies dancing with the ghosts' chains, free jazz shaking the chains of the black body who is in white history, invisible, off screen.

When we first published this book,
it was in 1971,
Blacks were Panthers,
the Ibarra family was celebrating Susie's first birthday and nobody could guess that she would play the drums alongside David S. Ware,
Malcolm had been assassinated and
his prophet was not quite born,
Julius Hemphill was forming his first band in St Louis
and Joe McPhee had already recorded his *Nation Time*,
with Clifford Thornton,
Spike Lee was in school and the iron curtain was drawn,
Ken Vandermark, then seven years old,
was not yet blowing into a saxophone,
LeRoi Jones was already called Amiri Baraka,
the Workshop de Lyon was still called Free Jazz Workshop,
George Jackson had been assassinated in jail and Mumia Abu Jamal was not yet
on death row,
here's for what hasn't changed, here's for what has changed.

Programming was advancing slowly,
the scenarios of the great surveillance of bodies,
the great alignment of minds,
were all but science fiction fantasies.

Fiction has become what it is now, and so has science. Frontal struggles have become fractal. Resistance, more than ever, is about crumbs. About slipping through the dragnet. Black Power has disseminated, and so has free jazz. Self-dissolution of the struggle fronts, whose fragments come back through a thousand resurgences. We have told a history of jazz that always slips through the dragnet of the present. The struggle of black Americans has not magically been erased; it has gone off screen, between the visible and the invisible, in the limbo of the consciences repressed by the media. Free jazz has not disappeared either; it has gone off stage. That lasted a few years. Silence without conscience. And then a renaissance. The return of the black question; counting black Americans dying slowly, or fast, in American prisons. The return of the free jazz question, listening to musicians of today who play freely and make it known. The return of the rebel voice, return of the rebel body. Neither one nor the other had ever disciplined themselves; return of the repressed.

This is where generalized programs
break their teeth.
On pieces of world,
on pieces of people
who do not want those programs.

No scenario, not even a commercial one
nor a military one or a disciplinary one
will prevent the human body to exit the frame
of laws to err in the real.
Improvisation is reality trumping body control,
i.e., the old fantasy of almightiness of the powers that be,
no matter what they are,
that only want human bodies to form masses,
publics, audiences, subscribers, sections, targets.
Audience is not the listener. It is not a collection of listeners.
To listen, to play, is to never cease being alone with others,
Other with oneself.

In 1971, we remember, the calibration of the man-consumer was not yet as advanced as it has become; neither was the calibration of jazz-consumption. This calibration has progressed. It has become lovable. We're not talking about desire: alienation works on love. There is in older and more recent free jazz a protest against jazz's alienated love. This is what hurt yesterday and hurts today. A jazz that loves music enough not to love what was once called jazz. The listener, the music lover, the fan all thrown into a divorce. We used to love and we still love that the beloved music is preserved, protected, sheltered, mothered, motherly, reassuring and lulling. Free jazz tears up the layette that comforts any listener in his love. To abandon the cherished object, the guaranteed insurance, established and recognized references, to abandon oneself to a music that goes beyond the state of "pleasure" and is not scared to open the door to self-assessment in an unpossessed alterity, ravishment, rapture. Who knows what loss the change might bring? What is there to lose? Possibly the frame that imprisons us.

This era more than any other has manufactured scenes and spectacles. Including for free jazz. Thirty years after the explosion, the fallout is here. Today

there is a free jazz scene. Something like a containment, a squaring off, has been put in place—often very well—to welcome excesses and improvisations more expected than ever.
Expectation dominates.
Expectation is a scenario.
Suspend expected expectation.
We expect a spilling off.
We pay for it, labels make up catalogues of unexpected jazz and magazines look out for the passage of the unforeseen; another way to say that in the great cultural store, free jazz also has found its section, that there is a commerce of refusal that very often trumps the refusal of commerce.
Cultural commerce's capacity for recuperation is infinite (we used to speak of recuperation as a threat: it has now become fate, if not a style).
But it does not stop it from being, first and foremost, the symptom of what is lacking to forbid recuperation: fear.
Fear, the companion of revolutions.
When black Americans are fearsome, commerce slows down.
Original free jazz, as this book will tell you, was a full-fledged actor in the struggle of black Americans for political rights and survival.
Music linked to political thought and action. The encounter of creative power and political consciousness. It happens every once in a while, though not so often. This encounter happens, it will always happen as a possibility, actualized.

Black or white, the imperfect man of free jazz advances into fear. Commerce is there to invoke fear. And maybe already there is no commerce but cultural commerce, trading frames for more frames?
Fear is the loss, the abandon, that which comes in spite of cultural commerce and sneaks into it like the evil whose end it keeps telling, in vain.

Let's call this ill love an "accident."
Improvisation links fear and accident,
fear as an inscription of the almightiness of the accident,
fear for all that is not planned, prepared, written down, expected, wanted,
And yet happens, surges.
Fear as the act of recording the spontaneous.

Accident: it is the part of the world that remains outside of calculation that instills fear.
What in reality has not yet been through representation,

through narratives, scenarios, market studies,
what has not yet completely folded to the orders of languages.
What we do not know,
what we do not understand,
what we do not want,
but still is there,
what comes, comes back, insists.
For example, you need a chord but your fingers slip,
open your eyes; a shadow passes,
fill your lungs with air: a burst of laughter,
you can manufacture wind with an electric fan but you cannot stop the wind
from blowing where it will.
Breath: here's something that cannot be completely controlled.
It can be lost, it can be short.

In the accident that threatens every constituted scene,
break-in, fear, risk of interruption, end of the show,
fear that the shadow might go.
And so the scene breaks,
the game ceases.

Yet, it is a fear of the opposite accident as well.
That the accident become promise might open the stage to slip onto it,
to take part.
Improvisation welcomes the threat and goes beyond it,
takes it away from itself, records it, power and threat.

Let's say that musical improvisations are but the sum of accidents tied to the
journeys of one or several bodies in real spaces and durations;
Music's body, its physicality.

In the specter of the audible
free jazz condenses all the invisibility of lives that are here and no longer here,
strata of buried experiences,
known and unknown, thought and unthought,
mechanical music and chaotic music.
Promise and threat that there will be
bodies in play and
with these bodies a whole
uncontrollable group of forces,

marks, cuts, retreats, traces, erasures, wounds,
all that is hardly describable and even less calculable,
an ensemble exceeding any possibility of a scenario.
The opposite of the triumph of the will and the powers of calculation: residual savagery of bodies, playing and played. Absent-present bodies are the reality of that music, life-carriers taken in histories and disturbing them.

Nowadays, the most synthetic, "techno" music programs can of course simulate real effects, errors, body effects, wrong notes and slips, why not.
But they cannot suffer from them.
The defects, the marks of reality they have imagined
and integrated in their lines of numbers
can never stop them from functioning,
from accomplishing themselves, from going
According to plan.
Chance can be simulated,
but bugs have to be eliminated.
The program that wants to imitate the real can reproduce its imperfections but these can never threaten the integrity and good functioning of the program.
We can hear synthetic music,
and why not synthetic jazz,
capable of reproducing perfectly mouth noises, beats on wood, on metal, blows, the bellows of a breath, why not, all the vibrations of a body or an instrument,
but never do those "impurities"
that are so important as real effects in the act of recomposition
come to compromise at any level the musical discourse.
Utterance without uttering
music without bodies
body effects but body without effect.
It seems to us that what has been called free jazz
constantly opposes the idea of a music that would go without crisis, without threatening its own journey, without strewing land mines on its own stage.
Clearly improvisation opposes the program; but today, it has become a war machine against the domination of programs.
In jazz, this war machine calls for the implication of the body into music, not as an extra rhetorical register, but as part of the real that won't let itself be completely reduced or canceled.
The body as what embarrasses and confuses,
what sticks out and needs to be transcended.

Improvisation is
what connects music to the accident
that is to be lived.

—Philippe Carles, Jean-Louis Comolli (2000)

Notes

Preface... And in 2014

1. Arthur Rimbaud, "Democracy," *Illuminations*, Trans. Louise Varèse (New York: New Directions, 1946).
2. In his preface to René Leibowitz, *L'Artiste et sa conscience: esquisse d'une dialectique de la conscience artistique* (Paris: L'Arche, 1950), Jean-Paul Sartre voices his doubt that music can be used for committed art, judging it "a non-signifying art . . . a beautiful mute with eyes full of meaning."
3. After Andrei Zhdanov, Russian politician in charge of cultural affairs under Joseph Stalin's dictatorship. He gave his name to the Soviet doctrine according to which, all art being a product of class struggle, it could therefore be divided bourgeois and socialist art.
4. See Pierre Bourdieu, *The Field of Cultural Production*, Randal Johnson ed. (New York: Columbia University Press, 1993).

Free Jazz/Black Power: An Introduction

1. Amiri Baraka [LeRoi Jones], "The Jazz Avant-Garde," *Black Music* (1968: New York: Da Capo Press, 1998), 69.
2. Alain Locke, "Art or Propaganda?" *Harlem* 1.1 (November 1928), 12.
3. W. E. B. Du Bois, "Criteria of Negro Art," *The Crisis* 32 (October 1926), 296.
4. Leroi Jones (Amiri Baraka), "The Myth of a 'Negro Literature,'" *The Saturday Review* (April 20, 1963), 20.
5. Ralph Ellison, "The Blues: Review of *Blues People*, by Leroi Jones," *The New York Times Review of Books* (6 February 1964), reprinted as "Blues People" in *Shadow and Act* (New York: Random House, 1964), 257.
6. See Gayatri Spivak's notion of "strategic essentialism" in "Subaltern Studies: Deconstructing Historiography," *In Other Worlds: Essays in Cultural Politics* (1987: New York; Routledge, 1998): 270–304.
7. See Eric Drott, "Free Jazz and the French Critic," *Journal of the American Musicological Society*, 61.3 (2008), 560–61.
8. Isabelle Leymarie, "Review of *Free Jazz/Black Power*," *Ethnomusicology* 18.1 (1974), 152.
9. Lehman, Stephen. "I Love You with an Asterisk: African-American Experimental Music and the French Jazz Press, 1970–1980." *Critical Studies in Improvisation/ Etudes critiques en improvisation* [Online] 1.2 (2005), 38.
10. Ibid., 47.
11. "Cette interprétation téléologique de sa musique fit du saxophoniste un avatar

de l'essence « prolétaire / musicien afro-américain » forgé par le système capitaliste." Jedediah Sklower, "*Rebel with the wrong cause*: Albert Ayler et la signification du jazz en France (1959– 1971)," *Volume!* 6.1–2 (2009), 208.

12. Eric Drott, "Free Jazz and the French Critic," 570.

13. Ibid., 571.

14. Frantz Fanon, *The Wretched of the Earth*, trans. Constance Farrington (Grove Press, 1963), 42.

15. LeRoi Jones (Amiri Baraka), "Black Art," *Black Fire: An Anthology of Afro-American Writers* (1968; Baltimore: Black Classic Press, 2007), 302.

16. George Lewis, "The AACM in Paris," *Black Renaissance* 5:3 (Spring 2004), 115.

17. Ibid., 116.

18. Mike Heffley, *Northern Sun, Southern Moon: Europe's Reinvention of Jazz* (Cambridge: Yale University Press, 2005), 209.

19. George Lewis, "Review of *Northern Sun, Southern Moon: Europe's Reinvention of Jazz* by Mike Heffley," *Current Musicology* 78 (Fall 2004), 80.

Epigraph

1. Georges Bataille, "Blackbirds," about the Negro Revue Lew Leslie's Blackbirds, at the Moulin Rouge, June–September 1929, in *Encyclopaedia Acephalica* (London: Atlas Press, 1995), Iain White trans., 36–37.

Introduction (1971)

1. LeRoi Jones (Amiri Baraka), *Blues People* (New York: Apollo, 1963).

2. Among them Jean Wagner (*Jazz Magazine*), Lucien Malson (*Cahiers du jazz, Le Monde*, ORTF), Yves Buin, Michel Le Bris, Bruno Vincent, Daniel Caux, Daniel Berger and Alain Corneau, Guy Kopelowicz (in the *Jazz Hot* team from 1966 to 1969). See also the following articles by Jean-Louis Comolli from *Jazz Magazine*: "Voyage au bout de la New Thing," *Jazz Magazine* 129 (April 1966): 24–29; "Les conquérants d'un nouveau monde," *Jazz Magazine* 131 (June 1966): 30–35; "Loin de Gunther Schuller, près de LeRoi Jones," *Jazz Magazine* 163 (February 1969): 47; by Philippe Carles and Jean-Louis Comolli: "Les secrets d'Albert le Grand," *Jazz Magazine* 142 (May 1967): 34–46; by Philippe Carles: "Champ et contrechamp sur (Paul) Bley," *Jazz Magazine* 141 (April 1967): 40–44; "Archie méconnu" *Jazz Magazine* 119 (June 1965): 50; "L'Opéra comique de Sun Ra," *Jazz Magazine* 159 (October 1968): 26–44.

3. Quoted in Ian Young, "Les Panthères Noires et la langue du ghetto," *Esprit* 396 (October 1970), 557. [Translator's note: this is a variation on Fred Hampton's famous phrase: "Political power does not flow from the sleeve of a dashiki."]

1. Jazz Today

1. Quoted in A. B. Spellman, *Four Lives in the Bebop Business* (New York: Pantheon Books, 1966), 150.

2. In "Shepp le rebelle," interview by Jean-Louis Noames, *Jazz Magazine* 125 (December 1965), 80.

3. Malcolm X, "After the Bombing," in *Malcolm X Speaks*, ed. George Breitman (New York: Merit Publishers, 1965), 175. [Translator's note: Carles and Comolli use the broad term "Black Muslim," though they are in fact specifically referring to the group called the Nation of Islam. It was founded by Wallace D. Fard Muhammad in 1930, and Elijah Muhammad assumed its leadership in 1934.]

4. The use of "man" to designate *the white man* originates in 1930s drug dealers' slang (Malcolm X was a drug dealer before he encountered Elijah Muhammad, as he discusses in *The Autobiography of Malcolm X*, New York: Grove Press, 1965). It then designated the Narcotics Bureau and, by extension, the federal government. For black cultural nationalists, as for Malcolm X, it means *the white man*. A famous slogan by Huey Newton (minister of defense for the Black Panther Party) says: "The spirit of the people is greater than the Man's technology." On the terminology of black militants in the United States, read Ian Young, "Les Panthères Noires."

5. Malcolm X, *The Autobiography of Malcolm X*, 171

6. Archie Shepp, "An Artist Speaks Bluntly," *Downbeat* (December 16, 1965), 11.

7. Malcolm X and Alex Haley, *The Autobiography of Malcolm X* (New York: Grove Press, 1965), 182.

8. H. Rap Brown, *Die Nigger Die!* (New York: Dial Press, 1969), 62–68.

9. Malcolm X, "The Black Revolution," *Malcolm X Speaks*, 51–2.

10. H. Rap Brown, *Die Nigger Die!* 104.

11. Ibid., 124–1245.

12. George Murray and Joudon M. Ford, "Black Panthers: The Afro-Americans' Challenge," *Tricontinental* 10 (January–February 1969), 108.

13. Quoted in Frank Kofsky, *Black Nationalism and the Revolution in Music* (New York: Pathfinder Press, 1970), 63.

14. H. Rap Brown, *Die Nigger Die!* 86.

15. In Jean Clouzet, Guy Kopelowicz, "Un inconfortable après-midi," *Jazz Magazine* 107 (June 1964), 32.

16. Michel Le Bris, Bruno Vincent, and Jean Frenay, "Marion Brown: l'Afrique a vaincu," *Jazz Hot* 235 (October 1967), 19.

17. Ornette Coleman, "'Round the Empty Foxhole," *Down Beat* 34 (2 November 1967), 16.

18. Philippe Carles, "Le don paisible," *Jazz Magazine* 119 (June 1965), 28.

19. Philippe Carles, "Qui es-tu Robin Kenyatta? Un saxophoniste qui rêve de découvrir l'Afrique," *Jazz Magazine* 172 (November 1969), 38.

20. Philippe Carles, "Archie méconnu," *Jazz Magazine* 119 (June 1965), 55.

21. "John Coltrane: 1926–1967," *Jazz Magazine* 145 (August 1967), 22.

22. Quoted in Ted Joans, "Black Power et New Thing," *Jazz Magazine* 150 (January 1968), 19.

23. Malcolm X, Speech at the Founding Rally of the Organization of Afro-American Unity, June 28, 1964.

2. Economic Ownership of Jazz

1. White musicians in blackface who mimicked the behavior and music of slaves for the entertainment of settlers and city dwellers. To the injury of economic exploitation of black labor, to cultural and racial depression, was added the insult of derision: the Negro becomes the target of entertainment and ridicule. White condescension in turn becomes proof of white superiority, and an easy way for slave masters to attain self-satisfaction.

2. In Charles Delaunay, Robert Aubert, and Kurt Mohr, "En bavardant avec Lucky Thompson," *Jazz Hot* 109 (April 1956), 9.

3. From the liner notes of *Black and Beautiful Soul and Madness: LeRoi Jones and the Jihad Singers*, Jihad 1001, Jihad Productions, Newark, 1968.

4. Harold Cruse, "Rebellion or Revolution? (Part One)," *The Liberator* (October 1963).

5. *Melody Maker*. [Translator's note: the original text dates the quote to a January issue of the *Melody Maker*. No issue that month or even that year featured Taylor, and I was unable to find the relevant source. The quote above is therefore my translation.]

6. This Afro-American musician was advertised as "the new Parker."

7. In A. B. Spellman, *Four Lives in the Bebop Business*, 94.

8. The AACM's aim according to Joseph Jarman was to "cultivate young musicians, and to create music of a high artistic level for the general public through the presentation of a program designed to magnify the importance of Creative Music; to create an atmosphere conducive to artistic endeavors for the artistically inclined by maintaining a workshop for the expressed purpose of bringing talented musicians together; to provide sources of employment for worthy creative musicians; to set an example of high moral standards for musicians and to uplift the public image of Creative Musicians; to increase mutual respect between Creative Artists and musical tradesmen (i.e., booking agents, managers); to uphold the tradition of elevated, cultured Musicians handed down from the past; to stimulate Spiritual growth in Creative artists through participation in programs, concerts and recitals." See liner notes to Joseph Jarman, *As if it were the Seasons* (Delmark Records DS-417, Chicago, 1968).

9. The Jazz Composers Guild is a proto-union created in New York in 1964 by Bill Dixon that counts as members Paul and Carla Bley, Burton Greene, Mike Mantler, Roswell Rudd, Archie Shepp, Sun Ra, Cecil Taylor and Jon Tchicai. Its original goal was to stop economic abuses against free jazzmen by cutting middlemen, agents and others. See "Quelques hommes en colère," *Jazz Magazine* 120 (July 1965), 16.

10. In Guy Kopelowicz, "Autumn in New York," *Jazz Hot* 214 (November 1965), 31.

11. In A. B. Spellman, *Four Lives in the Bebop Business*, 130–131.

3. Cultural Colonization

1. See "Vingt-six jazzmen nouveaux à la question", *Jazz Magazine* 125, (December 1965) 67.

2. Eric J. Hobsbawm, *The Jazz Scene* (New York: Monthly Review Press, 1960), 214.

3. Don L. Lee, "Introduction," in H. Rap Brown, *Die Nigger Die!*

4. Malcolm X, *Autobiography*, 265.

5. LeRoi Jones, *Jazz and the White critic*, *Black Music* (Cambridge, MA: Da Capo Press 1998), 11–12.

6. John O'Neal, "Motion in the Ocean," *Black Theater, Drama Review* 12.4 (1968), 73.

7. Symphony conductor Pietro Mascagni, quoted in André Coeuroy, *Histoire générale du jazz, strette, hot, swing* (Paris: Denoël, 1942), 7.

8. André Suarès, quoted in Coeuroy, *Histoire générale*, 22.

9. For example, critics soon focused on the *subject* of the musician, thus ignoring issues of social extraction and the historical determination of the subject's very existence, ignoring as well as the relativity of the notion of subject in non-Western ideological and cultural structures.

10. Our emphasis.

11. Our emphasis.

12. André Coeuroy, *Histoire générale*, 71–72.

13. Our emphasis.

14. Ibid., 75.

15. Jones is here targeting Hugues Panassié.

16. LeRoi Jones, "Jazz and the White Critic," in *Black Music* (1968; New York: Da Capo Press, 1998), 18.

17. LeRoi Jones, "The Last Days of the American Empire (Including Some Instructions for Black People," *Home: Social Essays* (New York: William Morrow and Co., 1966), 194.

18. LeRoi Jones, "Jazz and the White Critic," 12.

19. Panassié would come to fancy himself as the "pope of jazz."

20. Quoted in LeRoi Jones, *Blues People (Negro Music in White America)* (New York, William Morrow and Co., 1963), 235.

21. See Hugues Panassié's *La bataille du jazz* (Paris: Albin Michel, 1965); André Hodeir, *La religion du jazz (Hommes et problèmes du jazz)* (Paris: Flammarion, 1954), 315; Boris Vian, "Un certain Panassié," *Chroniques de jazz*, Lucien Malson ed. (Paris: la Jeune Parque, 1967): 155.

4. The Blind Task of Criticism

1. LeRoi Jones, *Blues People*, 8–9.

5. What the Blues Say

1. *Bessie Smith* (London: Cassell, 1959); *The Blues Fell this Morning* (London: Cassell, 1960); *Conversation with the Blues* (London: Cassell, 1965); *Screening the Blues: Aspects of the Blues Tradition* (London: Cassell, 1968); *The Story of the Blues* (London: Barrie & Jenkins, 1969).
2. Spellman, *Four Lives in the Bebop Business*; articles in *Down Beat*, *The Nation*, *Evergeen Review*.
3. Articles in *Down Beat* ("Don Cherry: Makin' in the Hard Way," *Down Beat* 30.30 (November 1963): 16–18; "Apple Cores," *Down Beat* 31.30 (November 1964): 21–40; *Down Beat* 32.40; 7 (March 1965): 34; *Down Beat* 33.17 (August 1966): 13. "Voice of the Avant-Garde: Archie Shepp," *Down Beat* 32.1 (January 1965): 18–36; "New Voices in Newark," *Down Beat* 33.5 (February 1966): 13), some of which were collected in *Black Music*; articles in *Jazz* ("Sonny Rollins: Our Man in Jazz," *Jazz*, April–May 1963: 18; "Archie Shepp Live," *Jazz*, January 1965: 8) and *Blues People*.

Poetry: *Preface to a Twenty-Volume Suicide Note* (New York: Totem Press, 1961); *The Dead Lecturer* (New York: Grove Press, 1964).

Short stories: *The System of Dante's Hell* (New York: Grove Press, 1963); *Tales* (New York: Grove Press, 1967).

Plays: *Four Black Revolutionary Plays* (Indianapolis and New York: Bobbs-Merrill Co., 1969). The author indicates that Sun Ra and Milford Graves's music must be used in the staging of the plays; *Dutchman, The Slave, The Baptism, The Toilet, Arm Yrself or Harm Yourself* (New York: Morrow).

Essays: *Home: Social Essays*

Born in 1934 in Newark, NJ, Leroi Jones also went to high school there, and studied at Howard University until he turned 19. In 1961, a John Hay Whitney scholarship helped him write his first poems. A novelist, short story writer and playwright, essayist, jazz critic, Jones participates in the creation of several cultural organizations in the early 1960s: *The Spirit House* in Newark, the *Black Arts Repertory Theater* in New York. He recorded with the New York Art Quartet his poem *Black Dada Nihilismus*

(E.S.P. 1004, 1970) and with Sunny Murray, Albert Ayler and Don Cherry, recorded "Black Art" on the album *Sunny's Time Now* (Jihad Productions, 1965).

4. Ulrich Bonnell Phillips, *American Negro Slavery* (New York: D. Appleton and Co., 1918), 401.

5. On slavery in the United States, see among others C. L. R. James, "The Atlantic Slave and Slavery: Some Interpretations of their Significance in the Development of the United States and the Western World," in *Amistad 1: Writings on Black History and Culture*, ed. John A. Williams, Charles F. Harris (New York: Vintage, 1970): 119–164; Eugene D. Genovese, *Political Economy of Slavery*; Matthew T. Mellon, *Early American Views on Negro Slavery* (New York: New American Library, 1969); John Elliot Cairnes, *The Slave Power* (London: Parker, Son & Co., 1862); Michel Fabre, *Esclaves et Planteurs dans le Sud Américain au XIXè siècle* (Paris: Julliard, 1970) and *Les Noirs Américains* (Paris: Armand Colin, 1967); Herbert Aptheker, *American Negro Slave Revolts* (New York: International Publishers, 1963); Stanley Elkins, *Slavery* (New York: The Universal Library, 1963); E. Franklin Frazier, *The Negro in the United States* (New York: MacMillan, 1963); Jean-Pierre N'Diaye et al., "Les Noirs aux Etats-Unis pour les Africains," *Réalités Africaines* 7 (May–July 1964); Daniel Guérin, *Décolonisation du Noir américain* (Paris: Editions de Minuit, 1963); Malcolm X, *On Afro-American History* (New York: Pathfinder Press, 1970); François Masnata, *Pouvoir Blanc, Révolte Noire* (Paris: Payot, 1968); *Slavery Defended: the Views of the Old South*, Eric L. McKitrick ed. (Englewood Cliffs, NJ: Prentice Hall, 1963).

6. The first anti-slavery association was created in England in 1823 [Translator's note: it is unclear what the authors are referring to. It is likely they are actually referring to the Society for the Abolition of the Slave Trade founded in 1787]. In 1833, the slaves of the British Empire were officially emancipated, but it was fully acquired in 1838, following clashes with slave owners. In 1817 a society for American colonization was created in the US with the purpose of transporting black slaves to Africa. After this aborted attempt, the abolitionist movement lay dormant until 1830, influenced in great part by British abolitionism. On American abolitionism, see Herbert Aptheker, *The Negro in the Abolitionist Movement* (New York: International Publishers, 1941); Gilbert H. Barnes, *The Antislavery Impulse: 1830–1844* (New York: Harbinger Books, 1964); Dwight L. Dumond, *Antislavery Origins of the Civil War in the United States* (Ann Arbor: University of Michigan Press, 1961). See Chapter 5. b.

7. E. F. Frazier, *The Negro in the United States*, 41.

8. Scott v Sandford, 60 U.S. 393 (1857). The slave Dred Scott filed suit in St Louis Circuit Court to obtain his freedom in 1847. About the Dred Scott decision, see Joanne Grant, *Black Protest: 1619 to the Present* (New York: Fawcett Premier Book, 1969), 121.

9. Dred Scott decision.

10. Excerpt from a speech at the Virginia House of Representatives, 1831 [Translator's note: speech by Henry Berry, Esq. January 20, 1832] quoted in Paul Oliver, *The Blues Fell this Morning*.

11. James Hammond of South Carolina, quoted In Herbert Aptheker, *The Negro People in America* (New York: International Publishers, 1946), 33–34.

12. Aptheker, op. cit., 45.

13. On the trade and breeding of slaves, see W. E. B. Du Bois, *Suppression of the Slave Trade to the United States of America* (New York: Longmans, Green & Co., 1896); Frederick Law Olmsted, *A Journey in the Seaboard Slave States* (New York: Dix and Edwards, 1856).

14. Malcolm X, *The Autobiography*, 4.

15. Ibid., 2–3.

16. For accounts of slavery by those who witnessed it, see Fanny Kemble, *Journal of a Residence on a Georgian Plantation in 1838–1839* (New York: Alfred Knopf, 1961); Charlotte Forten, *A Free Negro in the Slave Era: The Journal of Charlotte L. Forten* (New York: Collier, 1961). See also Chapter 5. e.

17. Malcolm X, "Message to the Grass Roots," *Malcolm X Speaks,* op. cit., 11.

18. On the living conditions of slaves, see Fanny Kemble, *Journal of a Residence*. "In 1850, average life expectancy was 25 for whites and under 21 for blacks. On the eve of war, merely 3.5 percent of slaves were over 60 years old, and slave mortality rate was 1.8 percent, compared to 4.4 percent and 1.2 percent respectively for whites. Taking into account the imprecision of statistics of the time, the amount of undeclared slave deaths, slave mortality rates were close to double those of whites. The image we have of old servants living out their last days peacefully must be radically changed." Michel Fabre, *Esclaves et planteurs*, 104.

19. The Society for the Extinction of the Slave Trade was created under the impetus of William Wilberforce, a young member of Parliament who took up the cause of slaves after defending poor children and prisoners. In 1786, Thomas Clarkson had published his *Essay on the Slavery and Commerce of the Human Species*). [Translator's note: the authors are getting different abolitionist societies mixed up: Wilberforce officially joined the Society for Effecting the Abolition of the Slave Trade in 1791. The Society for the Extinction of the Slave Trade and the Civilization of Africa was a different organization, created in 1839.]

20. In 1835, William Lloyd Garrison, the editor in chief of the *Liberator*, was attacked and beaten in Boston; on November 7, 1837, Rev. Elijah P. Lovejoy, editor of the *Alton Observer*, was shot down in Illinois.

21. The Underground Railroad was a network of clandestine relays helping escaped slaves from the South to reach cities in the North and in Canada. There, slaves were theoretically safe from arrest, extradition, or kidnapping. Among the passers in the Underground Railroad was Harriet Tubman, a slave who escaped Maryland when she

was twenty years old, and would become one of the heroes of black resistance to slavery (see W. E. B. Du Bois, *Dark Water: Voices from Within the Veil* (New York: Harcourt and Brace, 1920)). Thanks to this system, some hundred thousand fugitives escaped safely between 1850 and 1860, which, taking into account the cost of slaves at the time, represented about a $30 million loss for southern planters.

22. Quoted in Frazier, op. cit., 106.

23. Ibid., 107.

24. Three amendments were introduced in the Constitution to give a legal basis to black citizenship. The thirteenth proclaims, "Neither slavery nor involuntary servitude, except as a punishment for crime whereof the party shall have been duly convicted, shall exist within the United States, or any place subject to their jurisdiction." The fifteenth amendment states, "The right of citizens of the United States to vote shall not be denied or abridged by the United States or by any State on account of race, color, or previous condition of servitude." The 1875 Civil Rights Act, finally, declares that "all persons within the jurisdiction of the United States shall be entitled to the full and equal enjoyment of the accommodations, advantages, facilities, and privileges of inns, public conveyances on land or water, theaters, and other places of public amusement; subject only to the conditions and limitations established by law, and applicable alike to citizens of every race and color, regardless of any previous condition of servitude."

25. On the Reconstruction period, read Herbert Aptheker, *The Negro in the Civil War* (New York: International Publishers, 1962); George Bentley, *A History of the Freedmen's Bureau* (Philadelphia: University of Pennsylvania Press, 1955); John H. Franklin, *The Emancipation Proclamation* (New York: Doubleday, 1963); William Gilette, *The Right to Vote: Politics and the Passage of the Fifteenth Amendment* (Baltimore: Johns Hopkins Press, 1965); Booker T. Washington, *Up from Slavery* (New York: Doubleday, 1901); Joel Williamson, *The Negro in South Carolina during Reconstruction* (Chapel Hill: University of North Carolina Press, 1965); W. E. B. Du Bois, *The Souls of Black Folk* (Chicago: A. C. McClurg and Co., 1903); Godfrey Hodgson, *Carpetbaggers et Ku Klux Klan* (Paris: Julliard, 1966); Daniel Guérin, *Décolonisation du Noir américain*, 37–42.

26. W. E. B. Du Bois, *Black Reconstruction* (New York: The Free Press, 1898; 1935; 1962), 727.

27. Carl Schurz, *Report on the Condition of the South*, quoted in Hodgson, *Carpetbaggers et Ku Klux Klan*, 10; 241.

28. Wendell Phillips (1811–1884): president of the American Anti-Slavery Society from 1865 to 1870, he worked for the creation of a worker's party in the United States and was a member of the First Internationale.

29. Quoted in Hodgson, *Carpetbaggers et Ku Klux Klan*.

30. On the Ku Klux Klan, see Hodgson *Carpetbaggers et Ku Klux Klan*; J. Paul Mitchell, *Race Riots in Black and White* (Englewood Cliffs: Prentice Hall, 1970), 28–40;

Arnold S. Rice, *The Ku Klux Klan in American Politics* (Washington DC: Public Affairs Press, 1962).

31. B.A. Botkin, *Lay My Burden Down* (1945; New York: Delta, 1994), 248.

32. On disenfranchisement and the transformation of rural slaves into sharecroppers, read Gunnar Myrdal, *An American Dilemma: The Negro Problem and American Democracy* (New York: Harper and Row, 1944).

33. See II. 1. i. Also C. Vann Woodward, *The Strange Career of Jim Crow* (New York: Oxford University Press, 1957).

34. Tom Watson, quoted in E.F. Frazier, *Negro in the United States*, 153.

35. Beverly Nash, an ex-slave and member of the constitutional convention of South Carolina, quoted in Frazier, op. cit., 136.

36. E. F. Frazier, *Black Bourgeoisie*, (1957; New York: The Free Press, 1962), 96–97.

37. Du Bois, op. cit., 41–42.

38. See Guérin, *Décolonisation du Noir américain*, 138. Though severely criticized by most black leaders, Booker T. Washington's advice seem to have influenced moderates, "gradualists," and partisans of non-violence among blacks, such as Martin Luther King Jr: "Not all men are called to specialized or professional jobs; even fewer rise to the heights of genius in the arts and sciences; many are called to be laborers in factories, fields, and streets. But no work is insignificant. All labor that uplifts humanity has dignity and importance and should be undertaken with painstaking excellence. If it falls your lot to be a street sweeper, sweep streets like Michelangelo painted pictures, like Shakespeare wrote poetry, like Beethoven composed music; sweep streets so well that all the host of heaven and earth will have to pause and say, 'Here lived a great street sweeper, who swept his job well.'" In Martin Luther King Jr, *Strength to Love* (New York: Harper & Row, 1963), 71.

39. Booker T. Washington, quoted in E. Franklin Frazier, *Black Bourgeoisie*, 76.

40. Frazier would recognize in the 1962 edition that "this book dealt with behavior which is characteristic of middle-class people—white, black or brown." *Black Bourgeoisie*, 7.

41. Harry Johnston, *A History of the Colonization of Africa by Alien Races* (Cambridge: Cambridge University Press, 1899), 91.

42. "Ample evidence shows that slaves worked well below their capabilities.... The harsh treatment that slaves gave equipment shocked travelers and other contemporaries, and neglect of tools figured prominently among the reasons given for punishing Negroes. In 1855, a South Carolina planter wrote in exasperation: 'The wear and tear of plantation tools is harassing to every planter who does not have a good mechanic at his nod and beck every day in the year. ur plows are broken, our hoes are lost, our harnesses need repairing, and large demands are made on the blacksmith, the carpenter, the tanner, and the harnessmaker.'" Eugene Genovese, *Political Economy of Slavery: Studies in the Economy and Society of the Slave South* (New York:

Pantheon Books, 1965), 44–55. See also Karl Marx, *Capital* (Chicago: Charles H. Kerr and Co., 1915), Samuel Moore and Edward Aveling trans., 219.

43. From the end of the eighteenth century, a series of laws were implemented that established that conversion to Christianity would not help Negroes regain freedom. The Church had until then justified the enslavement of Africans with the fact that they were not Christians, but with these laws all original reticence soon disappeared. The Society for the Propagation of the Gospel in Foreign Parts, formed in 1701 by the Anglican Church, then inaugurated a program of mass conversion of slaves. The Moravian brothers, Presbyterians, Quakers, and, in Louisiana, French Catholics also partook in this systematic Christianization. On the topic, read E. F. Frazier, *The Negro Church in America* (New York: Schocken Books, 1963).

44. On slave revolts, read H. Aptheker, *American Negro Slave Revolts*; Jean-Pierre N'Diaye et al., *Les noirs aux Etats-Unis pour les Africains*; Joanne Grant, *Black Protest*, 51–56; J.-P. Mitchell, *Race Riots in Black and White*, 16–26.

45. See notes 14, 42.

46. Thomas W. Higginson, "Denmark Vesey," *The Atlantic*, quoted in E.F. Frazier, op. cit., 86.

47. *The Confessions of Nat Turner, the Leader of the Late Insurrection in Southampton, Virginia, as Fully and Voluntarily Made to Thomas R. Gray* (Baltimore, 1831).

48. Malcolm X, *Autobiography*, 177.

49. Malcolm X, *By Any Means Necessary* (New York: Pathfinder Press, 1992), 104–105.

50. *Letters on American Slavery* (American Anti-Slavery Society: 1860), 6. In this text, written in Hauteville-House in Guernesey on December 2, 1859, Victor Hugo also says:

> When our thoughts dwell upon the United States of America, a majestic form rises before the eye of imagination. It is a Washington!
>
> Look, then, to what is taking place in that country of Washington at this present moment.
>
> In the Southern states of the Union there are slaves; and this circumstance is regarded with indignation, as the most monstrous of inconsistencies, by the pure and logical conscience of the Northern states. A white man, a free man, John Brown, sought to deliver these Negro slaves from bondage. Assuredly, if insurrection is ever a sacred duty, it must be when it is directed against slavery. John Brown endeavored to commence the work of emancipation by the liberation of slaves in Virginia. Pious, austere, animated with the old Puritan spirit, inspired by the spirit of the Gospel, he sounded to these men, these oppressed brothers, the rallying cry of freedom. The slaves, enervated by servitude, made no response to the appeal. Slavery afflicts the soul with weakness. Brown, though deserted, still fought at the head of a handful of heroic men; he was riddled with balls; his two

young sons, sacred martyrs, fell dead at his side, and he himself was taken. This is what they call the affair at Harper's Ferry" (3).

Talking further about the trial (which pronounced five death sentences), he adds:

> Such things cannot be done with impunity in the face of the civilized world.... Let the judges of Charlestown, and Hunter and Parker, and the slaveholding jurors, and the whole population of Virginia, ponder it well: they are watched! They are not alone in the world. ... The executioner of Brown ... would be, though we can scarce think or speak of it without a shudder, the whole American Republic.... Viewed in a political light, the murder of Brown would be an irreparable fault. It would penetrate the Union with a gaping fissure that would lead in the end to its entire disruption. It is possible that the execution of Brown might establish slavery on a firm basis in Virginia, but it is certain that it would shake to its centre the entire fabric of American democracy (4; 6).

John Brown was hanged. Hugo wrote this epitaph: *Pro Christo sicut Christus*. Two years after his prediction, the Union did collapse and the Civil War started. Beyond Hugo's humanitarian response, most prominent abolitionists (William Lloyd Garrison, Wendell Phillips, Ralph Waldo Emerson, Henry David Thoreau, Frederick Douglass) approved of John Brown's action in spite of their dedication to pacifism. About John Brown, read Louis Filler, *Wendell Phillips on Civil Rights and Freedom* (New York: Hill and Wang, 1956), 107–8; W. E. B. Du Bois, *John Brown* (Philadelphia: Jacobs and Co., 1909); Joseph Déjacque, "La libération des Noirs américains," in *A bas les chefs!* (Paris: Champ Libre, 1971).

51. Charlotte Forten, "Life on the Sea Islands" *The Atlantic* (May and June 1864), quoted in Michel Fabre, *Esclaves et Planteurs*, 123.

52. In February 1970, John A. Williams and Charles F. Harris published the first issue of a journal dedicated to "texts on black culture and history." It was dedicated to the poet Langston Hughes, but also to Cinquez and his comrades through its title: *Amistad* ("friendship" in Spanish).

53. [Translator's note] The mutineers killed members of the crew and kept the rest hostage.

54. Aptheker, op. cit.

55. N'Diaye et al., *Les Noirs aux Etats-Unis*, 54–55.

56. Fabre, *Esclaves et Planteurs*, 11.

57. See Chapter 7. c.

58. See Rayford W. Logan, *Les Noirs américains et l'Afrique* (Paris: Centre Culturel Américain, 1961), 5.

59. The founding of this colony of freed American slaves on the African continent was supported by black and white abolitionists. Yet it was not very successful; fewer

than fifty thousand black Americans joined the new state. This semi-failure can be explained by the fact that freed slaves could find closer refuge and better living conditions in Haiti or in the Dominican Republic. Hope of gaining access to the material advantages of life in the United States certainly played a role as well, in spite of the injustice and violence from which blacks were suffering. See Rayford W. Logan, ibid.

60. Joanna Grant, *Black Protest*, 84–89.

61. Ibid., 89–92.

62. See note 85.

63. *A Brief Narrative of the Struggle for the Rights of the Colored People of Philadelphia in the City Railway Cars and a Defense of William Still Relating to His Agency Touching the Passage of the Late Bill* (Philadelphia: Merrihew and Son, 1867); Joanna Grant, *Black Protest*, 68.

64. He was also one of the organizers and authors of the *Petition for Equal Education*.

65. *Preamble of the Free African Society*, quoted in William Douglass, *Annals of the First African Church, in the United States of America: Now Styled the African Episcopal Church of St. Thomas, Philadelphia* (Philadelphia; King & Baird, 1862), 15–17; *A Narrative of the Proceedings of Black People during the Late Awful Calamity in Philadelphia in the Year 1793*, in *Negro Protest Pamphlets* (New York: Arno Press, 1969).

66. See note 72.

67. Following an idea proposed in the *Freedom's Journal*, the Negro National Convention was created. Its representatives met eleven times between 1830 and 1861 to discuss issues of segregation in schools and public places and political and civic improvement for Negroes. See Howard H. Bell, *A Survey of the Negro Convention Movement: 1839–1861*, PhD thesis, Western University, 1953.

68. Henry H. Garnet, quoted in Herbert Aptheker, *A Documentary History of the Negro People in the United States* (New York: Citadel Press, 1951), 232.

69. Frederick Douglass, *Resolution of the National Convention of Colored People and Their Friends*, (Troy, New York, 1847).

70. Frederick Douglass, "Letter to an abolitionist associate" (1849), in *Organizing For Social Change: A Mandate For Activity In The 1990s*, ed. K. Bobo et al. (Washington, DC: Seven Locks Press, 1991).

71. Frederick Douglass, *Narrative of the Life of Frederick Douglass, an American Slave, Written by Himself* (Boston: Anti-Slavery Office, 1845). About Douglass, read Michel Fabre, *ves et Planteurs*, 51–52; Joanna Grant, *Black Protest*, 111–14; Jay David, *Growing up Black* (New York: Morrow, 1968).

72. Frederick Douglass, op. cit., 33, quoted in Michel Fabre, *Esclaves et Planteurs*, 120.

73. *Slaves Petition for Freedom during Revolutionary War*, in Herbert Aptheker, op. cit.

74. About pamphlets and written protest, read Joanna Grant, *Black Protest*, and *Negro Protest Pamphlets*, op. cit.

75. *Negro Protest Pamphlets*, 19–21.

76. Ibid.

77. Ibid.

78. Frazier, *Black Bourgeoisie*, 175.

79. Quoted in Aptheker, op. cit., 255–56.

80. Gunnar Myrdal, *An American Dilemma*, 908.

81. See note 111; William Styron, *The Confessions of Nat Turner* (New York; Random House, 1967).

82. Olaudah Equiano, *The Interesting Narrative of the Life of Olaudah Equiano, or Gustavus Vassa, The African. Written By Himself* (London, 1789). Quoted in Paul Oliver, *Savannah Syncopators, African Retentions in the Blues* (London: November Books, 1970). See Chapter 6. a.

83. Charles Ball, *Slavery in the United States: A Narrative of the Life and Adventures of Charles Ball, A Black Man* (Lewistown Pa.: Taylor, 1836).

84. Henry Bibb, *The Narrative of the Life and Adventures of Henry Bibb* (New York, 1849).

85. *Narrative of the Life of Henry Box Brown, Written by Himself* (Manchester England: Lee and Glynn, 1851).

86. *Narrative of William W. Brown, A Fugitive Slave* (Boston: Anti-Slavery Office, 1847).

87. Henry Bruce, *The New Man: Twenty-Nine Years a Slave, Twenty-Nine Years a Free Man* (York: P. Anstadt and Sons, 1895).

88. Edited by Benjamin Drew (Boston: Jewett and Co., 1856).

89. *Narrative of the Life of Moses Granby, Late a Slave in the United States of America* (Boston: Gilpin, 1843).

90. *The Life of Josiah Henson* (Boston: Phelps, 1849); *Father Henson's Story of His Own Life* (Boston: Jewett, 1858).

91. *The Narrative of Lunsford Lane* (Boston: Torrey, 1842).

92. *The Reverend J. W. Loguen, as a Slave and a Freeman: Narrative of Real Life* (Syracuse, NY: J.G.K. Truair & Co., 1859).

93. *The Narrative of Sojourner Truth* (Boston: 1850).

94. *The Narrative of Henry Watson, a Fugitive Slave* (Boston: B. Marsh, 1848).

95. *Autobiography of a Fugitive Negro* (London: John Snow, 1850).

96. William Wells Brown, *Clotel, or The President's Daughter* (London: Partridge and Oakey, 1853).

97. Martin R. Delany, *Blake, or The Huts of America*, serialized in *The Anglo-African Magazine* (January to July 1859). See Robert A. Bone, *The Negro Novel in America* (New Haven, CT: Yale University Press, 1969).

98. Frank J. Webb, *The Garies and their Friends* (London: Routledge, 1857).

99. Frances E. W. Harper, *Iola Leroy* (Boston: James Earle, 1892); Sanda [Walter H. Stowers and William H. Anderson] *Appointed* (Detroit: Detroit Law Printing, 1894); John McHenry Jones, *Hearts of Gold* (Wheeling, VA: Daily Intelligencer Stream Job Press, 1896); Charles W. Chesnutt, *The House Behind the Cedars* (Boston and New York: Houghton Mifflin, 1900); *The Marrow of Tradition* (Boston and New York: Houghton Mifflin, 1901); *The Colonel's Dream* (New York: Doubleday, 1905).

100. Sutton E. Griggs, *Pointing the Way* (Nashville, TN: Orion, 1908).

101. Sutton E. Griggs, *Imperium in Imperio* (Cincinnati, OH: Editor Publishing Co., 1899).

102. On Dunbar's life, read Jean Wagner, *Black Poets of the United States*, trans. Kenneth Douglass (Champaign: Illinois University Press, 1973). This book must also be read for everything concerning black cultural activities in the United States until World War II. Very informed and precise, it was an indispensable source of information and a foundation for our research.

103. See Wagner, "Dunbar and the Plantation Tradition," 80–95.

104. Albert Memmi, *The Colonizer and the Colonized* (1957; Boston: Beacon Press, 1991), 87–88.

105. In *The Complete Poems of Paul Laurence Dunbar* (New York: Dodd, Mead and Co., 1913), 208.

106. Ibid., 219–220. See Wagner, "The Themes of Dunbar's Popular Poetry," 115.

107. Ibid., 178–179.

108. [Translator's note: the version sung by Abbey Lincoln is best known, but the song was actually composed by Oscar Brown.]

109. "Dely," 148–149.

110. Virginia Cunningham, *Paul Laurence Dunbar and His Song* (New York: Dodd, Mead and Co., 1947), 204.

111. See Wagner, *Black Poets in the United States*, 129.

112. Ibid., 17.

113. Quoted in Wagner, *Black Poets in the United States*, 19.

114. Quoted in Wagner, *Black Poets in the United States*, 22.

115. Wagner, *Black Poets in the United States*, 26.

6. Black Music before Jazz

1. When, in the 1920s, a movement appeared among black intellectuals and artists that meant to liquidate all memories from the slave period and valorize instead older connections with Africa, Alain Locke became a theoretician for what he dubbed a "Black Renaissance" (see *The Negro in American Culture*). Born in 1886 in Philadelphia, Locke (Alain Leroy) studied at Harvard. In 1907 he was the first black Rhodes Scholar

and went to England. After spending three years at Oxford, he studied for two years at the University of Berlin. Back in the United States in 1912, he became a professor at Howard University, then a philosophy professor in 1917 and eventually obtained a chair. The author of many books on black life and culture, he was interested in music and philosophy. His *New Negro* anthology became a sort of manifesto for the Black Renaissance at the beginning of the 1920s. After creating the *Associates in Negro Folk Education*, a group that anticipated black cultural nationalism and Black Studies, he wrote *A Decade of Negro Self-Expression*, *The Negro in America*, and *Frederick Douglass*. He also published an anthology of black theater, another dedicated to black poetry, and *When People Meet: A Study in Race and Culture Contacts*. He died in 1954 before he could finish a book on all-black contributions to American culture. On Alain Locke, read William Loren Katz, *The American Negro: His History and Literature*, New York: Arno Press, 1968); Wagner, *Black Poets in the United States*.

2. Equiano, quoted in Paul Oliver, *Savannah Syncopators*, 31–2.

3. Quoted in Oliver, ibid. According to Paul Oliver, the *stickado* is a sort of African xylophone specific to Ibo tribes.

4. Jones, *Blues People*, 18.

5. Melville Herskovits, *The Myth of the Negro Past*, quoted in Paul Oliver, op. cit., 81.

6. Oliver, op. cit.

7. Mezz Mezzrow and Bernard Wolfe, *Really the Blues* (New York: Citadel Press, 1946).

8. W. E. B. Du Bois, *Souls of Black Folk*, 2.

9. Words of an animist priest in Senegal, quoted in "Afrique Noire," *Encyclopaedia Universalis* vol. 1 (Paris: Albin Michel, 1970), 413.

10. W. E. B. Du Bois, *Souls of Black Folk*, 157.

11. Ibid., 155–156.

12. In *The Story of the Blues*, Paul Oliver cites one of the rare work songs to have reached us. It dates back to 1843: *(Lead:)* "De nigger trade got me . . ." (Choir:) "Oh, hollow!"

For lack of recording, two testimonies can help us imagine these songs, still African, and already close to the spirituals:

"The odd turns made in the throat, and the curious rhythmic effect produced by single voices chiming in at different irregular intervals, seem almost as impossible to place on the score as the singing of birds or the tones of an Aeolian Harp." (Lucy McKim, ca. 1850.) "[Their songs] have appeared to me extraordinarily wild and unaccountable. The way in which the chorus strikes in with the burden, between each phrase of the melody chanted by a single voice, is very curious and effective." (in Kemble, *Journal of a Residence*, 259)

13. Several recordings of prisoner songs have been made. Alan Lomax gathered the songs for *Negro Songs from the Mississippi State Penitentiary* (Tradition Records, Los

Angeles, TLP-1020) at the Mississippi State Penitentiary in Parchman. See also *Angola Prison Spirituals: Recorded at Louisiana Penitentiary in Angola* (77-Records, London, 77LA 12–13).

14. F. Kemble writes in her journal, "Except the extemporaneous chants in our honor, of which I have written before, I have never heard the Negroes... sing any words that could be said to have any sense. To one, an extremely pretty, plaintive and original air, there was but one line, which was repeated with a sort of wailing chorus." *Journal of a Residence*, 164.

15. W. E. B. Du Bois, *Dusk of Dawn* (New York: Harcourt, Brace & World, 1940), 111–115.

16. Quoted in Henry A. Kmen, *Music in New Orleans: The Formative Years 1791–1841* (Baton Rouge: Louisiana State University Press, 1966), 227. On Congo Square and New Orleans before 1900, read also Arlin Turner, *Creoles and Cajuns* (New York: Doubleday Anchor, 1959); Herbert Asbury, *The French Quarter* (New York: Alfred A. Knopf, 1936).

17. See Paul Oliver, *Savannah Syncopators*, 77.

18. Ibid.

19. See Richard Bardolph, *The Negro Vanguard* (New York: Rinehart, 1959), 43–44.

20. LeRoi Jones, *Blues People*, 33.

21. Thomas Wentworth Higginson, the white colonel of a black regiment, interested in hearing what his soldiers were singing, insisted that one of them sing a spiritual: "Then he began singing, and the men, after listening a moment, joined in the chorus, as if it were an old acquaintance, though they evidently had never heard it before. I saw how easily a new 'sing' took root among them." *Army Life in a Black Regiment* (Boston: Fields, Osgood & Co., 1870), 219, quoted in Oliver, op. cit., 10.

22. See E. F. Frazier, *The Negro Church in America* (New York: Schocken Books, 1964).

23. See Chapter 6. c.

24. See Sterling Brown, *Negro Poetry and Drama* (Washington, DC: Associates in Negro Folk Education, 1937).

25. See M. L. King Jr, *The Trumpet of Conscience* (New York: Harper's and Row, 1967): "Our spirituals, now so widely admired around the world, were often codes. We sang of 'heaven' that awaited us, and the slave masters listened in innocence, not realizing that we were not speaking of the hereafter. Heaven was the word for Canada and the Negro sang of the hope that his escape on the underground railroad would carry him there."

26. Higginson, *Army Life in a Black Regiment*, 217. Frank Kofksy also gives the example of *Bye Bye Blackbird*: the blackbird taking flight would be a fugitive slave whose fellows announced his escape without the knowledge of their masters.

27. N. I. White "Racial Traits in the Negro Song," *Sewanee Review* 28.3 (July 1920), 397.

28. Wagner, *Black Poets of the United States*, 28.

29. Quoted in Wagner, *Black Poets of the United States*.

30. Quoted in Oliver, op. cit., 10.

31. Quoted in Oliver, ibid.

32. Frederic Ramsey Jr, Liner Notes. *Music of the South, Vol.1–10*, ([Smithsonian] Folkways FA 2650–2659, 1955). LP.

33. Listen to "Street Cries of Charleston," *Riverside History of Classic Jazz* (BYG 529-061).

34. See Francis Bebey, *African Music: A People's Art* (New York: Lawrence Hill and Co., 1975); Paul Oliver, *Savannah Syncopators*; A.M. Jones, *Studies in African Music* (Oxford: Oxford University Press, 1959).

35. Sidney Finkelstein, *Jazz, A People's Music* (New York: Citadel Press, 1948), 68.

36. Archie Shepp, liner notes. *Mama Too Tight* (New York: Impulse A-9134, 1966).

37. [Translator's note: I was unable to identify the source for this quote. It is not in the English translation of Berendt's book.]

38. Quoted in Berendt, op. cit., 136.

39. Richard Wright, *White Man, Listen!* (New York: Doubleday and Co. 1957), 128–130.

40. Ibid., 133.

41. W. E. B. Du Bois, "Litany at Atlanta," quoted in Wright, *White Man, Listen!* 134.

42. This permanence, more or less clandestine or ignored by whites, has manifested itself through constant exchanges and borrowings, from one era to the next, and from one signer to the next. Take this blues recorded in the 1920s: "Nigger an' a white man playin' seven-up this mornin'/Well nigger win the money but he sacred to pick it up/This mornin' that too soon for me." This blues was an adaptation of a black song heard in 1876: "Nigger an' a white man playing seven-up/ White man played an ace; an' nigger feared to take it up/ White man played ace an' nigger played a nine/White man died, an' nigger went blind." Quoted in Oliver, op. cit., 21.

43. See Ian Young, "Les Panthères Noires."

44. See Jean Paulhan, "Les hain-tenys," *Oeuvres Complètes* (Paris: Gallimard, 1955).

45. See Richard Wright, *White Man, Listen!* 130–131; 135.

46. Brown, op. cit., 25–27.

47. Wright, *White Man, Listen!* 131–132.

48. See *The Chase* and *The Duel*, recorded in 1947 by saxophonist Wardell Gray with Teddy Edwards and Dexter Gordon.

49. See Jean Wagner, *Black Poets of the United States*, 161–210.

50. Ibid., 18. See also on serious black musicians: Alain Locke, *The Negro and his Music* (New York: Arno Press, 1969), 36–42.

51. On minstrels, see Jean-Christophe Averty's remarkable and very complete study "Les Minstrels," published in *Jazz Hot* 77 (May 1963): 8–10; *Jazz Hot* 78 (June

1963): 12–15; 22; *Jazz Hot* 79 (July-August 1963): 12–16; *Jazz Hot* 80 (September 1963): 14–16.

52. Zip Coon is the hero of several minstrel songs. Coon was one of the many pejorative terms used to call Negroes. It is a small rodent present throughout the southern states, hence the analogy some have seen with the term "raton" [rat] used by French colonizers in North Africa to designate indigenous people.

53. Constance Rourke, *American Humor* (New York: Doubleday, 1955), 74.

54. See Averty, *Jazz Hot* 77, 10.

55. Wagner, *Black Poets of the United States*, 45.

56. Averty, ibid.

57. See note 31.

58. Quoted Averty, *Jazz Hot* 79, 14.

59. See Wagner, *Black Poets of the United States*, 46–49.

60. James Weldon Johnson, *Negro Americans, What Now?* (New York: The Viking Press, 1934), 91–92.

7. In the Margins of Jazz History

1. James Baldwin, *Nobody Knows My Name* (New York: Dell Publishing, 1961), 18.

2. On the geographical distribution of blues centers in the United States, read Paul Oliver, *The Story of the Blues* (London: The Cresset Press, 1969). Another indication on the appearance of the blues, this quote from *A Free Negro in the Slave Era* (New York: Collier, 1961), the journal written in 1862 by Charlotte Forten, a black teacher who dedicated herself to educating young slaves, constitutes the first available written reference to the blues as a state of mind: "It seemed to me that I hadn't slept more than ten minutes when I was awakened by what seemed to me terrible screams coming from the direction of the [slave] Quarters." The following day, a Sunday, Charlotte Forten was still troubled by these screams; she came home from church in a state of deep sadness: "Nearly everybody was looking gay and happy; and yet I came home with the *blues*. Threw myself on the bed, and for the first time since I have been here, felt very lonely and pitied myself. But I have reasoned myself into a more sensible mood and am better now." Quoted in *The Story of the Blues*, 8.

3. *Le Monde du Blues*, title of the French edition of *Blues Fell this Morning*.

4. Quoted in Samuel Charters, *The Poetry of the Blues* (New York: Oak Publications, 1963), 35.

5. Charters, *The Poetry of the Blues*, 102.

6. Ibid., 99.

7. See Chapter 6, endnote 42.

8. Ibid., 101. Sung by Furry Lewis.

9. Quoted by Oliver, *Blues Fell this Morning*, 131. Another capitalist that inspired

blues lyrics was Rockefeller: "If you'll be my woman I will turn your money green,/ Show your more money, baby, than Rockefeller ever seen." Furry Lewis blues, quoted by Charters, *The Poetry of the Blues*., 31.

10. "Route 66" has become a standard, recorded by a variety of singers, one of the most recent versions being that of black singer and pianist Nat King Cole. The song is also an exemplary reflection of the great migrations and economic crises of the rural South. From Saint Louis, Missouri, Route 66 crosses Oklahoma; when travelers from Louisiana, Alabama, or Mississippi reach the route in Texas, they know they are going in the "right" direction: towards California. It is the itinerary followed by the characters of John Steinbeck's novel *The Grapes of Wrath*.

11. Charters, *The Poetry of the Blues*, 104. Sung at the Angola penitentiary in Louisiana by Guitar Welch in 1959.

12. Ibid., 94. "T Model Ford Blues," sung by Sleepy John Estes.

13. LeRoi Jones, op. cit., 101. "Put it Right Here or Keep Out There," sung by Bessie Smith.

14. Charters, *The Poetry of the Blues*, 95.

15. Ibid. Sung by Blind Lemon Jefferson.

16. Ibid., 78. Sung before embarking for Europe in 1918. Newport News was the harbor American troops left from when the United States entered the war. War is also the topic of Willie B.'s 1945 "Overseas Blues": 'I was 'way overseas/ I was 'way over in New Jerusalem/ General Eisenhower said: you soldiers got to go over Tokyo/ And do the best you can/ But I told him, no, little Willie don't want to go/ Said I had so much troubles with the Germans/ Don't send me over in Tokyo.' He said: Germany done fell now/ You soldier boys know what it's all about/ You go way over to the other islands/ And help General MacArthur out."

17. Ibid., 89. "Black Snake Moan," sung by Blind Lemon Jefferson.

18. Ibid., 85.

19. Cited in *The Selected Writing of W. E. B. Du Bois* (New York: Mentor Books, 1970), 117–118.

20. Du Bois was editor in chief for *The Crisis* from 1910 to 1934, when he left the NAACP.

21. See Mitchell, *Race Riots in Black and White*.

22. Prior to the Estates General in 1789 where representatives of the French aristocracy, clergy, and Third Estate were supposed to meet and discuss matters of the state, notebooks were sent around the country in which common people could express their complaints.

23. See Louis Madelin, *The French Revolution* (New York: G.P. Putnam's Sons, 1916), 41.

24. Quoted in Berendt, op. cit., 9.

25. *Melody Maker* (January 1967). [Translator's note: this issue of the *Melody Maker* does not contain the interview. I was unable to locate it.]

26. A French word derived from the Spanish criollo, designating whites born in the subtropical colonies, the term creole became in Louisiana synonymous with mulatto. Until the appearance of Jim Crow laws, creoles constituted a kind of sub-aristocracy or intermediary bourgeoisie between whites and free blacks in the hierarchy of New Orleans's good society." These nuances led creoles to a dramatic self-assessment when laws assimilated them to Negroes.

27. About *ragtime*, a piano style born of the encounter of European music and Negro rhythmic elements (which, when it appeared at the end of the nineteenth century, was more a composed genre than an improvised one), read Locke, *The Negro and his Music*, 57–59.

28. Alan Lomax, *Mister Jelly Roll: The Fortunes of Jelly Roll Morton, New Orleans Creole and "Inventor of Jazz"* (Berkeley and Los Angeles: University of California Press, 1950).

29. The form of snobbery that led some whites to go slumming for "Negro" music drew the hostility of more conservative whites: "A wave of vulgar, filthy and suggestive music has inundated the land. Nothing but ragtime prevails. . . . No seaside resort this summer has been without its ragtime orchestra, its weekly cakewalk. . . . Worse yet, the fashionable idle folk of Newport . . . have been the chief offenders. Society has decreed that ragtime and cakewalking are the thing, and one reads with amazement and disgust of historical and aristocratic names joining in this sex dance, for the cakewalk is nothing but an African *danse du ventre*, a milder edition of African orgies, and the music is degenerate music . . . Ragtime rhythm is nothing new, but its present usage and marriage to words of veiled lasciviousness should banish it from polite society," *Musical Courier* (1899), quoted in Leonard Feather, *The Book of Jazz* (1957; New York: Dell Publishing, 1976), 22.

30. In 1896, New Orleans alderman Sidney Story wrote legislation limiting prostitution to a thirty-eight block district close to Canal Street. The inhabitants instantly christened this area "Storyville."

31. According to James Weldon Johnson, several hundreds of people were killed, in *Black Manhattan* (New York: Alfred A. Knopf, 1930): 238–244. J. Paul Mitchell only notes 48 victims (39 blacks, 9 whites) in *Race Riots in Black and White*.

32. The United States are not the world, and democratic principles there being more shamefully violated than in other places, violence constitutes the only efficient response to violence—moreover, for the first time, they had been taught to fight scientifically. This "lesson in war" is comparable to the attitude of certain black GIs who assert that the war in Vietnam against communist guerillas will not be useless when they come back to the ghetto.

33. Du Bois, "Returning Soldiers," *The Crisis* 18.1 (May 1919): 13–14.

34. Quoted in Wagner, *Black Poets of the United States*, 167–168.

35. Ibid., 168.

36. Ibid., 169.

37. On the original ODJB, see Jean-Christophe Averty, "Contribution à l'histoire de l'O.D.J.B.," *Les Cahiers du Jazz* 3: 60–107; 4: 74–117.

38. Op. cit., from a letter to Averty written in 1956 by "Nick" LaRocca, cornet player and leader of the ODJB.

39. Beyond Carl Van Vechten's *Nigger Heaven*, which was one of the best sellers of the year 1926 (the author, a friend of poet Langston Hughes, meant to connect culturally the two communities), let us mention *Dark Laughter*, by Sherwood Anderson, Du Bose Hayward's *Porgy*, Julia Peterkin's *Black April*, E. C. L. Adams's *Nigger to Nigger*, and two plays by Eugene O'Neill: *The Emperor Jones* and *All God's Chillun Got Wings*.

40. "There is a definite implication that Louis had a primary interest in pleasing his audiences," said record producer George Avakian. "It is in line with this interest that he has become no only a great musician but also a great comedian and a showman." Quoted in Berendt, op. cit., 51.

41. Jelly Roll Morton in *Down Beat* (August–September 1938), quoted in Hugues Panassié, *The Real Jazz* (New York: Smith and Durrell, 1942), 38.

42. The standard in the United States designates a popular song often played by jazz musicians. Some (such as "Stardust," "The Man I Love," "My Favorite Things," etc.) are considered integral parts of jazz's thematic repertoire, if not "classics."

43. This style of vocal improvisation where words are replaced by onomatopoeia (chosen for their sound and rhythmic value) and through which singers imitate the flow of certain instruments is reminiscent of *tellana* in Indian music, a style of singing where "mnemonic syllables (bols) representing the different strokes on the drum (tabla or pakhavaja) are used to memorize the basic rhythm." In Alain Daniélou, *Northern Indian Music* (New York: Frederick A. Praeger, 1968), 67.

44. On Garvey, read Grant, *Black Protest*, 199–204; Wagner, *Black Poets of the United States*, 169–171; Yves Loyer, *Black Power* (Paris: Etudes et Documentations Nationales, 1968), 23–24.

45. *Survey Graphic* (March 1925).

46. These titles were all recorded between 1925 and 1936.

47. A theme such as "Air Conditioned Jungle," recorded by Ellington in 1947, dispels the last remaining doubts: Ellington refers first and foremost to the New York jungle in his works.

48. A suite in four movements recorded on September 12, 1935.

49. *The Crisis* (October 1926).

50. On the New Negro Movement, read R. A. Bone, *The Negro Novel in America*, 57–64.

51. Quoted in J. Wagner, *Black Poets of the United States*, 172.

52. Carter G. Woodson, founder of the Association for the Study of African American Life and History and of the *Journal of Negro History* and the *Negro History Bulletin*, appears as one of the most remarkable precursors of the cultural nationalists and propagandists of *Black Studies*.

53. "The Negro Artist and the Racial Mountain," first published in *The Nation*, 23 June 1926. Republished in *Amistad I*: 301–305.

54. Malcolm X, *Autobiography*, 40.

55. Ibid., 52.

56. Ibid., 54.

57. On the swing craze, read Benny Goodman's autobiography, *The Kingdom of Swing* (New York: Stackpole, 1939).

58. Oliver, *The Story of the Blues*, 102. This song was recorded in 1933: "It's hard time here, hard time everywhere, I went down to the factory where I worked for years ago/ And the boss man tol' me that I ain't comin' here no mo'." Many blues also focused on the New Deal: "Now I'm gettin' tired of sittin' around/ I ain't makin' a dime, just wearin' my shoe-soles down/ Now everybody's cryin' let's have a new deal/ Cause I've got to make a livin' if I have to rob and steal/ Now you go to your workhouse, put in your complaint/ Eight times out of ten, you know they'll say 'I cain't'/ They don't want to give you no dough, won't hardly pay your rent/ And it ain't costin' them one dog-gone cent/ Now I ain't makin' a dime since they close down the mill/ I'm sittin' right here waitin' on that brand new deal."

59. *Jazz Hot* 235 (October 1967), 19.

60. The first black union.

61. E. F. Frazier, *Black Bourgeoisie*, 2.

62. Billie Holiday with William Dufty, *Lady Sings the Blues* (1956; New York: Penguin Books, 1984), 81.

63. Malcolm X, *The Autobiography*, 298.

64. [Translator's note] The authors are likely referring to the 1937 Memorial Day Massacre, in which the Chicago Police Department opened fire on unarmed union demonstrators, killing ten.

65. Quoted in *U.S. Riot Commission Report: Report of the National Advisory Commission on Civil Disorders* (New York: Bantam Books, 1968), 222–223. A study of the riots of Summer 1965 ordered by President Lyndon B. Johnson on 29 July 1967, the report was written under the direction of Illinois Governor Otto Kerner (D) and New York Mayor John Lindsay.

66. A. Philip Randolph, "March on Washington Movement Presents a Program for the Negro, in *What the Negro Wants*, ed. Rayford W. Logan (Chapel Hill: University of North Carolina Press, 1944), 154–155. Quoted in Guérin, op. cit., 146.

67. From Randolph, "Keynote Address to the Policy Conference of the March on

Washington Movement, Meeting in Detroit, Michigan, September 26, 1942," quoted in Charles E. Fager, *White Reflections on Black Power* (New York: Eerdmans, 1967), 55.

68. Walter White, "What Caused the Detroit Riots?" in *The Crisis* (1943), quoted in J. Paul Mitchell, *Race Riots in Black and White*, 59.

69. Quoted in Mitchell, ibid., 66.

70. Ibid., 104.

71. Thurgood Marshall, "The Gestapo in Detroit," in *The Crisis*, August 1943, quoted in Mitchell, ibid., 129–130.

72. Ibid., 130.

73. *Detroit News*, July 30, 1943, quoted in Mitchell, ibid., 144.

74. *Wayne Dispatch*, July 2, 1943, quoted in Mitchell, ibid., 145.

75. Marshall, quoted in Mitchell, ibid., 130.

76. *Detroit News*, June 23, 1943, quoted in Mitchell, ibid., 169.

77. *Jackson Daily News*, July 3, 1943, quoted in Mitchell, ibid., 174.

78. This text associating Negroes, Jews, and Communsists was also circulated in Mississippi. [Hon. John Rankin, *Congressional Record*, July 1, 1943, quoted in Mitchell ibid., 175–176.]

79. See P. Allen Broyles, *The John Birch Society: Anatomy of a Protest* (Boston: Beacon Press, 1964).

80. "The Harlem Riot," *The Crisis* (September 1943), quoted in Mitchell, ibid., 95.

81. The title of a recording by guitarist Charlie Christian (also known under the title *Charlie's Choice*) made at Minton's Playhouse, New York, in May 1941, featuring pianist Thelonious Monk and drummer Kenny Clarke.

82. After renouncing all musical activity, Minton became the first Negro to be elected a member of Local 802 Musicians Union.

83. All these "bebopped" themes are part of Charlie Parker's recorded oeuvre.

84. In Nat Shapiro and Nat Hentoff, *Hear Me Talkin' to Ya* (New York: Dover Publications, 1956), 351, quoted in Lucien Malson, *Histoire du jazz moderne* (Paris: La Table Ronde, 1961), 25.

85. Ibid.

86. "I was always in a panic.... Worst of all was that nobody understood my music." He also said "I'd be happy if what I played were simply called 'music.'" "You know, it used to be so cruel to the musicians, just the way it is today—they say that when *Beethoven* was on his *deathbed* he shook his fist at the world because they just didn't understand.... But that's music." Quoted in J. E. Berendt, op. cit., 85, 89, 90.

87. See Kenneth B. Clark, *Dark Ghetto, Dilemmas of Social Power* (1965; Middletown, CT: Wesleyan University Press, 1989), 83: "The report on urban mental illness based on a neighborhood study conducted in mid-Manhattan and reported publicly in 1962 concluded that one in three in the area was, in some degree, emotionally disturbed."

The National Association for Mental Health estimates the proporition for the entire population of the United States to be one out of ten.

88. Langston Hughes, "Bop," in *The Best of Simple* (New York: Hill and Wang, 1961), 117–119.

89. Beyond the use of the word blues, references to other traditional jazz elements are worth noting, such as *hot, boogie*. . . .

90. Ibid.

91. *Victory-discs* were recorded or released by the army between 1943 and 1945 to boost troops' morale. The recordings were destroyed after the war, as musicians had worked for free. They are collection items now,

92. A member of the Communist Party of the USA in 1934, Richard Wright would quit it ten years later. First a supporter of the black nationalist project pushed by the Party among black intellectuals (which involved the creation of a black republic in the South), much like W. E. B. Du Bois Wright moved near the end of his life toward a form of Panafricanism nevertheless marked by his communist experience. In 1944, Wright wrote an article entitled "I Tried to Be a Communist" (*Atlantic Monthly* 174).

93. Though some of these musicians became famous under their chosen names, they are also known as: William Evans (saxophonist, born in 1920); Edmund Gregory (saxophonist, born in 1925), Walter Bishop Jr (pianist, born in 1927), Sun Ra, Absholm Ben Shlomo (a member of Sun Ra's Arkestra)—it is remarkable that the black musicians that changed their names in the 1960s, that is some fifteen years after the Islamized boppers, are more worried about erasing their "slave names": Ben Shlomo, the Ali brothers, and Kenyatta—Art Blakey (drummer, see chapter 7.g). Kenny Dorham (trumpeter, born in 1924), Kenny Clarke (the first bop drummer) and the trombone player Bernard McKinney (now K. Zawadi or Zwadi). Let us also mention Jamil Nasser or Jamil Suleiman (bassist George Joymen), Suleiman Saud (pianist McCoy Tyner), Aliya Rabiah (singer Dakota Staton), bassist Ahmad Khatab Salim (Atkinson), Ahmed Abdul Malik (bassist Sam Gill).

94. CORE in an interracial integrationist organization founded in Chicago in 1942 by students who wanted to organize anti-Jim Crow demonstrations. With its policy of nonviolent direct action, CORE anticipated the civil rights movement. In 1947, CORE organized the first *Freedom Ride* or *Journey of Reconciliation*. Black and white militants crossed the segregationist states, violating Jim Crow laws. In 1966, Floyd McKissick succeeded Farmer at the head of the movement. Contrary to the NAACP, which represents the interests of the black bourgeoisie, CORE became a kind of movement for the masses.

95. At the end of World War I, two years after the Russian Revolution, the Great Red Scare settled in the minds of American bourgeois, often mixed with the fears generated by the fledgling radicalism of black militants. If a poet such as Claude

McKay had early connections with the CPUS, only later did the Communists attempt to rally black votes. From 1928 to 1957 (when this project was abandoned during a Party Convention in Harlem), one of their objectives was to grant Negroes the right of self-determination in hopes of creating a black republic in the southern areas with black demographic majority. Along with supporting black nationalism, Communists also strove to revalue black culture. Poems, fiction, and articles written by Negroes were routinely published in the Communist press, and during the Harlem Renaissance the CPUS was predictably popular among black intellectuals and gaining an increasing audience among the masses. W. E. B. Du Bois, Langston Hughes, the singer Paul Robeson, Richard Wright were among black celebrities that either joined or sympathized with the Communist Party. The Party played a decisive role in the political maturation of black Americans, defending wrongly accused Negroes, naming James Ford, a Negro, as vice president on the Party's ticket in 1932 and 1936, and by adopting a separatist program that could only entice those who felt nostalgic about Garveyism. CPUS lost some of its audience when in 1943 it voiced disapproval for the Harlem riots in the name of national solidarity in the war against fascism. The Party's "popular front" project that implied a series of concessions on one or the other side further alienated the black masses. In 1970, nevertheless, the arrest and trial of Angela Davis, a Communist intellectual, gave an opportunity for good white Americans to express anew their fear of a Black-Red coalition.

96. For bluesman Lightnin' Hopkins, the Korean war was, it appears, completely predictable: "You know this world is in a tangle, baby, yeah I feel, they're gonna start war again/Yes there's gonna be many mothers and fathers worryin', yes there's gonna be as many girls that lose a frien'/I got the news this mornin', right now they need a million men/You know I been overseas, woman, po' Lightnin' don't want to go there again." Oliver, op. cit., 141.

97. John Birch was allegedly born in India in 1918, where his parents were missionaries. At the end of his studies in 1940, he left to evangelize China. During the war, his linguistic knowledge led him to help the American command. Now a captain, Birch was in charge of spying on Japanese troop movements. A few days before the end of the war, he left on a special mission at the head of a commando of Americans, Nationalist Chinese, and Koreans. It appears that on August 25, 1945, stopped on a road by Communist Chinese, Captain Birch vented his frustration and insulted the partisans. According to the biography drawn by Robert Welch (the founder of the John Birch Society), the leader of the Chinese partisans then shot him dead. Thus did the captain become the first "martyr of world Communism."

98. Berendt, op. cit., 18.

99. Beyond references in *On the Road*, *The Subterraneans*, and *Mexico City Blues*, the importance of jazz as background or source of inspiration must be noted in the novels of J. C. Holmes (*The Horn*) and the poetry of Gregory Corso ("For Miles"). Born in 1925

in New Orleans of a Jewish father and a black mother, the late bloomer Bob Kaufman represents both the Beat movement and a black American poetic tradition going back to Langston Hughes that is inseparable from jazz (see for example Kaufman's poems "Walking Parker Home," "Mingus," "Blues," and "San Francisco Beat" in his collection *Solitudes Crowded with Loneliness*).

100. The Third Stream is a branch of cool that expresses a mystical need for synthesis, either to give jazz full recognition and make it benefit from the wealth and formal diversity of Western music, or, much to the contrary, to add to certain avant-garde experiments warmth and emotional charge of Negro origin. These attempts so far have only resulted in the dilution of the black musical elements used by composers.

101. Like Leadbelly, many of these bluesmen appear to have lived on the margins of white society, choosing life as thieves or pimps over proletarian status. This attitude regarding the order established and imposed by whites must be tied to a certain characteristic of blues texts: they often feature outlaws terrorizing the "good people" with more or less overt admiration.

102. Not only was the blues the main inspiration for rockers, but young white listeners want to discover these "masters" their idols constantly allude to: Muddy Waters (whose "Rolling Stone Blues" inspired Brian Jones in naming his own band), John Lee Hooker, Buddy Guy, Sonny Boy Williamson, Herbert Sumlin, Son House, Skip James, T-Bone Walker, etc. . . .

103. Much like the boxer Muhammad Ali and Malcolm X, James Brown has become for the black masses living proof of their non-inferiority.

104. Rent being always very high in black neighborhoods (because of low wages and unemployment), as soon as they arrived in the North, Negroes began organizing paying musical parties in their homes, the money helping the hosts pay their rent.

105. A piano style appearing around 1928 in Chicago, boogie was among the first attempts to make the blues popular with dancers. The white public discovered it later and was immediately seduced by the virtuosity effects the genre encourages (the left hand plays a simple, almost obsessive accompaniment while the right hand improvises brief melodic variations). Commercialized and widely circulated in the early 1940s, boogie lost its novelty as the repetitive character of accompaniment grew increasingly mechanical.

106. The *Southern Christian Leadership Conference* (SCLC) was constituted in Atlanta in 1957 by southern black ministers led by Martin Luther King Jr, who in 1955 had organized the Montgomery, Alabama, bus boycott.

107. At the end of the nineteenth century, the American Federation of Labor (AFL) replaced the Knights of Labor (sixty thousand black members in 1886). In this new, traditionally racist trade union, only the miners of the United Mine Workers kept the humanitarian and egalitarian precepts of the Knights, who considered all workers

equal without race distinction. Created in 1936 following the Great Depression, the CIO easily trumped the AFL among black workers, inasmuch as it meant to be a mass union movement. The merger of the AFL and the CIO was felt as a betrayal and, in spite of Martin Luther King Jr's attempts to mediate, starting in 1955 black workers began losing all trust in them. From then on, black workers would equate white liberals, workers, and unionists with more "official" oppressors.

108. An advertisement by the Citizens Council of Greater New Orleans (New Orleans, LA, 1967) reads: "Help Save the Youth of America. Don't Buy Negro Records."

109. Georgia judge J. Robert Elliott once declared, "I don't want these pinks, radicals and black voters to outvote those who are trying to preserve our segregationist laws and other traditions." William H. Cox of Mississippi declared, "I am not interested in whether the registrar is going to give a registration test to a bunch of niggers on a voter drive."

110. Malcolm X began his speeches in the style of black ministers with a "brothers and sisters," and used those terms regularly. Nevertheless, the expression "soul brother" quickly became a commercial argument in black neighborhoods and ghettoes: "'I think most of that soul music is now being manufactured rather than felt,' said a Harlem record store owner, 'but at least this is one time in jazz history when the Negroes are popularizing their own music. It would take a lot of courage for Stan Kenton or Shorty Rogers to call one of their albums *The Soul Brothers*.'" Nat Hentoff, *The Jazz Life* (New York: Dial Press, 1961), 69.

111. Other pieces by Mingus indicate the nature of his concerns: "Freedom," "Meditation for Integration," "Prayer for Passive Resistance."

112. In Kofsky, *Black Nationalism and the Revolution in Music*, 120. The musician's "rage," associated with Malcolm X's skepticism, is also present in the writings (*If He Hollers Let Him Go*, *All Shot Up*, *Blind Man with a Pistol*) and the words of novelist Chester Himes: "I think the only way a Negro will get accepted as an equal is if he kills whites; to launch a violent uprising to the point where the people will become absolutely sickened, disgusted; to the place where they will realize they have to do something." In "My Man Himes: An Interview with Chester Himes," John A. Williams, Charles Harris eds. *Amistad 1* (New York: Random House, 1970).

113. *We Insist! Freedom Now Suite*, Max Roach and Oscar Brown Jr, with Abbey Lincoln, Coleman Hawkins, Michael Olatunji, etc.: "Driva' Man," "Freedom Day," "Triptych (Prayer/Protest/Peace)," "All Africa," "Tears for Johannesburg" (Candid Records 8002). Recorded on August 31 and September 6, 1960, in New York.

114. A rare attempt at escaping the bounds of the system of capitalist production, Candid was eventually bought by singer Andy Williams, and eventually revived to publish "nicer" records.

115. "Blue Soul," "Soul Brother," "Soul Sister," "Sister Sadie," "Sister Salvation,"

"Soul Meeting," "Soul Station," "Soul Me," etc. The word "soul" thus becomes a password and a quality label that lets musicians prevail with the black audience.

8. Free Fragments

1. In Philippe Carles, Jean-Louis Comolli, "Les admirables secrets d'Albert le Grand," *Jazz Magazine* 142 (May 1967), 47.

2. Jacques Bisceglia, Jean-Louis Ginibre, "La dent dure et les dents longues," *Jazz Magazine* 180 (July–August 1970), 27.

3. Liner notes to *Change of the Century* (Atlantic SD-1327, 1959).

4. The growl is among the traditional features of jazz treatments of sound. It is crucial to Duke Ellington's *jungle style*.

5. The drum set was born of the union of instruments that were used individually in marching bands (bass drum, cymbals, snare drum, etc.). The jazz drummer therefore became responsible for a series of accessories or, rather, for an ensemble of timbres. He then also had to invent a particular technique and physically adapt to his instrument.

6. The introduction in jazz bands of the string bass (as opposed to the wind bass) as instrument for rhythmical punctuation triggered a systematization of pizzicato play.

7. The instruments invented by the Belgian Adolphe Sax appeared in the late nineteenth century, and they played an especially important role in jazz in that they were virtually devoid of academic European conventions.

8. Delfeil de Ton, "Alan Silva and Dave Burrell," *Charlie-Hebdo* 8 (January 11, 1971), 13.

9. Ibid.

10. [Translator's note: "A term, derived from the present participle of the Italian verb concertare ('to arrange', 'to agree', 'to get together'), generally signifying music that is in some sense soloistic, with a contrasting element, or 'concerto-like.'" *Oxford Music Online*.]

11. *Jazz Magazine* 142.

12. In *Jazz Hot* 253 (1967), 19.

13. Daniel Caux, "Milford Graves et les paradoxes du nouveau drumming," *Jazz Hot* 251 (June 1969), 15.

14. Jean-Louis Noames, "Le système Taylor," *Jazz Magazine* 125 (December 1965), 38.

15. Milford Graves, op. cit., 17.

16. Lee Lockwood, *Conversations with Eldridge Cleaver* (New York: McGraw-Hill, 1970), 112–113.

17. Francis Bebey, *African Music: A People's Art*, trans. Josephine Bennett (1975; Chicago: Lawrence Hill Books, 1999), 122.

18. Liner notes from *Looking Ahead*, quoted in A. B. Spellman, *Four Jazz Lives* (1965; Ann Arbor: University of Michigan Press, 2004), 27.

19. Ibid., 34.

20. Cleaver, *Soul on Ice*, 224.

21. Ibid., 234–5.

22. BYG 529.330, "Actuel" 30.

23. Impulse A-97.

24. See the "impressionistic" and very clean use of soprano Kay Davis in "Transbluesency" in 1946.

25. *Jazz Magazine* 142, ibid.

26. Archie Shepp, liner notes to *The Magic of Ju-Ju* (Impulse A-9154, 1967).

9. Music/Politics

1. Ornette Coleman in Melvin Van Peebles, "Tête à tête avec Ornette," *Jazz Magazine* 125 (December 1965), 30.

2. When they do not, we get jaw-dropping interventions by *musicians* (Kenny Dorham in *Down Beat*, Martial Solal in *Jazz Magazine*, Jef Gilson in *Jazz Hot*) in the form of insults, snickers, and complete hostility. It is remarkable that it was felt necessary to summon experienced musicians in order to bring down free jazz musicians. This peculiar deference to "professionals" shows the incompetence of those critics who "didn't like it" on the topic of free jazz.

3. Co-opt free jazz and you get the same critics who did not want to hear about Ayler, Coleman, or Shepp praising a showman such as Charles Lloyd. The free jazz "effects" produced by a handy hack can convince doubters that free jazz can be... seductive music!

4. "At last one one must get used to not seeking everywhere only what is pleasant. Music is not made to charm the ears, even austerely, any more than painting is made to enchant the eyes. . . . Let us be rid, once and for all, of the hedonistic principle that can basically be found—in a form that is more or less disguised—at the root of almost every attack against innovation! Enough of those overly facile, weak, and fastidious 'voluptuaries,'" Michel Leiris, "The Case of Arnold Schoenberg," *Brisées: Broken Branches*, trans. Lydia Davis (San Francisco: North Point Press, 1989), 16.

5. [Translator's note: the source for this quote is not mentioned in the original text.]

6. Quoted in Berendt, op. cit., 51.

7. Quoted in Nat Hentoff, "Charles Mingus," in *These Jazzmen of Our Time*, Raymond Horricks ed. (New York: Jazz Book Club, 1960), 178.

8. Quoted in Frank Kofsky, "John Coltrane," *Jazz & Pop* (September 1967), 26.

9. In Jean Clouzet and Jean Wagner, "Trente questions à Max," *Jazz Magazine* 114 (January 1965), 21.

10. Quoted in Kofsky, *Black Nationalism*, 63.

11. Benoît Quersin, *Jazz Magazine* 119 (Juin 1965), 38.

12. In *Coda, Canada's Jazz Magazine* (Toronto: February 1968).

13. Igor Stravinsky, "The Composition of Music" in *Poetics of Music: In the Form of Six Lessons* (New Haven: Harvard University Press, 1970), 47; 117.

14. Stravinsky, "The Composition of Music." 11; 17.

15. A. Zhdanov, *Essays on Literature, Philosophy, and Music* (New York: International Publishers, 1950).

16. Francis Bebey, *African Music*, 2–5.

17. Quoted in Ted Joans, "Black Power et New Thing," *Jazz Magazine* (January 1968), 19.

18. Michel Leiris, "The Ethnographer Faced With Colonialism," 123-24.

19. On the importance of black theatre, read Franck Jotterand, *Le nouveau théâtre américain* (Paris: Seuil, 1970).

20. See Robinson Armstead L. et al., *Black Studies in the University* (New York: Bantam, 1969).

21. This is why defenders of "synthesis" speak, unawares, solely from the white point of view, whereby white culture was indeed enriched by black culture.

Preface to 1979 Edition

1. *Free jazz* was in fact on its way to being marginalized when this book was first published in January 1971, precisely because it was only barely recognized and accepted as yet another jazz style, replaceable as all the others. It seemed to us that much to the contrary, in the antagonized developments of *free jazz* something of a trans-stylistic truth of jazz was manifested, one that made *history* out of this series of styles, the history of a struggle in musical forms to put in relation to the history of the struggles of black people.

2. For example Mauricio Kagel with Peter Brötzmann, Krysztof Penderecki with the Globe Unity Orchestra, Luciano Berio with Michel Portal, Jean-Pierre Drouet with Jean-François Jenny-Clark, etc.

3. Black nationalism as a militant ideology has been replaced by more politicized analyses of the status of black struggles in the international fight against American imperialism: the most spectacular black American organization, the Black Panther Party, has gone underground and grown more radical, painstakingly destroyed by white police, torn apart by internal conflict: it is less visible, but not the least absent. If the struggles of black Americans now seem quieter, it is also because as they have

become less of a "good cause" and have to do without media attention. According to Don Pullen, "There are no leaders left, for whites or blacks. In the case of blacks it is a fundamental problem. If, for example, Huey Newton has changed, I think prison is to blame. Torture and beatings can change you. . . . You have to be superhuman to survive, to resist such an ordeal," in Giacomo Pelliciotti, "Mingus Dynasty," *Jazz Magazine* 233 (May–June 1975). Archie Shepp explains: "I have seen many radicals, or rather supporters of social change, destroyed because they put themselves forward, because they talked too much, on TV, in the newspapers . . . in short, because they trusted a system with no morals." [Translator's note: no source for this quote is indicated in the original text.]

Discography

Record titles are in italics, theme titles between inverted commas. Other musicians participating in the recording, the year of the recording, and the original recording label are also mentioned.

This alphabetical list is preceded by a short chronological inventory of records that, for being older than and foreign to free jazz per se, nevertheless point to numerous *encounters* between the different historical forms of African American music and of political and social demands of the black American community, as well as some explicit precursors to the modes of improvisation that would become inseparable from free jazz.

1

BESSIE SMITH: *The Complete Recordings* (1923–1933), CBS/SONY MUSIC.
BILLIE HOLIDAY: "Strange Fruit" in *The Complete Commodore Recordings* (1939–1944), COMMODORE.
DUKE ELLINGTON: "Black, Brown and Beige" (1944), RCA/BMG.
CHARLIE PARKER: *The Charlie Parker Story* (1945), SAVOY; *Bird: The Complete Charlie Parker on Verve* (1948–1954), VERVE/UNIVERSAL.
LENNIE TRISTANO: *Intuition* with Lee Konitz and Warne Marsh (1949), CAPITOL.
HORACE SILVER – ART BLAKEY: "Message from Kenya" in *Horace Silver Trio and Art Blakey* (1953), BLUE NOTE/EMI.
SHELLY MANNE: "Abstract No. 1" in *The Three* with Shorty Rogers and Jimmy Giuffre (1954), CONTEMPORARY/ ORIGINAL JAZZ CLASSICS.
SONNY ROLLINS: *Freedom Suite* (2958), ORIGINAL JAZZ CLASSICS/WEA.
MAX ROACH: *We Insist—Freedom Now Suite* (1960), CANDID.
CHARLES MINGUS: "Original Faubus Fables" in *Charles Mingus Presents Charles Mingus* (1960), CANDID.
JOHN COLTRANE: "Africa" in *The Complete Africa/Brass Sessions* (1961), IMPULSE.
J. B. LENOIR: *Alabama Blues!* (1965), BELLAPHON.
CHARLES MINGUS: "Don't Let It Happen Here" in *Monterey Jazz Festival 40 Legendary Years*, MALPASO/WEA.
JACKIE MCLEAN: *New and Old Gospel* with Ornette Coleman (1967), BLUE NOTE/EMI.

2

MUHAL RICHARD ABRAMS (piano, composition): *Levels and Degrees of Light* with Anthony Braxton, Leroy Jenkins, Maurice McIntyre, Charles Clark, Thurman Barker, etc. (1967), DELMARK; *Young at Heart/Wise in Time* with Leo Smith, Henry Threadgill, Lest Lashley, T. Barker (1970), DELMARK; *Sightsong* with Malachi Fa-

vors (1975), BLACK SAINT; *Blu Blu Blu* (1990), BLACK SAINT; *One Line, Two Views* 91995), NEW WORLD RECORDS.
AIR (Henry Threadgill: reeds, percussions; Fred Hopkins: bass; Steve McCall: drums): *Live Air* (1977), BLACK SAINT.
BYRON ALLEN (saxophone): *The Byron Allen Trio* (1964), ESP/CALIBRE.
BARRY ALTSCHUL (drums): *You Can't Name Your Own Tune* with George Lewis, Sam Rivers, Muhal Richard Abrams, Dave Holland (1977), MUSE.
ART ENSEMBLE OF CHICAGO (Lester Bowie: trumpet; Roscoe Mitchell, Joseph Jarman: reeds; Malachi Favors: bass, Famoudou Don Moye: drums): *A Jackson in Your House/ Message to Our Folks* (Lester Bowie, Joseph Jarman, Roscoe Mitchell, Malachi Favors, 1969), BYG ACTUEL/CHARLY RECORDS; *Reese and the Smooth Ones* (2969), BYG; *Tutankhamun* (1969), BLACK SAINT; *The Spiritual* (1969), FREEDOM; *Les stances à Sophie* with Fontella Bass (1970), NESSA; *Bap –Tizum* (Bowie, Jarman, Mitchell, Favors, Famoudou Don Moye, 1972), *Fanfare for the Warriors* (+Abrams, 1973), ATLANTIC/WEA.
ALBERT AYLER (saxophone): *My Name is Albert Ayler* with Niels Bronsted, Niels Henning Ørsted Pedersen, Roonie Gardiner (1963), BLACK LION; *Goin' Home* with Call Cobbs, Henry Grimes, Sunny Murray (1964), BLACK LION; *Spirits* with Sunny Murray (1964), DEBUT; *Ghosts* with Don Cherry, Gary Peacock, Murray (1964), DEBUT; *Spiritual Unity* with Peacock, Murray (1964), ESP/CALIBRE; *New York Eye and Year Control* with Cherry, Peacock, Murray, John Tchicai and Roswell Rudd (1964), ESP; *Bells* with Don Ayler, Charles Tyler, Lewis Worrell and Murray (1964), ESP; *Spirits Rejoice* with D. Ayler, Tyler, Grimes, Peacock, Murray (1965), ESP/CALIBRE; *Albert Ayler in Greenwich Village* (1966–67), IMPULSE; *Love Cry* with D. Ayler, Cobbs, harpsichord, Silva, Graves (19670, IMPULSE; *New Grass* (1968), IMPULSE; *Music is the Healing Force of the Universe* (1969), IMPULSE.
DEREK BAILEY (guitar): *Solo Guitar* (1971), INCUS; *Fairly Early with Postscripts* (with Kent Carter, John Stevens, Anthony Braxton, and solos, 1971/1998), EMANEM; *Bailey-Bennink* (1972), INCUS; *Lot 74 – Solo Improvisations*, INCUS; *London Concert* (E. Parker, 1975), INCUS; *Domestic& Public Pieces* (1975–77), EMANEM; *Bailey-Honsinger* (1976), INCUS; *Outcome* (with Steve Lacy, 1983), POTLATCH; *Lace* (1989), EMANEM; *Wireforks – Guitar Duets* (with Henry Kaiser, 1995), SHANACHIE; *The Sign of 4* (with Pat Metheny, 1996), KNITTING FACTORY WORKS; *No Waiting* (with Joëlle Léandre, 1997), POTLATCH.
GATO BARBIERI (saxophone): *The Third World* (1969), FLYING DUTCHMAN; *In Search of the Mystery* (1967), ESP; *Hamba Khale* (with Dollar Brand, 1968), TOGETHERNESS (CHARLY AFFINITY).
HAN BENNINK (drums): *Solo* (1972), ICP; *Serpentine* (with Dave Douglas, 1996).
KARL BERGER (vibraphone, piano): *From Now On* (with Henry Grimes and Ed Blackwell, 1966), ESP; *Peace Church Concert* (with Dave Holland, Richard Teitelbaum,

Garrett List, Ingrid, 1974), INDIA NAVIGATION; *All Kinds of Time* (with Holland, 1976), SACKVILLE; *We Are You* (with Peter Kowald, Allen Blairman, 1990), ENJA; *Crystal Fire* (with Holland and Blackwell, 1991), ENJA; *Conversations* (with James Blood Ulmer, Ray Anderson, Carlos Wald, Holland, Mark Feldman, 1994), IN & OUT.

JAC BERROCAL (trumpet): *Parallèles* (with Roger Ferlet, Michel Potage, Claude Bernard, Bernard Vitet, Peirre Bastien, Richard Marachin, Philippe Pocha, Vince Taylor, 1976), DAVANTAGE; *Hotel Hotel* (with Bastien, Clive Bell, Marc Dufourd, Daunik Lazro, Tony Marsh, 1986), NATO; *La nuit est le courant* (with Hubertus Biermann, Francis Marmande, Jacques Tollot, 1989), IN SITU.

ED BLACKWELL (drums): *Walls – Bridges* (with Dewey Redman and Cameron Brown, 1992), BLACK SAINT.

CARLA BLEY (piano, composition): *Jazz Realities* (with Mike Mantler, Steve Lacy, Kent Carter, Aldo Romano, 1966), FONTANA.

PAUL BLEY (piano): *The Fabulous Paul Bley Quintet* (with Don Cherry, Ornette Coleman, Charlie Haden, Billy Higgins, 1958), MUSIDISC; *Barrage* (with Dewey Johnson, Marshall Allen, Eddie Gomez, Milford Graves, 1964), ESP/CALIBRE; *Touching* (1965), DEBUT; *Time Will Tell* (with Evan Parker and Barre Phillips, 1995), ECM.

HAMIET BLUIETT (baritone saxophone): *Endangered Species* (with Olu Dara, Phillip Wilson..., 1976), INDIA NAVIGATION; *Birthright* (solo, q977), INDIA NAVIGATION.

ARTHUR BLYTHE (alto saxophone): *The Grip* (with Abdullah, Bob Stewart, Abdul Wadud, Steve Reid, 1977), INDIA NAVIGATION.

RAYMON BONI (guitar): *Pot-Pourri Pour Parce Que* (with Claude Bernard, 1977), HAT HUT; *Two Angels for Cecil* (with Eric Echampard, 1998), EMOUVANCE.

LESTER BOWIE (trumpet): *Numbers 1 & 2* (with Roscoe Mitchell, Joseph Jarman, Malachi favors, 1967), NESSA; *Fast Last!* (Julius Hemphill, Joseph Bowie, Phillip Wilson, Cecil McBee, John Hicks, etc., 1974), MUSE; *The Fifth Power* (Arthur Blythe, Favors, Wilson, Claudine Amina Myers, 1978), BLACK SAINT; *Duet* (Wilson, 1978), IMPROVISING ARTIST INC.

CHARLES BRACKEEN (saxophone): *Bannar* (with Dennis Gonzalez, Malachi Favors, Alvin Fielder, 1987), SILKHEART.

ANTHONY BRAXTON (saxophones, clarinets, composition): *Three Compositions of New Jazz* (with Leroy Jenkins, Leo Smith, Richard Abrams, 1968), DELMARK; *For Alto* (1968); DELMARK; *Silence* (Smith, Jenkins, 1969), FREEDOM; *B-X NOI 47 A* (Smith, Jenkins, Steve McCall, 1969), BYG; *This Time* (Smith, Jenkins, McCall, 1970), BYG; *Recital Paris '71*, FUTURA; *The Complete Braxton* (Chick Corea, Dave Holland, Barry Altschul, Kenny Wheeler, 1971), FREEDOM; *Dona Lee* (Michael Smith, Peter Warren, Oliver Johnson, 1972), AMERICA; *Town Hall '72* (Jeanne Lee, John Stubblefield, Holland, Altschul, Phillip Wilson), TRIO; *Together Alone* (with

Joseph Jarman, 1972), DELAMRK; *Four Compositions '73* (with Masahiko Sato, Keiki Midorikawa, HozumiTanaka), COLUMBIA; *In the Tradition* (with Tete Montoliu, Niels Henning Ørsted-Pedersen, Al Heath, 1974), STEEPLECHASE; *Live at Moers* (1974), RING; *First Duo Concert* (Smith, Richard Teitelbaum, 1974), SACKVILLE; *New York Fall '74* (Wheeler, Holland, Jerome Cooper, Jenkins, Teitelbaum, Oliver Lake, Hamiet Bluiett, Julius Hemphill), ARISTA; *Moers Festival* (Wheeler, Holland, Altschul, 1975), RING; *Five Pieces '75* (Wheeler, Holland, Altschul), ARISTA; *Duets* (Abrams, 1976); The *Montreux/Berlin Concerts* (George Lewis, Wheeler, Holland, Altschul, 1976), ARISTA; *Birth and Rebirth* (duet with Max Roach, 1978), BLACK SAINT; *Six Monk Compositions* (Mal Waldron, Buell Neidlinger, Bill Osborne, 1987), BLACK SAINT; *Eight (+3) Tristano Compositions* (John Raskin, Dred Scott, ecil McBee, Andrew Cyrille, 1989), HAT ART; *Wesleyan (12 Alto Solos)* (1992), HAT ART; *Trio (London 1993)* (Evan Parker, Paul Rutherford), LEO; *Charlie Parker Project 1993* (Ari Brown, Paul Smoker, Misha Mengelberg, Joe Fonda, Han Bennink, Pheeroan AkLaff), HAT ART.

PETER BRÖTZMANN (reeds): *Machine Gun* (with Willem Breuker, Evan Parker, Fred van Hove, Peter Kowald, Buschi Niebergall, Han Bennink, Sven Ake Johannson, 1968); *Couscous de la Mauresque* (Bennink, van Hove, Albert Mangelsdorff, 1971); *Brötzmann –van Hove – Bennink* (1973); *Outspan 2* (Bennink, van Hove, 1974); *Solo '76; 3 Points and a Mountain . . . Plus* (with Misha Mengelberg, Bennink, 1979); *Réservé* (with Barre Phillips, Gunter Baby Sommer, 1988); *Wie das Leben so spielt* (with Werner Lüdi, 1989); *No Nothing* (1990), *Nothing to Say* (solo, 1994); *Die Like a Dog* (1993); *Little Birds, Have Fast Hearts* (with Toshinori Kondo, William Parker, Hamid Drake, 1997)—all on FMP (FREE MUSIC PRODUCTION).

MARION BROWN (saxophone): *Capricorn Moon* (with Alan Shorter, Benny Maupin, Ronnie Boykins, Rashied Ali, 1965), ESP; *Three for Shepp* (1966), IMPULSE; *Afternoon of a Georgia Faun* (Anthony Braxton, Jeanne Lee, Andrew cyrille, Maupin, 1970), ECM; *Duets* (Leo Smith, Elliot Schwartz, 1970, 1973), ARISTA.

KENT CARTER (bass): *Solo* (1976), ICTUS; *Suspension* (1977), ICTUS; *The Willisau Suites* (with Carlos Zingaro, François Dreno, 19840, ITM PACIFIC; *K.C. & Albrecht Maurer* (1996), EMANEM.

ANDREA CENTAZZO (percussions): *Real Time* (with Alvin Curran, Evan Parker, 1977), ICTUS.

EUGENE CHADBOURNE (guitar): *Solo Acoustic Guitar* (1975–1976), PARACHUTE; *Patrizio* (with Paul Lovens, 1996), VICTO.

DON CHERRY (trumpet, flute, etc.): *The Avant Garde* (with John Coltrane, 1960), ATLANTIC; *Togetherness* (Gato Barbieri, Karl Berger, Jean-François Jenny-Clark, Aldo Romano, 1965), DURIUM; *Complete Communion* (Barbieri, Henry Grimes, Ed Blackwell, 1965), BLUE NOTE; *Symphony for Improvisers* (Pharoah Sanders, etc., 1966), BLUE NOTE; *Where is Brooklyn?* (Sanders, 1966), BLUE NOTE; *Eternal*

Rhythm (Eje Thelin, Sonny Sharrock, Berger, Joachim Kühn, Jacques Thollot, 1968), MPS; *Mu* (with Blackwell, 1969), BYG; *Human Music* (Jon Appleton, 1970), FLYING DUTCHMAN; *Old and New Dreams* (Dewey redman, Charlie Haden, Blackwell, 1977), BLACK SAINT; *Art Deco* (James Clay, Haden, Billy Higgins, 1988), A&M.

GUNTER CHRISTMANN (trombone)/DETLEF SCHÖNENBERG (drums): *Remarks* (Harald Boje, 1975), FMP; *Live at Moers* (1976), RING.

ORNETTE COLEMAN (saxophone, trumpet, violin, composition): *Tomorrow is the Question* (Don Cherry, Red Mitchell, Percy Heath, Shelly Manne, 1959), CONTEMPORARY/ORIGINAL JAZZ CLASSICS; *The Shape of Jazz to Come, Change of the Century* (Cherry, Charlie Haden, Billy Higgins, 1959); *This is Our Music* (Cherry, Haden, Ed Blackwell, 19610; *Free Jazz: A Collective Improvisation by the Ornette Coleman Double Quartet* (Cherry Freddie Hubbard, Eric Dolphy, Scott LaFaro, Haden, Higgins and Blackwell, 1961); *Ornette!* (1962); *Ornette on Tenor* (1962); *The Art of Improvisers* (1959–1961); *Twins* (1959–60); *To Whom Who Keeps a Record* (1959–60), or *Beauty is a Rare Thing—Ornette Coleman: The Complete Atlantic Recordings*, ATLANTIC/RHINO; *Town Hall Concert* (1962), ESP/CALIBRE; *Chappaqua Suite* (Pharoah Sanders, David Izenzon, Charles Moffett, 1965), SONY; *New York Is Now* (Dewey Redman, Jimmy Garrison, Elvin Jones, 1968), BLUE NOTE; *Friends and Neighbors* (Redman, Haden, Blackwell, 1970), FLYING DUTCHMAN/RCA BMG; *Science Fiction* (Cherry, Bobby Bradford, Haden, Higgins, Blackwell, 1971), SONY; *Skies of America* (1972), SONY; *Soapsuds Soapsuds* (Haden, 1977), HARMOLODIC/VERVE; *In All Languages* (Cherry, Haden, Higgins, Denardo Coleman, Calvin Weston, Jamaaladeen Tacuma, Al McDowell, Charlie Ellerbee, Bern Nix, 1978), HARMOLODIC; *Naked Lunch, Music from the Original Soundtrack* (Howard Shore, Barre Phillips, Denardo Coleman, 1991), MILAN/BMG; *Tone Dialing* (1995), HARMOLODIC; *Colors* (Joachim Kühn, 1996), HARMOLODIC.

JOHN COLTRANE (saxophones): *Ascension* (reddie Hubbard, Dewey Johnson, John Tchicai, Marion Brown, Archie Shepp, Pharoah Sanders, McCoy Tyner, Jimmy Garrison, Art Davis, Elvin Jones, 1965); *Kulu Se Mama* (1965); *Selflessness* (1965); *Meditations* (Sanders, Rashied Ali, 1966), *Cosmic Music* (1966–1968); *Live at the Village Vanguard Again* (Sanders, Alice Coltrane, Garrison, Ali, 1966); *Expression* (1967)—all on IMPULSE.

ANDREW CYRILLE (drums): *What About* (1969), BYG; *Dialogue of the Drums* (with Milford Graves, 1974), IPS (INSTITUTE OF PERCUSSIVE STUDIES); *Celebration* (Jeanne Lee, David Ware, Ted Daniel, Stafford James, etc., 1975), IPS; *Junction* (Daniel, Ware, Lyle Atkinson, 1976), IPS; *The Loop* (1978), ICTUS; *Nuba* (Lee, Jimmy Lyons, 1979), BLACK SAINT; *Special People* (Daniel, Ware, etc., 1980), SOUL NOTE.

COMPANY: *Derek Bailey - Tristan Honsinger – Maarten Altena – Evan Parker; Bailey –*

Anthony Braxton – Parker; Bailey – Han Bennink; Bailey – Steve Lacy (1976)—all on INCUS.

CREATIVE CONSTRUCTION COMPANY (Anthony Braxton, Leo Smith, Muhal Richard Abrams, Leroy Jenkins, Richard Davis, Steve McCall): *Muhal* (1971), *No More White Gloves* (2972), MUSE.

LOWELL DAVIDSON (piano): *Trio* (with Gary Peacock, Milford Graves, 1965), ESP/CALIBRE.

BILL DIXON (trumpet): *Septet* (1963), SAVOY; *Intents and Purposes* (with Byard Lancaster, Robin Kenyatta, Reggie Workman, Jimmy Garrison, Marc Levin, Bob Pozar, 1966-1967), RCA VICTOR; *Collection* (1970–6), CADENCE; *November 1981* (1981), SOUL NOTE; *Thoughts* (1985), SOUL NOTE.

ERIC DOLPHY (reeds): *Outward Bound* (1960), NEW JAZZ; *Out There* (1960), NEW JAZZ; *Far Cry* (with Booker Little, 1960), NEW JAZZ; *At the Five Spot* (with Little, Mal Waldron, Ed Blackwell, 1961), NEW JAZZ/PRESTIGE; *In Europe* (1961), PRESTIGE; *Memorial Album* (Woody Shaw, Prince Lasha, Clifford Jordan, Sonny Simmons, Bobby Hutcherson, Eddie Kahn, Richard Davis, J.C. Moses, 1963), VEEJAY; *Iron Man* (1963), DOUGLAS; *Out to Lunch* (Freddie Hubbard, Hutcherson, Davis, Tony Williams, 1964), BLUE NOTE; *Last Date* (Misja Mangelberg, Jacques Schols, Han Bennink, 1964), LIMELIGHT.

CHICO FREEMAN (reeds): *Morning Prayer* (Henry Threadgill, Muhal Richard Abrams, Douglas Ewart, Cecil McBee, Ben Montgomery, Steve McCall, Titos Sompa, 1977), INDIA NAVIGATION.

GIORGIO GASLINI (piano, composition): *Nuovi Sentimenti* (Don Cherry, Enrico Rava, Steve Lacy, Gianni Bedori, Gato Barbieri, Kent Carter, Jean-François Jenny-Clark, Frnaco Tonani, Aldo Romano, 1966), RCA.

GLOBE UNITY (Alex Schlippenbach, Peter Kowald, Evan Parker, Paul Lovens, Gerd Dudek, Paul Turherford, Kenny Wheeler, . . .): *Live in Wupperthal* (1973), FMP; *Evidence* (Steve Lacy, Albert Mangelsdorff, etc., 1975), FMP; *Pearls* (Anthony Braxton, Gunter Christmann, Mangelsdorff, etc., 1976), FMP; *Jahrmarkt/Local Fair* (Braxton, Christmann, Brötzmann, Mangelsdorff, etc., 1976), PO TORCH; *Improvisations* (Brötzmann, Tristan Honinger, Derek Bailey, etc., 1977), JAPO.

MILFORD GRAVES (drums, percussions): *Milford Graves Percussion Ensemble* (with Sunny Morgan, 1965), ESP; *In Concert at Yale University* (with Don Pullen, 1966), SRP; *Dialogue of the Drums* (Andrew Cyrille, 1974), IPS; *Bäbi* (Hugh Glover, Arthur Doyle, 1976), IPS; *Real Deal* (with David Murray, 1991), DIW.

BURTON GREENE (piano): *Quartet* (Marion Brown, Henry Grimes, Dave Grant, Tom Prince, Frank Smith, 1966), ESP; *Presenting Burton Greene* (Byard Lancaster, Steve Tintweiss, Shelly Rusten, 1969), COLUMBIA.

HENRY GRIMES (bass): *The Call* (Perry Ronbinson, Tom Price, 1965), ESP.

CHARLIE HADEN (bass): *Liberation Music Orchestra* (Perry Robinson, Dewey Redman,

Don Chery, Michael Mantler, Roswell Rudd, Bob Northern, Howard Johnson, Paul Motian, Andrew Cyrille, Sam Brown, Carla Bley, Gato Barbieri, 1969), IMPULSE; *Closeness* (Ornette Coleman, Alice Coltrane, Keith Jarrett, Paul Motian, 1976), HORIZON A&M; *The Golden Number* (Cherry, Coleman, Archie Shepp, Hampton Hawes, 1976), HORIZON A&M; *The Montreal Tapes* (Cherry, Ed Blackwell, 1989), VERVE; *Liberation Music Orchestra—Dream Keeper* (C. Bley, Redman, Joe Lovano, Branford Marsalis, Ken McIntyre, Tom Harrell, Motian..., 1990), POLYDOR.

GUNTER HAMPEL (vibraphone, bass clarinet, flute): *Gunter Hampel Groupe + Jeanne Lee* (1968), WERGO; *The 8th of July 1969* (Anthony Braxton, Lee, Steve McCall, etc.); *Dances* (1969); *Spirits* (Lee, Perry Robinson, 1971); *Familie* (Braxton, Lee, 1972); *Cosmic Dancer* (Lee, McCall, Robinson, 1975); *Enfant Terrible* (Braxton, Lee, etc., 1975); *Jubilation* (Lee, Marion Brown, Robinson. Manfred Schoof, Albert Mangelsdorff, Barre Phillips, etc., 1983)—all on BIRTH.

GERRY HEMINGWAY (drums): *Kwambe* (with Ray Anderson, Wes Brown, Anthony Davis, Mark Helias, Jay Hoggard, George Lewis, 1978), AURICLE RECORDS; *Special Detail* (Don Byron, Wolter Wierbos, Ernst Reijseger, Ed Schuller, 1990), HAT ART; *The Marmalade King* (Michael Moore, Wierbos, Reijseger, Mark Dresser, 1994), HAT ART.

JULIUS HEMPHILL (reeds, composition): *Dogon A.D.* (with Baikida Carroll, Abdul Walud, Philip Wilson, 1972), ARISTA; *Coon Bid'ness*. (Arthur Blythe, Hamiet Bluiett, Walud, Altschul, Carroll, Wilson, 1975), BLACK LION; *Blue Boyé* (1977), MBARI/SCREWGUN; *Blue Boyé* (1977) MBARI/SCREWGUN; *Roi Boyé* (1977) SACKVILLE. *Raw Materials and Residuals* (Wadud, Don Moye, 1977), BLACK SAINT; *Live from the New Music Café* (with Wadud and Joe Bonadio, 1991), MUSIC & ARTS; *Oakland Duets* (Wadud, 1992), MUSIC & ARTS; *Fat Man and the Hard Blues* (Carl Grubbs, James Carter, Marty Ehrlich, Sam Furnace, Andrew White, 1991), BLACK SAINT; *Five Chord Stud* (Tim Berne, Carter, Ehrlich, Furnace, Fred Ho, White, 1993), BLACK SAINT.

DAVE HOLLAND (bass): *Music From Two Basses* (with Barre Phillips, 1971), ECM; *Improvisations for Cello and Guitar* (Derek Bailey, 1971), ECM; *Conference of the Birds* (Anthony Braxton, Sam Rivers, Barry Altschul, 1972), ECM.

TRISTAN HONSINGER (cello): *Live Performances* (with Maarten van Regteren Altena, 1976), SAJ; *Map of Moods* (quintet, with Louis Moholo, 1994), FMP.

WILLIAM HOOKER (drums): *Is Eternal Life* (David Murray, Mark Miller, David Ware, Hasaan Dawkins, Les Goodson, 1976), REALITY UNIT CONCEPTS.

NOAH HOWARD (alto saxophone): *Noah Howard Quartet* (Rick Colbeck, Scotty Holt, Dave Grant, 1966), ESP.

HUMAN ARTS ENSEMBLE: *Under the Sun* (Lester Bowie, Oliver Lake, Charles Bobo Shaw, Carol Marshall, James Marshall, J.D. Parran, etc., 1973), ARISTA.

ISKRA: *1903* (Derek Bailey, Paul Rutherford, Barry Guy, 1972), INCUS.

MICHAEL GREGORY JACKSON (guitar): *Clarity* (Leo Smith, Oliver Lake, David Murray, 1976) BJA.
BOB JAMES (piano): *Explosions* (Barre Phillips, Bob Pozar, 1965), ESP/CALIBRE.
JOSEPH JARMAN (reeds): *Song For* (with Fred Anderson, Thurman Barker, Steve McCall, 1966), *As If It Were the Seasons* (Charles Clark, Barker, Muhal Richard Abrams, Anderson, John Stubblefield, John Jackson, Lester Lashley, 1968), *Together Alone* with Anthony Braxton (1971)—all on DELMARK; *Egwu Anwu*, (Don Moye, 1978), INDIA NAVIGATION.
THE JAZZ COMPOSER'S ORCHESTRA: *Communication* (Michael Mantler, Rudd, Tchicai, Lyons, Lacy, Kenyatta, Ken McIntyre, Shepp, Bley, Eddie Gomez, Kent Carter, Steve Swallow, Graves, 1964–1965), FONTANA; *Communications* (soloists: Don Cherry, Gato Barbieri, Larry Corryell, Pharoah Sanders, Cecil Taylor, 1968), JCOA.
LEROY JENKINS (violin): *For Players Only* (L. Smith, Bracton, M. McIntyre, Joseph Bowie, Dewey Redman, Sirone, Dave Holland, Charles Bobo Shaw, etc., 1975), JCOA; *Swift Are the Winds of Life* (Rashied Ali, 1975), SURVIVAL; *A Solo Concert* (1976); INDIA NAVIGATION; *The Legend of Aï Glatson* (1978), BLACK SAINT.
LEROI JONES (AMIRI BARAKA): *Black and Beautiful* (1965), JIHAD; *A Black Mass* (with Sun Ra & Myth Science Arkestra, 1968), JOHAD/SON BOY RECORDS.
ROBIN KENYATTA (reeds): *Until* (Mike Lawrence, Rudd, Walter Booker, Lewis Worrell, Horace Arnold, 1966), VORTEX; *Beggars and Stealers* (Abrams, etc., 1969–1975), MUSE.
LEE KONITZ (saxophones): *The Lee Konitz Duets* (Berger, Joe Henderson, Eddie Gomez, Elvin Jones, etc., 1967), MILESTONE.
PETER KOWALD (bass): *Quintet* (Rutherford, Gunter Christmann, Paul Lovens, etc., 1972), FMP; *Was Da Ist* (1994), FMP.
JOACHIM KÜHN (piano): *Transfiguration* (Rolf Kühn, Berger, Beb Guérin, Aldo Romano, 1967), MPS; *Sounds of Feelings* (Jean-François Jenny-Clark, Romano, 1969), BYG; *Abstracts* (1993), LABEL BLEU.
STEVE LACY (soprano saxophone):*Evidence* (Cherry, 1961), NEW JAZZ; *The Forest and the Zoo* (Enrico Rava, 1966), ESP; *Lapis* (1972—in *Scratching the Seventies*), SARAVAH; *The Gap* (Steve Potts, K. Carter, Irène Aebi, Noel McGhie, 1972), AMERICA; *Weal and Woe* (1972-1973), EMANEM; *The Crust* (Bailey, Potts, Carter, Stevens, 1973), EMANEM; *Saxophone Special* (Potts, Evan Barker, Trevor Watts, Bailey, Michael Waisvisz, 1974), EMANEM; *Flakes* (Potts, Carter, Aebi, McGhie, 1974), VISTA; *Stabs* (solo, 1975), SAJ; *Dreams* (Potts, Bailey, Carter, Aebi, Jean-Jacques Avenel, Kenneth Tyler, 1975—in *Scratching the Seventies*), SARAVAH; *Axieme* (1975), RED RECORDS; *Clangs* (Andrea Centazzo, 1976), ICTUS; *Lacy-Carter-Centazzo* (1976), ICTUS; *Sidelines* (Michael Smith, 1976), IAI; *Threads* (Alvin Curran, Frederic Rzewski, 1977), HORO; *Raps* (Potts, Ron Miller, Oliver Johnson, 1977),

ADELPHI; *Catch* (K. Carter, 1977), HORO; *N.Y. Capers & Quirks* (Ronnie Boykins, Dennis Charles, 1979), FMP; *Image* (Steve Argüelles, 1987), AH-UM MUSIC; *+16 Itinerary* (1990), HAT ART.

OLIVER LAKE (reeds): *Passing Thru* (solo, 1974), AFRICA; *Heavy Spirits* (Olu Dara, Joseph Bowie, Charles Bobo Shaw, etc., 1975), ARISTA; *Lake-Joseph Bowie* (1976), SACKVILLE; *Holding Together* (Fred Hopkins, Michael Gregory Jackson, Paul Maddox, 1976), BLACK SAINT; *Zaki* (Jackson, Pheeroan Aklaff, 1979), HAT ART; *Boston Duets* (Donal Leonellis Fox, 1989), MUSIC & ARTS.

BYARD LANCASTER (saxophone): *It's not up to us* (Sonny Sharrock, Jerome Huntler, Eric Gravatt, Kenny Speller, 1966), VORTEX.

PRINCE LASHA (reeds): *The Cry* (Sonny Simmons, Gary Peacock, Mark Proctor, Gene Stone, 1962), CONTEMPORARY.

JEANNE LEE (vocals): *Conspiracy* (Hampel, Rivers, Steve McCall, etc., 1974), EARTHFORMS.

GEORGE LEWIS (trombone, composition): *Solo Trombone Records* (1976), SACKVILLE; *Shadowgraph* (Roscoe Mitchell, Leroy Jenkins, Douglas Ewart, Muhal Richard Abrams, Anthony Davis, Abdul Wadud, 1977), BLACK SAINT.

SELWYN LISSACK (drums): *Facets of the Universe* (Mongezi Feza, Mike Osborne, Kenneth Terroade, Earl Freeman, 1969), GOODY.

GIUSEPPI LOGAN (reeds): *Quartet* (Don Pullen, Eddie Gomez, Milford Graves, 1964), ESP/CALIBRE.

PAUL LOVENS/PAUL LYTTON (drums): *Was It Me?* (1977), POTORCH.

FRANK LOWE (saxophone): *Duo Exchange* (Rashied Ali, 1972), SURVIVAL; *Doctor Too Much* (Leo Smith, Olu Dara, Fred Williams, Phillip Wilson, 1977), KHARMA; *Saxemble* (1995), QWEST; *Bodies & Soul* (Tim Flood, Charles Moffett, 1995), CIMP.

JIMMY LYONS (saxophone): *Other Afternoons* (Lester Bowie, Alan Silva, Andrew Cyrille, 1969), BYG; *Jimmy Lyons & Sunny Murray Trio- Jump Up* (1980), HAT ART.

KEN MCINTYRE (reeds): *Looking Ahead* (Eric Dolphy, 1960), NEW JAZZ.

KALAPARUSHA (MAURICE MCINTYRE) (reeds): *Humility* (Leo Smith, Malachi Favors, Thurman Barker, Claudine Myers, Ajaramu, etc., 1969), DELMARK; *Forces and Feelings* (1972), DELMARK; *Kalaparusha* (Berger, Ingrid, Tom Schmidt, Juma Santos, Jack DeJohnette, 1975). TRIO.

RADU MALFATI (trombone): *Thrumblin'* (Stephan Wittwer, 1976), FMP.

ALBERT MANGESLDORFF (trombone): *And his Friends* (Cherry, Elvin Jones, Berger, Konitz, etc.,1967-1969), MPS; *Tromboneliness* (solo, 1976), MPS.

GUIDO MAZZON (trumpet)/ ANDREA CENTAZZO (percussions): *Duets* (1976), ORCHESTRA.

MISHA MENGELBERG (piano): *Groupcomposing* (Benning, Brötzmann, E. Parker, Bailey, Rutherford, 1970), ICP; *Mengelberg-Bennink, Bailey-Tchicai* (1970), ICP;

Eineparlietischtennis (Bennink, 1974), SAJ; *Impromptus* (1988), FMP; *Who's Bridge* (Brad Jones, Joey Baron, 1994), AVANT.

JOUK MINOR (reeds): *Esprits du sel* (Jean Querlier, Josef Traindl, Odile Bailleux, Christian Lété, 1977), ELECTROBANDE.

ROSCOE MITCHELL (reeds): *Sound* (M. McIntyre, L. Bwie, Lester Lashley, Malachi Favors, Alvin Fielder, 1966), DELMARK; *Old Quartet* (Bowie, Favors, Phillip Wilson, 1967), NESSA; *Congliptious* (Bowie, Favors, Robert Crowder, 1968), NESSA; *Solo Saxophone Concerts* (1973–1974), SACKVILLE; *Nonaah* (Jarman, Braxton., Threadgill, Wallace McMillan, G. Lewis, Favors, Abrams, 1977), NESSA; *Hey Donald* (Albert Tootie Heath, Favors, Jodie Christian, 1994), DELMARK; *Sound Songs* (solo, 1994), DELMARK; *Nine to Get Ready* (Hugh Ragin, G. Lewis, Matthew Shipp, Craig Taborn, Jaribu Shahid, William Parker, Tani Tabbal, Gerald Cleaver, 1999), ECM.

DAVID MURRAY (reeds): *Flowers for Albert* (Olu Dara, Fred Hopkins, Phillip Wilson, 1976), INDIA NAVIGATION; *Low Class Conspiracy* (Hopkins, Wilson, 1976), ADELPHI; *3D Family* (Johnny Mbizao Dyani, Cyrille, 1978), HAT ART; *Remembrances* (Hugh Ragin, Dave Burrell, Wilber Morris, Tani Tabbal, 1990, DIW; *Death of a Sideman* (Bobby Bradford, Burrell, Hopkins, Blackwell, 1991), DIW; *Acoustic Octfunk* (Hopkins, Andrew Cyrille, 1993), SOUND HILLS; *Flowers Around Cleveland* (Bobby Few, Jean-Jacques Avenel, John Betsch, 1995), BLEU REGARD.

SUNNY MURRAY (drums): *Action* (with the Contemporary Quartet, 1964), DEBUT; *Sonny's Time Now* (Cherry, Ayler, Grimes, Lewis, Worrell, LeRoi Jones, 1965), JIHAD; *Sunny Murray* (Jacques Coursil, Byard Lancaster, Jack Graham, Alan Silva, 1966), ESP; *Big Chief* (Bernard Vitet, Becky Friend, Ronnie Beer, Kenneth Terroade, François Tusques, Beb Guérin, Silva, Favors, Earl Freeman, J. Lee, 1969), BYG; *Charred Earth* (Lancaster, Burrell, etc., 1977), KARMA; *13 # Steps on Glass* (Odean Pope, Wayne Dockery, 1994), ENJA; *Illuminators* (duet with Charles Gayle, 1996), AUDIBLE HISS.

MUSIC IMPROVISATION COMPANY (Bailey, E. Parker, Jaime Muir, Hugh Davies) (1968–1971), ECM.

MUSICA ELECTRONICA VIVA (Richard Teitelbaum, Lacy, Garrett List, Berger, Frederic Rzewski, Alvin Curran): *United Patchwork* (1977), HORO.

BOBBY NAUGHTON (vibraphone): *The Haunt* (L. Smith, Perry Robinson, 1976), OTIC.

JAMES NEWTON (flute): *Flute Music* (Clovis Bordeaux, Tylon Barea, Glenn Ferris, etc.), FLUTE MUSIC PRODUCTION; *Solomon's Sons* (D. Murray, 1977), CIRCLE; *The African Flower* (John Blake, A. Blythe, Olu Dara, Jay Hoggard, Pheeroan Aklaff, etc., 1986), BLUE NOTE.

NEW YORK ART QUARTET (Roswell Rudd, John Tchicai, Lewis Worrell, Milford Graves, LeRoi Jones, 1964), ESP/CALIBRE; *35th Reunion* (Rudd, Tchicai, Reggie Workman, Graves, LeRoi Jones/Amiri Baraka, 1999), DIW.

NEW YORK CONTEMPORARY FIVE: *At Jazzhus Montmartre* (Cherry, Tchicai, Shepp, Don Morre, J.C. Moses, 1963), SONET.

O.M.C.I. (Renato Gerermia, Mauro Periotto, Toni Rusconi): *Free Rococo* (1976), ORCHESTRA.

OVARY LODGE (Keith Tippett, Julie Tippetts, Harry Miller, Frank Perry): *Ovary Lodge* (1975), OGUN.

TONY OXLEY (drums): *Tony Oxley* (E. Parker, Bailey, Rutherford, etc., 1971–1975), INCUS.

EVAN PARKER (saxophones): *Topography of the Lungs* (Bailey, Bennink, 1970), INCUS; *At the Unit Theatre* (Paul Lytton, 1975), INCUS; *Saxophone Solos* (1975), INCUS; *Parker-Lytton* (1976), RING; *Atlanta* (Barry Guy, Lytton, 1986), IMPETUS; *Process and Reality* (1991), FMP; *50th Birthday Concert* (Alex Schlippenbach, Paul Lovens, Guy, Lytton, 1994), LEO RECORDS; *The Redwood Session* (Guy, Lytton, 1995), CIMP; *Natives and Aliens* (Guy, Lytton, Mailyn Crispell, 1996), LEO RECORDS; *Electro-Acoustic Ensemble* (Guy, Lytton, Philipp Wachsmann, etc., 1997), ECM.

WILLIAM PARKER (bass): *Flowers Grow in My Room* (Rob Brown, Assif Tsahar, Roy Campbell, Steve Swell, Billy Bang, Gregg Bendian, Susie Ibarra, etc., 1994), CENTERING RECORDS.

MICHEL PILZ (bass clarinet): *Carpathes* (Peter Kowald, Paul Lovens, 1975), FMP.

MICHEL PORTAL (reeds, bandoneon): *Our Meanings and Our Feelings* (Kühn, Jenny-Clark, Aldo Romano, Thollot, 1969), PATHÉ; *Alors!!!* (John Surman, Phillips, Stu Martin, Jean-Pierre Drouet, 1970), FUTURA; *Slendid Yzlment* (Howard Johnson, J. Minor, Barre Phillips, Runo Ericksson, Gérard Marais, Pierre Favre, 1971), CBS; *A Chateauvallon* (Vitet, Favre, Guérin, Léon Francioli, Tamia, 1972), LE CHANT DU MONDE; ¡Dejarme solo! (1979), DREYFUS JAZZ; *Arrivederci le Chouartse* (Francioli, Favre, 1980), HAT ART.

DUDU PUKWANA (saxophone): *Mbizo radebe (they shoot to kill)* (with John Stevens, 1987), AFFINITY.

DON PULLEN (piano): *Solo Piano Album* (1975), SACKVILLE, *Capricorn Rising* (Rivers, Alex Blake, Bobby Battle, 1975), BLACK SAINT (see also Milford Graves).

DEWEY REDMAN (reeds): *Look for the Black Star* (quartet, 1966), FONTANA; *The Ear of the Behearer* (Ted Daniel, L. Jenkins, Sirone/Norris Jones, Eddie Moore, 1974), IMPULSE.

REVOLUTIONARY ENSEMBLE (Jenkins, Sirone, Jerome Cooper): *Vietnam* (1972), ESP; *Manhattan Cycles* (1972), INDIA NAVIGATION; *The Psyche* (1975), RE; *The People's Republic* (1975), HORIZON; R.E. (1977), ENJA.

SAM RIVERS (saxophone, flute, piano): *Streams* (Cecil McBee, Norman Connors, 1973), IMPULSE; *Crystals* (full orchestra, 1974), IMPULSE; *The Quest* (Holland, Altschul, 1976), RED RECORDS; *Duets* (Holland, 1976), IAI; *Eight Day Journal* (with Tony Humas, Slyvain Kassap, François Corneloup, Henry Lowther, Noël Akchoté, etc., 1998), NATO.

SONNY ROLLINS (saxophone): *Our man in Jazz* (quartet with Cherry, 1962), *Three in Jazz* (1962), RCA.

ROSWELL RUDD (trombone): *Everywhere* (Logan, Kenyatta, Worrell, Haden, Beaver Harris, 1966—reissued with Cecil Taylor), IMPULSE; *Numatik Swing Band* (Jazz Composer's Orchestra, 1973), JCOA.

PAUL RUTHERFORD (trombone): *The Gentle Harm of the Bourgeoisie* (solo, 1974), EMANEM; *Old Moers Almanac* (solo, 1976), RING.

PHAROAH SANDERS (saxophone): *Pharoah's First* (1964), ESP/CALIBRE; *Tauhid* (Burrell, Sharrock, Grimes, Roger Blank and Nat Bettis, 1966), IMPULSE; *Karma* (Leon Thomas, Richard Davis, Julius Watkins, james Spaulding, Reggie Workman, Lonnie Smith, Billy Hart, Bettis, 1969), IMPULSE.

SEA ENSEMBLE (Rafael Garrett, Zusaan Fasteau): *Manzara* (1977), RED RECORDS.

SONNY SHARROCK (guitar): *Black Woman* (Ted Daniel, Burrell, Norris Jones, Richard Pierce, Graves, Peacock, Linda Sharrock, 1969), VORTEX.

ARCHIE SHEPP (saxophones): *Archie Shepp/Bill Dixon Quartet* (1962), SAVOY; *And the New York Contemporary Five* (Ted Curson, Cherry, Tchicai, Boykins, S. Murray, 1964), SAVOY; *Four For Trane* (A. Shorter, Rudd, Tchicai, Workman, Moffett, 1964), IMPULSE; *Fire Music* (Curson, Joseph Orange, M. Brown, etc., 1965), IMPULSE; *The New Wave in Jazz* (1965), IMPULSE; *New Thing at Newport* (Bobby Hutcherson, Phillips, Joe Chambers, 1965), IMPULSE; *Mama Too Tight* (Tommy Turrentine, Rudd, Grachan Moncur III, Perry Robinson, Howard Johnson, Haden, Beaver Harris, 1966), IMPULSE; *The Magic of Ju-Ju* (1967), IMPULSE; *Live at the Donaueschingen Music Festival* (Rudd, Moncur, Jimmy Garrison, Harris, 1967), MPS; *The Way Ahead* (Jimmy Owens, Moncur, Walter Davis Jr, Ron Carter, Roy Haynes or B. Harris, 1968), IMPULSE; *Blasé/Live at the Panafrican Festival* (1969), BYG ACTUEL/CHARLY RECORDS; *Black Gypsy* (Jenkins, Burrell, E. Freeman, S. Murray, 1969), AMERICA; *Attica Blues* (M. Brown, Cal Massey, Thornton, B. Harris, Bartholomew Gray, William Kunstler, Charles McGhee, Charles Stephens, Jenkins, Garrison Burrell, etc., 1972), IMPULSE; *The Cry of My People* (Joe Lee Wilson, Charles Greenlee, McGhee, Massey, Jenkins, etc., 1972), IMPULSE; *A Sea of Faces* (Greenlee, Burrell, Cameron Brown, B, Harris, etc., 1975) BLACK SAINT; *Bijou* (Arthur Jones, etc., 1975), MUSICA.

ALAN SILVA (bas, composition): *Skillfulness* (Berger, Becky Friend, Burrell, Mike Ephron, Lawrence Cook, etc., 1969), ESP; *Luna Surface* (Celestial Communication Orchestra, 1969), BYG; *Seasons* (Celestial Communication Orchestra, 1969), BYG (see Few, Wright).

SONNY SIMMONS (reeds): *Staying on the Watch* (Barbara Donald, John Hicks, Teddy

Smith, Marvin Patillo, 1966), ESP; *Ancient Ritual* (Charnett Moffett, Zarak Simmons, 1994), QWEST.

WADADA LEO SMITH (trumpet, etc.): *Creative Music* (solo, 1971), KABELL; *Reflectivity* (Anthony David, Wes Brown, 1974), KABELL; *Song of Humanity* (Lake, A Davis, W. Brown, Paul Maddox, 1976), KABELL; *Kulture Jazz* (solo, 1993), ECM.

SPONTANEOUS MUSIC ENSEMBLE (Trevor Watts, John Stevens): *Face to Face* (1973), EMANEM.

SUN RA (keyboards, composition): *Sound Sun Pleasure* (1953–1960), SATURN/EVIDENCE; *Sun Song* (1956), DELMARK; *Super-Sonic Jazz* (1956), SATURN/EVIDENCE; *Angels and Demons at Play/The Nubians of Plutonia, Visits Planet Earth/Interstellar Low Ways* (1956–1960), SATURN/EVIDENCE; *We Travel the Spaceways/Bad and Beautiful* (1956–1960), SATURN/EVIDENCE; *Sound of Joy* (1957), DELMARK; *Jazz in Silhouette* (1958), SATURN/EVIDENCE; *Fate in a Pleasant Mood/When Sun Comes Out* (1960–1963), SATURN/EVIDENCE; *The Futuristic Sound Of* (1961), SAVOY; *Cosmic Tones for Mental Therapy/Art Forms of Dimensions Tomorrow* (1961–1963), SATURN/EVIDENCE; *Other Planes of There* (1964), SATURN/EVIDENCE; *Heliocentric Worlds* (1965), ESP/CALIBRE; *The Magic City* (1965), SATURN/EVIDENCE; *The Magic City* (1965), SATURN/EVIDENCE; *Monorails and Satellites* (1966), SATURN/EVIDENCE; *Atlantis* (1967–1969), SATURN/EVIDENCE; *Outer Spaceways Incorporated* (1968), BLACK LION; *Holiday for Soul Dance* (1968–1969), SATURN/EVIDENCE; *My Brother the Wind* (1969–1970), SATURN/EVIDENCE; *The Solar Myth Approach* (1970–1971), BYG ACTUEL/CHARLY RECORDS; *Soundtrack to the Film Space is the Place* (1972), SATURN/EVIDENCE; *Sunrise in Different Dimensions* (1980), HAT ART; *Sun Ra and the Year 2000* (1990), LEO RECORDS.

TAMIA (vocals): *Tamia* (1978), T RECORDS; *De la nuit . . . le jour* (with Pierre Favre, 1987), ECM.

CECIL TAYLOR (piano): *At Newport* (Lacy, Dennis Charles, Buell Neidlinger, 1957), VERVE; *Hard Driving Jazz* or (under Coltrane's name) *Coltrane Time* (Kenny Dorham, Coltrane, Chuck Israels, Louis Hayes, 1958), UNITED ARTISTS; *The World of C.T.* (Shepp, Neidlinger, Charles, 1960), CANDID; *Nefertiti* (Lyons, S. Murray, 1962), FONTANA; *Unit Structures* (Eddie Gale, K. McIntyre, Lyons, Grimes, Silva, Cyrille, 1966), BLUE NOTE; *Conquistador* (Dixon, Lyons, Grimes, Silva, Cyrille, 1966), BLUE NOTE; *Nuits de la Fondation Maeght* (Rivers, Lyons, Cyrille, 1969), SHANDAR; *Spring of Two Blue J's* (Lyons, Sirone, Cyrille, 1973), UNIT CORE; *Akisakila* (Lyons, Cyrille, 1973), TRIO; *Indent* (solo, 1973), UNIT CORE (new release with FREEDOM); *Silent Tongues* (solo, 1976), ENJA; *Dark to Themselves* (Raphé Malik, Lyons, Ware, Mark Edwards, 1976), ENJA; *Embraced* (with Mary Lou Williams, 1977), PABLO; *In Berlin '88* (duets with Günter Baby Sommer, Lovens, Louis Moholo, Bennink, Oxley, 1988), FMP; *In Florescence* (William Parker, Bendian, 1989), A&M; *Momentum Space* (Redman, Elvin Jones, 1998), VERVE.

JOHN TCHICAI (saxophone): *Rufus* (Shepp, Don Moore, J.C. Moses, 1963), FONTANA; *Solo* (Mangelsdorff, 1977), SAJ; *The Real Tchicai* (Henning, Ørsted-Pedersen, Pierre Dorge, 1977) STEEPLECHASE; *Cassava Balls* (Hartmut Geerken, Famoudou Don Moye, 1985), LEO RECORDS; *Grandpa's Spells* (with Misha Mengelberg, 1992), STORYVILLE.

RICHARD TEITELBAUM (electronics): *Time Zones* (Braxton, 1976), ARISTA.

CLIFFORD THORNTON (trumpet, composition): *Freedom and Unity* (New Art Ensemble: Sonny King, Berger, etc., 1967), GOODY; *The Gardens of Harlem* (Jazz Composer's Orchestra, 1974), JCOA.

FRANÇOIS TUSQUES (piano, composition): *Free Jazz* (Vitet, François Jeanneau, Portal, Charles Saudrais, Guérin, 1965), MOULOUDJI/IN SITU; *Compositions de François Tusques avec Barney Wilen* (Wilen, Jenny Clark, Guérin, Romano, 1967), MOULOUDJI; *Piano Dazibao* (solos, 1970), FUTURA; *Intercommunal Music* (S. Murray, Louis Armfield, Silva, Guérin, Bob Reid, Shorter, Steve Potts, 1971), SHANDAR; *Le Piano Préparé*, CHANT DU MONDE; *Intercommunal Free Dance Music Orchestra* (Adolf Winkier, Michel Marre, Jo Maka, Guem), LE TEMPS DES CERISES; *Génération* (solo, 1988), KUIV PRODUCTIONS.

CHARLES TYLER (saxophone): *Ensemble* (Joel Friedman, Ronald Jackson, Grimes, C. Moffett, 1966), ESP; *Autumn in Paris* (+Brus Trio, 1988), SILKHEART; *Voyage from Jericho* (Boykins, Earl Cross, Steve Reid, Blythe, 1974), BLEU REGARD.

BERNARD VITET (trumpet): *La Guêpe* (Jean-Paul Rondepierre, Minor, Tusques, Bob, Guérin, Françoise Achard, 1971), FUTURA.

ALEXANDER VON SCHLIPPENBACH (piano): *Globe Unity* (Manfred Schoof, Brötzmann, Gerd Dudek, Breuker, Hampel, Berger, Kowald, Buschi Niebergall, Mani Neumeier, 1966), MPS; *Three Nails Left* (E. Parker, Kowald, Lovens, 1975), FMP; *Digger's Harvest* (with Tony Oxley, 1998), FMP.

PATTY WATERS (vocals): *Sings* (Greene, etc., 1965), ESP; *In Concert* (Logan, Burrell, Ran Blake, etc., 1966), ESP.

MARZETTE WATTS (reeds): *Backdrop for Urban Revolution* (Watts, Lancaster, Thornton, Berger, Sharrock, etc., 1966), ESP.

MIKE WESTBROOK (piano, composition): *For the Record* (Rutherford, Kate Barnard, Phil Minton, Dave Chambers, 1975), TRANSATLANTIC; *Piano* (1976–1977), ORIGINAL RECORDS; *Goose Sauce* (Brass Band, 1977–1978), ORIGINAL RECORDS.

WILDFLOWERS: *Volume 1* (K. McIntyre, M. McIntyre, S. Murray, Rivers, Air, 1976), DOUGLAS; *2* (Braxton, L. Smith, M. Brown, K. McIntyre, Flight to Sanity), *3* (Michael Jackson, Cyrille, Burrell, Randy Weston, Abdullah), *4* (Bluiett, Hemphill, Lyons, Lake, D. Murray), *5* (S. Murray, Mitchell).

BARNEY WILEN (saxophones): *Auto Jazz: Tragic Destiny of Lorenzo Bandini* (Tusques, Guérin, Eddy Gaumont, and tape recording of the 25th Monaco Grand Prix, 1968), MPS.

WORKSHOP DE LYON: *Tiens! Les bourgeons éclatent*... (Jean Bolcato-bass, Maurice Merle-saxophone, Christian Rollet-drums, trombone, Louis Scalvis, reeds, 1977), L'OISEAU MUSICIEN.

WORLD SAXOPHONE QUARTET (Bluiett, Hemphill, Lake, D. Murray): *Live in Moers* (1977), MOERS MUSIC/RING.

FRANK WRIGHT (saxophone): *Uhuru Na Umoja* (Noah Howard, Bobby Few, Art Taylon, 1970), AMERICA; *Last Polka in Nancy* (Few, Silva, Muhamad Ali, 1973), CENTER OF THE WORLD; *Shouting the Blues* (George Arvanitas, Jacky Samson, Charles Saudrais, 1977), SUN RECORDS.

Compilation: *Jazzactuel-a Collection of Avant-Garde/Free Jazz/Psychedelia from the BYG/ACTUEL Catalogue of 1969–71* (3 CD Charly). Sunny Murray, Archie Shepp, Steve Lacy, Sonny Sharrock, Grachan Moncur III, Clifford Thornton, Jacques Coursil, Dave Burrell, Sun Ra, Arthur Jones, Burton Greene, Art Ensemble of Chicago, Andrew Cyrille, Paul Bley, Frank Wright, Acting Trio (Philippe Maté), Dewey Redman, Don Cherry, Anthony Braxton, Jimmy Lyons, Claude Delcloo-Arthur Jones, Musica Electronica Viva, Kenneth Terroade, Alan Silva & The Celestial Communication Orchestra.

Works Cited

Aptheker, Herbert. *American Negro Slave Revolts*. New York: International Publishers, 1963.

———. *A Documentary History of the Negro People in the United States*. New York: Citadel Press, 1951.

———. *The Negro in the Abolitionist Movement*. New York: International Publishers, 1941.

———. *The Negro in the Civil War*. New York: International Publishers, 1962.

——— *The Negro People in America*. New York: International Publishers, 1946.

Armstead L. Robinson, Craig C. Foster and Donald H. Ogilvie. *Black Studies in the University*. New York: Bantam, 1969.

Asbury, Herbert. *The French Quarter*. New York: Alfred A. Knopf, 1936.

Averty, Jean-Christophe. "Contribution à l'histoire de l'O.D.J.B." *Les Cahiers du Jazz* 3 (1960): 60–107; 4 (1961): 74–117.

———. "Les Minstrels." *Jazz Hot* 77 (May 1963): 8–10; *Jazz Hot* 78 (June 1963): 12–15; 22; *Jazz Hot* 79 (July–August 1963): 12–16; *Jazz Hot* 80 (Sept. 1963): 14–16.

Baldwin, James. *Nobody Knows My Name*. New York: Dell Publishing, 1961.

Ball, Charles. *Slavery in the United States: A Narrative of the Life and Adventures of Charles Ball, A Black Man*. Lewistown, PA: Taylor, 1836.

Bardolph, Richard. *The Negro Vanguard*. New York: Rinehart, 1959.

Barnes, Gilbert H. *The Antislavery Impulse: 1830–1844*. New York: Harbinger Books, 1964.

Bataille, Georges. *Encyclopaedia Acephalica*. London: Atlas Press, 1995.

Bebey, Francis. *African Music: A People's Art*. Trans. Josephine Bennett. New York: Lawrence Hill and Co., 1975.

Bell, Howard H. *A Survey of the Negro Convention Movement: 1839–1861*. New York: Arno Press, 1969.

Bentley, George. *A History of the Freedmen's Bureau*. Philadelphia: University of Pennsylvania Press, 1955.

Berger, Daniel. "Cecil Taylor à la trace." *Jazz Hot* 228 (February 1967).

Bibb, Henry. *The Narrative of the Life and Adventures of Henry Bibb*. New York, 1849.

Bone, Robert A. *The Negro Novel in America*. New Haven, CT: Yale University Press, 1969.

Botkin, B. A. *Lay My Burden Down*. 1945. New York: Delta, 1994.

Brown, H. Rap. *Die Nigger Die!* New York: Dial Press, 1969.

Brown, Henry. *Narrative of the Life of Henry Box Brown, Written by Himself*. Manchester: Lee and Glynn, 1851.

Brown, Sterling. *Negro Poetry and Drama*. Washington, DC: Associates in Negro Folk Education, 1937.

Brown, William Wells. *Narrative of William W. Brown, a Fugitive Slave.* Boston: Anti-Slavery Office, 1847.

———. *Clotel, or The President's Daughter.* London: Partridge and Oakey, 1853.

Broyles, P. Allen. *The John Birch Society, Anatomy of a Protest.* Boston: Beacon Press, 1964.

Bruce, Henry. *The New Man: Twenty-Nine Years a Slave, Twenty-Nine Years a Free Man.* York: P. Anstadt and Sons, 1895.

Cairnes, John Elliot. *The Slave Power.* London: Parker, Son & Co., 1862.

Carles, Philippe. "Archie méconnu." *Jazz Magazine* 119 (June 1965): 50–55.

———. "Champ et contrechamp sur (Paul) Bley." *Jazz Magazine* 141 (April 1967): 40–44.

———. "Le don paisible." *Jazz Magazine* 119 (June 1965).

———. "L'Opéra comique de Sun Ra" *Jazz Magazine* 159 (October 1968): 26–44.

———. "Qui es-tu Robin Kenyatta? Un saxophoniste qui rêve de découvrir l'Afrique," *Jazz Magazine* 172 (November 1969).

Carles, Philippe and Jean-Louis Comolli. "Les secrets d'Albert le Grand," *Jazz Magazine* 142 (May 1967): 34–46.

Caux, Daniel. "Milford Graves et les paradoxes du nouveau drumming." *Jazz Hot* 251 (June 1969).

Charters, Samuel. *The Poetry of the Blues.* New York: Oak Publications, 1963.

Chesnutt, Charles W. *The Colonel's Dream* (New York: Doubleday, 1905).

———. *The House Behind the Cedars.* Boston and New York: Houghton Mifflin, 1900.

———. *The Marrow of Tradition.* Boston and New York: Houghton Mifflin, 1901.

Clark, Kenneth B. *Dark Ghetto, Dilemmas of Social Power.* 1965. Middletown, CT: Wesleyan University Press, 1989.

Cleaver, Eldridge. *Soul on Ice.* New York: Delta, 1968.

Clouzet, Jean and Guy Kopelowicz. "Un inconfortable après-midi." *Jazz Magazine* 107 (June 1964).

Clouzet, Jean and Jean Wagner. "Trente questions à Max." *Jazz Magazine* 114 (January 1965).

Coeuroy, André. *Histoire générale du jazz, strette, hot, swing.* Paris: Denoël, 1942.

Coleman, Ornette. "'Round the Empty Foxhole." *Down Beat* 34 (2 Nov. 1967): 16.

Comolli, Jean-Louis. "Les conquérants d'un nouveau monde." *Jazz Magazine* 131 (June 1966): 30–35.

———. "Loin de Gunther Schuller, près de LeRoi Jones" *Jazz Magazine* 163 (February 1969): 47–49.

———. "Voyage au bout de la New Thing." *Jazz Magazine* 129 (April 1966): 24–29.

Cruse, Harold. "Rebellion or Revolution? (Part One)," *The Liberator* (October 1963).

Cunningham, Virginia. *Paul Laurence Dunbar and His Song.* New York: Dodd, Mead and Co., 1947.

Daniélou, Alain. *Northern Indian Music*. New York: Frederick A. Praeger, 1968.
David, Jay. *Growing Up Black*. New York: Morrow, 1968.
Déjacque, Joseph. "La libération des Noirs américains." *A bas les chefs!* Paris: Champ Libre, 1971.
Delany, Martin R. *Blake, or The Huts of America*. Serialized in *The Anglo-African Magazine* (January to July 1859).
Delaunay, Charles, Robert Aubert, and Kurt Mohr. "En bavardant avec Lucky Thompson." *Jazz Hot* 109 (April 1956).
Dixon, Bill. "To Whom It May Concern." *Coda, Canada's Jazz Magazine* 8.4 (October–November 1967): 3–10.
Douglass, Frederick. "Letter to an Abolitionist Associate." *Organizing For Social Change: A Mandate for Activity in the 1990s*. Edited by K. Bobo et al. Washington, DC: Seven Locks Press, 1991.
———. *Narrative of the Life of Frederick Douglass, an American Slave, Written by Himself*. Boston: Anti-Slavery Office, 1845.
Douglass, William. *Annals of the First African Church, in the United States of America: Now Styled the African Episcopal Church of St. Thomas, Philadelphia*. Philadelphia: King & Baird, 1862.
Du Bois, W. E. B. *Black Reconstruction*. 1898. New York: The Free Press, 1962.
———. "Criteria of Negro Art." *The Crisis* 32 (October 1926): 290–297.
———. *Dark Water: Voices from Within the Veil*. New York: Harcourt and Brace, 1920.
———. *Dusk of Dawn*. New York: Harcourt, Brace and World, 1940.
———. *John Brown*. Philadelphia: Jacobs and Co., 1909.
———. *The Selected Writing of W. E. B. Du Bois*. New York: Mentor Books, 1970.
———. *The Souls of Black Folk: Essays and Sketches*. Chicago: A.C. McClurg and Co., 1903.
———. *Suppression of the Slave Trade to the United States of America*. New York: Longmans, Green & Co., 1896.
Dumond, Dwight L. *Antislavery Origins of the Civil War in the United States*. Ann Arbor: University of Michigan Press, 1961.
Dunbar, Paul Laurence. *The Complete Poems of Paul Laurence Dunbar*. New York: Dodd, Mead and Co., 1913.
Elkins, Stanley. *Slavery*. New York: The Universal Library, 1963.
Ellison, Ralph. "Blues People." *Shadow and Act*. 1964. New York: Random House, 1995. 247–58.
Feather, Leonard. *The Book of Jazz*. 1957. New York: Dell Publishing, 1976.
Granby, Moses. *Narrative of the Life of Moses Granby, Late a Slave in the United States of America*. Boston: Gilpin, 1843.
Fabre, Michel. *Esclaves et Planteurs dans le Sud Américain au XIXè siècle*. Paris: Julliard, 1970.

———. *Les Noirs Américains*. Paris: Armand Colin, 1967.
Fager, Charles E. *White Reflections on Black Power*. New York: Eerdmans, 1967.
Filler, Louis. *Wendell Phillips on Civil Rights and Freedom*. New York: Hill and Wang, 1956.
Finkelstein, Sidney. *Jazz, A People Music*. New York: Citadel Press, 1948.
Forten, Charlotte. *The Journal of Charlotte L. Forten: A Free Negro in the Slave Era*. New York: Collier, 1961.
———. "Life on the Sea Islands" *The Atlantic Monthly* XIII (May and June 1864): 587–596.
Franklin, John H. *The Emancipation Proclamation*. New York: Doubleday, 1963.
Frazier, E. Franklin. *Black Bourgeoisie*. 1957. New York: The Free Press, 1962.
———. *The Negro Church in America*. New York: Schocken Books, 1963.
———. *The Negro in the United States*. New York: MacMillan, 1963.
Genovese, Eugene. *Political Economy of Slavery: Studies in the Economy and Society of the Slave South*. New York: Pantheon Books, 1965.
Gilette, William. *The Right to Vote: Politics and the Passage of the Fifteenth Amendment*. Baltimore: Johns Hopkins Press, 1965.
Goodman, Benny and Irving Kolodin. *The Kingdom of Swing*. New York: Stackpole, 1939.
Grant, Joanne. *Black Protest: 1619 to the Present*. New York: Fawcett Premier Book, 1969.
Gray, Thomas R. *The Confessions of Nat Turner, the Leader of the Late Insurrection in Southampton, Virginia, as Fully and Voluntarily Made to Thomas R. Gray*. Baltimore, 1831.
Griggs, Sutton E. *Imperium in Imperio*. Cincinnati, OH: Editor Publishing Co., 1899).
———. *Pointing the Way*. Nashville, TN: Orion, 1908.
Guérin, Daniel. *Décolonisation du Noir américain*. Paris: Editions de Minuit, 1963.
Harper, Frances E. W. *Iola Leroy*. Boston: James Earle, 1892.
Heffley, Mike. *Northern Sun, Southern Moon: Europe's Reinvention of Jazz*. Cambridge: Yale University Press, 2005.
Henson, Josiah. *Father Henson's Story of his Own Life*. Boston: Jewett, 1858.
———. *The Life of Josiah Henson*. Boston: Phelps, 1849.
Hentoff, Nat. "Charles Mingus." *These Jazzmen of Our Time*. Edited by Raymond Horricks. New York: Jazz Book Club, 1960.
———. *The Jazz Life*. New York: Dial Press, 1961.
Higginson, Thomas W. *Army Life in a Black Regiment*. Boston: Fields, Osgood and Co., 1870.
———. "Denmark Vesey." *The Atlantic Monthly* VII (June 1861): 728–744.
Hobsbawm, Eric J. *The Jazz Scene*. New York: Monthly Review Press, 1960.

Hodeir, André. *La religion du jazz (Hommes et problèmes du jazz)*. Paris: Flammarion, 1954.

Hodgson, Godfrey. *Carpetbaggers et Ku Klux Klan*. Paris: Julliard, 1966.

Holiday, Billie and William Dufty. *Lady Sings the Blues*. 1956. New York: Penguin Books, 1984.

Hughes, Langston, "Bop." *The Best of Simple*. New York: Hill and Wang, 1961.

James, C.L.R. "The Atlantic Slave and Slavery: Some Interpretations of their Significance in the Development of the United States and the Western World." *Amistad 1: Writings on Black History and Culture*. John A. Williams, Charles F. Harris eds. New York: Vintage, 1970: 119–164.

Joans, Ted. "Black Power et New Thing." *Jazz Magazine* 150 (January 1968).

"John Coltrane: 1926–1967," *Jazz Magazine* 145 (August 1967): 16–23.

Johnson, James Weldon. *Black Manhattan*. New York: Alfred A. Knopf, 1930.

———. *Negro Americans, What Now?* New York: The Viking Press, 1934.

Johnston, Harry. *A History of the Colonization of Africa by Alien Races*. Cambridge: Cambridge University Press, 1899.

Jones, A.M. *Studies in African Music*. Oxford: Oxford University Press, 1959.

Jones, John McHenry. *Hearts of Gold*. Wheeling, VA: Daily Intelligencer Stream Job Press, 1896.

Jones, LeRoi [Amiri Baraka]. "Apple Cores." *Down Beat* 31 (19 Nov. 1964): 21–40.

———. "Archie Shepp Live," *Jazz* 4 (January 1965): 8.

———. *Black Music*. 1968. Cambridge, PA: Da Capo Press, 1998.

———. *Blues People (Negro Music in White America)*. New York: Apollo, 1963.

———. *The Dead Lecturer*. New York: Grove Press, 1964.

———. "Don Cherry: Makin' in the Hard Way." *Down Beat* 30 (21 Nov. 1963): 16–18.

———. *Four Black Revolutionary Plays*. Indianapolis and New York: Bobbs-Merrill Co., 1969.

———. *Home: Social Essays*. New York: Morrow, 1966.

———. "The Myth of a 'Negro Literature'." *The Saturday Review* (April 20, 1963): 20–21.

———. "New Voices in Newark," *Down Beat* 33 (10 March 1966): 13.

———. *Preface to a Twenty-Volume Suicide Note*. New York: Totem Press, 1961.

———. "Sonny Rollins: Our Man in Jazz." *Jazz* (April–May 1963): 18.

———. *The System of Dante's Hell*. New York: Grove Press, 1963.

———. *Tales*. New York: Grove Press, 1967.

———. "Voice from the Avant-Garde: Archie Shepp." *Down Beat* 32 (14 January 1965): 18–36.

Jost, Ekkehard. *Free Jazz*. Trans. Ekkehard Jost. 1974; Cambridge, MA: Da Capo Press, 1994.

Jotterand, Franck. *Le nouveau théâtre américain*. Paris: Seuil, 1970.

Katz, William Loren. *The American Negro: His History and Literature*. New York: Arno Press, 1968

Kemble, Fanny. *Journal of a Residence on a Georgian Plantation in 1838–1839*. New York: Alfred Knopf, 1961.

King, Martin Luther Jr. *Strength to Love*. New York: Harper & Row, 1963.

———. *The Trumpet of Conscience*. New York: Harper's and Row, 1967.

Kmen, Henry A. *Music in New Orleans-The Formative Years 1791–1841*. Baton Rouge: Louisiana State University Press, 1966.

Kofsky, Frank. *Black Nationalism and the Revolution in Music*. New York: Pathfinder Press, 1970.

———. "John Coltrane." *Jazz & Pop* (Sept. 1967), 26

Kopelowicz, Guy. "Autumn in New York." *Jazz Hot* 214 (Nov. 1965).

Lane, Lunsford. *The Narrative of Lunsford Lane*. Boston: Torrey, 1842.

Le Bris, Michel, Bruno Vincent, Jean Frenay. "Marion Brown: l'Afrique a vaincu," *Jazz Hot* 235 (October 1967).

Lehman, Stephen. "I Love You with an Asterisk: African-American Experimental Music and the French Jazz Press, 1970–1980." *Critical Studies in Improvisation/ Etudes critiques en improvisation* [Online] 1:2 (2005). 3 June 2013. http://jazzstudiesonline.org/files/Critical%20Studies%20in%20Improvisation%201-2--LEHMAN.pdf

Leiris, Michel. *Brisées: Broken Branches*. Trans. Lydia Davis. San Francisco: North Point Press, 1989.

Lewis, George. "The AACM in Paris." *Black Renaissance* 5:3 (Spring 2004), 105–121.

———. Review of *Northern Sun, Southern Moon: Europe's Reinvention of Jazz* by Mike Heffley. *Current Musicology* 78 (Fall 2004): 77–91.

Leymarie, Isabelle. Review of *Free Jazz/Black Power* by Pierre Carles and Jean-Louis Comolli. *Ethnomusicology*, Vol. 18, No. 1. (January, 1974), pp. 151–153.

Locke, Alain. "Art or Propaganda?" *Harlem* 1.1 (Nov. 1928): 12–13.

———. *The Negro and his Music*. New York: Arno Press, 1969.

Lockwood, Lee. *Conversations with Eldridge Cleaver*. New York: McGraw-Hill, 1970.

Logan, Rayford W. *Les Noirs américains et l'Afrique*. Paris: Centre Culturel Américain, 1961.

Logan, Rayford W. ed. *What the Negro Wants*. Chapel Hill: University of North Carolina Press, 1944.

Loguen, J.W. *The Reverend J. W. Loguen, as a Slave and a Freeman Narrative of Real Life*. Syracuse, N.Y.: J.G.K. Truair & Co., 1859.

Lomax, Alan. *Mister Jelly Roll: The Fortunes of Jelly Roll Morton, New Orleans Creole and "Inventor of Jazz."* Berkeley and Los Angeles: University of California Press, 1950.

Loyer, Yves. *Black Power*. Paris: Etudes et Documentations Nationales, 1968.

Madelin, Louis. *The French Revolution*. New York: G.P. Putnam's Sons, 1916.

Malson, Lucien. *Histoire du Jazz Moderne*. Paris: La Table Ronde, 1961.

Masnata, François. *Pouvoir Blanc, Révolte Noire*. Paris: Payot, 1968.
Marx, Karl. *Capital*. Trans. Samuel Moore and Edward Aveling. Chicago: Charles H. Kerr and Co., 1915.
McKitrick, Eric L., ed. *Slavery Defended: the Views of the Old South*. Englewood Cliffs, NJ: Prentice Hall, 1963.
Mellon, Matthew T. *Early American Views on Negro Slavery*. New York: New American Library, 1969.
Memmi, Albert. *The Colonizer and the Colonized*. Trans. Howard Greenfeld. 1957. Boston: Beacon Press, 1991.
Mezzrow, Mezz and Bernard Wolfe. *Really the Blues*. New York: Citadel Press, 1946.
Mitchell, Paul. *Race Riots in Black and White*. Englewood Cliffs, NJ: Prentice Hall, 1970.
Murray, George and Joudon M. Ford. "Black Panthers: The Afro-Americans' Challenge." *Tricontinental* 10 (January–February 1969): 96–111.
Myrdal, Gunnar. *An American Dilemma: The Negro Problem and American Democracy*. New York: Harper and Row, 1944.
Negro Protest Pamphlets: A Compendium. New York: Arno Press, 1969.
N'Diaye, Jean-Pierre, J. Bassens and B. Poyas. *Les Noirs aux Etats-Unis pour les Africains*. Paris: *Réalités Africaines* 7 (May–July 1964).
Noames, Jean-Louis. "Cecil Taylor: Le système Taylor." *Jazz Magazine* 125 (December 1965): 34–36.
———. "Shepp le rebelle." *Jazz Magazine* 125 (December 1965): 78–81.
Oliver, Paul. *Bessie Smith*. London: Cassell, 1959.
———. *Blues Fell This Morning*. London: Cassell, 1960.
———. *Conversation with the Blues*. London: Cassell, 1965.
———. *Savannah Syncopators: African Retentions in the Blues*. London: November Books, 1970.
———. *Screening the Blues: Aspects of the Blues Tradition*. London: Cassell, 1968.
———. *The Story of the Blues*. London: Barrie & Jenkins, 1969.
Olmsted, Frederick Law. *A Journey in the Seaboard Slave States*. New York: Dix and Edwards, 1856.
O'Neal, John. "Motion in the Ocean." *Black Theater, Drama Review* 12.4 (1968): 70–77.
Panassié, Hugues. *La bataille du jazz*. Paris: Albin Michel, 1965.
———. *The Real Jazz*. Trans. Anne Sorelle Williams. New York: Smith and Durrell, 1942.
Paulhan, Jean. "Les hain-tenys." *Oeuvres Complètes*. Paris: Gallimard, 1955.
Pelliciotti, Giacomo. "Mingus Dynasty," *Jazz Magazine* 233 (May–June 1975).
Phillips, Ulrich Bonnell. *American Negro Slavery*. New York: D. Appleton and Co., 1918.
"Quelques hommes en colère," *Jazz Magazine* 120 (July 1965).
Quersin, Benoît. "Walt Dickerson." *Jazz Magazine* 119 (June 1965).

Ramsey, Frederic Jr. Liner Notes. *Music of the South, Vol.1–10*. [Smithsonian] Folkways FA 2650–59, 1955. LP.
Randolph, A. Philip. "March on Washington Movement Presents a Program for the Negro." *What the Negro Wants*. Edited by Rayford W. Logan. Chapel Hill: University of North Carolina Press, 1944
Rice, Arnold S. *The Ku Klux Klan in American Politics*. Washington DC: Public Affairs Press, 1962.
Rourke, Constance. *American Humor*. New York: Doubleday, 1955.
Shapiro, Nat and Nat Hentoff. *Hear Me Talkin' to Ya*. New York: Dover Publications, 1956.
Shepp, Archie. "An Artist Speaks Bluntly," *Down Beat* 32 (December 16, 1965).
———. "Blindfold Test." *Down Beat* 33 (1966).
———. Liner notes. *The Magic of Ju-Ju*. New York: Impulse A-9154, 1967. LP.
———. Liner notes. *Mama Too Tight*. New York: Impulse A-9134, 1966. LP.
Spellman, A. B. *Four Lives in the Bebop Business*. New York: Pantheon Books, 1966.
Still, William. *A Brief Narrative of the Struggle for the Rights of the Colored People of Philadelphia in the City Railway Cars and a Defense of William Still Relating to His Agency Touching the Passage of the Late Bill*. Philadelphia: Merrihew and Son, 1867.
[Stowers, Walter H. and William H. Anderson]. *Appointed*. Detroit: Detroit Law Printing, 1894.
Stravinsky, Igor. "The Composition of Music." *Poetics of Music: in the Form of Six Lessons*. Trans. Arthur Knodel and Ingolf Dahl. Cambridge, MA: Harvard University Press, 1970.
Styron, William. *The Confessions of Nat Turner*. New York: Random House, 1967.
Ton, Delfeil de. "Alan Silva and Dave Burrell." *Charlie-Hebdo* 8 (January 11, 1971).
Truth, Sojourner. *The Narrative of Sojourner Truth*. Boston: 1850.
Turner, Arlin. *Creoles and Cajuns*. New York: Doubleday Anchor, 1959.
U.S. Riot Commission Report/ Report of the National Advisory Commission on Civil Disorders. New York: Bantam Books, 1968.
Van Peebles, Melvin. "Tête à tête avec Ornette," *Jazz Magazine* 125 (December 1965): 26–28.
Vian, Boris. "Un certain Panassié." *Chroniques de jazz*. Edited by Lucien Malson. Paris: La Jeune Parque, 1967.
"Vingt-six jazzmen nouveaux à la question." *Jazz Magazine* 125 (December 1965).
Wagner, Jean. *Black Poets of the United States*. Trans. Kenneth Douglass. Champaign, IL: Illinois University Press, 1973.
Ward, Samuel Ringgold. *Autobiography of a Fugitive Negro*. London: John Snow, 1850.
Washington, Booker T. *Up from Slavery*. New York: Doubleday, 1901.
Watson, Henry. *The Narrative of Henry Watson, a Fugitive Slave*. Boston: B. Marsh, 1848.

Webb, Frank J. *The Garies and Their Friends*. London: Routledge, 1857.

White, N. I. "Racial Traits in the Negro Song." *Sewanee Review* 28.3 (July 1920): 396–404.

Williams, John A. "My Man Himes: An Interview with Chester Himes." Edited by John A. Williams and Charles Harris. *Amistad 1*. New York: Random House, 1970.

Williamson, Joel. *The Negro in South Carolina during Reconstruction*. Chapel Hill: University of North Carolina Press, 1965.

Woodward, C. Vann. *The Strange Career of Jim Crow*. New York: Oxford University Press, 1957.

Wright, Richard. *White Man, Listen!* New York: Doubleday and Co. 1957.

X, Malcolm. *The Autobiography of Malcolm X*, New York: Random House, 1965.

———. *By Any Means Necessary*. New York: Pathfinder Press, 1992.

———. *Malcolm X Speaks*. Edited by George Breitman. New York: Merit Publishers, 1965.

———. *On Afro-American History*. New York: Pathfinder Press, 1970.

Young, Ian. "Les Panthères Noires et la langue du ghetto," *Esprit* 396 (October 1970): 549–73.

Zhdanov, A. *Essays on Literature, Philosophy, and Music*. New York: International Publishers, 1950.

Index

AACM (Association for the Advancement of Creative Musicians), 28, 154, 156, 166, 198n8
abolitionism, 56, 59, 66–72, 76. *See also* anti-slavery activism
Adderley, Cannonball (Julian), 28, 145
aesthetics, 50, 171, 180–81; black, 6, 30; bourgeois, 3, 175; idealist, 40, 176, 178; jazz, 33, 37, 45, 49; Western (white), 6, 40, 173
AFL (American Federation of Labor), 123, 221n107. *See also* AFL-CIO; CIO
AFL-CIO, 143. *See also* AFL; CIO
Africa, 67; Black Muslims and, 14, 15; civilizations of, 16–17, 24, 81; culture and traditions of, 48, 63, 80, 82–84; influence on black American music, 24–25, 42–43, 77, 88, 92, 106, 115–16, 131, 146, 158–63, 177; instruments from, 156, 160; movement back to, 68, 70, 113–14, 147, 160; valorization of, 15–20, 114, 147, 160
American Abolitionist Society, 67
American Anti-Slavery Society, 203n28
anti-slavery activism, 59, 61, 69; organizations, 201n6
Aptheker, Herbert, 56, 64, 67
Armstrong, Louis, 28, 31, 32, 104, 129, 140; instrumental style of, 43, 111–13, 153, 165; singing style of, 131; white society's image of, 20, 38, 111, 113, 121, 132, 134, 138
art: African American, 4, 24, 27, 39, 43, 47, 51, 63, 71, 77, 178–80; bourgeois characteristics of, 22, 40; history of, 50, 99; jazz as, 3, 25, 33, 37, 39–40, 128, 170, 178–80; politics and, 100, 115, 174, 178–79; Western notion of, 3, 40, 50, 77, 100, 117, 133, 170–76
Art Ensemble of Chicago, 3, 154, 156, 165, 166
avant-garde, 11, 23, 129–30, 136, 154, 168, 172, 176, 178
Ayler, Albert, 28, 153–57, 161, 163–66, 169, 170

Baldwin, James, 100, 134
Baker, Chet, 140
Baker, Josephine, 111
Baraka, Amiri. *See* Jones, LeRoi
Basie, Count, 122, 130
Bebey, Francis, 177
bebop, 12, 31; birth of, 122, 129; blues and, 133–34; characteristics of, 46, 129–32, 139, 152, 153, 158–59, 169; *hard bop*, 147; politics of, 133–35; quarrel over, 12, 44–46, 138, 170; white appropriation of, 129, 132–33, 137
Bechet, Sidney, 43, 110–11, 138, 165
Beiderbecke, Bix, 32
Berendt, Joachim Ernst, 99, 138
black masses, 4, 7, 58; culture and, 23, 178–80; Garvey and, 68, 113–15; Harlem Renaissance and, 115; music and, 21, 22, 28, 29, 32, 89, 94, 110, 141–42, 169, 170–71; NAACP and, 105, 120; politicization of, 15, 17, 19, 22, 29, 119, 141, 179; religion and, 23, 141
black music, 22, 26, 31–33, 63; African sources of, 5, 77–81, 82–83; blues foundation of, 121–22, 142, 144–48; characteristics of, 6, 22; cultural colonization of, 7, 25–27, 31–46, 82, 96,

251

131, 139, 180; free jazz as, 11–12, 155, 162, 164–65; history and, 51–52, 165, 174; jazz and, 32, 118–19, 121, 122; religion and, 84–87. *See also* blues; jazz

Black Muslims, 14, 15, 134–35, 143, 147, 160, 161, 175, 179. *See also* Islam

Black Panther Party (BPP), 5, 15, 17, 18, 19, 24, 68, 69, 92, 179

Black Power, 13–14, 17, 22, 68, 181, 189

black studies, 4, 15, 179, 209n1, 217n52

blackface. *See* minstrelsy

Blakey, Art, 133, 146, 160, 219n93

Bley, Carla, 29, 158

blues: bebop and, 122, 133–34; characteristics of, 82, 88–91, 100–104, 109–10, 112, 118, 141; free jazz and, 165–66; origins of, 87–89; piano, 122, 142; roots of jazz in, 5, 32, 39, 46, 106, 140, 144–46; singers, 109, 110, 113, 117, 121, 122, 140, 142; social commentary in, 34–35, 51, 101–4, 105–6, 117, 119, 121, 140–42; swing and, 118–19. *See also* black music; boogie woogie; jazz; rhythm and blues; rock and roll

Blues People. *See* Jones, LeRoi

boogie woogie, 122, 142, 164, 221n105. *See also* Kansas City, Missouri

bourgeoisie: black, 4, 34, 41, 58, 63, 71, 77, 107, 119, 141, 178; Western (capitalist), 38, 40, 47. *See also* Frazier, E. Franklin: *Black Bourgeoisie*

Brown, H. Rap, 16, 17, 18, 34, 92–93

Brown, Marion, 21, 28, 118, 158, 165

Brubeck, Dave, 26, 28, 140

Burnett, Chester. *See* Howlin' Wolf

capitalism: American (white), 4, 7, 8, 12, 14, 17, 18, 31, 49, 117, 120, 123, 128, 141, 142, 168; art and, 40, 50, 172; bebop and, 129–30; black, 18, 19, 25, 120; black activism and, 178–79; industrial, 25; music's relation to, 27, 29, 33, 47, 173; northern, 101, 103, 105; racism as effect of, 5, 8, 25, 81, 93–94; South and, 55, 59–62

Carmichael, Stokely (Kwame Ture), 5, 13, 22, 65, 160, 178

Carter, Benny, 117, 165

Carter, Ron, 29

Cherry, Don, 3, 21, 156, 160, 161, 164, 170

Chesnutt, Charles, 73

Chicago, Illinois: black migration to, 101, 103, 107; music scene of, 25, 41, 44, 109; race riot in, 108

Chicago Art Ensemble. *See* Art Ensemble of Chicago

Christian, Charlie, 118

CIO (Committee for Industrial Organization), 123; UAW-CIO, 125. *See also* AFL; AFL-CIO

civil rights movement, 13, 17, 19, 143, 175

Civil War, 60, 69

classical music: aesthetic standards of, 33, 36, 38, 42, 111; black musicians playing, 97, 121; in free jazz, 156, 164; influence on New Orleans music, 107

Cleaver, Eldridge, 19, 69, 82, 151, 160. *See also* Black Panther Party

Coeuroy, André, 38–39

Coleman, Ornette, 3, 135; critics' views on, 170, 171; *Free Jazz*, 11; free jazz pioneer, 11–12; multi-instrumentalist, 155–56, 161, 165; on musical technique, 155; political views of, 21, 25, 28–29, 99

colonialism, 18–19, 43, 48, 94, 179; American, 65; economic, 138, 153, 169; European, 43, 124

Coltrane, Alice, 156

Coltrane, John, 22, 45, 99, 170; bop background of, 153–54, 169; multi-instrumentalist, 156; musical approach of, 153–54, 160, 162, 166, 175

Communism: black America and, 116, 128, 134, 219n95; Communist Party of the United States (CPUS), 116, 134; threat of, 128, 136, 137

cool jazz, 28; *Birth of the Cool*, 139; reaction against, 142, 144–45, 147; rise of, 138–40, 143; white elements in, 161. *See also* Third Stream

CORE (Congress of Racial Equality), 135, 143, 219n94

criticism: on bebop, 45–46, 131–32, 152; black jazz critics, 3, 26; critique of jazz criticism, 6, 47–50; on economic exploitation of jazz, 29; on free jazz, 11–12, 170–73, 180; French jazz critics, 4, 38–39, 43–45; mainstream criteria of jazz, 3–4, 6, 31–32, 33, 36–40, 112, 117; white critics, 33–36, 41–43, 112, 137, 151, 170

Cruse, Harold, 26–27

Cyrille, Andrew, 29, 160

Davis, Miles, 139, 140. *See also* cool jazz

Depression, Great, 134; blues during, 119; effect on music, 117

Detroit: black ghetto of, 15; black migration to, 101, 103; riots in, 18, 124–28

Dixieland, revival, 138, 169

Dixon, Bill, 28, 158, 175, 199n9. *See also* Jazz Composers Guild

Dolphy, Eric, 146, 153, 156, 170

Dorsey, Jimmy and Tommy, 26, 118

Douglass, Frederick, 69–70, 71, 72, 73, 74, 86

Du Bois, W. E. B., 14, 53, 81, 119, 127, 160; on art, 115; black music according to, 81, 83, 91; Booker T. Washington seen by, 62; influence on Harlem Renaissance, 115–16; on lynching, 104, 108; political activism of, 13, 68, 104–5; Reconstruction seen by, 60

Dunbar, Paul Laurence, 73–76, 80

Ellington, Duke, 20, 32, 41, 43, 116, 134–35, 175; African references in music of, 115, 147, 160; European influences in music of, 162, 164; Garveyism and music of, 113–15; homage to, 164, 165

Ellison, Ralph, 134

Europe, James Reese, 110

Farmer, James, 135

folk music: African American, 25, 26; white American, 144

Frazier, E. Franklin, 34, 63; *Black Bourgeoisie*, 71

free jazz: African influence on, 177; birth of, 3, 11–13; black testimony in, 180; blues form in, 100; characteristics of, 151–67, 173–75; commerce and, 28–29; historical background of, 51–52, 146–48, 169; intellectuals and, 20; jazz and, 31, 152, 169–74, 177, 180; rejection of dominant ideology in, 12–13, 42, 180, 182; revolutionary character of, 4–6, 21–24, 46, 51, 146, 168, 178. *See also* criticism: on free jazz

funk, 144–45, 147

Garvey, Marcus, 68, 113–16, 135, 147, 160, 179

Gershwin, George, 27, 110

Getz, Stan, 140

Gillespie, Dizzy, 20, 45, 110, 132, 135, 139, 140, 160

Goodman, Benny, 116; "King of Swing," 26, 118
Graves, Milford, 28, 158, 160, 170
Griggs, Sutton, 73

Haden, Charlie, 29, 158
Hampton, Lionel, 118, 134
Handy, W. C., 106
Harlem, 31, 92, 163; birth of bebop in, 129; Harlem Renaissance, 114–17; riot, 15, 124, 128–29, 133
Hawkins, Coleman, 131, 146, 154, 165
Henderson, Fletcher, 43, 114, 118
Hentoff, Nat, 146
Herman, Woody, 26, 118, 139
Hines, Earl, 117, 129
Hodeir, André, defense of bebop by, 44, 132
Holiday, Billie, 121, 144
Howlin' Wolf (Chester Burnett), 90
Hughes, Langston, 116, 133, 137

improvisation, 112, 163, 171, 174, 185–94; African influence on, 92; collective, 11, 37, 87, 154, 159; controlled, 32, 38, 129; definition, 194; in bebop, 131–32, 133, 139, 153; in free jazz, 152–53, 157–58
integrationism, 4, 143; black bourgeoisie and, 34, 81, 105; black churches and, 85; jazz as symbol of, 113, 134, 172; music opposed to, 146; organizations supporting, 13–14, 143
Islam, 14–15, 44, 47, 130, 134–35, 143, 147, 160, 161, 175, 179, 197n3, 219n93

jazz: alterity of, 47, 170; as art, 3, 37; as black music, 4, 5, 20–22, 31–33, 35–38, 43, 82, 110; blues as basis of, 88–92; characteristics of, 4–5, 12, 27, 31–32, 37–40, 45, 114–15, 117–19, 129, 137, 151, 155, 165, 168, 172–74, 176, 181; "classic," 11, 43–44; exploitation of, 4, 5, 6, 25–30, 48–49, 109, 112, 169; history of, 4, 6, 20, 49–50, 51–98, 99–100, 165; "hot," 43; literature and, 116; "middle," 119–22; minstrelsy and, 96–97; "modern," 11, 146; as product of mass consumption, 112, 117; as social commentary, 11, 21, 142; "true," 32, 36, 43–46, 106, 111, 131, 138, 170; white, 31–33, 40–42, 161, 170–71; white critics and, 33–40. *See also* bebop; blues; free jazz; New Orleans, Louisiana; swing
Jazz Composers' Guild, 28–29, 199n9
Jazz Composer's Orchestra Association, 29
Jazz Messengers, 147
Jim Crow: laws, 61–62, 96, 104, 107, 124, 125, 143; minstrel show character known as, 95–96, 97
Jones, LeRoi (Amiri Baraka), 3–5, 15, 29, 33, 34, 35, 41, 43, 48, 51, 78, 85, 87, 92, 99, 200n3; *Blues People*, 5, 47, 77, 187; cultural nationalism and, 5, 160; denunciation of economic exploitation of jazz by, 26–27; musical recordings with, 28, 166, 198n3

Kansas City, Missouri, music scene in, 122, 142
Karenga, Ron, 5
Kenton, Stan, 26, 222n110
King, Martin Luther, 80, 86, 145, 204n38
Konitz, Lee, 140, 169
Korea, war in, 110, 123, 136, 139, 220n96
Ku Klux Klan, 61, 74, 104, 125, 127, 137, 143

Leadbelly (Huddie Leadbetter), 82, 90
Lincoln, Abbey, 75, 146, 166, 209n108
Locke, Alain, 77, 94, 97, 114, 115
Lunceford, Jimmie, 32, 117

Mantler, Mike, 29, 158, 199n9
March on Washington: in 1941, 124; in 1963, 143
McCarthy, Joseph, 108, 128, 137, 142
Miller, Glenn, 26, 118
Mingus, Charles, 21, 165, 166, 175; politics in music of, 146, 147
minstrelsy, 92, 95–97; exploitation of black culture in, 25, 80, 82–83, 89, 94, 109; Paul Laurence Dunbar and, 75, 80; representation of black people in, 94–97, 121
Modern Jazz Quartet, 11, 140, 144
Monk, Thelonius, 20, 45, 131, 139, 154, 155, 165
Morton, Jelly Roll, 107, 109, 111, 138
Moten, Bennie, 117
Muhammad, Elijah, 14, 44, 135, 197n3
Mulligan, Gerry, 26, 140
Murray, Sunny, 28, 156, 160, 166, 170

NAACP (National Association for the Advancement of Colored People), 13, 69, 105, 119–20, 124, 143, 219n94
"Negro question," 30, 189
New Deal, 119–20, 122, 123, 217n58
New Negro, 114, 115, 209n1
New Orleans, Louisiana, 26, 28, 111, 117; birthplace of jazz, 22, 25, 44–45, 106–7, 109–10, 138; Congo Square, 83–84; musical style, 157, 165–66; revival, 46, 138
New York Art Quartet, 28, 200n3
Newton, Huey, 19, 197n1, 225n3

Oliver, "King" (Joseph), 26, 109, 111
Oliver, Paul, 53, 106
Original Dixieland Jass Band (ODJB), 26, 43, 109, 110

Panassié, Hugues, 41, 170, 199n15; bebop and, 132, 138; search for jazz origins and, 44–45, 106; "true" jazz and, 43–46, 106
Parker, Charlie, 45, 133, 135, 139, 140, 155, 174; Kansas City and, 122; image of, 130–32
Powell, Bud, 131, 164
Prima, Louis, 28
propaganda: art as, 115; music as, 22, 110. *See also* radio

race records, 140
race riots, 15, 49, 68, 105, 108, 124–29, 133
radio, 20, 25, 110; jazz on, 26–29, 131, 181–82; as propaganda tool, 48, 141
ragtime, 75, 215n17
Randolph, A. Philip, 116, 120, 124
Reconstruction, 60–64, 73, 203n25
rhythm and blues, 20, 142–44, 163, 165, 166. *See also* blues
riots. *See* race riots
Roach, Max, 75, 133, 146, 175
rock and roll, 143–44, 163, 166. *See also* blues; rhythm and blues
Rollins, Sonny, 165, 169, 170

saxophone, 134; in jazz, 155, 156, 157, 165; in rhythm and blues, 142
segregation, 34, 49, 61, 62, 96, 107, 123, 142–43, 178
Sharrock, Sonny, 155, 158
Shaw, Artie, 26, 118

Shepp, Archie, 3, 11, 12, 22, 28, 65, 90, 146, 160, 161, 164–66, 168, 169, 170, 174, 175
slavery, 5, 11, 12, 36, 37, 40, 44, 47–48, 53–60, 64–68; music and, 77–88, 100, 106, 107, 131
Smith, Bessie, 100–101, 110, 121, 140, 144, 175
SNCC (Student Nonviolent Coordinating Committee), 13–14, 69, 143
solo, 97, 129, 157; soloist, 38, 93, 117, 133, 142, 157
soul, 20, 22, 28, 34, 42, 80, 142, 144–45, 147, 166
Spellman, A. B., 25, 29, 34, 45, 53, 99
spirituals, 39, 63, 75, 85–88, 91, 92, 97, 98, 106, 144–45, 175
Stollman, Bernard, 28
Sun Ra (Herman P. Blount), 28, 135, 152, 156, 158, 160, 162, 166, 170
swing, 28, 31, 45, 46, 106, 116–19, 121, 122, 129, 131, 132, 133, 142, 144, 158, 159, 160

Tatum, Art, 94
Taylor, Cecil, 3, 20, 27, 28, 31, 41, 140, 158, 159, 161, 162–63, 164, 199n9
Third Stream, 11, 140, 170, 221n100
trumpet, 155, 157
Tyler, Charles, 31, 160

Vietnam, war in, 11, 13, 15, 65, 110, 123
voodoo, 36, 78, 81, 147

Waller, Fats, 121–22
Washington, Booker T., 62–63, 71, 72, 73, 74, 81, 104, 113
Whiteman, Paul, 26, 36, 43, 111, 118
work songs, 53, 63, 81–82, 96, 97, 100, 106, 166, 210n12

World War I, 103, 106, 107, 113
World War II, 108, 110, 126, 134, 137
Wright, Richard, 90–91, 92, 93, 134

X, Malcolm, 14, 16, 17, 18, 34, 35, 57, 58, 65, 66, 69, 71, 73, 82, 97, 122, 135, 143, 160, 164, 189; on jazz, 22–23, 116

Young, Lester, 121, 122, 139

www.ingramcontent.com/pod-product-compliance
Lightning Source LLC
Chambersburg PA
CBHW030613230426
43661CB00053B/1974